Jesus and
the Quest for
Meaning

To Bernard Cooke

Contents

Preface

I wrote this book with four groups of readers in mind. First, I had in mind the students who register for one of my theology classes at the College of St. Catherine, a Catholic liberal arts college for women in St. Paul, Minnesota. Most of them are taking the class in order to fulfill the theology requirement. About 40 percent of them have Catholicism as their religious upbringing, though relatively few have gone to Catholic elementary or secondary school. Another 30 percent were raised in one of the mainline Protestant churches, with Lutherans the largest group. Fifteen percent have little or no background in any religion, and this percentage is on the increase. The remaining 10 to 15 percent are divided among evangelical Christians and recent immigrants from largely non-Christian cultures. I have to teach the course as if no one had any formal theological background. I can assume that many in the class will distrust organized religion but feel a deep spiritual longing. If I am to write a book that a class like this can use, I had better make it readable, nontechnical, ecumenical, and personal.

Second, I had in mind the students who register for our graduate courses. We offer a master's degree in theology with the option of a concentration in spirituality. The great majority of our eighty or so graduate students choose to do the concentration. Most are between thirty and fifty-five years of age, and although we admit men to the graduate program, over 85 percent of the students are women. Very few come into the program having majored in theology or religion as undergraduates. Their formal theological learning is minimal, and they come from a variety of denominational backgrounds. A book for them must be readable, ecumenical, and personal. Yet because they are graduate students, they will want to go deeper, and for them I have provided a quite formidable set of endnotes in which I add nuances to the main ideas of the body text, delve into more technical issues, offer suggestions for further reading, list primary and secondary sources, and give a sense of my intellectual pedigree. Because many of these graduate students will leave the college and work in some form of church ministry, I also include all those working in professional ministry as potential readers of this book. Indeed, I should think that this book would work quite well in a general theology course for first-year seminary students.

Third, I had in mind those laypersons in the pew who have a hunger for theology that goes beyond what they can learn from sermons. I am thinking, for example, of the kind of people who attended a talk on the Nicene Creed that I gave at St. David's Episcopal Church in Minnetonka, a suburb to the west of Minneapolis. I should want people like them to be able to read this book with profit, without requiring my presence as the professor to take them through it. Such a book has to be readable, nontechnical, ecumenical, and personal.

And fourth, I had in mind all those people who are on a quest for meaning. They are not sure what they believe in, but they know they have a hunger for something larger and deeper. Probably they have had at least some education past high school, and in their quest, they want to use their heads, not just their hearts. Books on spirituality that speak to the heart are flooding the market. I too want to speak to the heart, and this book is personal, with many examples from real life, but I also want to speak to the mind searching for meaning.

This book is not an introduction to theology in the conventional sense. It does not offer a textbook survey of theological sources, methods, doctrines, and creeds. It is not even a textbook, though it could be used as one of several books for a theology class. It offers the reader *one* way of entering theology, not *the* way. I make no claim to having the best approach or to saying the final word. I am simply adding my voice.

Though the book is not directed toward professional theologians, I hope they will read it, like it, and have their students buy it. They know, of course, that only a lunatic attempts to write a book that in three hundred pages tries to cover meaning, power, God, Christ, spirit, church, sacraments, faith, love, and hope. About any one of these topics, hundreds, maybe thousands of theologians know more than I do. Yet I should like to think that my take on theology might be of interest to the professionals. The book does show a way of organizing theology that, although not radically new, is, I hope, fresh and clear. I have been teaching for twenty-seven years and know that my approach works with a wide variety of students who are just entering theology.

Some readers will want to know a little about my religious and theological location. I am a Catholic with a strong ecumenical bent. As far as I know, I belong to no theological school or movement, but I count among my strongest influences Reinhold Niebuhr, Bernard Cooke, and Karl Rahner. Two close friends in the field, Larry Goodwin and Nancy Frankenberry, have brought me to an appreciation of process theology, though I would not classify myself as a process theologian. I wrote a book on the neo-Marxist Ernst Bloch and learned Spanish in order to read the liberation theologians: I emphasize social justice throughout this book, but I would not say that I do theology from a predominantly liberationist perspective. In the fall of 1964, I read Betty Friedan's *The Feminine Mystique* and was converted. I now teach at a college where 70 percent of my faculty colleagues and all but one of my bosses are women. I have been profoundly influenced by feminist theologians (Rosemary Radford Ruether is the one from whom I have learned the most), and I hope it shows in this book, but I would not say that I do theology from a predominantly feminist perspective.

The manuscript that became this book went through three drafts, and I had a lot of help along the way. Larry Goodwin, a former colleague of mine at what we call St. Kate's and now president of the College of St. Scholastica, was the first to encourage me to undertake a book like this. He also gave me a very close reading of the first draft. My first theology teacher, Bernard Cooke, read the first draft and sent a long list of corrections and suggestions. The same gift was given me by John H. Wright, S.J., my dissertation director, and Anthony Wilhelm, the author of the catechism *Christ among Us*. (Tony died in the summer of 1999 and left a hole in my heart and in the hearts of thousands of people across North America who knew him and his work.) Sister Catherine Litecky, C.S.J., read and responded to the first draft. Sister Eleanor Lincoln, C.S.J., read the first and third drafts very carefully and made numerous corrections. Mari Meyers, a theology major, gave a very precise reading of the second draft, and she helped me with the overall structure of the book. Michael Slusser of Duquesne University read and responded to chapter 5, and John Galvin of Catholic University did the same for chapter 6. Bea Palmer sent a very affirming letter after she read the first draft. Michael West, editor in chief at Fortress Press, forced me into a rather extensive revision that became the third and final draft—and made it a better book. During the editing and production process, Geneviève Duboscq and Zan Ceeley brought their sharp minds to the manuscript and caught a number of errors and infelicities. I thank all of them for their generosity and support.

I, of course, did not accept all of the corrections and suggestions offered by the readers of the manuscript. Do not blame any of them for the mistakes and errors that still remain.

To the College of St. Catherine, I am thankful for a sabbatical leave in the spring of 1994 that gave me the time to write the first draft and for a faculty grant in the summer of 1995 that allowed me to photocopy the manuscript and send it out to the readers. I have appreciated the support from the members of the theology department, especially Chris Franke, who showed continued interest in the project and provided help on key points. I owe a special debt of gratitude to my colleague Sister Catherine Michaud, C.S.J., who talked with me and listened to me about every aspect of the manuscript. She also offered prayers and continual encouragement. I thank the students of St. Kate's, upon whom I have inflicted the manuscript in whole or part over these past five years. They are sick of the photocopies and want to see the book!

My wife Kathleen read the first and second drafts of the manuscript and offered invaluable feedback. She was wonderful during the summer of 1999 when I virtually disappeared into the study to write the final draft. I send a salute of appreciation to my daughters Sarah and Kate, who were kind enough to ask periodically, "How's the book coming, Dad?"

I should like to hear the reaction of readers to the book. I welcome corrections, suggestions, criticisms, and reflections, and would be especially interested in hearing from teachers who have used the book. I can be reached by mail at the College of St. Catherine, Mail #4222, St. Paul, MN 55105, or by email at THWest@stkate.edu.

ONE

The Quest for Meaning

Human Being as the Tendency to Meaning

As a graduate student in California, I would watch from my study window the comings and goings of my next-door neighbor. Single, then in her forties, she drifted from job to job and from man to man. There were frequent eruptions of new activity: a return to school for retraining, a plunge into a new business, a stint as a special education teacher, a plan to move abroad, a rediscovery of Christianity. Each new venture was launched with much fanfare, and each new venture was soon abandoned. Several times the for sale sign went up on her front lawn as she felt the call toward a distant state or country. After a few weeks, the sign would come down. In backyard conversation, she was friendly enough but often appeared hurried and disoriented. One day I asked my wife, who knew her better than I, "What's going on with her, anyway? She seems to have no focus." My wife answered, "She is still in quest of her meaning."

My neighbor was not alone and would not be alone today. The quest for meaning is in fact a contemporary American obsession. Books on the quest for meaning pour out.[1] Talk shows are abuzz with people telling stories of meaning sought, meaning found, and meaning lost. The search for meaning has even flowed into our political discourse: Not long ago, then President Bill Clinton and First Lady Hillary Rodham

1

Clinton urged a "politics of meaning." Viktor Frankl's book, *Man's Search for Meaning*, has for years been a best-seller for the high school and college classroom.[2] As a college theology teacher, I have used his book for over two decades. Frankl was a successful psychiatrist in Vienna in the late 1930s, when the Austrians agreed to an *Anschluss* (union) with Nazi Germany. As a Jew, Frankl was in jeopardy. He turned down the chance to emigrate to a safe haven in the United States, not wanting to leave his parents alone and vulnerable. He ended up in the concentration camps. His father, mother, brother, and wife all died in the Holocaust.[3] Miraculously, he survived to give his account of his time in the camps. In his famous book, Frankl tells how he sought and found meaning even in the dehumanizing situation of a death camp where his captors systematically set out to strip him of all spiritual dignity. With great courage, he maintained his spiritual dignity and sought meaning. After the war, Frankl wrote many books on meaning and human life, and became the founder of a therapeutic movement called logotherapy, literally, meaning-therapy. He remarried, had children, grandchildren, and great-grand-children. In 1997, he died at the age of 92.

According to Frankl, the search for meaning is the "primary motivation" of human life.[4] We are more than biological instinct, more than psychological need; we are, in his words, the "will-to-meaning." The *will-to-meaning* is the dynamic tendency within us to seek meaning. It is a quality of the human spirit—and the essence of human dignity. By *spirit*, Frankl does not mean a dimension of the human being in opposition to matter; nor does he mean a dimension that is necessarily religious. Rather, he means a dimension that hungers for more than the satisfaction of biological instinct or psychological need.[5]

The tendency toward meaning is at once the deepest and most fragile thing about us. Although essential to our nature as spirit, it is not an overpowering drive or compulsion; it coexists with another aspect of our spiritual dimension, which is the freedom to oppose this tendency. Furthermore, certain extreme situations can lead to the loss of the spiritual dimension. In the concentration camps, Frankl saw many people reduced to a condition where the "primitive instinct"[6] for survival overpowered the other dimensions of the self, leaving barely a hint of freedom and the tendency toward meaning. Yet even in such extreme situations, where the crush of fate dehumanizes by despiritualizing, many individuals manage to preserve the spiritual dimension.[7]

The spiritual dimension thus shows its paradoxical nature: both vulnerable to oppressive forces yet in most extraordinary ways tenaciously alive, ever hungry for meaning, able to freely choose meanings.

Meaning and Freedom

In contemporary North America, we have to search for our meanings: they are not a given. We have been set loose from a simpler time when meanings were fairly well established by biological or social fate: the oldest son of a shoemaker followed in his father's footsteps; the oldest daughter married young and had children. Many of us, though not all, have been freed from the crushing weight of struggling most of the day merely to survive. We have the freedom to undertake the quest for meaning. This freedom is exhilarating, but also disorienting and dizzying.[8] We often end up nostalgic for an earlier time, when life's meanings were more fated, or we end up using our freedom to flit from one meaning to another.

But we have not completely thrown off the chains of fate. Freedom, even today, is never absolute in its range. All freedom is situated, and every situation, internal and external, has fateful elements that are not of our choosing and cannot be changed. By *internal situation*, I mean everything that exists within the individual self, from the outer skin to the deepest interior, limiting the choice of meaning. In my youth, I dreamed of being a professional golfer but soon ran up against the limits of my internal situation: I lacked the requisite athletic ability, the single-minded ambition, and the nervelessness that mark the truly competitive golf professional. By *external situation*, I mean everything outside our skin that pressures and restrains our lives. I dream now of an extended stay in a French-speaking country where I might finally achieve fluency in a language that I have been slaving away at for several years. But my external situation limits me: as a teacher at a small college, I have to manage on a salary that forbids the choice of this meaning. I even wonder if I shall be able to complete the modest meaning that I have set myself today, which is to write six pages of the first chapter of this book. My wife woke up ill today and is buried beneath a mountain of blankets only a few steps from my desk. Her illness, an instance of fate, has changed not only her internal situation, but also my external situation, limiting the range of my freedom.

So complex is the relation between our freedom and our situation that it is easy to stress one at the expense of the other. The philosopher Jean-Paul Sartre surely overstresses freedom when he writes: "I am absolutely free and absolutely responsible for my situation."[9] In contrast, the behaviorist B. F. Skinner saw freedom as an illusion.[10] In his view, we are completely at the mercy of our situation. Frankl tries to strike a balance. While insisting on human freedom, he remains equally aware of the constraints of our situation.

Indeed, he urges us to let these constraints guide our freedom toward a meaning. Otherwise, he says, the meaning chosen will be only a "projection of wishful thinking."[11] Look first not to the free play of the imagination but to the situation, which is "distinguished by its uniqueness."[12] Frankl gives special emphasis to the external situation. "Look outside yourself!" is his continual exhortation.

Yet surely we human beings should look not only to our external situation for guidance about the choice of meaning. We must also look at our internal situation. Each of us has a unique internal mix of temperament, energy, skill, native intelligence, ability, need, drive, health, sickness, wound, scar. Who we are is partly fate, and we cannot will away fate. We must attend to these fateful elements if our choice for meaning is to be realistic. One of my students is the oldest of nine orphaned children. She must factor in this external situation when choosing her meanings. But which meanings she chooses must also take into account her internal situation, especially her temperament and abilities.

Fate and freedom thus should enter into mediation with one another. As we imagine possible meanings, then, we should let this imagination be realistic, rather than gnostic, to adopt terms used by Jesuit literary theorist William Lynch. The human person, he writes, "is made not only to have a place but to make places, to make worlds, not out of whole cloth, not in terms of an isolated and sterile imagination, but in terms of an imagination that is in a constant and creative relationship with the world. It is on the side of mutuality that the facts depend, and out of this relationship they emerge."[13] We must then know our world, inner and outer. Knowing our world is a cognitive activity, making use of reason and imagination. To know our situation, we must use our heads.

When we make a free choice for a particular meaning in dialogue with our situation, this meaning, if realized, then becomes part of our situation. Earlier, I mentioned that my wife was sick in an adjacent room. Sickness is largely fate, but that she is my wife was a choice I once made (out of a situation full of fateful elements!) and continually renew. My current fate of having a sick wife is thus not entirely due to fate but also to freedom. To what degree any element of our situation is the result of fate or freedom is impossible to know with certitude,[14] yet this does not diminish the imperative to place the free imagination in dialogue with our whole situation, external and internal. It is a question here of preserving continuity of the self by allowing the accumulated reality of the self to weigh in on any decision.

Particular Meanings and Universal Values

Because our situations, both external and internal, are highly particular, so must be our meanings. On a given day, I can find myself at breakfast with my spouse, at school with my students, at dinner with in-laws, and in my study with my books. In each situation, I am called to choose the particular meaning or meanings that are appropriate. Life in general is the search for meaning, but in the daily round of situational shifts, this search is particularized in the search for many meanings. And because each situation is unique to each person, the meanings will be unique. Frankl in his psychiatric practice stressed the particularity of meaning. General meanings, he said, are of little help to the client. The meaning of life, Frankl says, differs "from person to person, and from moment to moment. Thus it is impossible to define the meaning of life in a general way."[15]

Frankl is surely correct to stress the particularity and uniqueness of each meaning. Situations are particular, so should be the meanings, because meanings are guided by the content of the situation. But we must be careful here to avoid situationism. Is the quest for meaning simply a matter of knowing our situation and choosing a meaning in light of it? Is our situation the sole guide to what we should choose for a meaning? Suppose someone were to say to Frankl, "I have analyzed my internal and external situation and decided to become a seller of heroin and cocaine." On what grounds could Frankl criticize such a choice unless there were some general meanings to life that could guide the choice of particular meanings? Surely he must say more than "You have not analyzed your situation accurately." The drug pusher could have analyzed his situation very accurately. Rather, at this point we would surely want the person to defer to one of life's general meanings, for example, "One should not sell a drug to human beings that does such terrible physical and psychological damage." And this general meaning could be further subsumed under a more general meaning: "Respect human life. Do what helps it flourish. Don't do what damages or destroys it." If Frankl forbids us to define the meaning of life in general terms, how can we refer a particular meaning to guidelines that go beyond the content of our particular situation? How could he judge the choice to sell cocaine as inauthentic, that is, morally wrong?

Yet Frankl is not afraid to make judgments about someone's choice of a particular meaning. Here is his account of the behavior of some of the prisoners after their liberation from the concentration camp:

> Now, being free, they thought they could use their freedom licentiously and ruthlessly. The only thing that had changed for them was that they were now the oppressors instead of the oppressed. They became instigators, not objects, of willful force and injustice. They justified their behavior by their own terrible experiences. This was often revealed in apparently insignificant events. A friend was walking across a field with me toward the camp when suddenly we came to a field of green crops. Automatically, I avoided it, but he drew his arm through mine and dragged me through it. I stammered something about not treading down the young crops. He became annoyed, gave me an angry look and shouted, "You don't say! And hasn't enough been taken from us? My wife and child have been gassed—not to mention everything else—and you would forbid me to tread on a few stalks of oats!"[16]

These men, he goes on to say, had forgotten the "commonplace truth that no one has the right to do wrong, not even if wrong has been done to them."[17] Here Frankl is clearly making a moral judgment of a particular meaning based on his commitment to a general life meaning, namely, "Respect the property of others," that goes beyond the particularities of the situation and should be heeded as a guide in the choice of particular meanings.

All his protestations to the contrary, Frankl is perfectly ready to make lofty declarations about the general meanings of life and to recommend them to his fellow human beings. I am thinking, for example, of those bleak moments in the concentration camp when Frankl was able to conjure up memory-images of his wife. Contemplation of those images became at those moments a particular meaning that brought him joy and consolation. In a later reflection on that meaning, he moves beyond its particularity to a generalization of great sweep: "A thought transfixed me: for the first time, I saw the truth as it is set into song by so many poets, proclaimed as the final wisdom by so many thinkers. The truth—that love is the ultimate and highest goal to which man can aspire. Then I grasped the meaning of the greatest secret that human poetry and human thought have to impart: the salvation of man is through and in love."[18] Frankl has come full circle. He has insisted that there is no general meaning to life but now he asserts that love is the one truth. Implied here is an exhortation from him to all human beings: as they survey their particular situations, they should let the general meaning of love, not just the situation, guide them in the choice of a particular meaning. Not every situation will offer the possibility of love—there are other general meanings besides that of love—but if it does, then they do right, indeed they move toward "salvation," by choosing love instead of indifference or hatred.

Part of the difficulty in understanding Frankl on the question of general meaning is terminological. It becomes clear as I read his other books that he really does believe in general meanings but uses the term *value* to denote them: "Meanings refer to unique situations—and the equally unique persons confronting them. In contrast to the meanings, which are unique, values are more or less universal in that they are shared by whole segments of a given population. I would even define values as meaning-universals."[19] Love for Frankl is thus a *universal* value. Hate would be a universal disvalue. Frankl is urging human beings to let their freedom be guided not only by the particularities of the situation but also by universal values. To choose a meaning that is not compatible with a universal value is to choose a meaning that is inauthentic. I have long thought that Frankl's best-seller should have been titled *The Human Search for Authentic Meaning*. The moral passion that suffuses his work shows a commitment to values—general meanings—that transcend the situation.

Not every universal value has to be a moral value. If that were the case, then every particular meaning would be judged as morally right or wrong. Every human choice would be charged with moral drama. There are indeed moralistic totalitarians who would have every choice be for or against a moral value, but Frankl does not number among them. He is aware of meanings that are aesthetic: we can find in his work references to the experience of the beautiful.[20] He is aware of meanings that are intellectual, meanings motivated primarily by the search for truth rather than the search for love and beauty. He refers, for example, to a lost manuscript, and throughout his stay in the camp he was generating the ideas he finally expressed in *Man's Search for Meaning*.[21]

As theology teachers, my colleagues and I have chosen many of our particular meanings as a response to the universal intellectual value of truth, pursued in a discipline that has a close relation to the universal moral values of love and justice. In the intense helter-skelter of our professional life, it is easy for us to neglect aesthetic values. After the end of last term and before beginning this book, I spent a great deal of time listening to music. In making this choice, I let myself be summoned by my situation and by the lure of the universal value of beauty. The creation and appreciation of the beautiful are particular meanings that fulfill a deep tendency of the human spirit. Not everything is or should be primarily moral.

Not even writing this book is primarily a moral meaning. I simply want to tell the truth as I see it. I hope to put it in a form that is aesthetically pleasing, but I would not want the book to be judged primarily by aesthetic criteria. Although I hope that my vision of the truth will have moral consequences in the lives of my readers, I would not want the book to be judged by the morality it effects in those who have read it. Rather, I hope to see the book judged by intellectual criteria. Have I told the truth in a clear and persuasive manner? Do my ideas hang together? Are they true to the evidence life offers? Does this book represent the views of others accurately? We are here in the realm of intellectual values, not primarily aesthetic or moral values.

When I wrote earlier of the creation and appreciation of the beautiful, I was alluding to the distinction between active and receptive meanings. Creating a piece of music is an *active* meaning: we must activate the body and place the notes on the score, and then someone must perform the piece. Appreciating this piece as performed is a *receptive* meaning: we receive it; we let the music come into body, psyche, and spirit. Being receptive does not mean we are passive. We must actively listen in a state of discriminating attention. Yet we are not actively composing or performing. This distinction between active and receptive holds as well for ethical and intellectual meanings. An old woman falls on the ice, and a young woman helps her back to her feet. In performing this ethical act, she has carried out an active meaning. But I may witness her action and be moved to appreciate it. In this appreciation, I realize a moral or ethical meaning, but it is realized in reception, not in action. So also with an intellectual meaning. A difference obtains between the active meaning of carrying out a scientific experiment and the receptive meaning of appreciating the intellectual rigor of that experiment.

The threefold division of universal values into the intellectual (truth), ethical (love and justice), and the aesthetic (beauty) is not new. This division goes back at least as far as Plato and found its way into the Christian tradition, achieving expression in the thought of medieval thinkers and their followers, for whom truth, goodness, and beauty are *transcendentals*, the values of being itself, which they identified with God.[22] In twentieth-century value theory, this threefold division has reasserted itself with surprising vigor. Frankl, who was influenced by value theorists like Max Scheler, gives implicit witness to it throughout his work. I find this threefold division persuasive. For years, I have asked my students in an introductory theology class to tell of the particular meanings they currently are carrying out. With the class's help, I am always able to subsume these meanings under the headings of the intellectual, the ethical, or the aesthetic, or a combination thereof.

In the same class discussions, however, other distinctions emerge. One day, a single mother of three blurted out, "My meaning is to make money, pure and simple. How does that meaning express universal values?" Another student asked her, "How are you going to spend the money?" She answered, "To give my kids a decent life." To which her interrogator replied with unconcealed delight, "But providing for your kids is an ethical meaning!" We must distinguish between intrinsic and instrumental values. The love that motivates the mother to provide for her children is an intrinsic value. It is an end in itself. It needs no justification by reference to other values and meanings. But making money is not, or at least should not be, an end in itself, but rather an instrument, a means, by which she realizes a particular meaning expressive of an intrinsic value like love.

Suffering and Meaning

No search for meaning can evade the issue of suffering. Only a masochist regards suffering as meaningful in itself. To seek out suffering for its own sake is a sign of mental illness. The healthy person avoids suffering and does not go out of her way to find it.

Yet some suffering should not be avoided. For example, we should not avoid the suffering attendant upon a life without meaning. Such a life ought to lead to a painful experience of what Frankl calls the "existential vacuum."[23] Such pain should not be repressed or evaded. A close friend tells me that the most agonizing period of his life came after graduating from college, when suddenly all the questions of who he was and what meanings he should seek came crashing down on him. College high jinks and the routine of classes had enabled him to escape the yawning abyss of the existential vacuum. For three months after graduation, he sought escape in sleep. He seized on quick answers: the impulsive reconciliation with an old girlfriend and an unthinking leap into graduate school—but the vacuum and the anguish remained. No authentic meanings emerged. What helped him turn the corner is that he eventually began to live in the pain and acknowledge its rights. He learned to face the vacuum and trust that his current hopelessness was not forever. Somehow, he resisted total denial of, or escape from, the suffering imposed by the absence of meaning. This kind of suffering was necessary for him if he was to struggle with the full depth and range of the question of meaning. And authentic meanings did finally emerge.

Suffering also comes from the choice of inauthentic meaning. Instead of filling the vacuum with a meaning compatible with universal values, we choose a meaning compatible with disvalues. Here, the matter of suffering becomes more complicated. If we human beings are the tendency toward authentic meaning, then surely the choice for inauthentic meaning will bring a spiritual suffering that is consequent on this frustration of the deepest tendency of our spiritual natures. But human beings are more than spirit: they are body and psyche, and the choice for inauthentic meaning often does bring bodily pleasure and psychological satisfaction. For example, a man can seduce and exploit a woman and derive satisfaction from meeting the challenge and pleasure from performing the act. Any spiritual suffering that should be consequent on the choice of such an inauthentic meaning can quite easily be overcome by this satisfaction and pleasure. Furthermore, the infinitely ingenious human self can convince itself that this inauthentic meaning is in fact authentic, that is, in the service of the highest values. Indeed, so powerful is the tendency toward authentic meaning that few who choose a meaning expressive of disvalue honestly say to themselves, Of course this is wrong and against the deepest values, but I simply choose to do it as a gratuitous act of perversity.[24] Rather, they mystify it; they ideologize it; they wrap it in the cloak of universal value. When I was a student in Berkeley, I was told by an aspiring novelist that he had carried out an emotionless seduction in order to experience it from within and thereby present it more convincingly in writing. He did not suffer remorse or regret. This seduction, he rationalized, was in service of the highest aesthetic value. Such is the self-deception that we will practice to avoid the spiritual suffering that ought to result from the choice of inauthentic meaning.

Yet it is difficult to avoid forever the suffering that should follow the choice for inauthentic meaning. Those moments arrive, perhaps in what some call the "hour of the wolf," those sleepless moments just before dawn, when the gnawing inauthenticity of one's life scratches through to consciousness, when the person choosing inauthentic meanings feels the spiritual pain of someone who has turned from value to disvalue. In addition, the biological, psychological, and spiritual dimensions of human beings are not sharply separated. They blur into one another and are interactive in fearsomely complex ways. Spiritual inauthenticity can spread its poison into body and psyche. Headaches occur; lethargy sets in; irritability increases; boredom invades.[25] Even the pleasure of body and the gratification of psyche wane with each seduction. This can spur the person to face spiritual suffering.

If the suffering that should result from inauthentic meaning does push through and is accurately named by the sufferer, then such suffering should be confronted, not avoided. A danger signal, an alarm, has sounded in the depths of the spirit. It is indeed a suffering that yields meaning because it is the spur to get back on the road to authentic meaning. This suffering is beneficial and necessary. Indeed, the larger a person's capacity for this kind of suffering, the larger the size of a person's spirit.

Suffering also accompanies the carrying out of an authentic meaning. Several years ago, a friend of mine made a heroic choice for a meaning. He gave up liquor. This was an authentic meaning, compatible with the universal moral value of love, a love toward others and toward self. His drinking was tearing at the fabric of his family life and had become for him a health risk. Carrying out this meaning entailed great suffering. He suffered the psychological loss of barroom conviviality: he is a people person and political enthusiast who loved to sit at the bar, drinking, talking, laughing. He suffered the biological pain of drying out a body that had come to crave liquor. He suffered the exhausting discipline of constant self-watchfulness. But he accepted all this suffering as required by this authentic meaning.

The realization of authentic meaning does not always bring suffering, but it often does, particularly with more noble and ambitious meanings. This suffering is worth enduring, for it is the price of a meaning. Sometimes, however, the suffering accompanying an authentic meaning becomes disproportionate to the meaning aimed at. The physical and psychological cost becomes too great. For known and unknown reasons, a person exceeds her threshold of suffering. I shall never forget my talk with a very serious and dedicated student who was taking a heavy course load and working thirty hours a week—all in the service of the particular meaning of finishing college. Hers was a noble meaning, expressive of the highest intellectual and moral values, for she wished to finish quickly in order to help out her large and poor family. But she was a physical and psychological mess, suffering enormously. I said, "Is this worth it? How about revising your meanings?" And she did. She took a hard look at her internal situation and decided to take a semester's leave from school and get a full-time job. She needed to make her meanings more proportionate to her capacity for pain.

The most difficult suffering to deal with is brought by fate. It is not chosen but simply strikes. A person breathes in a virus at a particular moment and is now in bed, miserable. A mood of depression, with no discernible cause, ambushes another and is ravaging her psyche—and invading her body and spirit. A beloved spouse in a fifty-year marriage steps out of this world into the dark unknown of Alzheimer's disease, and the spouse left behind loses his most cherished meaning: mutual love with his wife. Viktor Frankl was cast into a concentration camp because of the fate of his Jewish parentage.

Fateful suffering cuts deep because of its negative relation to meaning. It mocks our freedom to choose meaning because it invades without asking permission. It often overwhelms people and prevents the search for meaning. Or it prevents the completion of a meaning. I think of our family dentist who had finally gotten his practice up and running. His was an authentic meaning ennobled by his choice to practice in the inner city and serve many people on society's margin. One day, when I came in for my six-month checkup, he was not there. The receptionist told me he had a brain tumor and could no longer practice. He faced the real possibility of death. He not only could not complete a meaning but was threatened by death to be cut off altogether from meaning. Human life at its greatest depth is meaning sought, meaning undertaken, and meaning achieved. But fate knocks down the door and rushes in with a suffering that threatens not only to frustrate but even destroy the quest for meaning.

Does this mean fateful suffering is a region of human experience that cannot be penetrated by meaning? Frankl says no. Life, he says, has meaning unconditionally: life has meaning under all conditions, even the condition of fateful suffering. Yet he is careful to say that this meaning is "potential."[26] Fateful suffering does not automatically bring with it a meaning. There is no reason built into fateful suffering. Rather, the reason or the meaning is a potential that must be discerned, seized, and then carried out by the sufferer. The inner spirit of the sufferer must rise to the suffering and turn it into a bearer of meaning. True, fateful suffering can diminish the spirit, even crush it, but such suffering can also be an opportunity to enlarge the spirit. This opportunity is difficult to discover at first, when the sufferer is numb with pain, shock, and anger at the unfairness of it all.

When the composer Ludwig van Beethoven became aware that he was going deaf, his initial response was depression and paralysis. In these initial stages, pious sermonizing to the sufferer about "finding the potential meaning in your fate" heaps more suffering on the sufferer. But Beethoven did eventually "seize fate," using it to give his music more heroic beauty and depth.[27] Even if we are not great artists like Beethoven, there is a potential meaning in our suffering. Perhaps we can put our suffering at the service of a moral value and transform ourselves into more empathetic and generous human beings. We all at one time or the other are bushwhacked by suffering that we neither choose nor deserve. None of us fully escapes the tentacles of fate. Life addresses to us no more profound question than what we will do in the face of fateful suffering.[28] Will we find a way of transforming it into a meaning that serves universal values, especially the moral values of love and justice? Will we use our pain to deepen our solidarity with the pain of others? Will we use our own pain to alleviate the fateful suffering of others?

Penultimate and Ultimate Meaning

Until now, the particular meanings I have been discussing have been penultimate rather than ultimate, immanent within the world rather than transcendent beyond the world. Penultimate meanings are discovered, chosen, and carried out within the space and time of this world. Yet we human beings have a seemingly ineradicable tendency to move beyond the penultimate to the ultimate. The French existentialist philosopher Albert Camus found it "absurd," but it remains true that we finite beings can never rest content with the penultimate. We are ever restless within the confines of a universe limited to itself.[29]

By *ultimate meaning*, I mean a dimension of meaning that lies beyond the limits of this world. Ultimate meaning can enter into relationship with penultimate meaning in this world but is not confined to this world. It transcends the world. Frankl is convinced such a dimension exists. Here are two key passages: "In a last violent protest against the hopelessness of imminent death, I sensed my spirit piercing through the enveloping gloom. I felt it transcend the hopeless, meaningless world, and from somewhere I heard a victorious 'Yes' in answer to my question of the existence of an ultimate purpose." "Is it not conceivable that there is still another dimension possible, a world beyond man's world; a world in which the question of an ultimate meaning of human suffering would find an answer?"[30] Frankl raises the question of an ultimate meaning under the negative condition of fateful suffering, especially as it threatens life. Despite the potential penultimate meaning offered by situations of fateful suffering, the suffering exceeds this potential. Heroic appeals to seize fate and make it work for universal values sound empty in situations of extreme pain and imminent death. Even if some penultimate meaning is discoverable by the victims or their survivors, its yield pales in comparison to the enormity of the suffering. This harsh truth struck me again while recently watching Steven Spielberg's film, *Schindler's List*. Oskar Schindler saved eleven hundred Jews from the death camps and thereby discovered and carried out a penultimate meaning. On a wider scale, many thousands of people worked together after World War II to extract another penultimate meaning from the Holocaust: they established a homeland for the Jewish people. Moreover, millions of people, Jew and non-Jew, now show a greater sensitivity to racist and genocidal threats to humankind: their commitment to "Never again!" sounds repeatedly. These are all penultimate meanings compatible with the moral values of love and justice. But all these penultimate meanings will surely never be enough. Indeed, there is something deeply blasphemous in assuming that the yield of penultimate meaning could ever be enough.[31] We know almost instinctively that the suffering and death of so many innocent people in the Holocaust will forever be disproportionate to any yield of penultimate meaning. Here, we reach an abyss before which silence is perhaps the only genuinely respectful response.

Yet, with Frankl, I cannot help uttering the question: is there a dimension of ultimate meaning? Is there not a meaning in the sense that these deaths do not mean the absolute end of meaning for the victims? Do their deaths mean the death of all meaning for them, or do their deaths carry at least the potential for ultimate meaning beyond the limits of this world? Do the meanings they achieved live on only in our memories? Do the meanings they could have achieved suffer a stillborn death?

Frankl believes that a dimension of ultimate meaning exists. Yet he is silent on the question of what that meaning might be. "The ultimate meaning necessarily exceeds the finite intellectual capacities of man."[32] In chapters 5 and 6 of this book, when we consider the theology of death and resurrection, we shall explore an alternative view to Frankl's. In the light of Christian faith, we shall see that we are not completely in the dark about the ultimate meaning.

The question of an ultimate meaning raises itself not only as a response to the negative experience of innocent suffering and death. Are there not positive meanings which, though discovered and carried out within the penultimate, connect us with the ultimate? Do we not at times feel the presence of the ultimate in experience of the penultimate? I for one find it impossible to experience a particular meaning of depth and intensity without simultaneously sensing that the ultimate has broken into the penultimate and the penultimate has opened out into the ultimate. Last night, for example, I stepped out into the bitter cold of a Minnesota winter. The temperature was -25°F, and a foot of fresh powder covered the ground. It was clear, windless, utterly quiet. Usually, I go out into the Minnesota winter with stubborn resentment, but this time I surrendered to its terrible beauty. I stood there for several minutes, pervaded by the penultimate meaning of a beautiful winter night. And then I began to shudder, not because of the cold, but with that aesthetic thrill that crawls up and down the spine. And immediately, with an unmistakable self-authenticating certainty, I felt that this particular meaning was radiating out into the ultimate dimension, that my experience of beauty was pointing to an ultimate meaning as its source and coparticipant. I felt myself both in the world and in a dimension beyond the world, deeper than the world.

Beauty is a universal value. And there are other universal values such as love, truth, and justice. When we experience them in particular meanings, we often experience the interpenetration of the penultimate and the ultimate. Does this mean that the universal values reside in the ultimate dimension?

Ultimate Meaning and Universal Values

Years ago, when I was an undergraduate at the University of Minnesota, I fell into a lengthy and wrenching argument with a friend about why he had chosen to major in social work. Because he had no belief in God, I was hoping to maneuver him into an admission of a higher value. I did not succeed. We live in a world, he said, that can make no appeal to a standard that measures every situation. There was no universal standard anchored in human biology, psychology, or spirituality. Above all, no transcendent standard existed that speaks to the human spirit. In our world, he said, "We human beings have only the choice between power and pity, and I have chosen pity. And thus I will be a social worker." He went on to say to me, "It is your incurable religiosity that propels you to want to believe in God and attach your values to this God." He was an older man, one who had returned to college on the GI bill, much more experienced and better read than I. His words cut to my heart, and they still do as I recall them now. I take with complete seriousness the possibility that he may be right.

I often think of him when I find myself in class discussions with students about how difficult it is to judge a particular meaning as authentic or inauthentic. "People vary so much in their choices," a student will say. I point out that this is to be expected because every person is embedded in a situation that is particular to her and therefore unique to her. Particular meanings will vary accordingly. This helps, but often a student will push the question deeper. "But you say she is supposed to be guided by universal values. Where do we find these values?"

We cannot evade her question. She lives in a postmodern age, and she is raising the quintessential postmodern question. She is asking whether universal values have a universal ground or foundation, and , if so, what is it, and where is it? In the Middle Ages, this question was not nearly so knotty. A great medieval thinker like Thomas Aquinas reflected the confidence of the age: an untroubled belief in a universal foundation of values. They were founded first in human nature, and through reason one could know the fundamental desires and tendencies of this nature. Aquinas knew that human beings desired happiness and that the only way to happiness lay in the practice of certain virtues that are dispositions to choose particular meanings in harmony with truth, love, justice, and beauty. He knew further, by faith and not by reason, that God had instilled in human beings the universal desire to know and love God in this life and the next. The way to this "supernatural" happiness lay in the virtues of faith, hope, and love, and these virtues were gifts of God and tasks for us.[33]

Later, in the modern age, whose beginning is usually judged to be in the Enlightenment of the eighteenth century, the tendency was to ground values in reason alone. God could not provide anything that we did not already know by reason. God too had a reasonable nature. Those who did not believe in God possessed the same universal reason as those who did believe. Relying on reason, believer and unbeliever could agree that certain values made for human happiness and that these values were valid for all human beings. The foundation of universal values is therefore a universal human nature marked and known in its depths by reason.

Our postmodern age, by contrast, is anti-foundationalist in tendency.[34] We have difficulty believing, on several grounds, that we can reason our way to a foundation for universal values. First, as postmoderns we are historicists. We know our world constantly changes and therefore we are alert to how different things were in the past. Two hundred years ago, most so-called rational people in the United States had a value system that judged slavery as not wrong. Now, we think it is wrong. Second, we are sensitive to difference; that is, we are multicultural. We know that meanings and values differ from culture to culture, from ethnic group to ethnic group. Values and meanings change not only from one historical time to another but also from one cultural space to another. Third, we are social constructionists: we know that values and meanings change because in each age and culture human beings, especially those in power, construct a discourse that tells people what to value and how to act.[35] For example, in the South before the Civil War, the discourse, often dependent on the Christian tradition, enforced a belief in racial inferiority that privileged white power and marginalized African Americans to slavery. And fourth, we are disillusioned. The modern age emerged out of the eighteenth century with a widespread hope for progress based on reason, science, and technology. People believed in the grand narrative of history as the continued march into an ever better life for all. But then the twentieth century unleashed wars and genocides of unprecedented horror. Technology became a Frankenstein's monster hurling us toward environmental disaster. To every grand scheme for human progress, we postmoderns bring an understandable suspicion and skepticism.

Probably the best-known U.S. philosopher today is Richard Rorty. He is postmodern in his thoroughgoing anti-foundationalism.[36] For him, reason has no access to reality at all, let alone a realm of universal values. And as an avowed atheist, he does not turn to God for a foundation to values. For Rorty, when we make a decision for a particular meaning, all we have is our situation and our freedom. Values do emerge, but only as social agreements that supply us with a shared discourse about what we should do, that is, about preferred social practices. For example, the current consensus of our group might declare that a heartless sexual seduction solely to bring pleasure to the seducer is morally wrong because it violates the values of mutual consent and love. In Rorty's version of anti-foundationalism, the would-be seducer is free to accept or reject these values, but he cannot call on a universal foundation for support. He cannot appeal to a universal human nature or a transcendent realm of values. He cannot call on God's will. Values for Rorty are strictly dependent on continued social acceptance or rejection. As society changes, so do values.

None of us escapes the influence of postmodernism. But the radical anti-foundationalism of a Rorty makes me very uneasy. In the spring of 1998, many people were horrified and angered by the so-called ethnic cleansing of the Albanians in Kosovo. Did they respond this way because of a value that is merely a social agreement? Is not the value of justice, which they saw so brutally violated, anchored in a foundation deeper and more secure than a shared discourse?[37]

It has been instructive to watch Frankl over the years trying to ground his values. In the 1963 edition of *Man's Search for Meaning*, he says we are beings "whose main concern is fulfilling a meaning and actualizing values."[38] These values have an independent existence, hovering over us as a lure and standard. Values, then, do not drive us from within but lure us from without.[39] In a book published a few years later, he appears to have adopted Max Scheler's beliefs in the independence of universal and eternal values, although he continues to be reticent about the foundational location of these values.[40] That book, however, is followed not long after by another in which he unflinchingly and without nostalgia says "that values are disappearing because they are transmitted by tradition and we are facing the decay of traditions,"[41] which would appear to bring him close to Rorty's view of values as social agreements. In the 1984 edition of *Man's Search for Meaning*, Frankl has excised all those passages that imply the existence of values independent of us in favor of a foundationalism that anchors universal values in a universal biology:

> Logotherapy conceives of conscience as a prompter that, if need
> be, indicates the direction in which we have to move in a given life
> situation. In order for us to carry out such a task, conscience must

apply a measuring stick to the situation one is confronted with, and this situation has to be evaluated in the light of criteria and in the light of a hierarchy of values. These values, however, cannot be espoused or adopted by us on a conscious level—they are something that we are. They have crystallized in the course of the evaluation of our species; they are founded on our biological past and are rooted in our biological depth.[42]

I find all this perplexing, for in the same book Frankl continues to refer to the human "spirit" and to avoid all reductions of the human being to biological "drive" and "instinct."[43] Furthermore, he clearly believes in God and speaks approvingly of those who "consider themselves accountable before God" when they choose a meaning. But if people are accountable to God, then God must in some way be accountable to universal values. How could God call us to follow the call of justice if God did not also practice justice? Yet Frankl never links God with values, and thus he is back to anchoring these values in human biology. But when we choose a meaning that is compatible with value, are we really simply following the unconscious call of our genes?

Biological foundationalism is an interesting way of combating the postmodern distrust of all foundations. When I read a very skillful expositor of biologism like Robert Wright, I am convinced that values are in part grounded in our genetic heritage.[44] Yet I cannot agree with those who claim that the lure of universal values is founded solely in our biology. Biology does not account fully for the challenge and summons we feel as we face a situation calling for an authentic meaning. Moreover, if values are fully anchored in the genes, I do not understand why conscience, which responds to the call to value, is so difficult to form, and even when fairly well formed, to follow. If someone like Frankl were to respond by saying that it is because we are free, then I have to ask: is it not precisely freedom that allows us to rise above the dictates and predispositions of our biology? Freedom leads great martyrs and prophets to defy the biological instinct for survival and give up their lives for a noble cause. How could this freedom be itself rooted solely in biological instinct? Finally, how is it that we choose *in*authentic meanings? How do we in freedom oppose values if our freedom is biologically grounded along with those values? How could biological evolution produce a freedom that then could defy biology?

Perhaps Rorty is right: we are left only with values constructed and sustained by social consensus. But surely social consensus is not enough to account for the pull and lure of values. If social consensus is the sole source of values, then it is difficult to understand the achievement of those great heroes of human history who have pushed human beings forward into a deeper discovery and awareness of values precisely because they defied the social consensus. Socrates, Gautama Buddha, the Hebrew prophets, Jesus, even Oskar Schindler in his faltering, ambivalent way, discerned and carried out values that put them at odds with the dominant social consensus. I find myself drawn toward believing it more reasonable to conclude that their human spirit was responding to the lure of values that transcend any social agreement and that these values reside in the ultimate dimension.

The transcendence of values finds further support in the universal tendency of human beings to assure themselves that they are right not just with themselves and their world, but also with the ultimate order of things. Individuals and societies build "sacred canopies" of value and meaning.[45] Or to put it another way, they anchor their meanings and values in religion. This is done even when, especially when, their meanings are inauthentic. Individuals and societies dress up the most warped meanings and disvalues in the finery of cosmic or sacred value.[46] In doing so, they provide a perverse yet powerful demonstration of the inexorable tendency of the human spirit toward a realm of transcendent value. For centuries, Christians supported slavery with references to God's will. Why did they so eagerly seek divine approval for such an inhuman institution? Power and greed are not enough to explain it. We see also a flight from an uneasy conscience. Conscience is the response of the human spirit to the lure of transcendent value. To pacify their consciences, human beings forge a false compatibility between inauthentic meaning and universal value. But in doing so, they give ironic and terrifying testimony to the pressure of the transcendent value on the human spirit.

Finally, we experience the inexhaustibility of meaning. Particular meanings when carried to completion do yield joy, yet also what the German philosopher Ernst Bloch called the "melancholy of fulfillment."[47] The human hunger for meaning reasserts itself, and we find ourselves propelled forward into ever new penultimate meanings. The values of truth, love, justice, and beauty are inexhaustible: no penultimate meaning can fully express any one of these values. Our yearning for value is therefore infinite, and the only satisfactory explanation for this infinite yearning is that these values are not only universal but also ultimate. They transcend not only the human situation but also the penultimate world. Values are realized in the world, but they exceed the world. Human beings go beyond themselves, transcend themselves, because there is a dimension of value that exceeds the limits of the world.

I am not proposing here a knockdown proof for the ultimate foundation of universal values. The evidence of our experience is too ambiguous to yield neat, rational proof. After all, many human experiences indicate the absence of ultimate and transcendent values. Chaos and terror, death and destruction, lies and hatred, ugliness and violence—they appear at times to rule the world. Authentic meanings are often so precarious and so easily frustrated and destroyed that the belief in the continuous luring presence of a transcendent realm of values to the world can seem like only a pious dream. The mind cannot move smoothly and rationally from such an ambiguous world to transcendent value. Some people indeed are tempted to postulate not a transcendent foundation of values but of dis-values. My anti-foundationalist college friend to whom I referred above once told me, "If there is anything that transcends the world, it is something bad, not something good."

Again, I am not offering a rational proof. Postmodernism has broken us of an easy confidence in a reason that claims to provide infallible certitude about foundations. Also, postmodernism has stimulated us to greater tolerance of and sensitivity to the variations of meaning and value among the world's cultures.[48] Strong conviction about our own values must now coexist with a willingness to sympathetically understand the values of others. We must be modest about the formulation of how the values we claim as universal apply to situations faced by other cultures. Here, postmodernism in its multicultural sensitivity to the difference of the other has had a good influence.

Nevertheless, it is not against reason to believe that transcendent values do break into this world and that we can dimly apprehend them. Human beings inch forward into richer and more sustained authentic meaning. Despite this ambiguous world, we feel a call, even a challenge, from beyond it. And in response we feel the weight of ultimate responsibility. We encounter a dimension that is calling us to account. To make sense of this experience, we seek an ultimate foundation for the presence and success of values in the penultimate world. This move is not compelled by reason alone—nor is it a leap of irrational faith. This move to the ultimate is a choice, inspired and confirmed in feeling, that is reasonable, though not strictly rational.

The Ultimate Foundation of Universal Values: God

To say that universal values have their foundation in the ultimate dimension would appear to lead to some form of Platonism. Plato believed that the values of truth, goodness, and beauty reside in a transcendent realm of ideas and that all penultimate meanings are imitations of these ideas.[49]

Varieties of Platonism continue to this day. The U.S. philosopher James K. Feibleman (1904–1987), is an "axiological realist"; namely, he believes that values dwell in a realm that transcends the empirical world.[50] The French philosopher René Le Senne (1882–1954) has a variation on the same theme.[51] The British philosopher Iris Murdoch (1919–1999) fashioned an interesting version of Platonism.[52]

Although I find myself believing that values are transcendent and anchored in the ultimate dimension, I find unconvincing the notion that such values exist in this dimension unanchored in anything but themselves. Values, after all, are static and inert. How is it that one feels their call, their summons, their pressure on conscience? Values cry out for some coordination with consciousness. How can anything be of universal value unless universal consciousness values it?[53] How do we account for the depth of our guilt when we violate the conscience, which is responding to the lure of values? The violation of an impersonal realm of inert values, no matter how lofty or noble, could not arouse such depth of spiritual anguish.[54]

Here, the question of a personal God arises. We have learned already that although Frankl in his private self clearly has a relationship to God,[55] he is vague on the nature of God and God's relationship to values, which of course is to be expected, given his reluctance to link universal values with the ultimate. "God is not dead, He is silent," Frankl has written. He thus prays to a God whose character remains unknown.[56]

Here, the human mind comes to a limit, to make way for the possibility of religious faith. Because this book offers a theology of Christian faith, it is that faith, the faith in the God of Jesus Christ, who was the God of Abraham, Isaac, Jacob, and the prophets, that I wish to begin exploring now.

Christians believe that we human beings cannot on our own intellectual power scale the heights and enter the mystery of God. On our own, we stand with respectful silence before the mystery of God. On our own, we have no mental grasp of the nature of God. On our own, we can only reach that point where it would seem reasonable to believe that these values find their ultimate foundation in God. We need to know more but cannot know more on our own.

The initiative, then, must come from God's side. If we cannot on our own enter the divine mystery, then we must wait for God to speak to our inquiring readiness to know. Christians believe that God has not remained silent, but has taken the initiative and come close to us. They believe that God communicated to human beings, not in such a way that the mystery of God is exhausted or neatly conceptualized, but in such a way that they really do know God, however dimly.[57]

God has communicated that God has an intrinsic relationship to universal values. In God, the values of truth, love, and beauty find their foundation. God does not simply approve of these values but is identified with them. In an inexhaustibly mysterious way, these values define the very being of God. Above all, the value of love (with justice as its further specification) is at the center of God's mystery.[58] God communicates not just about the values but communicates God's own being as characterized by these values. And if self-communication is precisely the definition of love, then love is at the heart of the divine nature. We are pushed then to say that the ultimate truth and the ultimate beauty is that God is love, which is the basis for the Christian conviction that the moral value of love enjoys a relative priority over the intellectual value of truth and the aesthetic value of beauty. Yet because these same values are united in God, they cannot always be sharply distinguished when we express them in authentic meaning: we apprehend not only truth in an elegant mathematical proof, but also beauty; not only beauty in a great film, but also truth; not only love in a truly good person, but also beauty.

Faith in God is faith in the living God. The God of the Hebrew and Christian Scriptures is Spirit, full of emotive energy. God energizes values and makes them flow into the world. When these values flow and press down on our consciences, their energetic call is the energy of God. When, therefore, we choose a particular meaning compatible with universal values, we do God's will, and the life of God dwells in us. Those who believe in the living God, "do not," says Frankl, "interpret their own lives merely in terms of a task assigned to them but also in terms of a taskmaster who has assigned it to them."[59] Indeed, if we build up a history of choosing authentic meanings in the world, we build up an identity as God's companion in the world, as God's daughter or son carrying out God's life in the world.

But we can know all this only if God has chosen not to be silent. Everything that I have said assumes that God has revealed God's self, that God has communicated God's self, or to use traditional theological language, that God has spoken a Word in the power of the Spirit, most perfectly in the life, death, and resurrection of Jesus. I do not mean that with God's Word the mystery of God has been exhausted. All language about God, even the language that seeks to express the experience of the Word and Spirit is analogical and symbolic, and therefore can never contain God's awesome depth.

Meaning and Self-Actualization

It is a commonplace today to speak of the meaning of life as self-actualization. Yet with Frankl I agree that self-actualization is not the meaning of life, but the consequence of finding and carrying out authentic meanings.[60] We should not then aim primarily at self-actualization but at meaning. Nor should we aim primarily at the wonderful feelings—the bodily pleasure, the psychic contentment, the spiritual joy—that accompany self-actualization. Rather, we should concentrate on the meaning and give ourselves over to it. The pursuit of meaning demands a loss of self, not certainly a self-abnegating denial or diminishment of the self, but a free, vital giving of the self over to the meaning. By aiming too consciously at actualization and its feelings, the self intrudes too much, threatening to turn the meaning into a mere instrument for the self. Suddenly, no meaning is worth it unless it gives the explicit promise of providing a feel-good "growth experience." Furthermore, the realization of meaning is often painful and difficult. And the nobler the meaning, the more frequent the accompanying physical and psychological discomfort, even anguish. If we focus too much on the pleasure, happiness, and joy flowing from meaning accomplished, we will be less likely to accept the suffering and deprivation often required to accomplish a meaning, particularly a lofty one.

This subordination of the self to the meaning is most obviously required when the meaning is in service of an ethical value. Genuine love and all the values that flow out of love (justice, fairness, sincerity, empathy, trust, courage, discernment, reliability, loyalty, and so on) are not realizable by the self that is too focused on the self as the final aim of it all. Even love directed toward the self, which indeed is an authentic meaning, will not be spiritually fruitful unless the self aimed at is the self that seeks meaning compatible with universal value. In other words, if you wish to love yourself, then you will be zealous that this self learns to give itself over to authentic meaning. One of the great paradoxes is that true love of the self requires that the self break out of the circle of self-love.[61]

I am reminded here of a conversation several years ago with a former student. She had been a person of intense self-preoccupation. And she took a delight in it: "I am taking a lifelong seminar," she once said, "and I am the topic." Psychologically acute and charming with people, she found herself as an adult drawn to a career in social work. Yet she had great difficulty in this career from the beginning. She quickly became impatient with her clients, finding them selfish for taking up so much of her time with problems she found either trivial or too close to her own. She was even jealous of them for having the time to make her listen to their problems. One day, she decided to quit social work and spend her life savings in a full-time pursuit of herself: "I need to find the real me" was her plea.

And her plea was plausible. She had been emotionally neglected as a child and went out into the world with a fragile understanding and possession of her adult self. Adding to her difficulty was that she was a woman in a culture in which energetic self-possession and assertion are not prized as so-called feminine virtues. Surely she was wise to step out of normal life to gain a more secure grasp of her internal situation. But her sabbatical from the normal course of life quickly stretched into weeks and then months. She spiraled down into an unfathomable abyss of self-concern, isolating herself from virtually all human contact. Finally, slowly, she began to climb out of the abyss, but only after concluding that the search for self could not forever be her sole focus. The search for self had to be accompanied by the search for meanings that can get the self out of the self. She eventually returned to the world of people and to social work. She proved the truth of the great line from John Donne: "The self is the Babylon that I must out of lest I perish."[62]

Not only the pursuit of ethical values requires getting outside the self. The scientist in pursuit of truth as an intellectual value must give herself to the object of her research. She must control the assertion of self-interest in order not to poison her inquiry with bias. She must bracket thoughts of quick self-gratification in order to persevere and not to seize precipitately on incomplete evidence. She must become one with her object so that she will be subliminally attuned to all its facets, so that she merges her mind with the object. The true scientist has a devotion to the object that is akin to love because it requires what love requires, the gift of the self and the frequent willingness to defer gratification.

The same is true for the artist in pursuit of an aesthetic value. To succeed, he must become one with the aesthetic project before him. A concert pianist, for example, must become the music; the music must become him. If he thinks only of the self-gratification of seeing the audience moved and elevated, he will not have the self-forgetfulness sufficient to ensure concentrated communion with the work he is performing.[63] He must practice, and often he must suffer. Only in this way, when he is finally onstage in performance, can he be fully surrendered to the work. One then can see him playing, in semimystical sympathy with the music, and at the end watch him hesitate for that brief moment when the music has ended but he still is in union with the music. When he turns to the deliriously appreciative audience, it is only then that he in full self-consciousness can bask in the radiant joy of self-actualization. But if from the beginning his attention had been only on this moment of joy, he would never have reached this moment. He needed to lose himself in the meaning of the music, rather than think only of the joy the self would garner when and after the music was performed.[64]

Meaning and the Power of Feeling

Frankl rejects the "will-to-power" and affirms the "will-to-meaning."[65] Surely, he is correct: to make power itself into a meaning, particularly power over others, is a deformation of the human spirit. Power alone is an inauthentic meaning. Yet power has a positive relationship to meaning that Frankl does not explore.

Let me go back to the beginning. As spirit, we are the tendency to meaning compatible with values. This is a dynamic tendency toward penultimate and ultimate meaning. This tendency has the felt quality of desire, yearning, aspiring. Not only our minds and wills but also our hearts are restless for authentic meaning. Nothing lies deeper in us than this desire, which is why the existential vacuum is so intolerable. The quest for meaning is energized by passionate desire.[66] G. W. F. Hegel, the great German philosopher, said, "Nothing great has been accomplished without passion."[67]

But desire needs the direction of concrete, particular meaning. The search for a particular meaning begins with a cognitive act: using reason and imagination, we discern in our situation a potential meaning. Guided by the lure of universal values, we choose an authentic meaning to be realized. It could be an active meaning: we might join the Peace Corps. It could be a receptive meaning: we might watch the fog roll in from the sea. Whether the meaning is active or receptive, we must move our will to seize it, and then our will must move the mind and body to carry it out. All this requires power. The meaning by itself cannot fulfill itself. We must move toward it and on it, but to move is to be empowered to move.

The power I am talking about here is not the same as powers, that is, talents and skills. Talents and skills are of course necessary to realize meaning. If I wish to practice medicine, I must have a sizeable set of talents and skills. Rather, I am talking about the power that moves us toward a meaning and sustains us in the realization of meaning. It is in part the power of feeling. Feeling is active even before we make a choice for a meaning, for when we turn our minds to our situation, not only the head goes to work, but also the heart. The heart accompanies the head in its search, responding to potential meanings with varying degrees of felt attraction. The most attractive meaning evokes the strongest desire, and this desire helps move the will toward choosing this meaning.[68] A colleague of mine recalls the day when she first felt the rush of desire toward the career of college teaching. After days of examining her situation, she suddenly felt a lively and energizing upsurge attach itself to this meaning.

So strong was the heightened desire for this meaning that her will came to a decision quite spontaneously. So full of feeling, so passionate, was her desire that she overcame her intellectual self-doubts and started on the long and arduous road toward the doctorate. It was this passionate desire that kept her on that road. She also needed the continued help of the will to keep her feeling focused and resolute. When feeling went slack for a stretch, her will kicked in and kept her slogging on until the feeling surged again with all its energizing power. In the end, she did something great, thanks to the power of feeling.

As we move through the day scanning our emerging life-situation for possible meaning, there occur thousands of large and small movements of feeling, many of which take place without reflective self-consciousness. If our basic predispositions to feel are well tuned to values, we feel curious, interested, and attracted to meanings compatible with truth, beauty, and love. If they are mistuned, we will be drawn toward meanings that serve disvalues. I am not saying that we are *ruled* by feelings. Feelings are not all-powerful. Feelings are indeed spontaneous and thus can seem at times overpowering, yet there remains deep in our spirit the unfathomable mystery of freedom, by which we choose to avow or disavow a feeling.[69] If we avow it, then we go with its flow and act on it. Each time we avow a feeling, we strengthen our predisposition to have it again. If someone, for example, sees a person lying in a ditch moaning with pain and goes with the feeling of compassion that wells up within him, he strengthens the predisposition to feel compassion again, in time turning it into a habit, that is, a virtue.[70] He becomes a compassionate person. If he disavows the feeling of compassion, resists its flow, and acts against it, and does that again and again, the predisposition to feel the compassion appropriate to the situation weakens, and he can lose his predisposition to that feeling. His heartlessness will become a bad habit, that is, a vice. He will become a heartless person. Virtues and vices are habits of feeling with pervasive influence on our choices of meaning. Yet choices turn back on feeling and influence its flow: feeling needs the cooperation of the will.

In the previous section on self-actualization, I spoke of the feeling of joy that the pianist feels as he finishes his performance and shares with the audience his and their joyful exaltation. But we do not have to wait for achieved meaning to have that joy. This joy can begin to occur while we are still in the process of achieving that meaning, and this joy feeds and strengthens the desire to persevere to the end when the joy will be fully ours. I am reminded of Barbara McClintock, who won the Nobel prize in 1983 for her work on the genetic makeup of corn. This was an authentic meaning in service of the intellectual value of truth. Yet her work in the early stages was met with incomprehension by most of her colleagues. Undaunted, she returned to her research with a desire even more resolute and concentrated. A colleague, Evelyn Wilken, remarked: "It was really a great thing to see. She was really getting such intense joy out of it." The philosopher W. Jay Wood comments: "Clearly she [McClintock] embodies the virtue of perseverance. She is not much discouraged by her failure to garner her colleagues' recognition. But notice how this appears to be grounded in the joy she derives from her work, her deep delight in the subject matter itself."[71]

The power of feeling that searches for meaning, desires meaning, sustains meaning, and results from meaning can be communicated to others. And when we do that, we communicate not only the meaning but also the feeling that clothes this meaning. In this way, we can empower and energize people. A friend of mine who has made civil rights his lifelong passion frequently tells the story of his having been there in person to hear Martin Luther King Jr.'s "I Have a Dream" speech. It was August 23, 1963. He had come primarily out of curiosity and as the afternoon wore on became rather bored. When King came to the podium, there was a great stir and tremendous applause, but the first fifteen minutes or so of King's speech were rather subdued. Then the words rang out, "I have a dream!" and, as my friend put it, "He really started smokin'." My friend's curiosity gave way to excitement and then, with King's last soaring words, "Free at last, free at last, thank God almighty, free at last!," to the most elevated feeling. He was stirred, inspired, transported. The effect of the speech was to jolt him out of his complacency and move him into a meaning to which he has been attached with indeflectable devotion. What moved him was King's passionate desire for interracial justice and peace. This was his meaning, and he passed it on charged with his feeling. King empowered my friend.

King's meaning was authentic. It expressed the universal moral value of love, whose public expression is justice. Earlier, I argued that it is reasonable to believe that the universal values are anchored in God. God beholds these values in consciousness and identifies with them. Would it be unreasonable to believe that God also *feels* these values and thereby energizes them with divine feeling? I think not, though here again the human spirit reaches a limit and has to wait upon God's Word. And this Word does come but not alone. It comes empowered by God's Spirit, which in faith and love we can understand to be God's feeling made resolute and decisive by God's will. Spirit is that invisible and elusive power attached to God's Word that empowers us to feel and act as God's sons and daughters.

The quest for meaning issues finally in hearing God's Word and feeling God's Spirit. Christian faith understands God's self-communication in Word and Spirit as having reached a climax in the life, death, and resurrection of Jesus Christ. To that Word and Spirit we respond in faith, love, and hope. We shall examine all this in greater depth in the following chapters.

TWO

Meaning and the Formation of Human Identity

Christians believe that God exists and is not silent. They believe that God speaks through a Word in the power of the Spirit. In this Word, God communicates universal values with which God is fully identified. God clothes these values in feeling that gives them their power as they come to human beings. God thus animates the Word with the power of God's Spirit. Christians believe further that this Word and Spirit are spoken with special meaning and power through Jesus of Nazareth. Indeed, they believe that Jesus is so identified with God's Word that they do not hesitate to confess in faith that Jesus is God's Word in the power of the Spirit.

How are we to understand this? What does it mean to say that God speaks? And how are we to understand how the divine speech shapes the identity of Jesus? These are the questions that I shall be concerned with in this chapter and the next.

But before dealing with the issues of divine speech and Jesus' identity, I should like to explore the nature of human speech. Only after having gained some understanding of the human word can we then go on to understand the divine Word. There are similarities and differences between the two, and thus we shall be exploring the human word as an analogy to the divine Word. Yet only to some degree is either word explicable in human language, for we are dealing here with complex and mysterious realities. Neither the human word nor the divine Word can be neatly pinned down into categories that make them fully comprehensible. Yet reason illumined by faith can bring some understanding of the human and divine word and the analogy between them.

The Human Word

The human word has an intrinsic connection with meaning. Through word, human beings attempt to communicate meaning. Human beings have meanings they have sought and now live by, and through a word they can take these meanings and communicate them to others. My wife has among her meanings that of being a nurse. She can take this meaning and express it in word to another.

But not only human life has meanings. From my desk I can look out my window at the silver maple that canopies our backyard. It is huge. Last summer I measured its girth: fourteen feet! It has a meaning, not a meaning it had to search for and then freely choose, but a meaning that was built into its genetic inheritance. It grew into the full stature of its meaning by a necessary development that did not require choices. I can take the meaning of this tree and visualize it within my mind as an image, subsume it under a concept, and express it as an inner word to myself.[1] I can say in my mind, This is a tree. When I express this inner word to another person, I externalize the inner meaning, the inner word, in an outer word. I can say to another person, "This is a tree." I can do this with any region of reality, not only the world of nature where I find trees, plants, and animals, but also the world of human culture where I find houses, stores, and the stock market. I can also look to the world within the human self where I find moods, feelings, and images. These too have meaning that I can conceptualize and then express in inner and outer word. Or I can look to that region of reality that transcends nature and culture and try to find, internalize, and express the meanings I find there. I can discover and express to myself and others the meanings of angels, God, purgatory, and departed souls. Finally, there is the region of possible reality, where I try to grasp and express the meanings of what might be or is imagined to be.[2] Language, therefore, is the attempt to communicate to self and others the meanings found in all regions of reality.

We have then a four-step process: we discover meaning in some region of reality, give birth to this meaning within ourselves, express it to ourselves in inner word, and then communicate it to others in outer word.

This is a mysterious process: our reason can never neatly and exhaustibly understand or express it.[3] And this is an active process: we do not just passively reflect the meaning of reality, but actively distill it and then reproduce it within our minds. Because the mind is active and not just passively reactive, mistakes and distortions are possible. And since each individual mind is in part shaped by the thought and language of the community to which it belongs, the individual is prone to repeat the mistakes and distortions of the community mind. Yet this should not lead us to a postmodern despair about the capacity of the mind to grasp the real.[4]

If the human word is the attempt to communicate meaning—I say "attempt" because not every word is successfully communicated—then a word can be verbal or nonverbal. Usually when we think of a human word we think of a verbal word, of human speech, or of the translation of speech into a code such as writing or Morse. But there is also what we might call nonverbal speech. I can tell someone verbally where the nearest grocery store is, but I also can communicate the same meaning nonverbally by pointing my index finger. Verbal language dominates communication because of the enormous range of its vocabulary. Verbal language, however, is based on a rather narrow exercise of the body: larynx, throat, mouth, nose, and tongue. Nonverbal language, by contrast, can mobilize the whole body—a full body hug, for example—and thereby communicate meaning with great power.

Whether words are verbal or nonverbal, they are always *outer* words; that is, they are events out in the world of space and time that are perceived by one or more of the senses of hearing, sight, touch, smell, or taste. The speaker has to do something with his or her body: vibrate the larynx, point the finger, wrap the arms around someone, apply the cologne, or serve the cake. If human beings were to lose all movement of their bodies, language would cease. I cannot communicate the meaning of love for someone by standing before her in a mute, motionless state. I must get that meaning into my body; I must incarnate it; I must create an outer word that strikes the senses of the body of the person I love. I must verbally say "I love you" or nonverbally say it with an ardent look or energetic hug.

The movement of meaning from speaker to hearer is the purpose of language. Without meaning, one does not have language. But it would be a mistake to regard the purpose of language as only the transference of meaning. We do things with words other than merely communicate meaning.[5] To use the technical terminology favored by linguists and philosophers of language, language goes beyond semantics (meaning) into pragmatics (doing).[6]

To illustrate the pragmatics of language, let me give an example. A mother is on a riverbank with her seven-year-old son. It is springtime, and the water is high and swift. They are a safe distance away when suddenly the boy begins to run toward the water. She quickly says, "Daniel, the water is deep and fast." She has conveyed meaning through outer word. She has distilled a meaning from the natural world—the condition of the water, given birth to it within her mind, and then through her body created a verbal word that conveys this meaning to her son. She thereby intends to transfer this meaning from her mind to his and in doing so inform him of the condition of the river.

Suppose, however, that Daniel responds by saying, "Thanks for the information, Mom" and then continues to run toward the river. Would the mother believe that she had accomplished all the purposes of her word? On one level, certainly. She made an assertion about the river, and he believes her, and so he has been informed. But clearly, she has some other purpose in mind: she is trying to get her son to do something, namely, to stop running toward the water. If, then, we judge the success of her word solely by the meaning that informs, she will fail in the primary function of her word, which is to direct the boy to act in a certain way. For she was not simply asserting something about the river with the intention to inform, but warning the boy with the intention to direct the boy's actions. The final judgment, therefore, of whether she accomplished her purpose rests on how the boy acts. Language has been enlisted here to serve a function that goes beyond the mere transference of meaning.[7] The mother's word here carries not primarily the *informative* function, but the *directive* function: she desires to direct him to act in a certain way.[8]

Another function of language is the *emotive*. The speaker expresses an emotion or feeling for the purpose of arousing a particular feeling or emotion in the hearer. Suppose the mother, in a state of exaltation and wonder, exclaims to Daniel, "Daniel, observe the mighty rush of the swift and deep river! The renewal of life is making its entrance!" She intends to inform him, yes, and she intends to direct him to observe, yes, but the primary function of her word here is emotive: she wants to evoke in him her feeling of exaltation and wonder. If in response he looks at the river and then says with an indifferent shrug, "Yeah, Mom, nice river," then her communicative purpose is not fully successful.

With the emotive function, therefore, the speaker is trying to communicate the emotion, not merely the meaning of the emotion. She wishes the hearer not only to be informed about the feeling but also to feel the feeling. There is a difference, for example, between communicating a detailed and precise description of an exalted feeling and communicating the feeling itself. In the first case, the speaker is informing the hearer about the exaltation and thus tries to be accurate, precise, and nuanced. In the second case, the speaker wants the hearer to feel his exaltation and thus tries to be vibrant, poetic, and high-flown.[9]

Words that aim to arouse feeling are emotive; words that aim to move the hearer to action are directive. Words that carry the emotive or directive function have not only meaning but also power. Not all words carry emotive and directive power. Most, perhaps, have the clean transmission of meaning as their sole or primary function.[10] But many words aim to arouse feeling or effect action and, to be completely successful, require power.[11]

The Language of Self-Communication

Like many of my generation, I have on occasion sought out a psychological counselor for help. When I am with a counselor, I try above all to be informative. The counselor wants to know about my deepest feelings, images, and thoughts. She wants to know about my psychological needs, about my meanings and values. To give the counselor what she wants, I have to be as clear and precise as possible. I must ensure that I have grasped the meaning of my inner reality and found the correct outer word to express that meaning. To be sure, the wise counselor will also be alert to the texture and power of my feelings. She will even try to enter into empathetic identification with my feelings. But all this is at the service of her becoming better informed about my inner reality. Informative success is my primary aim.

To be informatively successful with my counselor is a more complex process than one might first think. It requires the steps on her side of understanding, belief, and trust.

First, my counselor must understand the verbal and nonverbal code that my outer words are using. If I am speaking in English, she must understand English. This is a cognitive act; she must use her head to understand what I am saying. Even within our shared English, she and I must have a considerable overlap in our agreement about what certain English words mean. This may require some learning and adjustment on the spot. For example, she will probably discover quite early on that I am quite fussy and conservative in my use of words. Thus, I make it a point of linguistic honor always to use the word *disinterested* in its older meaning of "impartial," and never in its newer meaning of "uninterested" or "indifferent." If I use nonverbal words, if, for example, I deliberately shrug my shoulders to communicate indifference, then she must know this as part of my nonverbal code.

Second, she and I must share a belief in the existence and possibility of the realities my words are referring to. There must, in other words, be considerable overlap in our respective reality-horizons. She may *understand* what I mean when I say that my astrologer told me to consult Elvis and then my guardian angel before choosing a counselor, but if she does not believe in astrological influences, the terrestrial return of Elvis, and guardian angels, then I am not going to succeed in fully informing her, that is, convincing her. Our general beliefs on what is real and possible are simply too different at this point in the conversation.

Third, she must trust me. Even if she believes in the existence of guardian angels or is at least open to the possibility, she may not trust me when I tell her that an angel told me to seek counseling. She may believe that I am telling her that to curry favor with her or manipulate her ideas of me. In a word, she may believe that I am not sincere, that I am telling a lie.[12] Or she may believe that I am sincere but self-deceived, not about the existence of angels, but about my report that an angel told me to seek counseling. She may feel and intuit that I am terrified of counseling and have tricked myself into believing that an angel has told me to seek it out.

If, however, my counselor understands my language, shares my general beliefs, and trusts me, I will accomplish my intention to inform her. If there is a significant breakdown at any point—if I cannot make myself understood, if our general beliefs are radically different, if she consistently distrusts my ability and willingness to see things and tell things as they really are—then my intention to inform her will suffer. In the extreme case, the counselor and I may decide to break off the counseling relationship.

With my counselor, I am engaged primarily in communicating about myself. I am animated primarily by the purpose to inform her. This communication is indeed complex, but it takes on considerably more complexity when my purpose is not simply to communicate about myself but to communicate my *self* to another in order to elicit a communication of the other's self back to me. I am referring to the language of reciprocal self-communication, which is the language of deepest communion, participation, and mutual indwelling. I am referring to the language of love, to those deeply personal words in which the self goes out to the other with the aim that the self of the other will come back. These are the words between I and Thou, between lover and beloved.[13] These words intend far more than informative success. Let me explain.

Deeply personal words are words of self-communication, not just words about the self. As such, they are informative, but not merely or primarily informative. With these words, the emotive and directive functions are as important as the informative function. Meaning alone is not enough. The meaning must ally itself with emotive and directive power, for the speaker here is not only trying to inform the hearer but also move the hearer to feel and act toward him the way the speaker feels and acts toward her. To accomplish this, he must ensure that the meaning he speaks in outer word be clothed in the power of his feeling. When he says "I love you," he must infuse his word with the energy, the spirit, the élan of his meaning, which is the feeling of love.

The outer word *I love you* is extraordinarily complex. It carries a meaning that dwells in the inner self of the one who loves. The one who loves senses his whole self tending and moving toward the one he loves. This love is a tending and moving of the mind and will propelled by a rush of feeling. There is no love without the power of feeling. The meaning then is the deepest self in its psychological and spiritual feeling-movement toward the other. It is the movement of desire. Somehow, this movement must be translated into outer word.

The self that loves is the whole self: biological, psychological, and spiritual. If he as lover is to communicate this whole self, then he first must be informative. Deeply personal words go beyond the informative, but they include the informative. He need not say much about his biological self—she can observe that. He does need to talk about his psychological self: his temperament and why it developed the way it did; his unique constellation of needs and abilities; his instabilities, fears, and neurotic tendencies. Most important, he must tell her about his spiritual self, about his meanings, past, present, and future, and how they express his attachment to values. He must tell her about the history of his choices and how they arose out of the intersection of situation and freedom.

Yet he must do more than inform her of his meanings and values. Since he is communicating himself and not just about himself, he needs to infuse these meanings with the feeling power that moves him toward the realization of these meanings and values. She must not only know about, but feel, the power of the feeling he attaches to these meanings and values. She must be able to feel the depth and intensity of his feelings. Above all, she must feel the energizing feeling of his love for her. He cannot say "I love you" as if he were merely passing on a trivial piece of information. Rather, he must energize that meaning with the feeling. Only then can he have any hope that his word will not just have informative success, but also emotive and directive success.

I do not intend to say that the informative success is unimportant. Indeed, in the typical communication it enjoys a certain chronological priority over the emotive and directive functions, thereby lending truth to the old adage, *nihil amatum nisi prius cognitum* (nothing is loved unless it is first known). Informative success means first that the meaning gets across to the hearer. The speaker, the lover in this case, must make himself understood. The hearer as the beloved must understand his code when he verbally or nonverbally tells her he loves her. Second, she must share his general belief in the reality and possibility of love between two human beings. Love must exist within the reality-horizon of speaker and hearer. Finally, she must trust that he is sincere and not self-deceived. If at any point in this informative transfer things break down, then the whole communication breaks down. But if he can succeed with her informatively, then she will be at least open to allowing emotive and directive success to occur.

Emotive success also has its steps. First, the hearer must feel the speaker's feeling for her. This moment is more receptive: she allows his feeling to flow in and touch her. In the second step, she must feel her feeling for him. This moment is more active: her feeling of love flows out to him. Each step requires her capacity and willingness to feel. She may lack the capacity to feel his feeling flowing into her because she is emotionally numb as the result of a recently failed relationship. Perhaps she has a long history of failed relationships going back to childhood when her parents failed to love her properly, which diminished, even virtually extinguished, her capacity to feel love from another. She may have the ability to feel receptively and actively, and indeed may already be feeling an incipient rush of emotion from him and toward him, but may decide to disavow it, to cap it, and in doing so, gradually shrink her capacity to feel love from him or for him.[14] And she may have a perfectly good reason for choosing this way: perhaps she is a first-year medical student who does not have the time or energy right now for a deep love relationship. In her freedom, she can choose to prevent his self-communication from having full emotive success.

Even if his word is emotively successful with her and she is aroused to feel love in return, she still has to act on it. For she also feels the directive power of his word. She feels the urgency of his desire that she not only feel love for him but also act on that feeling. She knows that he wishes ardently to hear the same outer word from her that he spoke to her. She may, however, lack the capacity or ability to speak that word. She may lack skill in the language of love. She may be a pervasively shy person for whom any outer word, especially one so personal, is frightening and thereby paralyzing.

Or she may have the ability to act but not the willingness. She may feel the love and welcome it, but choose not to act on it, waiting instead for a better time or place. Perhaps she is self-deceived about her capacities: she is able to speak the outer word of love but doubts her ability to do so. So she chooses not to speak. She may be that medical student mentioned above: part of her strategy to avoid intimacy will have to include not only disavowing and capping her incipient feeling for him, but refusing to express it. Expression of feeling in outer word would mislead him. The expression of feeling has this strange way of bending back and strengthening feeling. So she chooses not to act, even though she has the capacity. All of this shows that the directive power of the speaker's love is communicated out of his freedom and to *her* freedom. The power of genuine love is always persuasive, never coercive.[15]

It would be a mistake to conclude from the outline above that informative, emotive, and directive success occur in neatly chronological and distinguishable steps. Typically, informative success enjoys a chronological priority, but it does not always happen that way. It is possible, for example, for the hearer to feel the speaker's feeling for her, to feel that feeling in return, and to act on it, that is, to allow the speaker's word to have emotive and directive success, even before she explicitly and self-consciously understands the meaning of her feeling flowing toward the speaker. The emotive and directive power may begin to be effective before its meaning is clear and known to the mind. Heart often precedes head in this kind of deeply personal communication. So in response to his "I love you" she may say, "But I don't love you," even though in fact she is already beginning to feel love in return and indeed expressing it in nonverbal action. We get a glimpse here of the complex relation that can obtain among the three functions. They can be quite neatly demarcated in theory, but in practice they blur into one another, with each function highly interactive with the other.

The important point here is that all three functions must enjoy success if the circle of self-communication is to be fully completed. The deepest self of one person goes out to the other and elicits from the other person a return of the deepest self. The speaker clarifies his meaning in outer word and infuses it with emotive and directive power. The hearer is informed by the meaning and moved to feeling and action by the power. The functions fold in upon each other without losing their distinctiveness. Freedom pervades the whole exchange. Two persons become I and Thou in mutual self-communication.

Word and Human Identity

In chapter 1, I spoke of the three dimensions of the human being: biological, psychological, and spiritual. To each dimension, there corresponds a dimension of human identity. Let us look at each in more detail.

First, human beings have a *biological* identity. It is universal and it is unique. It is universal because all human beings share the same DNA code that forms the foundation of a universally shared anatomy and physiology. They have the same brain structure, the same circulatory system, the same glandular secretions, and the same two-legged gait. They have the same instincts: the groping and sucking reflex, the fear response, the survival impulse, the drive to reproduce. And yet the biological identity is also unique. When one sperm fertilizes one egg, the respective universal DNA codes merge into a configuration that is unique to the new human zygote. This zygote will develop into a human being that is biologically unique. This human being will have a hair color, skin hue, musculature, height, gender, athletic ability, energy level, and physiognomy in a combination that will distinguish him or her from others.

Second, human beings have a *psychological* identity. It is universal and it is unique. It is universal because all human beings share the same psychological needs for solitude and conviviality, challenge and achievement, love given and love received, autonomy and mutuality, surprise and routine. All have the capacity for humor, intelligence, and language. All have a temperament or personality. Nonetheless, psychological identity is unique. The temperament of each person is a unique constellation of extroversion and introversion, dreaminess and practicality, rationality and emotion, coolness and effervescence, spontaneity and order.[16] The unique temperament of each person in turn affects the strength of his or her psychological needs. An extrovert has a greater need for conviviality. An orderly type has a greater need for routine, predictability, and closure.

Third, all human beings have a dimension of spirit and thus a *spiritual* identity. They all have the dynamic tendency toward particular meanings compatible with universal values. This is the deepest level of human identity. Both human beings and animals have biological and psychological identities, but only human beings have a spiritual identity.[17] In the depths of the spiritual identity is also found freedom, and thus spiritual identity is always at least in part the consequence of free choice. A further ingredient of the spiritual identity is the power of feeling that the person attaches to each meaning and the value each meaning expresses. Except when feeling diffuses itself into unnameable mood, feelings are intentional; that is, they are attached to and shaped by meanings. When, for example, I conjure up an image of my mother, I feel admiration and love. Or when I think on the meaning that is this book in progress, I feel stubborn and passionate desire (I *will* get it finished). A person's meanings and the intensity and endurance of the feelings she brings to them constitute a person's character. A strong character has a commitment to his or her meanings that is suffused with steadfast feeling. If the meanings are authentic, then such a character is not only strong but good. Some people have a passionate commitment to inauthentic meanings and thus to disvalues. Their characters are strong but not good.

Human identity on all three levels is the result of the intersection of fate and freedom. Fate operates with special effectiveness on the biological level. Our biological identities are largely the result of the sexual union of our biological parents, which occurred without our consultation. Granted, their union probably occurred because of their free choice, but they had no control over which sperm struck which egg. The environment (for example, the availability of food or incidence of disease) we grow up in can also affect our biological identity, and during the crucial early years that environment is not a matter of our choice. I was born with the biological predisposition toward spinal curvature, facial acne, and myopia. Today, I woke up with a back spasm so bad that I cannot straighten up. Just before I sat down today to work on this book, I looked in the mirror and saw a bent-over person with thick glasses and acne scars. Such a fate!

Somewhat less obviously, yet more so than we might suspect, fate shapes our psychological identity. Part of the temperament we each possess is first of all the result of our biological identity. My mother gave birth to nine children. She insists that each child showed a different temperament from day one. "It's in the genes," she says with utter certainty. Yet I think she would, if pushed, be willing to admit the added influence of social environment on psychological identity.[18] A child born with a disposition toward introversion may find this introversion strengthened if the sibling order has placed her between two very rambunctious extroverts. Not only individual siblings have their own temperaments, the whole family has a temperament, a certain family style, that leaves its mark on all its members. In addition, there are ethnic, regional, and national temperaments. Those of us who have been raised in Minnesota, a state profoundly influenced by Northern European immigration, cannot help but be tilted in the direction of stoicism, reticence, and ingratiating nonassertiveness (known around these parts as "Minnesota Nice"). Whole nations display temperamental leanings. Seventy-five percent of all Americans score "extrovert" on the Myers-Briggs Type Indicator: surely this results in a social environment that pressures individual personalities in that direction, even if they have been genetically endowed with a predisposition toward introversion.[19]

Even the spiritual identity, which resides in that dimension of the self where freedom also resides, is partly the consequence of fate. Long before we exercise our freedom to choose certain meanings and values, other people were shaping our spiritual identities according to their meanings and values.[20] Typically, they were our biological or adoptive parents, especially during our formative years. They had meanings and values that were energized, more or less, with feeling. If they were energetically engaged in the meaning of parenthood, they tried to pass their spiritual identities on to us. They, or others who played a surrogate parental role, gave us our primary spiritual identity. How many times have you heard someone say "I got my values from my parents"? The older we become, the more likely we are to say this. The more we see of the past behind us, the heavier weighs the hand of fate.

In the ideal situation, the primary spiritual-identity givers have made a conscious and energetic commitment to authentic meanings expressive of the universal values of truth, love, justice, and beauty, and then passionately embraced the meaning of parenthood. They have developed deep and consistent predispositions to think, feel, and act authentically when encountering a situation with a meaning-potential. These virtues in turn motivate them to launch and sustain the project of communicating their meanings and values to their children.

These ideal parents are in effect engaged in a project of self-communication. Self-communication in this context is parental love, and loving their children is their particular meaning. This means that one of the values that is going to come across to their children is the value of love itself. The parents may also endeavor to pass on the values of truth and beauty; indeed, their own lives may be so caught up in these values that the value of love might receive less explicit attention. They may then express their love for their children somewhat more indirectly by shaping them more explicitly around the value of truth or beauty. For example, a family of musicians could find that much of the love that is communicated is done through music and for music. Or a family of great naturalists who spend a great deal of time doing research in the African bush could find that the focus on truth is the medium for their love. Still others might give the highest explicit attention to love as the highest value, and frankly, this would be my preference, as the reader might guess from my earlier remarks in chapter 1 where I placed love and justice, the moral values, at the pinnacle of the hierarchy of values. Doing so does not mean that the values of truth and beauty are or should be neglected. Indeed, the examples just given of the musicians and naturalists show that truth and beauty can be at the service of love. But love should be the core value that both encourages and unifies the other values. For this reason, when parents communicate their spiritual identities, they are loving, but ideally they are very self-consciously focused on love as the value they want most to see their children take on and make the core of their spiritual identities. What animates the self-communication, love, should also be the core meaning of the communication. Loving parents, it seems to me, should above all be dedicated to rearing loving children.

Parents who wish to communicate love as a meaning must translate the meaning into their bodies and then produce outer words with those bodies. If love is to be an identity-forming meaning and value, then it must be communicated. Since this is a self-communication, the language used must be deeply personal: it must be at once informative, emotive, and directive. Their parental words, whether verbal or nonverbal, must say in effect, "I love you and I want you to be loving" and say it with power.

To illustrate this process of parental self-communication in more detail, let me focus on one of the parents, the mother, even though the father is or ought to be equally engaged. The process begins with the mother's secure and conscious grasp of her own meanings, especially the meaning of love and the universal value it expresses. We can imagine that well before the birth of her first child she comes to full awareness of this meaning by self-consciously expressing it to herself in the following inner word: *My core meaning and value is love and I wish to communicate that meaning and value to my child.* This interior self-expression in inner word is a complex act of self-doubling, for when she utters this inner word about herself, she then sees herself in this word, as if she were looking at herself in an interior mental mirror. Philosophers would say that she, the subject, has made herself into an object, not a material object outside herself but a spiritual object inside herself. The I-subject looks at the me-object, and in this way comes to a conscious grasp of the identity of the I-subject. In this case, she as the expectant mother sees expressed in her me-object one who is committed to love as a meaning and value.

Yet there is more to this process of self-doubling in inner word. I am sure all of us have looked at ourselves in the mirror and not liked what we saw. I look in the mirror and wish I had better skin, a flatter stomach, a less prominent chin. At that moment of looking, a feeling of sour dissatisfaction flows from the I-subject to the me-object in the mirror. This dissatisfaction can also well up when I look at myself in my interior mirror. On certain days, I see in the me-object someone not living up to my meanings and values. This evokes negative feelings from the I-subject, feelings of aversion, shame, and guilt. I find myself not loving what I see. My whole day is affected. I walk around down in my spirit, affecting others for the worse by my negative energy. On other days, I see in the me-object a reasonably good person committed to meanings and values. The flow of feeling from the I-subject to the me-object is then warm and affirmative.

I walk around up in my spirit, affecting others for the better by my positive energy. I am particularly high when my I-subject sees in the me-object someone committed to love as a meaning and value. Love evokes love, and the I-subject embraces the me-object, and this embrace opens out to include the whole world. What we have are two operations: the I-subject expresses itself in inner word and thereby mirrors itself, and then the I-subject evaluates the me-object, which evokes a flow of positive or negative feeling toward that me-object.[21]

This is what happens to our expectant mother. Her I-subject expresses and embraces her me-object as loving, and this evokes a flow of positive feeling toward her me-object. She then pledges to communicate her me-object to her child. When that child comes into the world, she will activate her body and create deeply personal words, charged with feeling, that will communicate her loving self to her child. She hopes thereby to shape the child's spiritual identity around the value of love. Thus, she is doing more than loving the child; she is giving identity.

Her outer word of self-communication can be nonverbal and verbal. Much of the identity-forming love that parents communicate to infants is in fact nonverbal: hugs, kisses, caresses, massages, powderings, and various bodily ministrations—all "spoken" with feeling. As the years go on, however, the verbal word becomes increasingly more prominent in communicating with the developing child.[22]

All three functions—the informative, the emotive, and the directive—are ingredients in the identity-forming word of love from parent to child. The parent is not only informing the child that she or he is loved, but infusing it with emotive and directive power. The parent wants the child to feel the parent's love, to feel love for the parent in return, and then to act on it. And since the particular meaning of love from this particular parent to this particular child is also an expression of a universal value, the parent desires that the child love not only the parent but others as well. If the parent's particular meaning is not consciously grasped by the parent as the expression of a universal value, there is the danger that the child will see his or her spiritual identity as adequately expressed only by returning love to the parent.

Spiritual identity-formation takes time. A parent is fully communicating the meaning and power of love from the beginning to her infant child, but the infant cannot take much of it into his or her own spiritual identity. Much of the biological identity is already established with the nine-month gestation in the womb, whereas the spiritual identity has hardly begun when the child is born. The spiritual gestation will take many years, with an uncertain outcome. A parent, therefore, can communicate much more of herself to a ten-year-old than a five-year-old. A parent can expect that her fifteen-year-old will have gone far in receiving the value of love and all those values (justice, honesty, fairness, compassion, thoughtfulness, etc.) that flow from love. A parent is fully communicating her spiritual identity to the child from the beginning, but only gradually can this identity dwell in the child as the child's self-possession. Only over many years does the child develop the capacity to take on the spiritual self offered by the parent.

Spiritual identity descends upon the child as fate. As infants, we human beings are given no choice about who will be our primary spiritual-identity givers. In the lottery that is life, some of us are reared by people of good but weak character, who have a halfhearted commitment to authentic meanings, or by people of bad but strong character, who have a fierce attachment to inauthentic meanings. The possible mixtures of good and bad, strong and weak are infinite, and the mixture imposed on us is a luck of the draw. Even if our identity-givers are relatively good people, they are influenced by the wider cultures of clan, region, ethnic group, and nation that are always to some degree corrupted by inauthentic meanings and disvalues. These wider cultures tilt identity-givers toward inauthentic meanings in ways often invisible to the identity-givers. Fate, then, imposes upon us not only our spiritual identity-givers, but also the culture in which these identity-givers are embedded. Life is not fair!

Yet we are free, are we not? Yes, but even freedom is partly the result of fate. Some identity-givers in their single-minded zeal to pass on identity become terrified that their child will choose to reject what they are communicating. They restrict freedom and try to turn out clones. But a spiritual identity that is not possessed in freedom is not truly possessed; rather, it is passively tolerated in slavish conformity or brusquely rejected in aggressive rebellion. In either case, the child is in thrall to the parent and not in possession of herself. The wise parent, therefore, offers not only meanings and values but allows the child gradually to exercise more and more freedom. Only a spiritual identity freely received is truly possessed. Not only the values, therefore, are received from the parents, but the freedom as well. Freedom itself is to some extent a matter of fate!

One of the ways the parent educates the child into freedom is by taking care to stress that what is ultimately most important are the universal values that stand behind particular meanings. The particular meanings, after all, are very much a function of particular situations, and the particular situations of the identity-givers are different from those that the child will grow into. A father, for example, who believes passionately in the values of love and justice may choose the particular meanings of parenthood, social work, and volunteer counseling to express those values; whereas his daughter may examine her internal and external situation and choose the particular meanings of the single life, medical doctor, and Peace Corps volunteer. The meanings differ, but the values are the same and perhaps infused with the same passion and given the same priority. If he is a wise parent, he welcomes this exercise of her freedom and indeed has from the beginning encouraged it. Precisely by stressing that the values are universal he has helped her see beyond the limited range of meanings he has chosen.

If parents offer values in an ambiance of freedom, their children become increasingly free as they develop and thereby become increasingly responsible for their spiritual identities. Not solely responsible—to our dying day we remain marked by fate—but enough responsible to be held accountable for the meanings and values that constitute the core of our spiritual self.[23]

Receiving Identity from God

No one would deny that human beings receive identity from other human beings. Some people may not admit that this identity-formation goes beyond the biological and psychological into the spiritual, but few would deny that to some degree at least we are what we are because of what we have been given by others.

I should like now to raise the possibility of receiving identity also from God. Is it part of human nature to be open to receiving identity not only from human others but from God, the transcendent Other?

The most influential Catholic theologian of this century, Karl Rahner, answered yes to this question and explained his answer at length, especially in his earlier writings.[24] Rahner's view is that all human beings have the "supernatural existential." They have the capacity to receive into their own identity God's gift of self-communication in Word and Spirit, and they have this capacity precisely because God is always giving this gift, even before we make the choice to accept or reject it. God's gift is the "supernatural," our capacity to receive it is the "existential."

Rahner took the term *existential* from the philosopher Martin Heidegger, whose seminars Rahner attended in the early 1930s. According to Heidegger, human existence is characterized by basic structures called existentials. Possibility for example, is one of the existentials of human being.[25] Human beings are not predetermined, but open to new possibilities that they freely choose or reject. Their lives therefore are marked by historicity, by a movement through time that is not predetermined. Human beings thus have no fixed essence that simply unfolds through time. Unlike acorns, whose future as mature oak trees is predetermined and closed, human beings have a future that is indeterminate and open, that waits upon their free decisions. Acorns are marked by development, not historicity. Human beings can choose who they want to be.

Rahner is proposing that the capacity to receive God's self-communication is the result of a divine self-communication that has been going on since the beginning. It is like watching children growing up under the influence of loving parents. Usually, they turn out to be adults with the capacity to be loving. And why? Because from the beginning they were loved, and this created in them the capacity to love. To use the language of Heidegger, one could say that they now have the existential of being loving. Loving has become a structure of their very being. But it is a parental existential, that is, it is a gift from loving parents. By analogy, God is the loving parent, who transcends the world and is therefore supernatural. This God loves humankind from the beginning as a gift, not as something that we can demand of God. This gift creates in us the capacity to love God and to love others in and with God's love. We can resist this capacity and even defy it, but we forever remain marked by it. It is a basic structure of our being, it is an existential.

In theory, we could imagine human beings without the supernatural existential; but in fact, God has freely chosen to make human beings the object of God's own self-communication in Word and Spirit. Given this divine choice, human beings are marked by it in their innermost center. The call from God stimulates the human desire and capacity to hear the call. Indeed for Rahner, all of creation has been the object of God's self-communication in Word and Spirit from the beginning, long before human beings came on the scene. The evolutionary process can therefore be understood as the movement of nature toward a creature who has the fully developed capacity to hear and receive the Word and Spirit of God.[26] The supernatural existential is the result of an original act of divine freedom. The capacity for God is not simply a human possession built into human nature as a "natural right," but the culminating response to a primordial divine gift.[27]

God thus freely decides to communicate the divine self in love to the world, though this does not mean that God needs the world in order to be loving. Let us recall that the universal values are anchored in God. God by nature loves and affirms God's self as true, good (because loving), and beautiful, and does so apart from the world.[28] By nature, God can do nothing else but affirm these values. But with the divine choice to create and love the world, God ties freedom and love together, adding a new dimension to love. Love becomes a good given and received only in freedom. We human beings enjoy a freedom that God respects. We can only be persuaded, not coerced, into a loving response.

Rahner does not arrive at the supernatural existential using philosophical reason alone. In his writings, he insists that such an existential is only fully discernible and nameable by religious faith, and specifically Christian faith. He believes that in Jesus God has found that perfect recipient of the divine self-communication in Word and Spirit. Only when we see in Jesus the full realization of the divine self-communication do we become fully aware of the depth and scope of human capacity. Belief in Jesus as the Son of God, as the one who has received God's identity, thus throws retroactive light on the history of human possibility. I am reminded of people who, after breaking through to unprecedented achievement, cause others to exclaim, "We did not realize that human beings were capable of that!" So too those who have experienced Jesus say, "We did not realize that human nature had that capacity!"

We come again to Jesus. Christian theology always returns to Jesus as the center of Christian faith. We need to explore in more detail the formation of Jesus' identity. That is the subject of the next chapter.

THREE

The Identity of Jesus

At the center of the Christian faith is Jesus of Nazareth, who is Messiah, the Christ, the Son of God. Jesus is at the intersection of two movements, one flowing from God to the world, the other flowing from the world to God. In Jesus, God communicates the divine self fully to humanity, and humanity communicates the human self fully to God. In this double movement, the meaning of God and the meaning of human nature are decisively revealed.

Although Christians believe that Jesus has received his identity from God, they do not define Jesus solely in terms of God. Jesus is a human being and as such he shares the fate of all human beings, which is to receive biological, psychological, and spiritual identity from other human beings.

In this and the following two chapters, I shall attempt a theological reconstruction of the identity and mission of Jesus. This reconstruction is theological because it is a reflection on the self-communication of God (the Greek word for God is *theos*) as it shapes Jesus' identity and mission. It is constructive because it constructs or builds up a conceptual and narrative scheme that attempts to give a coherent understanding of God's self-communication to Jesus. Finally, it is reconstructive because it builds on the constructions and reconstructions of other Christian thinkers, past and present.

To theologically reconstruct the identity of Jesus is to reconstruct a *Christology* (the Greek word for messiah is *christos*); to theologically reconstruct the mission is to reconstruct a *soteriology* (the Greek work for savior is *soter*). Admittedly, the distinction between Christology and soteriology is abstract and artificial. But for the sake of analytical clarity, I shall consider them separately, while not neglecting to show how identity and mission interconnect, how each implies and reinforces the other.

My theological reconstruction is governed by the criteria of *fidelity* to the Christian tradition and *plausibility* to contemporary people.[1] The Christian tradition is the history of Christian witness to Jesus as the one who communicates the Word of God in the power of the Spirit. This tradition gives special authority to the witness of the earliest Christian community, who responded to Jesus in faith and expressed this faith in words, at first orally, then in writing. Later, the Christian community, that is, the church, decided that some of these writings were an especially accurate and powerful expression of the earliest Christian witness. These writings were canonized as the New Testament,[2] to which now the church has pledged fidelity. As a Christian theologian working within the church, I too pledge fidelity to the New Testament and to the tradition that flows into it and out of it.[3]

In the New Testament, we find the first theological reconstructions of the identity and mission of Jesus. Jesus, of course, constructed a theology of his identity and mission; that is, he had his own understanding of what God was calling him to be and to do.[4] Later, in continuity with Jesus' self-understanding, and under the effect of his resurrection, his followers reconstructed theologies of their own that spoke to and out of their situation. Down through the centuries, Christians have continued reconstructing Christology and soteriology, but always in pledged fidelity to the previous reconstructions, especially to those found in the New Testament. As a Christian, I now attempt a reconstruction that I hope meets the criterion of fidelity to this tradition of reconstruction.[5]

I am also obliged to meet the criterion of plausibility. I shall try to reconstruct Jesus' identity and mission in a way that is plausible to you, the contemporary reader. Thus while being faithful to the tradition, especially to the New Testament, I need not be slavishly servile to its language and conceptuality. To be plausible, I shall have to use the language of today and speak to the situation of today. And this situation is marked by the quest for authentic meaning.

Faith and the Historical Jesus

I recall a conversation I had with a neighbor at a community meeting. He was retired from the railroad and had lived in this part of town all his life. I told him I was a theology teacher at the College of St. Catherine and had lived in the community for twenty years, long enough to see the neighborhood become much more ethnically diverse. People of differing skin color were moving in, among them African Americans. Somehow, the conversation turned to Martin Luther King Jr. My neighbor had grave doubts about King: "He caused a lot of mischief. He loved the limelight. And I have heard stories about him and other women." I said, "He had his moral weaknesses, but I think he was a sincere person of God who was working for God's justice on earth." He replied brusquely, "How do you know that? You cannot get inside a man's soul. How do you know God was working through him?" I told him that I had read the historians and the biographers, watched films and listened to tapes of King's speeches and sermons, and decided that he was a person of God. This did not convince my neighbor. Our conversation turned to another topic, his grandchildren. From the way he talked, he was obviously a good and caring man. And probably in his own deep way, a man of God. But he had his doubts about King.

On my way home, I thought about this conversation. How do we decide that King was a person of God doing God's work? A historian can study King's words and deeds and even to some degree imaginatively feel her way into his inner self, but she cannot write his history in a way that would oblige us to believe that King was a person of God doing God's work. We are dealing here with realities that exceed historical reason and judgment. When I say King was a person of God doing God's work, I am making a decision about the man based not only on history but also on my religious faith in God and in God's work in the world. To King's story, I bring my theology, which is a reflection of my faith, and faith is a mysterious surrender of the whole self to the mystery that is God. Yet I certainly would not want my theology of King's person and work to be contradicted by what I know historically of King. Let us suppose, for example, that the historians could show with high probability that King was indeed motivated primarily by the desire for the "limelight." Or suppose that his understanding of his calling could be shown to contradict how Christians historically have understood God and God's work. If I want my theology of King to have intellectual integrity and not just be the assertion of a willful and blind faith, then surely I will have to place it in dialogue with the history of King. And the same holds for my theology of Jesus.

For centuries, Christians assumed that the New Testament reconstructions of Jesus were not only theologically true but also historically accurate, and that therefore their faith in Jesus as the Word of God was consistent with the history of Jesus. Like the New Testament writers themselves, they made no sharp distinction between theological truth and historical fact. But influenced as we are today by the rise of modern critical history, we make the distinction.[6] Take, for example, this passage from the Gospel of Luke: "Jesus, full of the Holy Spirit, returned from the Jordan and was led by the Spirit in the wilderness, where for forty days he was tempted by the devil" (Luke 4:1-2). Pretend you are a modern historian. Can you refer to the inspiration of the Spirit of God to explain Jesus' sojourn in the wilderness? Try to sell that to a group of professional historians! As a historian, you cannot explain events in the world by reference to powers that exist outside the world: you cannot bring in gods, angels, or demons.[7] And therefore, the most you can say is that Jesus, during his days in the wilderness, believed himself to be inspired by the Spirit of God. Of course, you may also be a Christian who would be willing to confess that Jesus not only believed he was led by the Spirit, but he was in fact led by the Spirit. But you confess that out of your faith in God's Spirit, not out of your reasoning as a historian.

But in this case, at least what you say to your fellow historians is consistent with what you confess in faith. Suppose, however, another historian, whose skills you respect, claims that Luke's story of Jesus' temptation was completely lacking in historicity, that is, it simply did not occur at all. He argues that the story was invented by Luke to make a theological point and therefore did not literally happen. If you as a historian find yourself persuaded by his argument, what then happens to your faith that the Spirit led Jesus in the wilderness? Unless you want to preserve your faith at the price of your intellectual integrity, you will probably say to yourself, Well, I'll give up my faith that in this instance the Spirit led Jesus.

But how much faith we give away to the historians? Suppose they claim the following: that Jesus was conceived naturally, that Jesus was born in Nazareth and not in a manger in Bethlehem, that Jesus harbored no hope for the coming reign of God, that Jesus did not walk on water, that there was no last supper, that Jesus did not intend to die for our sins. Can we give up the historicity of all these and still have faith in Jesus? Right here, things become dicey, and the believing Christian becomes nervous. In the modern quest for the historical Jesus, will we find Jesus only to lose our faith?

Several options lie before us. We could take flight from historical reason and return to a precritical reading of Scripture. In every class I teach, I have at least two or three Bible-believing students, good and devout people, who accept everything the New Testament says about Jesus as simple, literal truth, no matter what the historians say. Faith requires that we accept it all, no questions asked, no doubts expressed.

A more subtle approach was taken by Rudolf Bultmann (1884–1976), the great German biblical scholar, historian, and theologian. For him, the New Testament writers were more often making a theological point than writing reliable history. Inspired by enthusiastic faith in the risen Christ, empowered by the authority of the Spirit, and moved by the urgent needs of a young and vulnerable community, they put words into Jesus' mouth, moved incidents of his life into different contexts, exaggerated the tension between Jesus and his Jewish opponents, and endowed Jesus with a rich theological understanding of his own death. Moreover, they saturated their whole narrative with a "mythological" worldview that allowed easy acceptance of spectacular miracles, heavenly voices, angelic visitations, and the fiery end of the world.[8] Yet Bultmann, despite his suspicion of the historical reliability of the New Testament, shared the New Testament faith in the crucified Jesus who is resurrected by the living God, because, he argued, the resurrection was not, strictly speaking, an event that took place in history, but an act of God beyond history and therefore not open to historical denial or affirmation. The resurrected Jesus, he said, was the "Christ of faith." We have faith in that Christ, not in the "Jesus of history." The historical reconstruction of Jesus' earthly life, though valuable as an intellectual enterprise, has no positive connection to faith and theological reconstruction.[9] For Bultmann, this is no cause for alarm: let the historians reconstruct the history of Jesus however they wish, Christian faith is safe![10]

Bultmann was so influential that for three decades very few Christian scholars undertook the search for the historical Jesus. That changed in the 1950s. Ever so gingerly, followers of Bultmann began to move away from the master's strict separation of history and faith. They initiated the "new quest for the historical Jesus."[11] Along with this came the growing realization that a sharp separation of the Jesus of history from the Christ of faith was not good for faith. To cut off Christian faith from historical reason leads to a kind of *fideism*, to faith as pure decision, as pure leap, beyond or even against what reason may tell us about Jesus. Cutting off history from faith opens Christians up to the charge of inventing the Christ of faith as a consoling myth. Most important, it undermines their claim that in the man Jesus the Word of God became incarnate, became flesh, and therefore has truly entered history and is not just a fabrication.

In the last twenty years, the new quest has given way to the *third* quest for the historical Jesus, which in our day has resulted in an explosion of books and articles. The books by John Dominic Crossan and Marcus Borg have become best-sellers, prominently displayed in huge chain book-stores like Barnes & Noble and colorfully highlighted on the Web pages of Amazon.com. Originating in the Jesus Seminar, this third quest has been carried out with growing confidence in our ability to paint a historically reliable portrait of Jesus.

I am not a historian, nor am I a biblical scholar, but as a theologian I do not believe I can take flight from historical reason. I believe that any theological reconstruction of Jesus' identity and mission should be con-sistent with the historical reconstruction. Consistent with it, not com-pelled by it.[12] Theologians must go beyond the historians' judgment, for they engage mysteries that historians cannot grasp because they have limited themselves to worldly causes. Not only that, theologians have to engage the questions and concerns of their own time, which may not have been those of Jesus' time. Nevertheless, theologians must check in at the bar of history if they are to avoid fanciful speculation. As we shall see in this chapter and the two that follow, I reconstruct a theologi-cal view of Jesus that departs somewhat from the formulations of classi-cal Christology and soteriology, and I do so in part because of what I have learned about the history of Jesus. I must also be open in principle to having my faith in Jesus disconfirmed by historical reconstruction. When the Dead Sea Scrolls were found (primarily in the late 1940s and early 1950s), there was speculation that they would result in a historical recon-struction so radical that traditional Christian faith would be shattered. This did not happen. But it is possible that there are undiscovered scrolls out there that might have this effect. I doubt such scrolls exist, yet for the sake of intellectual integrity I must be willing to let my faith be ques-tioned and chastened by new historical evidence and interpretation.

With respect to all those new historical reconstructions now in the bookstores, I remain cautiously appreciative. I am inclined to trust histor-ical reconstructions that display the following characteristics. First, they place Jesus very much within his Jewish context. Jesus lived and died a devout Jew; he was not the first Christian. Second, they give proper weight to Jesus' eschatological hope, that is, to his hope that the reign of God inaugurated by his own mission will arrive fully at the end (that is, the eschaton) of the present age.[13] Third, they do not deny a genuine conflict between Jesus and his Jewish opponents, but insist that this conflict is between parties whose worldviews were both recognizably Jewish. Fourth, they acknowledge that Jesus was a religious and theological genius whose theological ideas, while usually not new when looked at singly, were put together in a new and creative way. Fifth, they are careful not to read back into Jesus' self-understanding concepts developed by later Christologies: it is not historically convincing to suppose that Jesus walked around knowing he was the second person of the Trinity who had come down from heaven. This fifth point should not be taken to mean, however, that later Christologies (and soteriologies), especially those of the New Testament writers, are largely inventions. True, these writers had an experience that the historical Jesus did not yet have, the experience of Jesus as resurrected, but I find it unreasonable to conclude thereby that they were so dazzled by the resurrected Jesus that their memories of the earthly Jesus suddenly became largely unreliable. I have never found Bultmann, and all those like him who continue to regard the New Testament as a meager historical source, convincing in this respect.[14]

Let me turn now to the theological reconstruction of the identity and mission of Jesus as the communicator of God's Word and Spirit. This reconstruction goes beyond, yet I hope is consistent with, the historical reconstruction of Jesus' life and death. It is a comparatively brief reconstruction, in keeping with the aim of this book, which is to provide only an entrance into theology.[15] And since it is a theology for our time, it will have to speak in the language and to the questions of our time.

The Biological Identity of Jesus

As a human being, Jesus had a biological identity: he had the DNA that gave him the anatomy and physiology of a human being. He had therefore all those biological instincts and needs that universally mark human nature. His biological identity was also unique: he was a male with a unique combination of skin color, body type, energy level, and facial shape. Unfortunately, we know little of his biological identity in its uniqueness. No historical document has been left to us with a physical description, and thus we cannot be certain of how he looked. Given the time and place of his birth, he was probably a little over five feet tall with a complexion that was olive or even darker. Many males in that era wore beards, and perhaps he did too. But this is guesswork: we just do not know very much about the biological Jesus apart from his possession of universal traits.

Jesus received his biological identity by fate, not by his own choice. Who gave it to him? Biological identity is the result of that mix of genes and chromosomes received from a human male and female who have entered into sexual union. The Gospels of Matthew and Luke, however, tell the story of Jesus' virgin birth, or more precisely, his virginal conception.[16] According to this story, Jesus did not have a human father. He had only a human mother, Mary, who conceived him not through sexual union with Joseph, the man to whom she was engaged,[17] or with another man, but through the power of the Holy Spirit, through the power of God (see Matt. 1:20; Luke 1:35).

For centuries, virtually all Christians believed the story of the virginal conception to be literally true and binding on faith. They thus believed in a miracle in the classical, literal sense of the term. With the virginal conception, God performed a miracle by interrupting, suspending, or exceeding the normal connection of cause and effect. The normal chain of cause and effect is a law of nature, and surely one of the laws of nature is that a human conception occurs only if one male sperm fertilizes one female egg. This in turn can happen only if there is a sexual union between a human male and female, at least this was the case in first-century Palestine, long before the technology of in vitro fertilization. But according to the infancy narratives of Matthew and Luke, as interpreted down through the centuries by most Christians, the event of male and female intercourse did not occur, and thus a law of nature was broken or exceeded. And therefore God, who transcends the world and the rule of nature's laws, supplied the causal power to effect the conception of Jesus. A worldly event, the conception of a human being, had an otherworldly cause, God. This is a miracle in the classical, literal sense.[18]

It is important to stress that Christians have not believed that in the virginal conception God supplied divine sperm. Unlike Zeus, the chief Greek god, Yahweh, the God of the Jewish people, is spirit who totally transcends matter and biology, and therefore cannot have sexual intercourse with human females. Yahweh has no biological sex. Yahweh is neither male nor female, and therefore those masculine names that have been given to God in Scripture and tradition, such as father, king, and shepherd, are strictly metaphorical, having no literal attribution: God is no more literally a male than a female.[19] This means that the basis for Jesus' biological identity cannot be genes and chromosomes supplied directly from God's own male-configured DNA. God cannot make a direct biological contribution to Jesus' identity because God is not biological. We have here a stupendous miracle, not a male god sexually consorting with a human female.

Over the past two or three hundred years, there has been a growing minority of Christians who have expressed skepticism about the literal truth of the story of the virginal conception.[20] In their view, science has proved the universal reign of nature's laws, a reign that even God, the creator of these laws, respects. God thus respects the law that a human conception requires a male sperm and a female egg. These Christians say that belief in a virginal conception of Jesus should not be regarded as essential to Christian faith. They point out that the two other Gospels in the New Testament, those of Mark and John, do not mention a virginal conception of Jesus. These Gospels were clearly written out of and to Christian communities for whom the belief in a virginal conception was not present or not important. The writer of John's Gospel, for example, had an extraordinarily lofty view of Jesus' identity yet appears to have managed without such a belief. The stories of Matthew and Luke are just that, stories, meant not to communicate the literal truth about Jesus' conception but the religious truth about his relationship to God.

There does remain one problem for these skeptics. They have to face the possibility that the story of the virginal conception has behind it the embarrassing fact that Jesus was in fact born "too early."[21] To conceive a child during the engagement period with a man who was not the fiancé would have been a serious breach of Jewish law and would have made Mary an adulterous sinner against God's covenant. How could a Christian accept that Jesus the Messiah was conceived in sin?

Two Catholic thinkers, James P. Mackey and Jane Schaberg, do not recoil from such a question. Mackey admits as possibly historical Mary's early pregnancy but does not feel compelled to redeem it by referring it to God's miraculous activity. He grants therefore the possibility that Jesus' conception occurred in morally dubious circumstances. Perhaps Mary was not the pure vessel of honor that Christians have historically believed. This still would not have prevented her from being the mother of the one who had been called to be the Son of God. Mackey points out that there is a great and wonderful mystery in God's working through an event of such moral ambiguity. It would not have been the first time. Schaberg takes her speculations in a feminist direction and raises the possibility that Mary was a victim of rape and that Jesus thus is conceived and born out of a situation marked by the sin of male domination and oppression of women. Mary is not the sinner but the one sinned against. Through this situation, God then creates a redemptive situation where Jesus the Son mediates God's power to save both men and women. Mary's fateful suffering at the hands of a patriarchal society is transformed into a vehicle for the climactic communication of God's redemptive love. Jesus' conception is not a miracle, therefore, but a scandal that God works in and through. What is revealed here is the redemptive potential of even the most scandalous human events.[22]

The proposals of Mackey and Schaberg are highly speculative and, because of the paucity of confirming or disconfirming historical data, will remain speculative. There are other ways of accounting for the existence of the stories of the virginal conception, not the least of which was that there was indeed a miraculous event.

The position one takes on the virginal conception will be influenced by many things: by the authority one invests in Scripture and tradition, by one's metaphysical understanding of how God acts in the world, and by the weight that one assigns to the virginal conception relative to other Christian doctrines. The important thing is that Jesus was a human being with a human biological identity and that God made no direct contribution to this identity as a "male" partner of Mary. I confess to having doubts at times about the literal truth of the virginal conception, but I applaud the important theological role the doctrine has served in the struggle against adoptionism, the view that Jesus was called to his sonship later in his adult life (for example, at his baptism) after God had judged his life as meriting adoption. With the tradition, I agree that the identity-forming Word and Spirit of God were present in a special way to Jesus from the beginning. Yet I believe, along with the bishops at the Second Vatican Council, that there is a "hierarchy" of Christian truths, and for me the virginal conception is not near the top of that hierarchy. For this reason, I do not think that Christians should impose on one another a uniform interpretation of the biblical accounts of Jesus' conception.[23] They should focus on the heart of Christian mystery, which is that Jesus is the spiritual, not the biological, Son of God.

The Psychological Identity of Jesus

Jesus had a psychological identity. He shared with all human beings the psychological needs for solitude and conviviality, love and friendship, autonomy and mutuality, challenge and repose, surprise and routine. No evidence suggests that he had these needs any less than we do. But the precise shape and strength of these needs occurred only in interaction with his temperament, about which we know virtually nothing. Students have told me that Jesus must have been an extrovert because he was unafraid to go out and preach publicly. How do we know that he was not afraid? How do we know that he was temperamentally suited to public interaction with people? Jesus would not have been the first introvert to have his aversion to public activity overcome by his passion to communicate his values and meanings. Other students have told me that he must have been a "thinker" rather than a "feeler" because of the tight logic he exhibited in his arguments with his opponents. Yet this "thinker" is shown as a person of strong feeling, weeping over Jerusalem and moved by compassion. Furthermore, he did not just argue but told stories called parables, which operate not by strict logic but by a strange paradoxicality. These parables are more like hot bursts of imaginative feeling than cool productions of logical reason.[24] The truth is that we do not have enough evidence to chart a personality profile of this man. In a mock serious tone, I have argued to students that a person of his greatness must have been an Extrovert-iNtuitive-Feeling-Judging type on the Myers-Briggs Type Indicator, and have gone far toward persuading many of them, until I told them with a smile that ENFJ were my letters.

Jesus received his psychological identity from other human beings: first, from his genetic inheritance, insofar as temperament is determined by genes; and second, from his social environment. His family, both immediate and extended, undoubtedly had a style of thinking, feeling, talking, and laughing that marked Jesus. And then too there were the influences of the ethnic and regional temperament, though we know little or nothing of the temperamental style of first-century Galilee. Did he receive his psychological identity from God? Having defined psychological identity quite narrowly as the mixture of need and temperament, I think we have to say no. I find myself unable to define God in psychological categories. Would we really want to say that God has, for example, a need for solitude? That God is an extrovert ("Only an extrovert would want to create a world," a student of mine once said)? That God is decisive rather than easygoing and playful, rather than tense and sober? Talking about God this way seems a bit silly. I do not think we can attribute to God a psychological identity in this sense. And therefore God did not influence the formation of Jesus' psychological identity by passing on to Jesus God's own psychological identity.

The Spiritual Identity of Jesus

Jesus' spiritual identity also came from other human beings. All the available evidence suggests that Jesus' parents, Mary and Joseph, were devout Jews who would have believed that all their particular meanings were anchored in values that are God's values. Just as God was loving, kind, compassionate, just, and righteous, so also should human beings imitate God in these values. The practice of God's values, made explicit in the Torah (*Torah* is the Hebrew word for law or instruction), was the foundation for the relationship or covenant between God and the people, and among the people themselves, for the Torah was the cement of the community. These values at their root were moral, for they forged and governed relationship between persons. True, many of the particular meanings detailed in the Torah governed cult, that is, worship, prayer, sacrifice, and fasting, and directed daily routines, such as eating, drinking, and working; but at its base the Torah was at the service of covenant, and covenant at its heart is the reign of love and justice. The moral values thus were summed up in personal and relational terms: "You shall love the Lord your God with all your heart, and with all your soul, and with all your might" (Deut. 6:4-5). "You shall love your neighbor as yourself" (Lev. 19:18). In Judaism there was little or no talk about values in the abstract, for all values were rooted in God, who is personal and relational. When, therefore, God communicated to the Israelite people through the great prophets, God communicated God's very own life as values that demanded realization. The Word came in the power of the Spirit with the aim of empowering the Jews to live out God's justice in the world. Those who let this Word have its effect, who let themselves be not only informed by its meaning but also moved by its power to feeling and action, became sons and daughters of God and brothers and sisters of one another.

This Judaism Jesus received because of his upbringing at the hands of devout Jewish parents.[25] From early on, then, his parents would have been speaking deeply personal, identity-forming words that would have passed on to Jesus the values and meanings of their religious tradition. Jesus would not have been able to hear and accurately interpret God's Word unless he had been first formed into the Jewish identity by other human beings, especially his parents. Just because Jesus disagreed with certain interpretations of Judaism does not mean that he repudiated Judaism. It is widely thought by Christians that the incarnation of God's Word in Jesus occurred simply because God wished it. All God had to do was choose to become incarnate in a human being, and it was done, a bolt out of the heavenly blue, a quick descent from above. To be sure, the incarnation of God's Word and the consequent formation of Jesus as the Son was a divine possibility, but only because it was also a human possibility by virtue of a Judaism passed on to Jesus by Jews engaged in the formation of his spiritual identity.[26]

God does not only pass on spiritual identity through others. The Jewish tradition allows for God's direct communication to persons, most dramatically the prophets. Prophets are those who combine a lively religious sensibility with the insistent feeling of having been singled out by God for an especially intense and intimate communication. Jesus takes his place in a long line of prophets who felt themselves addressed by God, not only indirectly through the community and its traditions, but directly. As his conviction about this communication became ever more intense, his parents, family, and other human identity-givers receded in importance.[27] I am not saying that Jesus was "just a prophet." I see in him an instance of divine self-communication unprecedented in its intimacy and intensity. The New Testament writers had it right when they saw Jesus as not only proclaiming God's Word, but identifying with it and being identified by it to a unique degree. They saw him as the one who communicated the Word with power and authority precisely because he had allowed it to define the very core of his spiritual self. He proclaimed the good news of God's reign because he first lived it and incarnated it.[28]

God's Self-Communication to Jesus in Word and Spirit

In chapter 2, I talked about the formation of a child's spiritual identity as a self-communication from parent to child.[29] Self-communication demands a special use of language whereby the self first grasps itself in inner word and embraces itself with the power of feeling, and then expresses this as outer word infused with power. Such a word aims to be not only informative but emotive and directive, for it comes to the hearer as the meaning and power of love. Self-communication is love, and this love forms spiritual identity.

By analogy, the Christian sees God as doing something similar with Jesus, though since we are dealing here with a great mystery, the difference is greater than the similarity.[30] But if we take the plunge into this mystery and attempt to gain a glimmer of understanding, I think we can at least point to the truth by imagining that God, who is *self*-conscious and personal being, first grasps Godself in an inner Word. Indeed, it is the very generation of the inner Word that makes God self-conscious. Standing back from the self expressed in inner Word would also seem to be the necessary precondition for God's free self-communication to Jesus.[31] If the divine self that is communicated to Jesus is not to be lost in or fully absorbed by Jesus, then prior to the communication this self must have already doubled itself by expressing itself in inner Word: "In the beginning was the Word, and the

Word was with God, and the Word was God" (John 1:1). The divine self as doubled in the inner Word "bec[omes] flesh" (John 1:14) in Jesus, not the self "prior" to the doubling.[32] In human life, the fundamental "I-subject" that is the source of all inner activity expresses itself as a "me-object" that the "I" can look at and have a relation to, and it is this "me" that the "I" sends out to the other in outer word. Meanwhile, the self as the "I" is retained and not lost in the other because it remains as enduring active source of the inner act of doubling and the outer word of self-communicating.

In traditional theological language, God thus Fathers his own other as Word and then the Father communicates in and through this Word to Jesus. In this way, God can be both transcendent to the world as the Father in heaven and yet simultaneously fully present as the Word made flesh in Jesus. Again, I invite the reader to think on his or her own mystery. How is it that you are able to give yourself over to another without losing yourself in the process? Your interior life must be structured to allow your self to go out and yet stay back, to dwell in the other and yet dwell in the self, to be both self-given and self-retained. This presupposes a continuously inner act of self-doubling of your "I" into your "me." And by analogy, we can imagine that a similar process occurs in God, without of course presuming that we have even begun to exhaust the mystery of God's inner life (or even our inner life) with the use of these categories.[33]

When we think of Word, however, we think of meaning. But more than mere meaning is being communicated when God communicates God's spiritual identity to Jesus, for this is a deeply personal Word that comes suffused with the power of feeling. When God grasps Godself in inner Word, the meaning of that Word is God's core value or meaning, which is love and justice. But love is not only a meaning but also a feeling, so this meaning is clothed in divine feeling. Another more anthropomorphic way of saying it is that the self that God sees expressed in inner Word is fully loved by God. Divine feeling is poured out over divine meaning because the meaning is fundamentally the meaning of a self affirmed in love, which is feeling. That same feeling is poured out over the divine values of truth and beauty that enjoy a mysterious unity with the value of love. The divine self that is doubled in inner Word is also poured out in feeling over the Word. Traditionally, theologians have called these the "processions" of the Word and Spirit, through which the divine "I" is eternally expressing itself. The Word enjoys a certain logical priority, and in this sense the Word proceeds first, but the Spirit is equally and fully expressive of the one divine self.[34]

The inner Word of God in the power of the Spirit then goes out to Jesus as a deeply personal self-communication that aims to form Jesus' spiritual identity. Here, the analogy between human and divine self-communication begins to break down. When a human parent communicates herself, she translates her inner word into outer word, into a meaningful event that can be heard, seen, touched, smelled, or tasted, and this she does by activating her body. Human beings have an immediate relationship to their bodies that allows them to use their bodies as a medium for self-communication. But God is spirit and has no body. How does God communicate God's self to Jesus? How could God produce an outer word without a body?

At this point, we return to the question that occupied us when we were dealing with the virginal conception: How does God act in the world? Persons who have no difficulty believing that God acted in the world miraculously to cause Jesus' virginal conception will have no difficulty imagining that God could and did speak to Jesus through outer words. Since God has no body, any outer word produced by God would have to be a miraculous event. One of the laws of nature is that a human word has to be traced back to a human body as its cause. When, therefore, the Scriptures tell of God's outer word to Moses through a voice out of the burning bush (Exod. 3:1-22), then they tell of a miracle. A miracle is also implied in this account of Jesus' baptism: "In those days Jesus came from Nazareth of Galilee and was baptized by John in the Jordan. And just as he was coming up out of the water, he saw the heavens torn apart and the Spirit descending like a dove on him. And a voice came from heaven, 'You are my Son, the Beloved; with you I am well pleased'" (Mark 1:9-11). If this story is literally true, then God caused an event that exceeded natural and human power, producing an outer word that communicated to Jesus.[35] God, though lacking a body, can speak an outer word because God is able and willing to exercise miraculous power in the world. Just as God exercised miraculous power to cause a conception without the cooperation of a human male, so now God exercises this power to communicate to Jesus without the mediation of a human voice.

Earlier, when analyzing the virginal conception of Jesus, I pointed out that in the modern era a growing minority of Christians, influenced by the success of science, believe that God does not disrupt the continuities of worldly cause and effect. Yet not only the success of science has led people to believe in such a God, but also the increased sensitivity to the problem of evil. For this is a century of monstrous evils, of which the most shattering was the Holocaust of six million Jews. This evil presents difficulties for believers in the God of the Jews. This God had chosen the Jews for a special covenant, for a special relationship. This God, Yahweh, for centuries was depicted as able and willing to intervene in nature and history on behalf of the Jews. Yet Yahweh did not intervene in history to save the Jews from Hitler's genocidal project. This undeniable fact raises serious questions for those devout Jews and Christians who believe in a God who can and does exercise miraculous power in the world on the behalf of the innocent. According to the Hebrew Scriptures, this God intervened to speak to Moses and to lead the Israelites out of Egypt into the promised land. According to the Christian Scriptures, this God intervened to speak an outer word to Jesus at his baptism. If God was able and willing to intervene for the sake of Moses, the Israelites, and Jesus, why not for the Jews who were enslaved in the concentration camps? Is there not an inconsistency here that raises grave doubts about God's justice and fairness?

Some say that it is blasphemous to demand that God meet our standards of fairness. They ask us to accept God's answer to Job, which is that Job has no right to question God: God's ways are beyond the reach of human moral inquiry. "Shall a faultfinder contend with Almighty?" God thunders to Job out of the whirlwind (Job 40:1–2). Others say that at least to some extent we do know about God's ways. After all, we are called by God to work with God to make the world more just. How can we do that if we do not know God's ways? How could God enjoin us to do justice if God is not just or had left us in the dark about the content of divine justice? If we visit injustice upon people, God will condemn us. If we cause the innocent to suffer or fail to rescue them from suffering, God will condemn us. If God will not excuse us for causing the innocent to suffer or failing to rescue them from suffering, how can God be excused? Surely, God must be held to God's own moral standards if God is to hold us to them.

The friends of Job have an answer, of course, a very logical answer. God does hold to God's own moral standards, they insist. God does not visit suffering on the innocent or fail to alleviate their suffering. Therefore, Job must not be innocent! A virulent form of Christian anti-Semitism has extended this calculus to the whole Jewish people and applied it to the Holocaust. The Jewish people, it is said, are collectively responsible for the murder of Jesus Christ and therefore deservedly suffered divine punishment and nonintervention in the Holocaust. This argument is pernicious, and Jews rightly proclaim their innocence of the charge. Romans were as much or more directly involved in Jesus' death than Jews. Does anyone dare say that modern-day Italians deserve a Holocaust?

If God did not directly cause the Holocaust as punishment, why did not God at least intervene in the Holocaust and stop it? How can anyone believe in an all-powerful and all-just God who would fail to alleviate the suffering of innocent people? Many would say that we cannot believe in such a God. Even before this century's evils deluged us, this argument against belief in God received unforgettable expression by the Russian novelist Fyodor Dostoyevsky through the words of one of his most famous characters, Ivan Karamazov. Ivan argues that the suffering of one innocent child is enough to sustain his passionate atheism.[36] And the Holocaust has supplied us with an incomprehensible amount of innocent suffering. How can we not be convinced by Ivan?

Another possibility is proposed by Jewish and Christian believers who say that we must revise our conception of God's power and how it is exercised in the world. An example of this rethinking can be found in the best-seller *When Bad Things Happen to Good People* by Harold Kushner, an American Reform Jewish rabbi.[37] Kushner believes in God and believes that God is just and fair. He also believes that God has power but does not believe that God exercises the power to act miraculously in the world to cause or alleviate suffering. God does not influence the laws of nature to reward friends or punish enemies. Or to strengthen someone's faith or to lead him or her to faith. Or to make a person of strong faith a greater witness to faith. Or to summon people to greater moral achievement. Or to bring a family closer together or build a person's character. If a gust of wind blows out the windowpane of a skyscraper, God is not going to step in and suspend the law of gravity as the glass plunges toward a God-fearing person below. God also shows an absolutely consistent respect for the exercise of human freedom. If a person wishes to abuse his freedom by shooting another, God will not intervene in the shooter's freedom. Kushner also argues that there are events in the world that cause suffering that are the result neither of nature's laws nor of human freedom, but of pockets of physical chaos where effects do not follow neatly from causes, where nature gratuitously "misbehaves" for no cause at all.[38]

Kushner's main point is that God does not break into the world and override the results of natural law, human freedom, or random chaos. God does not exercise power in this coercive way. Rather, God's power is active on the inner, spiritual selves of people persuasively, so their freedom might be preserved. God is continuously present to people offering empathy, encouragement, and inspiration. In being thus present, God in no way interrupts, suspends, or exceeds any law of nature. If people are open to God's power, they will learn to accept suffering in a world where nature, human freedom, and chaos do bad things to people. They will be energized to transform suffering into a meaning that serves self and others. They will be emboldened to create a world in which there is less suffering. Instead of blaming God for acting or failing to act, they will avail themselves of what God is doing, inspiring them spiritually to gird up their loins and do some good.

Over a thousand of my students have read Kushner's book, and on the whole they find his revised version of God's action in the world persuasive. Yet they always raise this question: according to Kushner, does God not intervene miraculously in the world because God cannot do so or because God freely chooses not to do so? On this question, Kushner's text is ambiguous, although he appears to lean in the direction of saying that God cannot intervene even if God wants to.[39] God is therefore limited by God's own nature, not by choice, from intervening in such a way. If this is indeed his view, then Rabbi Kushner is very close to the views espoused by process theology, a theological movement, strong in North America, inspired by the philosophers Alfred North Whitehead and Charles Hartshorne.[40] Process theologians, with their neoclassical theism, insist that God is metaphysically constrained from intervening coercively in the world to interrupt natural law or freedom. Each event in the world has a private creative power that is inviolate: God could not override it even if God wanted to. If, however, Kushner takes the more classical view—and there is some textual support for saying that he does—then God is limited with respect to natural law and human freedom because of God's own choice to be limited.[41] God, in creating a world ruled by natural law and subject to human freedom, has undergone a voluntary self-limitation. God in theory could intervene miraculously in the world but has freely chosen not to.[42]

Whether Kushner takes the neoclassical or the classical view of God, it is clear from his book that he does not expect God to intervene miraculously in the world. He certainly does not believe that God ever intervenes directly to cause suffering and death. That would contradict God's moral goodness. Kushner is willing to accept a world in which nature and freedom operate without divine tampering. But how about a rather harmless intervention, indeed an intervention that serves the good, as when God spoke to Moses through a burning bush or to Jesus at the river Jordan? According to classical theism, such interventions would be possible in theory and undoubtedly occurred in fact. Kushner would surely say that even these harmless interventions raise difficulties. Why speak an outer word to Moses and Jesus and not to others? The Jews in the death camps would have been deeply consoled and encouraged by the voice of God telling them, "You are still my people. Do not lose heart. I will be with you through this dark time and bring you into the light." Not much of an intervention, you say, but surely many would have found it of great inspiration. But God was silent in the camps. God neither spoke nor acted miraculously. In the face of this divine silence, when a consolatory outer word could have helped thousands, even millions, is it easy to say without ado that God spoke outer words to Moses and Jesus?[43] Some contemporary people have become skeptical of all reports of this kind of divine speech.

Even those Christians who believe that God did speak miraculous outer words admit that according to the New Testament, such outer words do not seem to have been God's primary mode of self-communication to Jesus. The primary mode must have been a more spiritual, more mystical communication directly from God to the inner spiritual self of Jesus. On good historical grounds, we can judge Jesus as a person of prayer. He taught his followers how to pray, and he is often shown at prayer (see Mark 6:46; 14:32; Matt. 14:23; 26:36-44; Luke 3:21; 5:16; 6:12; 9:18; 9:28-29; 11:1). We can imagine that at these moments of prayer Jesus was particularly receptive to God's identity-forming Word suffused with the power of the Spirit. Jesus would have felt a Word that was deeply personal, not merely informing him about the meaning of God, but moving him emotively and directively by the power of God. The Word and Spirit of God descended on Jesus and called him to make God's life his life, to make God's values his values, above all the value of self-giving love, which is the core of God's spiritual identity. In order for this self-communication to be fully success-ful, Jesus had to understand it, believe it, trust it, and let its power move him to feeling and action. It was therefore a Word not only to be heard and understood, but also felt and obeyed. For Jesus to be truly the Son of God, he had to receive God's Word and Spirit in faith and love. Openness to God in faith and love was the essence of the prayer that streamed directly from the interior self of Jesus to God. And God's inner Word in the power of the Spirit streamed directly to Jesus without the mediation of outer word, by analogy with the experience of the prophets in the Old Testament.

Jesus' primary spiritual-identity giver was thus increasingly the tran-scendent Other whom he called Abba or Father.[44] Jesus was not a passive object of God's self-communication: his identity was not simply the con-sequence of divinely directed fate. If we are to affirm his humanity, then his own freedom played an active role in the person he became. His iden-tity was a process unfolding in time and completed only in death.

The spiritual identity of Jesus was not complete at his conception or birth. He was a human being, and he had to grow into the capacity to accept the identity that God was offering. In the New Testament, there is the ten-dency to keep pushing the key moments of Jesus' identity-formation back in time and then back into eternity before his time. But the earliest preaching about Jesus by his followers puts the key moment at his death and resurrection, as can be seen in this excerpt from Peter's sermon: "This Jesus God raised up, and of that all of us are witnesses. Being therefore exalted at the right hand of God, and having received from the Father the promise of the Holy Spirit, he has poured out this that you both see and hear. . . . Therefore let the entire house of Israel know with certainty that God has made him both Lord and Messiah, this Jesus whom you crucified" (Acts 2:32-34, 36). The clear import of this text is that Jesus is not fully Messiah, Lord, Son, until he surrenders in death to God and God exalts him in resurrection. But as the earliest preaching develops, earlier moments in Jesus' career are given increasing emphasis: the transfiguration, the baptism, the birth, the conception, and finally, in the Gospel of John, Jesus' identity as the Son of God is shown as having already been established from eternity, even before incarnation in humanity. This tendency was continued and strengthened by the early church, which, in combat against the Arian heresy, formulated the doctrine of the eternal generation of the Son as the second person of the Trinity. Arius, a priest of Alexandria in the early third century, taught that Jesus was indeed the incarnation of the preexistent Son, but this Son was not eternal and therefore not divine in the same exalted way as the Father, who created the Son. The church rightly rejected Arius' views on grounds that if Jesus is to save us, then the true and eternal God must be at work in Jesus and not a created divinity, for only the true God can save us. The Council of Nicaea ruled that the Son incarnate in Jesus is "of the same being" as God the Father. God's eternal begetting of the inner Word was the eternal begetting of the fully personal Son.[45]

This tendency to push the identity-formation of the Son back in time and then before time was understandable in historical context and was required to counter Arius, but I agree with those contemporary theologians who think it resulted in formulations that devalue the earthly development of the personhood of Jesus.[46] Christians came to believe that when the infant Jesus lay in the manger he already was fully the Son of God. How could he be? Spiritually, he was not even fully the son of Mary and Joseph. And if he had not come fully into his human sonship, how could he have come fully into his divine sonship? To be sure, God was fully present within Jesus, communicating God's self through the Word and Spirit. The divine self-communication that God wanted Jesus to make his own was there from the beginning, as deeply personal Word, poured out over Jesus in full meaning and power. But Jesus, the human infant, did not yet have the capacity to let that Word form the core of his identity.[47]

I wish to see a return to that strain of New Testament preaching that puts more accent on Jesus' development in time. According to the Gospel of Luke, Jesus "increased in wisdom and in years, and in divine and human favor" (Luke 2:52); according to the Epistle to the Hebrews, Jesus "learned obedience through what he suffered; and having been made perfect, he became the source of eternal salvation for all who obey him"

(Heb. 5:8); and according to the Epistle to the Philippians, only after Jesus had "humbled himself and became obedient to the point of death" was he then "highly exalted" (Phil. 2:8-9). Jesus therefore grew into his capacity to take on the spiritual identity God was communicating to him in Word and Spirit, a development that was not completed until death.[48]

When we talk of the unfolding of Jesus' capacity for the divine identity, we necessarily talk of the unfolding of his capacity for free choice. Like that of all human beings, Jesus' identity-formation in the early stages is much more a consequence of fate than freedom. Fate receives particular emphasis in the New Testament, which was written in a milieu influenced by apocalyptic writing, a genre that stressed human powerlessness and transhuman power. The evil cosmic powers had considerable control over cosmos and history, and there was little that human beings could do but wait in faith and hope. For God was ultimately in control, even though surface events did not always appear to testify to that control. God had a plan to save the world, and God would carry it out. Only God knew the plan in detail; only God knew the day and hour when God would arrive and carry out the final act of salvation, establishing the reign of God forever. The whole course of human events had then been predetermined by the divine plan, and there was little human beings could do to hinder or hasten its fulfillment. Jesus was therefore "handed over . . . according to the definite plan and foreknowledge of God" and then "raised . . . up" (Acts 2:23-24). The divine plan made it "necessary that the Messiah should suffer these things" (Luke 24:26), and even after the resurrection of Jesus those who accept Christ have in fact been destined to do so "before the foundation of the world" (Eph. 1:4–5). Given this apocalyptic determinism,[49] it is no surprise that the New Testament gave more stress to divine doing than to human choosing. Jesus' choosing did not receive the attention that we would give it today with our heightened sense for the role of human freedom in the unfolding of all human events, including the event of one's identity-formation.

In our thinking about the identity of Jesus today, we must not overstress fate at the price of freedom. Jesus' identity as the Son of God is not simply a consequence of God's choice but also Jesus' choice. His laying hold of the identity pressing down on him was done in freedom. It was therefore his destiny to be the Son, not simply his fate. He truly felt the attraction of other identities and freely chose to reject them—how else can it be if we are to take seriously the stories of his temptations (Matt. 4:1-11; Luke 4:1-13)?[50] The greatest temptation was his death, for there is no greater challenge to one's meanings and values than the threat of death. The strongest proof of his commitment to an identity is his willingness to suffer and die for it. Jesus' lifelong commitment showed itself in one last excruciating recommitment.[51] We really do not know how secure Jesus was in his grasp of his sonship until we see him surmount this final challenge, until we see him "obedient to the point of death—even death on a cross" (Phil. 2:8). In death, Jesus showed he was secure in his sonship, and in death, he definitively secured it: "Therefore God also highly exalted him / and gave him the name / that is above every name" (Phil. 2:9). In resurrecting Jesus, God establishes him forever as the divine-human Son, the risen Lord, who is worshiped and glorified.

For good reason, the church has always extolled Good Friday, Holy Saturday, and Easter Sunday as the climax of the liturgical year. In doing so, the church has ascribed greater theological significance to the end of Jesus' life than to the beginning or prebeginning. But over the centuries, as earlier turning points in Jesus' identity-formation were given increasing emphasis, the Christmas story and its attendant liturgies and symbols became increasingly prominent in Christian piety. As this logic pressed its rights further, not just the birth but the conception of Jesus became more important, which in turn encouraged within the Catholic tradition especially a dramatic expansion in devotion to Mary. Her yes to the conception became for some Catholics more important than the yes that Jesus said on the cross. Indeed, this Marian emphasis, allied with a view of Jesus that has his sonship fully established from eternity, led to making the conception, the moment of incarnation, the most important moment of Jesus' earthly career. The yes of the human Jesus had scarcely a role to play. Mary's exercise of freedom became more important than Jesus' exercise of freedom.

We must be careful here to avoid a misunderstanding. When we speak of the freedom of Jesus as he faced death, we do not mean that Jesus faced his death with a neutral freedom, as if this supreme challenge to his identity as the Son were simply one more fork in the road where he could have gone just as well one way as the other. From the beginning, God had chosen him and through the Word was drawing him into divine sonship. As Jesus ratified God's choice of him, his identity as the Son became so securely anchored that a sudden no to this identity became inconceivable. I tell my students about Mozart, whose precocious and prodigious musical genius has been rightly interpreted as not just genetic luck but divine gift. This gift then came under the solicitous cultivation of Mozart's father, Leopold, and Mozart responded willingly and became a virtuoso musician and composer at an early age. It is impossible to imagine that suddenly at age thirty Mozart would have decided to quit composing and become, let's say, a lawyer. We would not, however, want to say that Mozart was a great composer solely by fate and not also by freedom. He was a composer by destiny, and destiny occurs out of the mix of fate and freedom. While acknowledging that the mystery of Jesus' identity as the Son of God far surpasses the mystery of Mozart's identity as a composer, I think we can say that Jesus, like Mozart, achieved his identity by destiny, by a fate accepted in freedom.

I also tell the students about the Old Testament prophet Jeremiah, though again I warn them that all analogies offer only a dim understanding of the mystery of Jesus. Jeremiah felt God's call as an all but overwhelming fate. Indeed, he saw himself as having been anointed in his mother's womb to be a prophet to Israel (see Jer. 1: 4). He could not imagine his life in any other way. And yet, if he was human, then he was free, and thus he accepted the call in freedom and transformed his fate into destiny. According to the infancy narratives of Matthew and Luke (Matt. 1:18-24; Luke 1: 26-38), Jesus was anointed by the Word and Spirit of God before his life in the womb and thus the Word and Spirit were uniquely forming his identity and mission from the first moment of his existence. Surely, then, he was the incarnate Word by overwhelming fate! And yet, if he was truly human, he was free, and thus he accepted the Word in freedom and transformed his fate into destiny. And this acceptance could be accomplished in him and by him only through a life climaxing in death. Therefore, the incarnation of the Word at Jesus' conception is not simply an accomplished fact that is then revealed in his life and death, but is an incarnation that is accomplished in and through his life in freedom, and the final act of this accomplishment is his death.

Earlier, I warned that a discussion of the identity of Jesus apart from the mission can become abstract and artificial. Well, I have proven it in this discussion of Jesus' death, for in no other event is the identity of Jesus more closely tied to his mission, which is the subject of the next chapter.

FOUR

The Mission of Jesus

In the previous chapter, we examined the formation of Jesus' identity as the spiritual Son of God. The formation of Jesus' identity begins within the inner life of God who grasps Godself in inner Word and infuses this Word with the power of the Spirit. God's self grasped in Word and Spirit is then communicated to Jesus who has the capacity and willingness to make the Word in the power of the Spirit the very core of his own identity. God communicates a self whose very being is determined by the universal values of truth, love, and beauty, especially the value of love, which unifies the values of truth and beauty. The value of love becomes the animating center of Jesus' self. In this way, God's center becomes Jesus' center.[1]

Why did God undertake this formation of Jesus' identity? Most fundamentally to fulfill the purpose of creation. From the beginning, creation is pervaded by God's desire to engage the world in an intimacy that will form the identity of the world. Human beings then emerge in the evolution of the world as those beings with the greatest capacity for such an intimacy with God, and Jesus emerges as the human being most fully capable and willing to receive God's offer of intimacy and identity-formation. And thus the incarnation of the Word in Jesus by the power of the Spirit is the realization of God's intention for creation.[2]

70

God's identity-formation of Jesus is also undertaken for the sake of other human beings. The identity of Jesus is one that reaches out to others to involve them in the process of identity-formation. God intends Jesus to take on the value of love, which is God's value. As God's value, it is universal and suffused with God's feeling. God therefore loves not only Jesus but everyone. And therefore when Jesus takes on God's identity, he loves not only God but everyone whom God loves. When Jesus responds fully to the informative, emotive, and directive purposes of God's identity-forming Word, he not only completes the circle by loving God in return but opens the circle out to other human beings.

Loving someone fully in return involves identifying with the values they espouse. I recall a long and difficult discussion with a young couple whose relationship had become very rocky. After talking to both together, I talked to each separately. The young man complained to me that she was "too much of an idealist." She was a social worker who, he said, "loved the whole world." Yet later in our conversation, he confessed that he loved "everything about her." To which I responded, "Except that part of her that loves the world." The contradiction here is obvious: if he really loved "everything about her," he would above all love her generous, world-embracing spirit. He would be proud of her commitment to the value of love and encourage her in those particular meanings that she had chosen to express this value. He would be drawn into aligning his loves with her loves. Instead, he resented her loves. And as the conversation with him continued, I learned that in fact he loved her only insofar as she loved him and attended to him alone. His love for her was insecure and narcissistic: he loved her as an instrument to fulfill his own childish needs. His own lack of generosity and maturity prevented him from getting outside himself to love her for her own sake, in the fullness of her spiritual identity.

When Jesus responds to God's informative, emotive, and directive Word of love, Jesus returns love to God. But the love Jesus receives from God is a love of cosmic generosity. To love such a God fully is to identify with a love of universal scope and to dwell within and be committed to God's values in their universal intent. To love God is to identify oneself with God's love, and God loves all of one's neighbors, indeed all beings on this earth and beyond. Those who say that they love God and yet do not love their neighbors really do not love the whole God. Rather, they love only that part of God that loves them. They are immature and morally stunted narcissists, who need all the attention, even from God. Indeed, they really do not love the true God. When they insist that they do, they are either lying or they are self-deceived. "Those who say, 'I love God,' and hate their brothers or sisters, are liars" (1 John 4:20). Jesus, however, loves God in God's fullness, and therefore he loves those whom God loves. He identifies fully with God's identity and thus spontaneously reaches out to others.[3]

God Commissions Jesus to Go Public with the Word of Love

Because Jesus made God's identity his own, he loved not only God but all those whom God loved. As a human being, he communicated this love by activating his body and speaking nonverbal and verbal outer words. In theory, Jesus could have confined the range of these outer words to the relatively narrow sphere of life that was his as a carpenter's son in Nazareth. He would have loved all persons within that sphere, but the number of persons he would have encountered would have been quite limited.

Sometime in Jesus' life, perhaps gradually over time, he felt not only God's call to identity but also God's call to mission. He felt the call to communicate God's love not only to those whom he encountered in the daily round of his small town life but to the whole people of Israel. In a word, Jesus felt the prophetic call. He felt commissioned by God to go out to the wider public. Responding obediently to this call put him in the long and honorable tradition of the Hebrew prophets. Like them, he became a willing instrument of God's purpose for the whole people.

God has no body and thus no way of speaking outer words except through miraculous interventions, which even in Scripture are shown to occur rather rarely. More usually, God seeks out somebody, the body of a human being, through whom God can speak God's Word in outer word. To a degree, all human beings receive the call to go public with the Word, but some, in a mysterious confluence of their religious sensibility and God's inexplicable choice, feel this call more insistently and choose to devote their whole adult lives to the prophetic mission. Jesus was one of those who accepted this call. Indeed, according to his followers, he accepted this call so fully and definitively that he deserves to be called the final, or eschatological, prophet.[4]

Jesus the final prophet is a messenger of God's Word, but not a mere messenger. In commissioning Jesus, God has chosen someone who in his spiritual depths is identified with the Word in the power of the Spirit. Because of this shared identity, Jesus can be uniquely effective when he goes out and speaks the Word publicly.

The difference between being a mere messenger of a word and being a messenger deeply identified with it can be illustrated by the following situation from ordinary human life. Picture that a woman named Anne, living in Minneapolis, receives a phone call from the husband of her longtime and dearest friend, Kate, who tells her that Kate has suffered a stroke and is now in a New York hospital. Anne is the mother of five children, four of whom are still at home. She also has a career outside the home and is thus in no position to drop everything and go to New York in order to speak words of love and concern in the flesh to Kate. She decides therefore to commission a mere messenger to speak these words: she decides to send flowers. Later, the delivery person arrives at Kate's hospital room as Anne's messenger and hands over the flowers saying, "These are from Anne in Minneapolis." He is not speaking this word of flower-giving on his own behalf but solely on behalf of Anne. He is a mere messenger of Anne's word.

Anne decides to go further. Her oldest daughter, Sarah, is a college student in New York. Anne has had extraordinary success in communicating her spiritual identity to Sarah. She has endeavored to pass on her most cherished values to Sarah, who has shown a lively capacity and willingness to make them her own. Anne's most cherished value is love, and thus in the love she has shown Sarah she has been communicating a particular meaning that participates in a universal value. So completely has Sarah accepted the meaning and power of her mother's identity-forming words that friends of the family often comment, "Sarah is so generous, just like her mother. It's uncanny, to be with Sarah is almost to be with her mother!" In the deepest spiritual sense, Sarah is truly the daughter of her mother. Having reared a daughter with whom she shares identity so fully, Anne's next move is all but inevitable. She calls Sarah and tells her about her friend Kate in the hospital. Sarah's reaction is one of spontaneous sympathy, not only for Kate but also for her mother. Anne then calls her to a mission: "Could you do something for me? Could you drop by and see Kate on my behalf? And would it be possible for you to do so on a regular basis?" Sarah says, "Of course!"

The key words spoken by the mother are "for me" and "on my behalf." Sarah will speak to Kate for her mother's sake, on her mother's behalf. Anne the mother, who cannot be there to speak outer words through her own body, will speak outer words through her daughter's body. And daughter Sarah will carry out this mission not as a mere messenger, but as someone who identifies with the love that her mother speaks through her. She dwells in her mother's love; her mother's love dwells in her; and thus she participates in the love that the mother feels for another person. She is thus uniquely positioned to carry out this mission with maximum authority and power.

Sarah the daughter can also carry out the mission with maximum spontaneity and freedom. A mere messenger who delivers a bouquet of flowers carries out precise instructions agreed on by Anne and the floral service. The outer word is fixed by Anne's wishes and by company protocols. But her daughter enjoys an intimacy and shared identity with her mother that allows her considerable freedom. Her mother does not hesitate to allow this freedom. Precise instructions from mother to daughter are not required. And thus Sarah chooses when to visit and which outer words to say. It is she who decides to go to the hospital three times a week during the lunch hour. It is she who decides to feed Kate lunch (the stroke has left Kate paralyzed on her right side), read her the *New York Times*, chat with her, and give her a back rub. And since she is there "in the name of the mother," all these outer words are not only hers but her mother's. The love that Sarah speaks through outer word is ultimately her mother's love.

Like Sarah, Jesus is not a mere messenger. When he goes out in public to speak God's Word in the power of the Spirit, he goes as one who is spiritually identified with God's Word and Spirit, as one who claims that "all things have been handed over to me by my Father" (Matt. 11:27).[5] The Word he speaks in outer word he lives. He speaks then with "authority,"[6] for he responds to and speaks not only the truth about God's coming reign of love, mercy, and forgiveness, but responds to and speaks its power in feeling and action. He incarnates in being what he speaks in outer word.[7] He is not simply passing on information about God but God's very own life. It is true that Jesus, particularly in the earlier strata of the New Testament, refers everything to God and says little about himself, that he is more focused on what God is saying rather than on himself as the incarnation of what God is saying, but even in these earlier strata, the identity of Jesus is important. He is not a mere conduit for God's Word: he has identified with this Word in the deepest dimension of himself, and thus the reign of God's love that Jesus announces is already successful in Jesus' spiritual identity. How else can we account for his power and authority? When, for example, he makes the rule of God present through his forgiveness of the sinful woman (Luke 7:36-49), he is not a mere messenger of God's forgiveness but identifies so completely with God's attitude toward sinners that his forgiveness comes as God's forgiveness. Jesus does not simply announce the reign of God but brings it to people in his own words and deeds.[8] This unity of identity and mission gives to the mission its special power: "Whoever welcomes you welcomes me, and whoever welcomes me welcomes the one who sent me."[9]

Jesus also shows the freedom of one who is not a mere messenger. Secure in his intimate identity with God, Jesus carries out his mission with genuine freedom. He is not shown as one who makes only those moves that have been predetermined by God, which is remarkable given the influence at that time of the apocalyptic worldview, according to which God exercises considerable control over everything. The New Testament writers depict a Jesus who has great latitude in the precise how and when of his mission. He does the will of the "one who sent" him, in full human freedom. In the words of the English theologian Keith Ward: "Jesus has a free mind and will, which makes its own decisions and performs its own creative actions. He is united to God in such a way that, in freely obeying his distinct calling, he expresses what God is, becoming a living revelation of Supreme Value."[10]

The Two-Directionality of Jesus' Words

I should like to return to mother Anne, daughter Sarah, and Anne's friend Kate. The reader will recall that Sarah had decided to visit Kate three days a week on her mother's behalf. On these three days, she arrives at noon and immediately activates her body to communicate in outer word her own and her mother's love. In and through these words, she gives herself over to Kate as the embodiment and continuation of her mother's giving of herself to Kate. She does this with a skillful blend of verbal and nonverbal words: she speaks verbal words of encouragement and reads the *Times* aloud; she speaks nonverbal words by feeding her, helping her back in bed, and giving her a back rub.

Yet something else is going on here of which all the parties involved are more or less aware: Sarah is not only communicating her mother's love for Kate, but also her love for her mother. This second communication is not always obvious, but it is there implicitly. Kate certainly is able to pick it up as a continuous undertone, and after a few days of watching Sarah carry out her mission, she tells her husband, "In everything Sarah does for me I can feel not only her mother's love for me but her love for her mother. She positively radiates it!" And when Kate's husband passes this on to Anne back in Minneapolis, Anne too feels the power of the love that her daughter feels for her and is expressing precisely through the mission that Anne has called her to.

This love that Sarah the daughter on her mission expresses implicitly to Anne the mother can also be made explicit directly from daughter to mother. We can easily imagine periodic phone calls from Sarah to her mother, perhaps from a pay phone down the hall from Kate's room, in which she sums up her latest series of outer words. Her mother of course says, "Thanks so much for doing this for me, Sarah." And Sarah says, "I am doing this because I love you, Mom." And thus she expresses explicitly to her mother the love that she expresses implicitly in her mission to Kate.

What therefore seems at first glance to be a rather simple human activity reveals itself to be more complex. Sarah's mission to Kate is a self-communication that simultaneously moves in two directions. In one direction, she continues in her self-communication to Kate her mother's self-communication. In the second direction, she communicates herself back to her mother. She does so in and through her outer words to her mother's friend, though in a way that is largely implicit. This of course does not prevent her from stepping aside from her self-communicative mission to Sarah and communicating her love for her mother explicitly and directly by phone, though even that direct and explicit communication remains connected to the mission.

In this way, the mission serves to deepen not just the relation between Sarah's mother and her mother's friend, but the relation between Sarah and her mother. Throughout this mission, Sarah is finding herself moving into an even deeper participation in her mother's spiritual identity, and her mother has found her relation with her daughter taking on even greater depth and complexity. Anne, to be sure, loves all her children. You would never get her to say that she loves one more than the other. But having called her oldest to a special mission and watched her carry it out with such undeviating generosity and determination, she is finding that her love for Sarah is developing a unique intimacy.

Jesus' words spoken while on his mission are also two-directional. First, they continue the self-communication toward human beings from God through Jesus. And thus, in Jesus' outer words of love, mercy, and forgiveness, God's Word of love, mercy, and forgiveness is communicated. Second, in continuing God's self-communication, in saying yes to the mission, Jesus communicates himself back to God. In giving himself and God to others, Jesus gives himself to God. This second direction back to God is largely implicit in his outer words to human beings, but sometimes Jesus steps aside from his mission and speaks directly to God, as we know from frequent references in the New Testament to Jesus praying.[11] Undoubtedly, many of Jesus' prayers were simple declarations of love and thanksgiving to God, but we can easily suppose that Jesus connected many of these prayers with his mission.[12] The key point here is that when Jesus speaks outer words to others as part of his mission, such words are two-directional. In offering and giving himself to others in God's name, he simultaneously offers and gives himself to God: "I do as the Father has commanded me, so that the world may know that I love the Father" (John 14:31).

Furthermore, we can easily imagine that in carrying out his mission, Jesus, like daughter Sarah in the example above, deepens his identity with the one who sent him on the mission. His public mission, with its high points and low points, its joys and sorrows, its successes and failures, and especially its final acceleration toward suffering and death, undoubtedly brought his identity with God to a new depth and complexity. Would we be too anthropomorphic if we were to imagine that this could also be occurring from God's side? To be sure, God loves all human beings and wants them all to share God's identity as sons and daughters, friends and companions. But with those called to special mission, to dramatic and risky public communication of divine meaning and power, surely God's identity-forming relationship takes on unique depth and intimacy even from God's side. In Jesus, God has chosen someone willing to speak the Word publicly with fearless clarity and total commitment, even unto suffering and death. Did this not give to the sharing of spiritual identity between God and Jesus a unique intimacy and depth felt by both?[13]

Jesus Communicates the Word Verbally

Jesus is able and willing to accept the mission to speak the Word of God in the power of the Spirit. He goes public and speaks outer words that are verbal and nonverbal. In and through these words, he makes the meaning and power of God's reign present to people as reality and promise. He invites people to surrender to the power of his words and thereby to come under God's rule of love, mercy, forgiveness, and acceptance. Jesus' words are therefore informative, emotive, and directive; they aim to change not only how people think but how they feel and act.

In the New Testament accounts of Jesus' public life, the verbal words predominate. He spent much time preaching. The Gospels depict an outpouring of stories, parables, admonitions, epigrams, proverbs, and scriptural citations. Scholars debate which of these words go back to the very words of Jesus. The Gospels did not begin to receive final form until at least four decades after Jesus' death. Between his death and the four Gospels, there developed oral and written traditions about what Jesus said and did. These traditions varied according to the community that produced and assimilated them. The writers and final editors of each Gospel also added their point of view, shaping the material they had received according to their interests and the interests of the communities for which they wrote. Furthermore, the communities and their traditions developed after they had experienced Jesus as resurrected by God from the dead. They believed that Jesus was at the "right hand of God" (Acts 2:33), still communicating with them in the power of the Spirit. When, therefore, the early followers of Jesus met with a new historical situation—for example, the destruction of the Temple in 70 C.E. or the expulsion of the Jesus Party from the synagogues in the last decades of the first century—they put on the mind of the risen Christ and confidently uttered what they believed Jesus was speaking to this situation and then projected both the situation and the words of Jesus back into his historical life. No one during the time of Jesus would have seen anything wrong with this, but it does present difficulties for us now as we try to talk about the outer words that Jesus actually spoke during his mission.

No one word, therefore, can be invested with absolute historical certainty. Nevertheless, scholars are convinced that there is a core of verbal preaching that can reliably be traced back to Jesus. About the general shape of this preaching there is much agreement.[14] I shall proceed, therefore, with some confidence that when I talk about what Jesus said I am not engaging in airy speculation.

Jesus preached that God was making a renewed initiative in God's relationship with the Jewish people. God's invitation to come under the rule of God's love was coming again with special power and urgency through his agent, Jesus the Son and anointed one,[15] whom God has commissioned to speak the Word in the power of the Spirit. This did not mean a repudiation of God's previous initiatives: God's covenant with Israel, inaugurated through Moses, renewed through David, and vigorously promoted by the great prophets, was not annulled by Jesus. Earlier, God had called the Israelites to a relationship of love and justice with God and with each other. Thus the essence of the original covenant was the twofold law: love God and love the neighbor (see Deut. 6:5 and Lev. 19:18). Jesus in his preaching ringingly reaffirmed the twofold law, and he enjoined people to make it the essence of their belief, feeling, and action (see Mark 12:28-34; Matt. 22:34-40; Luke 10:25-28).

Out of the twofold law, the Hebrew religion elaborated over the centuries many commandments and rules governing ethical, cultic, and everyday behavior in great detail. These received classical expression in the Torah (the reader will recall that *Torah* is the Hebrew word for law or instruction), which is found in the first five books of the Hebrew Scriptures. This Torah, as the written law, found further elaboration in new rulings to meet new historical situations. Thus, by the time of Jesus there was a written Torah and an oral Torah.

In his preaching, Jesus did not advocate the annulment of the written and oral Torah, but he did relativize it by placing the stress on love and justice as the essence of God's relationship with human beings and their relationship with one another. And thus all the rules that flow out of and further specify love and justice are important only insofar as they serve love and justice. Jesus, then, like many of the prophets of an earlier time and the proto-rabbis[16] of his own time, stressed that interior disposition is as important as exterior action, for ultimately love and justice are qualities of the inner spiritual self in its tendency toward God and others. The transformation of this inner disposition is the aim of the reign of God that in the words of Jesus is breaking in anew upon the Jewish people.

I am reminded of a conversation I had several years ago with a Catholic woman who had entered middle age feeling a little insecure about her attractiveness to her husband. He was a strict Catholic, very resolute in his adherence to the ethical principles and rules propounded by his church. Most of the time, it would have never dawned on her to think he could be unfaithful, but one night, when she felt especially low in self-confidence, she blurted out, "Honey, would you ever be unfaithful to me?" He replied, "Sweetheart, I would never break any of the commandments, and you know that." She was cheered by the *sweetheart* and calmed by his tone, which was nondefensive. The next day, however, she thought again about what he had said and became very agitated. She was a student in one of my theology classes, and she decided to bring her agitation to me. I asked her, "Well, what did you want him to say?" She hesitated and then said, "I wanted him to tell me how much he loved me!"

We all can perfectly understand her response. She wanted him to go to the heart of the covenant that she hoped existed between them. Not that she thought the commandments and rules governing sexual fidelity were unimportant. Indeed, she was on one level very relieved to know that he kept those commandments. But she knew intuitively that the rules flow out of and back into the relationship. Sexual fidelity is the expression of love, not the love as such. True, sexual fidelity bends back on the love and deepens it; yet it is subordinate to the love in a way that the love is not subordinate to the sexual fidelity. She did not want, therefore, to hear about his strict conformity to rules governing his outer behavior, but about the reality and intensity of his inner love toward her. She wanted him to grasp the meaning of his love toward her in inner word, infuse it with the power of his feeling, and then pour this love-feeling into a deeply personal outer word: "Sweetheart, I am faithful because I love you so much."

Nothing in the Gospels suggests that Jesus was engaged in a sweeping attack on the commandments and rules of the Torah.[17] But he placed special emphasis on the inner spring of action, which is the interior movement of love toward God and others. At times, apparently, it led Jesus to suspend a particular rule (see Mark 2:23-28; Matt. 12:1-14; Luke 6:1-11), but it did not lead him to a wholesale dismantling of the Torah. His teaching and his lived example consistently accent self-giving as the essence of Judaism, a self-giving that does not abolish the Torah but that in extraordinary situations could go beyond all rules and expectations.[18]

Jesus also taught that God takes the initiative in the offer of relationship and that the offer is unconditional. It is offered to all people. They do not have to prove themselves worthy of the offer. But Jesus was acutely aware that many are not willing to respond to the offer. Many fail in their relationship to God and to others. They do not live under God's rule of love. They are sinners, but they do not admit their sin.[19] Jesus is not as harsh as John the Baptizer,[20] but he is no sentimentalist about human beings. Jesus looked into people's hearts and saw their hardness. He called people to judgment and repentance (see Matt. 3:2-12; 4:17; Mark 1:15; Luke 13:3, 5) as the necessary precondition for accepting God's forgiving love. God was there, offering relationship to human beings, inviting them into the present and future reign, but many were saying no and thus would not enter into relationship with God from their side. That was their sin. And thus the first aspect or moment[21] of Jesus' preaching is a moment of judgment, spurring people to repentance.

Yet in his preaching Jesus gave more stress to announcing God's forgiving love than to judging people's refusal to accept it. God through Jesus' words welcomed everyone into the reign of God's love and justice. God is the Good Shepherd (Matt. 18:10-14) who seeks out the one lost sheep rather than resting content with the ninety-nine who are found, the father who welcomes back his prodigal son (Luke 15:11-32) without first demanding a long confession of his sin, the woman who seeks her lost coin (Luke 15:8-10),[22] the generous vineyard owner (Matt. 20:1-16) who offers full pay to all the workers no matter when they come on duty. Everyone is invited to come under the tent of God's love. Jesus showed particular solicitude for those whom conventional religion had stigmatized not just as sinners, but as sinners unworthy of divine favor: the tax collector, the Samaritan woman, the prostitute, the poor people of the land who were not strict Torah observers. Jesus did not idealize them—he never said they were not sinners—but he did see in them a tendency toward greater honesty. They were aware of their sin, and this awareness led them to be more open to God's offer of forgiving and accepting love than those who in their self-righteousness were smugly unaware that they too needed forgiveness.

Thus, Jesus did not separate the moment of judgment from the moment of forgiveness. His intuitive religious genius enabled him to see that unless judgment of sin is immediately followed by the offer of forgiveness, judgment is unlikely to elicit repentance. Judgment alone simply scares people. Told only that they have put themselves outside the covenant of God's love and that there will be dire consequences, they lie to themselves and to others and protest that they are good, that they have not sinned. They hide themselves from themselves, from others, and from God. To bring them out of hiding and self-deception, Jesus emphasizes that God's judgment is a judgment made by the God who is always there offering forgiveness even as this love is being refused. The good shepherd is always in pursuit. The old woman is always looking for her coin. God is always there forgiving the sinner; the sinner need only accept God's offer to be forgiven from his or her side. Sins can then be confessed without fear and in total honesty, like the woman who boldly entered the Pharisee's house and bathed the feet of Jesus with tears of remorse and repentance.[23]

The verbal words of Jesus do not only judge and forgive the sinner but also aim at the sinner's moral transformation. He calls the Israelite people to a life in conformity with the renewed covenant now drawing near. Jesus is not a hectoring moralist, and yet his words have an emotive and directive power. If sinners are to come under God's reign, they must let this power change their hearts and move them to a new way of feeling and acting.[24] Nor does he leave his hearers without guidelines to how someone who responds fully to the Word and Spirit ought to act. Coming under God's rule is to do what God is trying to do in the world: spread the rule of love and justice to others. To do that means that hearers of the Word ought to transform their own verbal and nonverbal words into expressions of love and justice. Jesus therefore spells out a moral ideal of extraordinary challenge: "Be perfect, therefore, as your heavenly Father is perfect" (Matt. 5:48). Be forgiving, accepting, loving, merciful, and just as God is. This is tantamount to demanding that people imitate Jesus himself in his obedient sonship. When people ask Jesus what they must do to come under the reign of God's saving love, he says feed the hungry, give drink to the thirsty, welcome the stranger, clothe the naked, take care of the sick, and visit those in prison (see Matt. 25). To put it in the terminology of this book: embrace particular meanings that are compatible with the universal values of love and justice. Jesus' hearers thus are called not only to hear Jesus' words but to do them. He offers not only an ideal, but as the one "full of the Holy Spirit" (Luke 4:1) offers the power to carry it out.[25]

It remains, however, a very exacting ideal that is difficult to carry out consistently. Human beings fall short, and when they do, the ideal embodied in Jesus' words is received by hearers as words of judgment calling them to repentance, which is the first moment of Jesus' preaching.

But judgment is paired with the offer of forgiveness, and thus the ideal that convicts them is an ideal that God through Jesus lives out perfectly in those outer words that forgive and reconcile human beings. Jesus' words in turn ready them for the third moment, the Spirit-filled transformative power of the Word. Judgment, forgiveness, and transformation: these three moments are thus folded into Jesus' preaching and form a complex unity.

We see the moments of judgment, forgiveness, and transformation coming together in one of Jesus' most powerful parables, the parable of the unforgiving slave. Here it is as told by Matthew's Gospel:

> The kingdom of heaven may be compared to a king who wished to settle accounts with his slaves. When he began the reckoning, one who owed him ten thousand talents was brought to him; and, as he could not pay, his lord ordered him to be sold, together with his wife and possessions, and payment to be made. So the slave fell on his knees before him, saying, "Have patience with me, and I will pay you everything." And out of pity for him, the lord of that slave released him and forgave him the debt. But that same slave, as he went out, came upon one of his fellow slaves who owed him a hundred denarii; and seizing him by the throat, he said, "Pay what you owe." Then his fellow slave fell down and pleaded with him, "Have patience with me, and I will pay you." But he refused; then he went and threw him into prison until he would pay the debt. When his fellow slaves saw what had happened, they were greatly distressed, and they went and reported to their lord all that had taken place. Then his lord summoned him and said to him, "You wicked slave! I forgave you all that debt because you pleaded with me. Should you not have had mercy on your fellow slave, as I had mercy on you?" And in anger his lord handed him over to be tortured until he would pay his entire debt. So my heavenly Father will also do to every one of you, if you do not forgive your brother or sister from your heart. (Matt. 18:23–35)

This extended story is driven by a simile, namely, the reign of God is like the reign of this lord.[26] A slave comes to this lord with a debt that is enormous: the annual income of Herod the Great, the king of Judea, was nine hundred talents a year and this slave owes ten thousand! Imagining ourselves as the Jewish audience hearing this parable, we would gasp at this amount.[27] Such a debt is unpayable; the lord will surely modify his demand. But he shows himself heartless, and our sympathies are with the slave when he throws himself at his lord's mercy. But we hold out no hope for a reprieve. For we know that in strict justice the lord has a right to be heartless; this is what the slave owes, and in justice he must pay the price if he does not pay the debt. Such is the rule of ordinary life. Yet parables are full of unexpected turns in plot that jolt us out of our normal way of looking at life. The heartless lord suddenly does a 180-degree pirouette, bestows a marvelous mercy, and forgives the whole debt. He had every right to exact full payment, but he wipes the slate clean in a gesture of unimaginable generosity. In like manner, God will deal with our sins, if we only repent and humbly ask for mercy.

Then we are surprised by another twist in the story: the slave, instead of feeling grateful and generous, turns to a fellow slave and refuses to forgive a debt of hundred denarii. He seizes him by the throat and throws him in debtors' prison. The lord had forgiven him a debt that was forty-five thousand times greater than the debt he now refuses to forgive. We are stunned by this flagrant ingratitude, and our earlier sympathies for the slave turn to a demand for strict justice. We thus watch approvingly when his rightfully distressed fellow slaves hand him over to the lord for judgment and punishment. The unmerciful slave has missed the moment of transformation; he has squandered the lord's mercy and failed to see that a mercy accepted is a mercy that now must be practiced: "From everyone to whom much has been given, much will be required" (Luke 12:48). Indeed, practicing the mercy one has received is the surest sign that one has truly received it. Mercy is a complex mystery that can only be fully understood and appreciated in the practice of mercy.

We see in this parable many aspects of Jesus' teaching of the reign of God. The dominant motif is God's mercy and forgiveness, God's bounty and immeasurable generosity. All the slave has to do is honestly admit his debt, and mercy will flow over him. Yet the moment of judgment is starkly present. The reign of God welcomes all, but repentance must be genuine and the plea for mercy sincere. Mercy cannot "take" in a person who does not have true repentance. The slave suffers a self-imposed judgment and punishment. In our day, when we are inclined to sentimentalize God's love, we are likely to overlook the moment of judgment that is in Jesus' teaching: those who say no to the reign of God's mercy as offered by Jesus will suffer the consequences.[28]

At the deepest level, this parable is not about a money debt, but about the debt that is incurred when one is treated with generous mercy. When the slave's debt is forgiven, he incurs a debt of gratitude to the lord and a debt of mercy to those who are indebted to him. God expects more from those who have been given so much. We see with stark clarity the moral rigor of the demands of God; we are asked to do nothing less than treat others the way God treats us. The very mercy that God shows us is the mercy by which our treatment of others will be judged. The reign of God offered by Jesus is thus at once a gift of boundless mercy and a demand for the highest moral transformation: "Be merciful, just as your Father is merciful" (Luke 6:36).[29] Yet we are the most fortunate of all creatures; for the ideal by which we are judged is the ideal that God carries out. When we fall short of this ideal, as we inevitably do, God is always there, offering forgiveness.

Jesus Communicates the Word Nonverbally

Jesus did not only preach; he acted. Commentators on the New Testament text often say that Jesus made God's rule of love present in word and deed. It would be just as accurate to say that Jesus made this love present in verbal and nonverbal word. For Jesus' deeds were nonverbal words that communicated God's meaning and power. In Jesus' culture, something as simple and everyday as sharing food and drink with someone carried communicative significance—in idiomatic English we would say that it spoke volumes. To refuse to share table fellowship was to say, You are not worthy of my company, you are outside the circle of my love and concern.[30] By the standards of his day, Jesus was downright promiscuous in table fellowship. He spoke with great meaning and power when he sat down and broke bread with observers and nonobservers of Torah, with Pharisee and non-Pharisee, with tax collector and prostitute. He was also wonderfully receptive to the company of women.[31] He made a lot of room at his table and spoke thereby a nonverbal word that showed the universality and unconditionality of God's love.

Another nonverbal word full of meaning and power was spoken through Jesus' miracles. The miracles depicted in the New Testament are of two kinds. First, the *nature miracles,* in which Jesus is shown to have the power to act directly on the natural world to cause an event that cannot be explained by reference to nature's laws or human powers. The nature miracles are the multiplication of the loaves and fishes (Mark 6:33-44), the astonishing catch of fish (Luke 5:1-11), the changing of water into wine (John 2:1-11), the walking on water without sinking (Mark 6:45-52), the calming of the storm (Mark 4:35-41), and the withering of the fig tree (Mark 11:12-14). Second, the *healing miracles,* in which Jesus heals a human being of an illness or disability by giving sight to the blind, restoring hearing to the deaf, exorcising the demons of the possessed, stopping the hemorrhaging of the woman, and so on.[32]

Many today find it difficult to believe in Jesus' miracles. Rudolf Bultmann and his followers ruled out the historicity of Jesus' miracles on the grounds that a modern view of the world simply has no room for them. By contrast, the Catholic scholar John P. Meier, after exhaustively analyzing the miracles on strictly historical grounds, concluded that many of the miracle stories of exorcism and healing go back to events that were astonishing enough to lead witnesses to believe that Jesus could have performed them only with the help of a supernatural power.[33] Some witnesses thought he was performing these miracles by the power of God; others thought it was by the power of the devil or demons. But whatever the explanation, witnesses resorted to supernatural explanations and thus saw these great works as miracles. Meier has much more doubt about the historicity of the nature miracles: "With the sole exception of the feeding of the multitude, all these stories appear to have been created by the early church to serve various theological purposes."[34]

What is the purpose of Jesus' miracles? They bring to people the Word and Spirit of God. They are expressions of the coming eschatological reign of God's mercy and love. Jesus, says N. T. Wright, "never performed mighty works simply to impress. He saw them as part of the inauguration of the sovereign and healing rule of Israel's covenant god."[35] The miracles are a protest against physical evil and a genuine foretaste of the coming new age in which, according to E. P. Sanders, "pain, suffering, and death would be overcome."[36] They represent the defeat of Satan and the demonic powers. The coming reign of God, therefore, does not bring only a spiritual transformation, which is the forgiveness of sins and a renewed heart, but also a transformation of the whole self.[37]

In the New Testament, we find many more accounts of healing miracles than of nature miracles. Is a healing miracle nothing but a nature miracle applied to the human body or psyche? If so, then it is a miracle in the classical sense: Jesus healed a body or psyche by interrupting, suspending, or exceeding the physical and psychological laws of nature. I know of no case where a completely severed optic nerve reconnected itself solely by virtue of the normal operation of nature's laws. If in curing a blind man Jesus caused a severed optic nerve to reconnect, then he did something with God's power that nature or human power could not do. Such a healing, therefore, would be nothing more than a nature miracle applied to the human body.

Yet Jesus on more than one occasion of a healing miracle said, "Your faith has healed you" (Mark 5:34; 10:52; Matt. 9:22; Luke 7:50; 8:48; 17:19;

18:42). This raises the possibility that Jesus' healing miracles were not simply a species of nature miracle. A nature miracle is a direct intervention in the normal operations of the natural world, but if faith is required then perhaps the intervention is not direct but occurs through the person's faith. Faith is an act that rises out of the spiritual dimension, where freedom and the tendency toward meaning dwell, where the laws of nature do not fully rule. And thus the power by which Jesus performed a healing miracle may be a power that entered the person by way of the person's spiritual act of faith. Once this power had entered the person's spirit, then it moved on to work the psychological or physical healing. Jesus may have effected the healing miracle of a kind of spiritual-psychosomatic power, a power that flowed first to the spirit and then through to the psyche and the body.[38] And the faith of the person healed was not only a faith that Jesus could heal, not only saying, "I believe you can do it, Jesus," but a faith in the core meaning of Jesus' word, which is the meaning of God's love for humankind and the triumph of that love in the coming reign of God. It was a faith that said, I believe that you can do it, Jesus, and that you do it as a communication of divine love. It was a faith that saw the healing as an invitation to come under the rule of God's mercy and to assume full membership in God's covenantal community.[39] The healing was therefore not a wonder performed for its own sake but a communicative sign of the inbreaking reign of God. The miracles were intended then to move people into new life under the rule of forgiveness and love.[40] Jesus was more than a wonder-worker; he was the communicator of God's Word of love in the power of the Spirit.

I am not saying that Jesus performed healing miracles solely as a way of transforming the spiritual self into believers in the Word. Jesus was no dualist who sharply separated the spiritual dimension of the self from the psychological and biological dimensions. The love of God that Jesus communicated to people was intended to save the whole self, not just the spiritual self. For human beings need to be saved not only from the spiritual suffering that is the effect of sin, but also from the psychological suffering that is the effect of madness (or demons), and from the physical suffering that is the effect of leprosy. Jesus, as a Jew, had a holistic view of the human self. He could not restrict the aim of God's love to judging, forgiving, and transforming the self in its spiritual dimension. Jesus saw the Spirit-power of the Word reaching down deep into matter, into the body, but this power could have its full effect only if let in by the faith of the person healed.

Jesus therefore continued to heal, even though he knew thereby that he continually ran the risk of being seen solely as an instrument for psychological and bodily healing to the neglect of spiritual healing. Jesus walked a fine line here, and we can sense in the Gospels occasional doubt on Jesus' part that his miracles were requested for the right reasons and interpreted in the right way.[41] Moved by compassion (see Mark 1:41; 6:34; Matt. 20:34; Luke 7:13) and impelled by a holistic vision of salvation,[42] he healed. But if the blind person sees and does not in the end become a more loving and faithful servant of God's reign, has he or she been truly healed? Not in the deepest, spiritual sense. A sane psyche and a healthy body do not constitute the full rule of God's healing love.[43]

Yet Jesus' attention through the healing miracles to the psychological and physical is remarkable and serves as a warning to all those who try to overspiritualize the effects of God's Word and Spirit. Love gives *primacy* to evoking love in the spiritual self, but love at times gives *priority* to psychological and physical healing. For love is expressed through outer word, and the spiritual self communicates and receives the outer word with full effectiveness only through a sound mind and body. If mind or body is debilitated or ill or in pain, the word's meaning can be muddied and its power diminished. Psychological and physical suffering not only make the communication of spirit difficult but can batter down the spirit and reduce it to an obsessive concern for mental and physical recovery. My wife is a nurse, and I worked for many years as a nursing assistant. We have both witnessed how pain can numb and even shatter the spirit, making all but impossible the full flourishing of the spiritual self. Here indeed love must give the priority to healing the ill person. After sufficient healing, love then turns to the spiritual transformation, which has primacy.

The healing miracles are nonverbal words that have the power to reach into all dimensions of the human self. However we interpret their precise mode of causality—as a nature miracle or as a spiritual-psychosomatic miracle—the presence and promise of holistic salvation is the key point. Those who are skeptical about Jesus' virginal conception and the outer word of God spoken at Jesus' baptism will be inclined to see the healing miracles as somehow occurring through the spirit of the recipient, rather than as miracles in the classical sense, though even that interpretation leaves room for much mystery. I understand their skepticism, but I would not want to see Christians separate from one another on the question of the precise causality of Jesus' healing miracles. For the fundamental import of Jesus' nonverbal words of healing is, I think, clear and inescapable: God in Jesus loves the whole person, and it is the whole person who is being invited into the coming reign of God.

One final point. Jesus' healing miracles provide an entry point into the modern work of social justice. Let me tell of an incident that occurred at our place. One summer evening, my wife spotted a man lying on the boulevard grass not far from our back door. Moved by compassion and concern, she went out to help. He looked as if he were a Native American, and my wife, knowing the high incidence of diabetes in the Native American community, asked if he were a diabetic. It turned out that he was not; rather, he had been injured by a car and had dragged himself to the boulevard. As a registered nurse, my wife had some medical skill she could bring to him, but she became aware immediately that his injuries exceeded her skills, so she told me to call 911. In five minutes, the county emergency service arrived and quickly applied to this injured man a massive amount of skill and equipment. After stabilizing him, they rushed him off in the ambulance to the county hospital. It was all very impressive.

Jesus had the miraculous power of healing and perhaps could have applied this power to the injured man on our boulevard and healed him. My wife does not have this kind of healing power but, like Jesus, was moved by compassion upon seeing someone in pain. She then applied her limited human powers to a person in need of healing. She performed an act of charity. But she quickly came to the limit of her powers and therefore enlisted the help of our county's emergency service, which is a complex social structure. Creating and maintaining a social structure like this is the modern work of social justice. Many years ago, people in our county saw a problem that could not be solved by individual acts of charity, and they initiated a social movement to create a new structure. Jesus was not a social reformer or revolutionary in the modern sense, but he used the power of the Word and Spirit to combat and alleviate psychological and physical suffering. In the spirit of Jesus, we too should use all our powers to help individuals and to create just social structures.

To sum up: Jesus' mission was to speak the verbal and nonverbal words of God. With these words, Jesus intended to draw people into the rule of God's love. When people believed, felt, and acted on these words, they were healed; they were made whole; they were saved. Saving people was his mission—and he had success. Indeed, during his mission he commissioned some of his followers to continue his saving mission. The Gospel of Mark speaks of those who were "sent out to proclaim the message, and to have the authority to cast out demons" (Mark 3:14-15). It is routine for Christians to say that Jesus saved human beings through his suffering and death, but long before suffering and dying, Jesus was saving human beings and commissioning others to help him. He saved them by the Word spoken in the power of the Spirit, which moved people to faith and love. If the death of Jesus was an event that saves human beings, it must be an event that continues the communication of the Word and Spirit. How this might be is the topic of the next chapter.

FIVE

The Death of Jesus as the Final Word of Mission

In this chapter, I shall argue that the suffering and death of Jesus is an outer word that sums up and culminates all the previous words of his mission. I shall also place the suffering and death in the closest possible connection with the last supper, the final meal Jesus shared with the innermost circle of his followers.

Jesus' Death Completes His Saving Mission

Jesus' suffering and death should not be isolated from the previous unfolding of his mission.[1] Such an isolation has occurred in the history of Christian theology and has led to soteriologies[2] that made Jesus' death into *the* saving act. These soteriologies implied that prior to Jesus' death God was not saving people, indeed could not save people because until Jesus' death on the cross the price and debt of sin had not yet been paid. In the popular Christian imagination, this has led to a soteriology that sees God as withholding mercy and love from Adam and his descendants until Jesus' death. Indeed, in the wake of the Fall of Adam, the hearts of the Israelites and all human beings had become so hardened that God feels as much wrath as mercy toward them. God would like to begin anew with Israel and with all humankind, but divine justice demands that divine wrath against sin be discharged and that human beings pay off the debt for sin. God therefore is in a bind: God wants to begin anew with the human race but is stymied by God's undischarged wrath against sin. Fortunately for the human race, the merciful God has provided the solution: God initiates a plan that God infallibly carries out whereby Jesus is chosen to represent the whole human race. By his suffering and death, Jesus makes the satisfaction for sin, pays the debt for sin, and absorbs God's punishing wrath against sin. God's justice having been satisfied, God is now free to bestow on humankind the Word and Spirit of love, mercy, forgiveness, and reconciliation. God could not do this before the death of Jesus, and thus the ministry of Jesus becomes little more than a preparation for death.[3]

But it is abundantly clear in the New Testament that God through Jesus was saving people long before his death. Jesus was drawing people into the rule of God's love by communicating the meaning and power of the love to people he met along the way. It is true that Jesus also had an expectation for the future. He was aware during his earthly mission that he was not yet making God's rule fully effective. Jesus' preaching manifests a tension between what God was already accomplishing through him and what God had yet to accomplish, and this tension understandably increased as the conflict between Jesus and his opponents increased and his death loomed as ever more likely.[4] Jesus knew that the definitive, final (eschatological) completion of his mission was in the future, a future that he came to believe was only reachable through his death. But that does not mean that before his death salvation was not happening. Salvation did not begin with the death of Jesus.

Yet it is appropriate to give special emphasis to the death. My reaction here against the popular tendency to overstress the death should not be taken to mean that the death does not have surpassing significance. The death was the final word of Jesus' earthly mission, summing up all his previous outer words and giving to these words new depth and power. In the light of his death, his followers could now see with full clarity the meaning of his mission: "We know love by this, that he laid down his life for us" (1 John 3:16). And later, under the influence of Jesus' resurrection, they could see in his death the eschatological victory of God.

Jesus' Death as His Final Word

Despite all my talk about words being verbal and nonverbal, it may still strike the reader as strange to say that Jesus' death was a word (and since Jesus spoke this word on God's behalf, also simultaneously God's Word).

When we think about a word, we imagine the speaker directly activating his or her body to produce the outer word, whether verbal or nonverbal. The speaker is therefore seen to be the direct agent of the event that is the outer word. Jesus, however, was not the direct agent of his death. He did not take his own life. In theory, he could have done so and thereby spoken a word that could have carried, let us say, this meaning: up until now I have wished to carry out the mission to speak God's Word, but I am not willing to do so in the face of death at the hands of my enemies. I wish not to go through the pain and shame of public torture and execution. I will take my own life. One could perhaps feel considerable understanding and sympathy for such a death-word, but one would see this word not as the culmination of his mission but its termination. His death would not sum up the meaning of the previous words of his mission but would convert these previous words into a self-contained series broken off by suicide.

But to speak a word through death does not require the speaker to be the direct agent of his death. Suppose the speaker were killed by others precisely because the speaker was speaking a word and refusing to stop speaking it. The speaker would not be the direct agent of his or her death—the direct agents would be those who killed the speaker—but the speaker would be the indirect agent because the speaker could have avoided the death if he or she had stopped speaking the word.

When I say "speaker" or "speech," I am referring to the complete spectrum of action by which meaning is communicated. During World War II, in those lands under Nazi rule, some Christians (sadly, very few) harbored Jewish families. This action communicated meaning. It was a nonverbal word more powerful than any verbal word of love. In expressing their love in this nonverbal way to their Jewish brothers and sisters, these Christians very consciously ran the risk of discovery, torture, and death at the hands of the Nazis. When the Nazis did discover them, as they often did, they did indeed torture and kill them, stringing them up in the town square for all to see. And what did townspeople see? Or better, what did they hear? Those who had ears to hear, heard this word: we loved our Jewish neighbors enough to give our lives. This is what those hanged said as the indirect agents of their word of death. Not everyone had the ears to hear their communication. Many heard only what the direct agents, the Nazis had to say: these people are traitors to the *Vaterland* and the Aryan cause; this too could be your fate.

What is important is the causal chain: for a person to speak a word through death without being the direct agent of her death, her speaking of the word must be a necessary, contributing cause of the death. The other day, a colleague and I were discussing the death of Martin Luther King Jr.

by an assassin's bullet in April 1968. We were in our twenties at the time and had fiercely supported King and his cause. We felt his death as a devastating tragedy that struck a hard blow at our hopes for racial justice in America. Yet when our numbness and grief subsided, we found our strength and hope revitalized, partly because of the death, which deepened our commitment to his cause. For King was struck down while carrying out his mission, which was to speak the word of interracial love and justice. He was on the balcony of that motel because he had come to Memphis to plead justice for the virtually all-black sanitation workers' union. He was there knowing that every word of his public mission brought with it the risk of death: from the earliest days of his mission he had passed hardly a day without a death threat. James Earle Ray, his assassin, was there in Memphis with his rifle to stop King in his mission. He was the direct agent of King's death, but King was the indirect agent and thus a contributing cause of his death, for his mission entailed the risk of death, and he knew that. Thus the irony, at once terrifying and inspiring: Ray killed King to silence him, but the death then became King's final and most powerful word of love and justice.

All this would change if the chain of causality were different. Imagine for a moment that an enterprising reporter had discovered that King was addicted to gambling and that the primary purpose of his visit to Memphis had been to participate in a high stakes card game. Imagine further that on an earlier visit King had lost heavily to a James Earle Ray and had refused to pay what he owed, taking refuge in his celebrity. For months Ray had been dunning King for payment and threatening him if he did not pay. It all came to a head that day in Memphis when Ray decided to carry out his threat. If this chain of causality were true, my colleague and I would find ourselves reacting differently to King's death. His death would still be a terrible tragedy—we would mourn him profoundly—but his death would not be a word that communicates the meaning and power of his mission.

I want to be very careful here not to be misunderstood. When I say that King was the indirect agent of his death, I do not wish to imply in the least that King was on a suicide mission or that he manipulated his public life out of a masochistic wish to die a martyr. King loved life and hated death. But he risked his life and lost his life out of love for God and loyalty to God's call to mission. He willed the death only insofar he willed the mission.

If the death of Jesus is to be heard as a word communicating the meaning of his mission, which is to announce and bring God's reign of love and justice, then there must be a causal connection between that mission and his death. The connection is supplied by the intentions of Jesus and his executioners. In going up to Jerusalem to confront the power elite, Jesus must intend to carry out his mission. Also, his executioners must intend to stop him in his mission. If, however, Jesus had gone to Jerusalem with the sole intention to expel the Roman occupiers and secure political power for himself and his followers, then his death, as ordered by the Roman legate Pontius Pilate, was not a word of God's love but a word that communicated a purely political meaning.[5] If Jesus had caused a ruckus in the Temple precincts (see Mark 11:15-19) merely as a protest against the economic power of those who benefited from Temple cult and sacrifice, then his death, as urged on Pilate by the Temple priesthood, was not a word of God's kingdom-love but a word intended only to incite social and economic revolution.

We are confronted with a classic instance in which a theological reconstruction based on faith intersects with a historical reconstruction based on reason. No amount of historical evidence can compel a person to believe that Jesus had gone to Jerusalem with the sincere intention of speaking the Word of God to the centers of power. No amount of evidence can compel us to believe that he was in Jerusalem carrying out the intention of God. Yet the decision to believe that he was sincere in his mission and that his mission was from God must be consistent with the historical reconstruction of the events leading up to his death in Jerusalem. If he were there solely on a political, social, or economic mission, and not as the Messiah charged with ushering in God's eschatological rule, then we would have to radically redefine the meaning of his death. If at least some key people behind his execution had not been motivated to stop Jesus in his mission, if, for example, they had totally misread the meaning of his action in the Temple or had regarded Jesus merely as a deluded disturber of the peace, then Jesus' death as a religiously significant event begins to dissolve into a cruel and tragic farce.[6] It would be analogous to learning that James Earle Ray had killed Martin Luther King Jr. because the arrival of King and his entourage at the motel had caused too much noise in the neighborhood.

The historical reconstruction of Jesus' intentions is therefore important to the theologian.[7] Of course, we have no direct access to Jesus' inner mind and heart (or to anyone else's for that matter), but it is possible to infer with considerable confidence the nature of these aims by reconstructing the history of his verbal and nonverbal words. When we do that, we begin to see that the words spoken on his mission quite early on aroused an opposition that could make Jesus fearful for his life. Even though in theology and worldview he was closer to the Pharisees than to any other group in Israel, he clashed with them, especially with the hard-line Shammaites,[8] whose intensification of Torah practice and militant opposition against Rome were not shared by Jesus. So far as we know, none of these Pharisees threatened him with death, and even if they had, they did not have the political power to carry out the threat, but their distrust had to impress on Jesus the riskiness of his mission. We must also recall that early in his public mission Jesus learned of the fate of his predecessor and mentor, John the Baptizer, whose pointed words of judgment to Herod the King had led to his arrest and death (see Mark 6:14-29).

Jesus began his mission in his home province of Galilee. He won many followers and drew enthusiastic crowds, but he was not a complete success. Whole towns refused to accept his offer of the reign of God.[9] His reception in his hometown was frosty: his family thought him crazy, his listeners "took offense at him" (Mark 6:3). He soon left, "amazed at their unbelief" (6:6). This did not deter him from bringing the good news to all of Israel, but when he "set his face to go to Jerusalem" (Luke 9:51), the religious and political center of Israel, he must have reckoned with the possibility of seeing not only his message rejected but also his life put at risk.[10]

Prior to going up to Jerusalem, Jesus acted as the Messiah. He spoke verbally and nonverbally of God's coming reign, and he spoke with the authority of one anointed to be the agent of that coming. He appears, however, to have avoided publicly designating himself as the Messiah. He often spoke in riddles about the coming reign and his role in it, in part to avoid being misunderstood as a nationalistic messiah who would forcefully drive out the Romans, and in part to avoid arrest before his mission was complete.[11] But as he entered Jerusalem, he decided to behave in a more overtly messianic way. He arranged for his entry on a donkey and in doing so made an unmistakable allusion to the prophet Zechariah's vision of that day when God will dwell in Zion (that is, Jerusalem) as king:

> Rejoice greatly, O daughter Zion!
> Shout aloud, O daughter Jerusalem!
> Lo, your king comes to you;
> triumphant and victorious is he,
> humble and riding on a donkey,
> on a colt, the foal of a donkey. (Zech. 9:9)

Then, in a very provocative action, Jesus went to the Temple, the holiest place in all of Israel, to symbolically cleanse it of activity inimical to the intentions of his Father in heaven.[12] During his mission, he had forgiven sins, bypassing entirely the official channel for forgiveness that is the

Temple and its system of sin offerings. Some of the Gospel writers have him predicting that with the coming of God's reign the Temple will be destroyed. We can be quite sure that he made mutterings in that direction, giving voice to his conviction that his role of God's agent called him to lead an anti-Temple movement.[13] This was not new to Judaism; years before Jeremiah relentlessly attacked the Temple, and Jesus' contemporaries, the Essenes, saw the Temple and its priesthood as deeply corrupted. But in Jesus' Temple action, a cluster of aims came together that could not have failed to arouse the most intense opposition among the religious elite. Jesus was not only attacking one of the most cherished symbols of the Jewish religion but doing so while making implicit the claim to be the Messiah, the agent who would help God regain the throne and usher in a new rule where the "first will be last, and the last will be first" (Matt. 19:30). Such arrogance; indeed, such blasphemy![14]

Jesus was not the first Jew of his time to ride into Jerusalem acting as the Messiah intent on saving his people. Many before and after him urged the people to rise up violently against the hated Roman occupiers, to "take it [the kingdom] by force" (Matt. 11:12).[15] Some of them promised the downtrodden and oppressed masses an upheaval in the whole social structure. They made the Roman and Jewish leadership nervous, and the leaders crushed them with merciless cruelty. Memories and fears of such messianic pretenders led Pontius Pilate to pronounce the sentence of death on Jesus, which was a terrible injustice, for Jesus did not intend to lead a violent revolution against Rome. He did indeed promise a radically new world under God's rule, but this was a rule that would not come through human force. Jesus counseled the very opposite of force: love, mercy, justice, peace, trust, patience, and nonviolence.[16] He did not doubt that God's reign was coming, and would come, through him, but its coming was God's work, in God's good time: "But about that day or hour no one knows, neither the angels in heaven, nor the Son, but only the Father" (Mark 13:32).

Last Supper and Death

Many historians are convinced that the immediate cause of Jesus' death was his action at the Temple.[17] Jesus had long reckoned with the possibility of death, but now he knew of its inevitability. The machinery was in motion. Judas, his betrayer, had met with the chief priests. The priests had hastily arranged an informal nightly trial to bring their charges against

Jesus. Jesus meanwhile had planned a Passover meal, or at least a meal with strong Passover connotations, where he would initiate the speaking of the final word of his life. I am talking here of the last supper, at which Jesus showed his theological originality in a supreme way. There are still historians who argue that the theological content of the last supper was almost entirely the creation of early Christians who retrojected the meaning of one of their own liturgies into Jesus' death.[18] Granted, the scriptural accounts of this supper show in places a soteriology that comes out of later Christian reflection, and, granted, the accounts show traces of a later, more formal liturgy, but I find implausible the claim that the early Christians were so much more theologically and liturgically inventive than Jesus himself.

Accounts of the last supper, though they vary from author to author, can be found in all four Gospels (Matt. 26:20-29; Mark 14:17-25; Luke 22:14-23; John 13–17) and in one of the epistles of Paul (1 Cor. 11:23-26).[19] Mark reports (14:22-25): "While they were eating, he took a loaf of bread, and after blessing it he broke it, gave it to them, and said, 'Take; this is my body.' Then he took a cup, and after giving thanks he gave it to them, and all of them drank from it. He said to them, 'This is my blood of the covenant, which is poured out for many. Truly I tell you, I will never again drink of the fruit of the vine until that day when I drink it new in the kingdom of God.'" Something extraordinary is occurring here: Jesus is incorporating his death into his mission. He has come to believe that his death will be not the termination of his mission but its climax. He believes now that the definitive reign of God will come not before his death but in some mysterious way through his death. Ben Meyer said it well: "Jesus did not aim to be repudiated and killed; he aimed to charge with meaning his being repudiated and killed."[20] Precisely by sharing the bread and wine, he charged his death with the meaning of his mission. Not only, therefore, was there a causal connection between his mission and his death, but this connection was brought to conscious expression when Jesus shared the bread and wine at the last supper. And this sharing of bread and wine was itself a word, a complex verbal ("Take, this is my body") and nonverbal (the sharing of the bread and wine) word in which Jesus communicated the meaning and power of the kingdom-love coming from God, the same love Jesus had been speaking throughout his mission. Furthermore, Jesus continues to offer eschatological hope: his death will be "for the many" who will drink wine with Jesus in the kingdom that will come after his death. The last supper then is a continuation of the mission, another outer word spoken "for the sake of the One who sent me" (see John 12:45; 12:49; 13:16; 16:5; 17:25), though in this case placed in the tightest possible connection with the impending death. Indeed, I think the connection between the word of the last supper and the word of the death is so tight that the two can be seen as two stages of one final word. Perhaps an analogy from human life would help explain what I mean.

Imagine two people involved in a courtship. During the courtship, the meaning and power of the love they feel for one another intensifies and deepens. This love is communicated through outer words that carry the informative, emotive, and directive functions. As their love grows, their mutual commitment grows. If their courtship comes to a successful completion, then this process of mutually intensifying commitment culminates in a word by which the couple communicate their love with special meaning and power. This word occurs when each officially says to the other, "I do give myself to you in marriage."[21]

What interests me here is that the word of marriage is spoken in two stages, and neither stage is complete without the other. In the first stage, the two persons speak the word of self-giving marital love ceremonially, through a ritual, whose meaning of love has been established by the community and accepted by the couple. In the ritual, they speak their self-giving in a complex verbal and nonverbal word. They nonverbally exchange rings and verbally utter their commitment in love. Their choice of how they speak this meaning is not entirely theirs: the essential elements of the outer word have been determined by the community, though nowadays the community tends to be quite flexible about other elements of the ceremony.

But with the ritualized speaking of the outer word, the word of marriage is not complete. The couple is required, at least by most communities, to complete the public, ceremonial word with the private act of bodily love. This is indeed a requirement. If one of the two refuses to go through this second stage, then the community regards the first stage as null and void. This private act is the most intimate and profound word two people can speak. The whole body is invested with the inner meaning of love, and the word created impinges on all the senses of the partners. This is a word that is seen, heard, touched, tasted, and smelled. The inner meaning and emotive power of the word are translated into a code involving every part of the body. Each partner is giving and receiving. Each is informing with meaning and moving the other with feeling; and each is being informed, moved, directed. With the completion of this private act, the word "I give myself to you in marriage" is completed, and not before.[22] We have one word here, even though it is spoken in two stages separated in space and time. The church is not the marital bed; the early morning ceremony is not the late night lovemaking; but the two spaces and two times are united by the one intention to speak the one word of love as the initiation of a marriage.

At the last supper, after the main meal was finished, Jesus shared bread and wine, accompanied by words of thanksgiving. Jesus did not invent this ritual. It was a complex nonverbal and verbal word that had been ritualized by the Jewish community. In verbal words, Jesus thanked the God of Israel for all that God had done for Israel as the covenanted people.[23] Sharing bread and wine, accompanied by these words, meant that Jesus affirmed the meaning that the community had given this ritual. But then Jesus added a new dimension of meaning. Jesus brought the bread and wine into the tightest possible connection with the giving of his body and blood in his impending death. Just as God communicated meaning and power through his past words to Israel, so now this God was communicating through Jesus' death. In Israel's past, God had communicated the Word through liberating the people from Egypt and passing on the Torah at Sinai. But God had not finished speaking: the Word in the power of the Spirit was being uttered through Jesus' death, whose meaning was now being ceremonially expressed in the sharing of the bread and wine. Everything we know of Jesus' own understanding of his mission leads us to believe that he would not have regarded this new dimension as constituting a break with Judaism. Indeed, the idea of the prophet dying for his people or of the servant communicating God's redemptive love through suffering was not alien to the Jewish tradition.[24] Even the idea of a suffering messiah was not totally alien, though to be sure it was not usual to link suffering with the messiah. Yet it cannot be denied that Jesus was introducing a new level of meaning here, using his liturgical and theological creativity to bring his followers and perhaps even himself into a fuller consciousness of the death not as the termination of his mission but as its fulfillment.

When Jesus shared the bread and wine, he shared himself. It was an outer word of self-communication, and because it was spoken by one commissioned by God, it was simultaneously God's self-communication. The tradition that has come down to us about what Jesus said verbally captures the intimacy of the connection between the nonverbal action of sharing bread and wine and the self that is given in that action. While sharing the bread, he said, "This is my body," and while sharing the wine he said, "This is my blood." Human self-communication is bodily. To give ourselves we have to activate the body. We can also take things like bread and wine and use them to communicate the self. At that moment, the bread and wine become extensions of our bodies and take on the functions of our bodies. Not just bread and wine go over to the receiver, but the self. Jesus in effect is saying: in this bread and wine now being shared with you, I want you to see the gift of myself. But this giving of the self through bread and wine is then linked inextricably to his impending death. Jesus in effect is saying: the same self I am giving to you through this bread and wine will be given to you in my death. The last supper and death are then two stages of the one final word of a mission whose meaning was God's self-giving through Jesus' self-giving.

In the Christian theological tradition, Jesus' final word of self-giving has also been termed a self-offering or even a self-sacrifice, in order to link Jesus' final self-communication more closely with Jewish traditions of sacrifice. People today are reluctant to call the self-giving in Jesus' final word a self-sacrifice, or even a self-offering, because such language connotes a masochistic eclipse of the self.[25] But etymologically, *sacrifice* comes from the Latin words *sacer*, holy or sacred, and *facere*, to make, and thus when something is sacrificed, it is given over to God's holiness, into the orbit of God's meaning and power. God's meaning and power are suffused with the universal value of love. To give oneself in love to God and others is to do the thing most acceptable to God. It is a holy and sacred thing. It is a sacrifice.

The last supper and death are the final word of Jesus' earthly mission. God has commissioned Jesus to speak the Word in the power of the Spirit. God freely wills this mission, and Jesus freely accepts it. Neither God nor Jesus directly wills the death, but they do directly will the mission. God is the God of life, who sacrifices no one on the altar of death. God does not glorify death but glorifies those who die for the reign of God's love and justice. God is not a sadist who believes in the redemptive power of suffering and death for their own sake.[26] Nor was Jesus a masochist with an eager desire to be the slaughtered lamb. But God and Jesus did will the mission, and in this very restricted sense they are the indirect agents of Jesus' death and thereby able to speak through it. In this sense, what God does not will, the suffering and death of Jesus, becomes part of what God does will, the speaking of the Word through Jesus, in the power of the Spirit.

Jesus' Death and the Consequences of Sin

God did not will the death of Jesus; rather, God willed the mission of Jesus. The mission, not the death, was God's plan. Yet there is about the death of Jesus a certain mysterious fittingness. This most negative event in human life, the killing of an innocent person, is transformed into the most positive event, the Word of God's coming reign of love. We can understand why Christians down through the centuries have wanted to see the death as part of God's providential plan.

On the negative side, the killing of Jesus was the very antithesis of meaning. It was the defeat of love. It was not the rule of God but the rule of darkness. To die on a cross after being tortured for having preached the rule of God's love was surely proof that God's love does not rule the world. Deserted by most of his followers, rejected by his people, abandoned by God, Jesus suffered a death that the greatest sinner, not the most loving Son, would deserve. Does not sin by its very nature cut off the sinner from God and others? Is not sin a distancing from God? Is not a sinner's death deservedly a lonely death, one from which God is absent?[27] Yet lonely death is what Jesus experienced. How can this death be fitting? How could God's will be any way involved in the lonely death of a good man?

On the positive side, the death of Jesus on the cross is the final word of his saving mission and prepares the way for the arrival of God's reign. Yet how do we get from the negative side of Jesus' death, which sees it as a death that in justice only a sinner should suffer, to the positive side, which sees it as a word of mercy that saves sinners? The answer given by some of the most influential soteriologies is that Jesus in his death takes on sin and its consequences as a substitute for humankind. What should befall us, a death cut off from God, Jesus takes on freely, in our place, and thereby saves us from sin. These soteriologies describe Jesus' death as ransom for sin, satisfaction for sin, paying the price for sin, pouring out of blood for sin, sacrifice for sin, propitiation for sin, punishment for sin.[28] In one of its most popular formulations, the theory states that God planned the death of Jesus, laying upon Jesus, the innocent Son, the punishment for sin that in justice should be laid upon the sinful human race.[29] As the substitute for the whole human race, Jesus in his death suffered what human beings should suffer, and, in consequence, God relieves human beings of the just punishment due to sin and brings them into the embrace of his merciful love. Justice is served in order that mercy may reign.

This theory has two weaknesses. First, it directly implicates God in the planning of Jesus' death by turning it into a divine requirement: if God's justice is to be served and God's mercy is to flow freely, sin must be punished by someone's death, and God chose Jesus to be that someone. Second, it promotes the idea that salvation is a once-and-for-all objective transaction between God and Jesus that takes place apart from our subjective response. But surely Jesus' death will not be a word that saves unless we say yes to that word. And if we in our recalcitrant sinfulness say no to that word, we shall have to bear the consequences of this no, regardless of what Jesus has done.[30] It is precisely here that this theory is open to a revision that might free it of these weaknesses.[31] Let me explain.

In this imperfect world, the consequences of sin are not always neatly and justly enacted. Bad people turn on good people and cause their suffering, even their death. God, of course, does not cause bad people to cause suffering, but God allows it out of respect for the integrity of worldly causation and human freedom. God did not intervene to save Jesus, a good person, from those who visited on him a lonely death. They made a good person suffer what they, in a world of neat justice, would suffer. Jesus, a good person, suffered not only the physical pain of crucifixion, but worse, the psychological and spiritual pain of rejection, abandonment, and loneliness. In a terrifying reversal of justice, sinners visited upon Jesus a death that by strict justice should have been theirs.

The consequences of sin thus fall on the one who does not deserve them. Jesus not only suffered at the hands of sinners but suffered what sinners should suffer. The Gospel of Mark has Jesus on the cross crying out, "My God, my God, why have you forsaken me?" (Mark 15:34). I do not want to make too much of any one Gospel passage—it cannot be verified with certainty as reporting Jesus' very words—but surely we can surmise that when Jesus journeyed this far into the dark and lonely region of death, he felt forsaken by God and by others. The lonely and loveless death of a good person is enough to drive anyone to feel forsaken by God, and Jesus was a good person. Such a death brought Jesus (and God with him) into an identification with sinners in their darkest moments, even though it was not Jesus' sin that put him there but rather the sin of others. It even may have led him to understand in the most excruciating way the nihilism and terror that drive the sinner to isolate and destroy good people. Perhaps it is the fear of abandonment that tempts people to cause others to suffer what they most fear. Can we doubt that Jesus felt this fear, this anxiety, this abandonment?

Yet we have learned that Jesus as the indirect agent of his death converts his death into a word. At the last supper, he lays hold of the negative of death and shapes it into the positive of mission. Followers of Jesus hear in his death the Word of God's love that reaches out to sinners, to judge them, yes, but also to forgive and transform them.[32] We sinners therefore are supposed to see in that death what we deserve and then feel through that death the forgiving love that will ransom us from the consequence of sin, which is to be cut off from God and others. This ransom will not occur without our repentance and cooperation; salvation flows from God through Jesus but is not automatically successful in us human beings. Jesus suffered and died for sins so that we might be able and willing to suffer and die for our sins, and then enter into the joy of forgiveness. In Jesus' death, a Word is spoken in the power of the Spirit that can take us through death into new life. Jesus takes on the consequences of sin, converts them into a word of forgiveness, in the hope that we will hear that word, accept forgiveness, enter the reign of God, and thereby escape the consequences of sin. In doing this, Jesus does not convert a wrathful God to a merciful God but rather communicates God's everlasting mercy. In dying, Jesus does not save the human race once and for all, in one objective action, but rather makes God's saving love definitively present in history as a deeply personal word whose power is fully effective only in our subjective response.

All this assumes that Jesus remained loyal to his mission even in death. Scholars know that his words on the cross, "My God, my God why have you forsaken me?" are in fact the opening verses of a psalm (Ps. 22) from the Hebrew Bible that finish with faith and trust in God. We do not have any direct access to Jesus' consciousness during this time, or anytime for that matter, but we do have the previous record of his mission and other accounts of his last hours. All the evidence suggests that he was a person of God who resisted the temptation to stray from his identity and mission as the Son. It is therefore consistent with the evidence to believe that Jesus did not in the end abandon God. Even though in the depth and darkness of his final misery he may have felt cut off from God, he did not cease loving God and others. He was therefore able to sustain the communication of the Word of love and did not turn against that Word and fall into despair and hatred. Sustained by the power of the Spirit, he carried the meaning of his mission into and through his death. To believe that a human death has the potential to carry such a meaning, and to believe that this potential was actualized in the death of Jesus, is to embrace an extraordinarily optimistic view of Jesus' life and of life in general. It says that the worst that can happen can be a vehicle of the best. It says that God was there speaking through the death of a good person. The potential of death to communicate love is realized here in such an inexhaustibly fitting way that we can almost be led to believe that God planned it that way.

Almost, but not quite. It is precisely the aim of God's Word through Jesus to transform sinners into people who will not cause suffering and pain and death to others. How could God choose to do that by planning the suffering and pain and death of Jesus? If God wants us to fight against innocent suffering and death, then God too must fight against innocent suffering and death. God does not want people to suffer and die, even sinful people, who are all of us. God the good shepherd seeks out everyone, especially the lost sheep. God through Jesus knows the pain of sinners and is willing to journey into the farthest region of sin to rescue them from a lonely death. This is Jesus' mission, a mission that ends in death. God and

Jesus did not plan it this way, but once the mission came into confrontation with death, they transformed that death into the climax of the mission.

Jesus' Death as Victory over the Powers

When I talked above about sinners visiting a lonely and painful death upon Jesus, I opened myself up to a misinterpretation. Evil is not as simple as that. It is a mistake to imagine that evil comes solely out of the minds of individuals fully conscious that what they intend to do is evil. Many individuals first deceive themselves that what they are doing is good, not bad. All individuals come out of groups and to some extent have been corrupted by these groups. The group tells them that what they are doing is normal, indeed moral, and required for the good of the group. The New Testament writers were fully aware that evil is more than the sum of bad things done by malicious individuals acting with full consciousness. Evil is also a force that is there, tempting and bending individuals in the wrong direction even before they add their own individual choice. In the New Testament, evil is often seen as coming from cosmic, nonhuman forces that can sometimes act with ill intent in human life without any need of human cooperation. These forces are variously named demons, dominions, thrones, or powers.[33] Often, they are summed up in one figure, such as Satan, the devil, or the antichrist. These forces could take over persons, twisting them not only spiritually but psychologically and physically. These forces could also take over historical institutions: the early Christians were convinced that these forces had taken over the social and political structure of the Roman Empire (see 2 Thess. 6–7 and the Book of Revelation). So strong was the belief in these nonhuman sources of evil that no one would have followed Jesus as the one who spoke the saving Word in the Spirit unless he or she believed that his Word and Spirit could also defeat these forces.[34]

Jesus' followers believed that when Jesus culminated his mission in death he defeated the evil powers. He, of course, was defeating these powers before his death—see all those stories that have him casting out the demons and have the demons admitting his superior power—but the final blow against them comes with Jesus' death. This part of his saving work formed the basis for that strain in the theological tradition that speaks of *"Christus victor,"*[35] that is, of Jesus Christ as the one who is victorious over the nonhuman evil forces. The stress here is not on his victory over individual hearts but over those forces operative before the heart decides. It is a victory over an evil that is already resident in objective reality before it becomes resident in the human subject. This evil comes from outside us and appears to work its way into us insidiously, quietly, almost irresistibly. We are being bent toward evil and even drawn into evil long before our conscious cooperation. Indeed, one of the reasons for the great and efficacious power of these evil forces is that they can operate so long without our conscious awareness.[36]

In the New Testament, the evil forces are depicted either as purely cosmic or as closely linked to historical institutions. I think we should see them more in their connection with historical institutions, for the source of this objective evil is more human than nonhuman.[37] I am open to the possibility that demons and devils exist, and, if they do, I trust completely that the Word and Spirit of Jesus can defeat them. But when I look on the human world, past and present, and see all the evil, I am strongly inclined to trace most of it to human beings. It is an objective evil, but it is produced by human subjects, in such a way that is often invisible to these subjects. It is that structured evil that insinuates itself into our religious, social, political, and economic systems. This evil is therefore the culture insofar as it shapes human behavior toward disvalues and inauthentic meanings. Culture is always there as a given, pressing down on choice and advertising itself as the way we have always done things. And each culture has its own fiendish variation on how it corrupts its members.

Jesus spoke his Word into a culture whose most powerful members, both in the Jewish establishment and the Roman administration, believed there was a right way to think and act, and that this right way had to be enforced, by violence if necessary. Jesus was destroyed and thereby silenced (at least that was the hope of his silencers) as least as much by a cultural system operating with full correctness as by conscious individual maliciousness. Indeed, it is very likely that most of the chief actors involved in Jesus' torture and death acted as sincere defenders of public order and religion. Jesus was a popular figure. Unrest could follow in his wake. He said he spoke for God. His message was recognizably Jewish, but radical and demanding. His followers appeared especially attached to his person. His Word was a disturbance and a threat, both religiously and politically.[38] He had the conviction that through his words something new and sweeping was starting to occur. He talked of God's new rule and that the "last shall be first." It is historically understandable why certain social and religious powers would want him out of the way.

In the early church, Jesus the *Christus victor* is often depicted has having won a once-and-for-all victory over the evil forces. But if we understand these evil forces as corrupt structures created by human beings, then clearly his victory was not once and for all.[39] For the battle against the demon of twisted social structures continues into our day. Indeed, our own time has witnessed the epitome of structured evil, as, for instance, in the Turkish massacre of the Armenians, the Nazi terror, the Japanese conquest of China, the Stalinist gulag, the killing fields of the Khmer Rouge, the institutionalization of hatred in Northern Ireland, the slaughter in Rwanda, the communal killings in India, and the ethnic cleansing of Albanians by Serbs in Kosovo. On a less spectacular but more pervasive scale, think of the millions of acts everyday whereby we degrade and hurt others because some racist, sexist, or classist structure has worked its way so deeply into our spirit that dehumanization of the other not only seems normal but even moral. Or think only of the North American way of life, surely in some ways a good way of life yet also in many subtle and not so subtle ways deeply corrupting of the spirit and an obstacle to expanding the rule of God's love and justice.

Jesus in his death clearly did not defeat all these demons once and for all. The battle continues. But Jesus did accomplish the following: first, he exposed the evil powers and thereby brought them to the full consciousness of those willing to hear in his death not just the word of those who wished to silence him but the word of a love that does not seek the domination and death of other human beings. In the New Testament, it says that Jesus has made a "public example" (Col. 2:15) of the evil powers. In the death of this innocent person, evil overreaches itself and exposes its true character.

Second, Jesus was loyal to God alone. In preaching the rule of God's love as the only object worthy of the surrender of one's whole self, Jesus exposed all the social structures demanding total loyalty as idols, as false gods. The Roman Empire demanded total obedience and made each new emperor into a god as he ascended the throne. Nazism and Stalinism turned their systems and their leaders into cult idols that demanded total worship and obedience. The U.S. gospel of wealth defends unfettered capitalism as God's own economic system; some forms of Christian socialism identify socialism with the definitive coming of God's rule to earth. Down through the centuries, enslaving the conquered, dehumanizing people of different color, disempowering women, privileging the poor (as either sinners or saints) and thus keeping them poor—all have been given the sacred aura of religious correctness. By contrast, Jesus gives total loyalty only to the God who passionately seeks the rule of love and justice. Jesus thus undercuts the idolatrous pretension of any social structure to religious inevitability. Those who have been informed, moved, and directed by the Word and Spirit of Jesus can no longer see any system as normal.

Third, Jesus in his last supper and death communicates the final word of his mission, which is a word of love and justice. If the word is successful in sinners, which are all of us, then we will repent, accept forgiveness, and be transformed into persons who are more loving and just. Not only will we treat those individuals whom we encounter in daily life more lovingly, but we will work for more just social structures.[40] The battle against evil is never just a battle against the evil hearts of individuals but also against those structures that corrupt the heart. Evil is more than the sum of individual choices for inauthentic meaning. A mysterious kind of multiplier effect occurs when individual choices coalesce with the passions and biases of the group. Empowered by Jesus' Word spoken in the Spirit, we can sustain the battle on both fronts and with Christ not only hope for victory but work for victory.

But we sustain the battle with Christ only because Christ is still with us, not just in our memory of his earthly mission climaxing in death but also in our experience of his continuing presence to us in Word and Spirit. We experience him not only as the crucified Jesus but also as the risen Christ. God's resurrection of Jesus definitively establishes Jesus as Christ the victor over death and means that Jesus is now alive, drawing us to victory over sin and death. Christ victorious is Christ risen. This is the theme of the next two chapters.

SIX

The Resurrection of Jesus

The Resurrection and History

At the last supper, Jesus tried to communicate to his followers that his death would be the only way he could be the Messiah and usher in the rule of God. To be the Messiah meant physical suffering and death, not political revolt and rulership. This was lost on his disciples. Right to the bitter end, they wanted revolt against the Romans and rule over Israel. They even squabbled over who would be in top positions of power, and did so long after Jesus had told them that his reign would come through service, weakness, and death, not through revolutionary action.[1] We are not surprised, therefore, when we learn that before and after Jesus' crucifixion his followers distanced themselves from their leader, terrorized by their own fear of death and devastated by this blow to their messianic hopes.[2] Yet, soon after Jesus was buried, these same disciples came out of hiding and courageously preached Jesus as the messianic agent of God's eschatological reign. Not only had their faith in Jesus as the Messiah revived, but they now felt the Word and Spirit of Jesus moving them to continue Jesus' mission.

This change in the disciples, which is accessible to historical reason, can be explained by their belief that God had raised Jesus from the dead. How did the disciples come to this belief? Whenever I raise this question in class, almost invariably someone pipes up, "The tomb was empty!

107

The women went to the tomb on the third day and it was empty. That proves the resurrection." But does the tomb offer sufficient ground for belief in the resurrection? Not really. True, the tradition of an empty tomb goes back to early in the history of the post-Easter community, and in all probability a nucleus of historicity lies behind this tradition.[3] But by itself the empty tomb proves nothing except that a body has disappeared (Jesus' body was not buried in the ground but placed in a tomb hewn out of a rock and then covered by a stone that could be rolled away by some-one strong). Mary Magdalene, arguably the first visitor to the tomb, was perplexed and wondered where the body had been taken (see John 20:13). Even if we imagine that a video camera had been placed in the tomb after Jesus' burial, and that later this videotape recorded the presence of his body and then its sudden absence, we viewers would have a cause for wonder but not direct or sufficient evidence of God's raising Jesus from the dead.[4] In fact, we never could have direct historical evidence of Jesus' resurrection. All the evidence, of whatever kind, would be indirect at best. Let me explain.

Historical reason focuses on an event in this penultimate world and searches for its causes within this penultimate world. If President Kennedy is shot, we look for the gun and the shooter. If someone has a heart attack, stops breathing, but then comes back to life, we look for the cause in the recuperative power of her body or in the resuscitative skills of someone who knew CPR. But a resurrection is not resuscitation. When Peter preaches that "God raised him up, having freed him from death" (Acts 2:24), he does not mean that Jesus has been brought back to life to live as he had before in this penultimate world. Rather, God has raised him into the ultimate dimension, has "taken him up to heaven" (Act 1:2). The resurrection, then, is an event that begins in God's active intent to raise Jesus and ends in Jesus' coming to live with God as the risen Lord (see Phil. 2:11); that is, it begins and ends in the ultimate dimension. For this reason, the resurrection of Jesus should not be classified as a miracle. Miracles occur in this penultimate world, in this space and time. Something spectacular and inexplicable hap-pens: the liquid once water is now wine; the person once blind now sees. Granted, to accept it as a miracle, we must have religious faith that God's power has affected the penultimate world, but the result is imme-diately tangible to our senses: the water tastes like wine; the blind man sees. But our senses have no direct access to the heavenly realm where the risen Jesus dwells with God.[5] The resurrection begins with a dead body in this world, but it concludes with a risen body beyond this world, "exalted at the right hand of God" (Act 2:33). Historical reason, which always initially rests on the testimony of the senses, has no direct access to this transformation of the crucified Jesus into the risen Christ.

How about the appearances of the risen Jesus to the disciples? According to the New Testament, the risen Jesus made the following appearances: to three women (including Mary Magdalene) at the tomb (Matt. 16:9-11), to Mary Magdalene alone at the tomb (Mark 28:9-10; John 2:14-18),[6] to Peter (Luke 24:34; 1 Cor. 15:5), to Cleopas and another person (his wife?) on the road to Emmaus (Mark 16:12-13; Luke 24:13-35), to the disciples (Luke 20:19-23; John 20:19-23; 21:1-25), to the eleven or twelve apostles (Mark 16:14-18; 1 Cor. 15:5; Matt. 28:16-20), to "more than five hundred brothers and sisters" (1 Cor. 15:6), and to James (1 Cor. 15:7). Do not these appearances take place in this space and time? The Jesus who appears is bodily and therefore tangible to the human senses. Here, surely, is a very tangible appearance recounted by Luke:

> While they were talking about this, Jesus himself stood among them and said to them, "Peace be with you." They were startled and terrified, and thought that they were seeing a ghost. He said to them, "Why are you frightened, and why do doubts arise in your hearts? Look at my hands and my feet; see that it is I myself. Touch me and see; for a ghost does not have flesh and bones as you see that I have." And when he had said this, he showed them his hands and his feet. While in their joy they were disbelieving and still wondering, he said to them, "Have you anything here to eat?" They gave him a piece of broiled fish, and he took it and ate in their presence. (Luke 24:36-43)

According to N. T. Wright, a biblical scholar whom I respect and from whom I have learned much, we should take this account fairly much at face value.[7] Without denying that Luke and other Gospel writers added many of their own colorful details and apologetical emphases, Wright insists that these appearances in all their sensible tangibility are historical. There is no other way of explaining how the disciples came to believe that Jesus was the resurrected Messiah.

With Jesus' death and resurrection, Wright argues, the grand narrative of God's covenant with Israel came to a final or eschatological climax. Jesus' followers confessed boldly that Jesus was the Messiah and insisted that God's reign had come. Such a confession was possible, says Wright, only if they believed that Jesus has been raised bodily from the dead. For bodily resurrection was a nonnegotiable element in the Jewish hope for the eschatological rule of God: the dead must be raised bodily if Jews were to participate in the new age and the new creation.[8] There was no room for Jesus' followers to redefine the embodied resurrection of the dead: a purely spiritual resurrection of Jesus would not be enough to convince first-century Jews that the reign of God had come through Jesus.[9]

And thus, according to Wright, the followers of Jesus who believed that Jesus was indeed Messiah by virtue of God's confirming act of resurrection had to believe that the resurrection was bodily. But how could they believe this? They had no direct access to the transcendent realm. Somehow the transcendent realm had to make contact with them. And, says Wright, it did: the risen Jesus appeared to them and in a way that made his bodiliness unmistakable. True, this body was exceedingly odd: it could suddenly appear in, and disappear from, a closed room (ohn 20:19, 26); it was often unrecognizable (Luke 24:16; John 20:14-15); it could quickly vanish from the table (Luke 24:31). This Jesus clearly was not a resuscitated Jesus who had returned fully to this life, but a resurrected Jesus whose body had undergone a remarkable transformation. Yet Jesus appeared in his transformed body: he did not appear to his followers in a vision, as he did with Paul (1 Cor 15:8; Acts 22:6-11), but rather in perceptible bodily form. His body was not left behind in the tomb but was raised up, transformed, and appeared in this space and time. And, therefore, the tomb, Wright insists, had to be empty—and it is compatible with historical reason to believe it was empty.

Wright would not, I believe, say that he has offered a historical proof for the bodily resurrection of Jesus. Rather, he is saying that we can make full sense of his followers' Easter faith only if we accede to the historicity of the New Testament accounts of the empty tomb and the appearances. Conversely, we can make full sense of the historical evidence—the appearances of Jesus and the empty tomb—only if we accept in faith what his followers accepted in faith, that God had raised Jesus bodily from the dead. Faith is crucial—faith in the covenantal God, faith in God's acting through the earthly Jesus, faith in God's power over death, faith in God's promises to transform history and cosmos, faith in God's willingness to redeem the innocent dead.

Wright's historical and theological reconstruction of the resurrection narratives carries persuasive power. Yet I am a little uneasy. He has insisted on such a tight fit between resurrection faith and the biblical accounts of the empty tomb and the appearances! And it is a fit so dependent on the apocalyptic worldview of first-century Judaism. Do we as contemporary Christians have to accept an empty tomb to believe that Jesus is resurrected in his body? If we push Wright's logic to its end and accept as he does that our resurrection hope is grounded in the resurrection of Jesus, are we not asked to believe that at the end of this age we all will be raised bodily out of our graves? Don't we then have to say that God will have to reassemble and transform the body of John F. Kennedy Jr., whose ashes are scattered in the vast tomb of the sea? Would our resurrection faith collapse if we were to learn that the body of Jesus had in fact been stolen?

It is true that the empty tomb is less important to Wright's argument than the tangible objectivity of Jesus' appearances. With Wright, I refuse to reduce these appearances to subjective visions that could be exhaustively explained by worldly causes, as would be the case if a sociologist were to argue that the death of Jesus led to the temporary disenchantment of his followers, which they overcame and then, in a fit of apocalyptic enthusiasm, generated the hallucinatory vision that Jesus was resurrected bodily. The sociologist might direct our attention to the widespread phenomenon of social delusion in our time. She would need only to refer to all those who believe that Elvis is making regular appearances to his devotees on earth.

A psychologist might offer an explanation of Jesus' appearances based on bereavement theory, pointing out that many people in our day have received deeply consoling visitations from departed loved ones.[10] These visitations are often very vivid in their objective tangibility and yet like Jesus' appearances often have a strange, otherworldly quality, and thus are not mistaken for literal returns to this world. For the secular psychologist, such visitations do not point to the existence of a bodily afterlife but show simply that the survivor's painful sense of loss can, in a healthy person, lead to self-healing visions of the departed loved one.

Again, with N. T. Wright, I find such reductionistic explanations (that is, explanations that reduce the possible causes solely to worldly causes) unconvincing when used to exhaustively explain the biblical accounts of Jesus' appearances, though I think I might be more open than he is to a modest contribution from bereavement theory. But Wright pushes the literal objectivity of the appearances too far. He talks about them as if they were observer-neutral events, as if a person with no faith in the God of Jesus would have observed exactly what the disciples observed. Since he believes that a camera could have recorded the vanishing of Jesus' body from the tomb,[11] I am inclined to think that he would agree with the Christian philosopher Stephen T. Davis that photographs of Jesus' appearances would show what was shown in the biblical accounts. For example, a snapshot would show the doubting Thomas (see John 20:27) putting his fingers and hands into Jesus' wounds.[12] Granted, Davis insists that once an appearance of Jesus is perceived, it must then be interpreted correctly, that is, illuminated by faith,[13] but I believe that even before one stands back to interpret an appearance, one's very perception of it is already marked by a religious faith-readiness to observe what is there to observe.[14] True, the faith of the disciples had been weakened by Jesus' death, but they continued to be devout people who believed in the living God of the Jesus they had known and loved. They were ready to have their faith revived.[15] They were not atheists believing only in the material world of ordinary sense experience. Would the famous atheist Bertrand Russell have seen what the disciples saw in Jesus' appearances? I doubt it.

I do not want to go to the other extreme and dissolve the stories of the appearances into stories created by the early disciples to dramatize a purely spiritual experience of Jesus' resurrection. These stories speak of appearances that must have had enough tangible objectivity to allow the disciples to believe that the risen Jesus was not a pure spirit, but was, in some mysterious way, an embodied spirit.[16] We have no analogy from our lives now that can provide much insight into precisely how Jesus' embodied spirit made itself present in the appearances.[17] I think we are justified in saying that they "saw" something objective that is remarkable but that their seeing was in part already a faith experience.

Important as it is to show that resurrection faith is consistent with the history of the first Christians, I think we should avoid obsessive attention to the empty tomb and to the bodily appearances. Let me say it again: the resurrection is not a historical event in the strict sense. The effects of the resurrection are to some degree historical, but the resurrection in itself is not historical. With respect to Jesus' resurrection, therefore, historical reason is less helpful to faith than it is with respect to his death. We can, however, still use reason to undergird and make sense of the resurrection faith, but we must go beyond historical reason into a broader reason that reflects on whether God has remained faithful to Jesus, on whether death has ultimate meaning, and on whether the mission of Jesus continues. Here reason works closely with faith, both pointing to faith and drawing out the implications of faith. In the next three sections I shall put this broader reason to work.

The Resurrection as God's Final Word to Jesus

I should like to return to a point I made in chapter 4: the outer words Jesus speaks on his mission are two-directional. First, they are his words and therefore God's Word to human beings. The Word and Spirit of God come to human beings through Jesus, whose identity and mission have been formed by that Word and Spirit. Second, because the outer words that Jesus speaks on his mission are spoken on behalf of the God who sent him, these words speak not only Jesus' (and God's) love for human beings but also Jesus' love for God. His mission, then, is a continuous act of self-communication and self-giving, even a self-sacrifice, to human beings and to God. This two-directional self-communication climaxes in Jesus' last supper and death, a word in which Jesus most completely gives himself to human beings and to God.

In the word of last supper and death, Jesus gives himself into the mystery of God,[18] trusting that God will respond to him. This is, of course, a word spoken throughout his mission, but there is a definitiveness about this final word in which Jesus gives his whole body over to God. Perhaps the only thing in human life that comes close to this is the complete bodily self-gift that occurs when two persons in love give themselves sexually to each other.

If someone were to speak a word of love through death, how would we respond to such a word? Dying is a word that is spoken in this space and time, but dying is the departure of the speaker from this space and time. The speaker who has so profoundly spoken to us in dying for us is no longer here to receive our answer. It would be wonderful to be able to answer the speaker with the nonverbal word of bringing him or her back to life. It is impossible to think of a more appropriate way of expressing one's love and gratitude. But we human beings do not have the power over life and death. If someone speaks love for us by dying for us, we do not have the power to speak a nonverbal word of revivification in return.

But the God of the Jewish people does have power over death. This is the firm belief of that strain of Judaism that was strong in Jesus' day and to which Jesus' own theology and piety were very close.[19] I am speaking here of the Judaism of the Pharisees, who believed that God had the power to raise the dead and establish them in a new mode of being, beyond this old world, in the new world, "at the right hand of God."[20] In raising the dead, God brings them into "glory" (Heb. 2:10), into fulfillment of their human nature as sons and daughters of God. Therefore, the God to whom Jesus spoke his love in death had the power to give the most appropriate answer: Jesus dies into the mystery of God, and God answers by resurrecting him in glory at God's right hand. Jesus in his final word of last supper and death communicates himself to God, and God, in response, takes Jesus into a life-giving embrace.

If we today are to have faith in the resurrection of Jesus, we must go against a widespread skepticism about an afterlife, which in turn is based on a widespread skepticism about the existence and power of God. But if we can let ourselves be drawn into the story of Jesus, whose faith was in a

God who enters into a relationship of unconditional love with human beings, then we are made ready to believe that such a God would not let this relationship be broken by death.[21] Resurrection faith tells us that those who die saying yes to God, and especially those like Jesus whose very suffering and death is a word of yes to God, do not die into nothingness but into God's life-giving embrace.

If we can believe that God is personal and loving, and invites all human beings to respond with love, then it seems to me that the vectors of our thought and feeling converge on the probability that God said a life-giving yes to Jesus and to anyone else like Jesus who has in life and death said yes to God. We are therefore primed for resurrection faith by our remembrance of God's relationship with the earthly Jesus.

Faith in Jesus' resurrection is also, to some extent, dependent on believing that Jesus lives now and is present in Word and Spirit. Unless the Word and Spirit are experienced now, here in this penultimate world, then talk of Jesus' resurrection and our future resurrection rings hollow. Experiencing resurrection now means experiencing the movement from death to new life. Only by dying now to the old, unloving self and rising into the new, loving self does the anticipated resurrection become real and credible.[22] Unless we love now in imitation of the way Jesus on earth loved, which is a dying to self that others may live, we shall not be able to recognize the risen Jesus who carries the scars of crucifixion. Imitating Jesus is made possible by the presence in our lives of God's Spirit, who is the Spirit of the risen Jesus. The Scriptures closely connect the resurrection faith of the disciples with their experience of a new empowering presence of Jesus' Spirit.[23] According to Paul, the power of the Spirit that raises us out of the death that is sin is the same power that raises Jesus and us from the dead: "But if Christ is in you, though the body is dead because of sin, the Spirit is life because of righteousness. If the Spirit of him who raised Jesus from the dead dwells in you, he who raised Christ from the dead will give life to your mortal bodies also through his Spirit that dwells in you" (Rom. 8:10-11).

The Resurrection Gives
Ultimate Meaning to Death

A death can have penultimate meaning; that is, it can have meaning for us left behind in this world. Persons who die for a great meaning can inspire present and future generations to embrace that meaning. When I was a student in Germany in the 1960s, I attended lectures by the renowned

German biblical scholar Willi Marxsen, who told us that resurrection faith is faith in the continued *cause* of the earthly Jesus, not faith in the continued *life* of the risen Jesus. The death of Jesus inspires others to carry on his cause in the penultimate world; his death, therefore, does not have the ultimate meaning of his entering into a transformed life with God.[24] Jesus in his death does not enter into God's life-giving embrace, but his values live on in the lives of others. Listening to Marxsen back then, I said to myself, This is a rather thin brew! Does it really capture the richness of the biblical witness?

I do not believe that the death of Jesus would have rung its meaning down through the centuries if his followers had not believed that God answered Jesus' death with resurrection. It is possible, though unlikely, that some slim historical memory of his death as noble and courageous could have survived. After all, we know that for some time after his death, the followers of John the Baptizer kept his memory and cause alive. But his followers were few, and they are now forgotten. Jesus would have suffered the same fate if God had not answered his death with resurrection in a way that could be experienced by his followers. Without the resurrection of Jesus, sin and death would have the last word. In the face of the death of the innocent, God would have nothing to say to Jesus' survivors except "I could do nothing about Jesus' death, but carry on!" God would provide no entrance into the ultimate dimension.

Perhaps it is too good to be true, but Christians believe that God does resurrect the dead. This means that death is fully redeemed. It is more than a penultimate expression of universal values; it is the entry into the ultimate dimension. Death is eternal life with God. After all, the deaths of most innocent people, especially those deaths caused by human beings in the grip of their own conscious sin or driven by unconscious cooperation with a sinful social structure, are quiet, hidden, and largely unheard by those left behind in the penultimate world. Faith in resurrection is the faith that God hears the death cries of innocent and good people and responds with life-giving love.[25]

The yes God says in the resurrection of Jesus is not the first time God says yes. The yes that resurrects Jesus is the culmination of a yes that God has been saying to the human race from the beginning. This yes finds the perfect human response in the obedient yes that Jesus says to his identity and mission. Jesus' obedience is evoked, not compelled: the emotive and directive power of God's Word is indeed very persuasive, but it is not coercive. The love Jesus speaks in the last supper and death evokes God's culminating yes of resurrection. Because resurrection is God's response to Jesus' free obedience and love, resurrection is partly Jesus' own achievement.[26] Yet everything begins with the initiating movement of God's love in the Word and Spirit toward Jesus, a movement that culminates in the resurrection of Jesus. So the resurrection is really God's grand achievement, yet mediated through Jesus' free yes. Through Jesus' yes, the movement of God out of the ultimate into the penultimate achieves its furthest reach, but through Jesus' yes in death the penultimate achieves its furthest reach into the ultimate. God stretches out to meet this reach with the yes of life-giving embrace, which is resurrection. In this way, an apparently meaningless event in this penultimate world, the defeat of a good and innocent person, is an event heaviest with ultimate meaning. It is a meaning that Jesus discerned and freely chose in his last supper and death, and then realizes fully when God completes Jesus' death with the life-giving response of resurrection.

The Resurrection Universalizes and Eternalizes Jesus' Mission

As a cradle Catholic, I was taught by the catechism that the risen Christ is present "in the Spirit," not "in the flesh." To be sure, I was also taught that Jesus appears to his disciples in a way that was perceived as in some way bodily, but these appearances were not literally in the flesh: his followers were not led by these appearances to believe that Jesus' resurrection was really nothing but a return to "the days of his flesh" (Heb. 5:7). Somehow, despite these appearances, Jesus as resurrected was believed to be in a new mode of bodily being that exceeded this space and time. His main mode of presence to the world after the resurrection is therefore not in the flesh but in the Spirit.

Nevertheless, this should not be taken to mean that only the Spirit of the risen Christ is present and that the Word is not. As risen, Jesus continues to communicate the Word of God's love in the power of the Spirit. The Gospel of John gives to the Spirit of the risen Christ an implicit Word-function: "When the Spirit of truth comes, he will guide you into all the truth; for he will not speak on his own, but will speak whatever he hears, and he will declare to you the things that are to come. He will glorify me, because he will take what is mine and declare it to you. All that the Father has is mine. For this reason I said that he will take what is mine and declare it to you" (John 16:13-15).[27] When, however, Jesus moves from the earthly to the risen mode of being, something is lost with respect to his communicative mission. On earth, Jesus had a body that he could activate to communicate the Word of unconditional love. His body located him in space and time and enabled him to create outer words that could be heard, seen, touched, tasted, and smelled. This was a wonderful advantage for the communication of God's Word, for the Word found a body that God as pure spirit lacked. It also was a disadvantage. For the body that locates a person in a particular space and time also limits a person to a particular space and time. Even with the technology of print, telephone, audio, video, and computer, the human person is still limited in communicative range by the body. Jesus was even more limited, living as he did in an age relatively lacking in communicative technology, which limited the range of his Word and Spirit to a small area of land called Palestine and to a small number of hearers reachable by foot or on mule. Not only that, he appears to have committed nothing to writing.

As risen, Jesus no longer suffers the limitations of space and time. The range of his Word and Spirit has exploded out of the particularity of Palestine into the universality of all spaces and times. This may be the deepest reason for all those references in the New Testament that depict the resurrection as a freeing up of the Spirit. Only as risen can Jesus universally "pour out [his] Spirit" (see Acts 2:17-18, 33) and thereby fulfill the eschatological hope. In John's Gospel, there may be theological significance to the portrayal of Jesus' death as "giv[ing] up his spirit" (see John 19:30): it may signify the departure of the Spirit from the confines of Jesus' flesh to the universality of the risen Lord. In the same Gospel, Jesus' death and resurrection are seen as the necessary precondition for the full and definitive sending of the Spirit or Paraclete. This should not lead us to think that Jesus was not already bearing the Spirit and acting in its power while in his earthly body, but there does seem to be an effort by the New Testament writers to differentiate between the bearing of the Spirit through Jesus in the flesh from the sending of the Spirit through Jesus in the mode of the risen Christ.[28] I think we can understand this difference as the movement from a mode in which the Spirit of Jesus is limited to a particular space and time to a mode in which the Spirit burst out of these limitations into universal presence. Resurrection, then, resulted in the universalization of Jesus' mission.

With the resurrection, Jesus' mission is not only universalized, but also eternalized. Jesus has been established in his "eternal kingdom" (2 Peter 1:11), as mediator between God and humanity "through the power of an indestructible life" (Heb. 7:16-17). Jesus as the risen Lord continues to speak the Word in the power of the Spirit. Jesus as the risen Christ continues to communicate himself in love to human beings and to the God who commissions him. This has the retroactive effect of vindicating his claims to messianic identity and mission while on earth. Indeed, as we have learned, his followers were not secure in their belief in Jesus' messiahship until they had experienced Jesus as risen and as continuing his mission. Furthermore, it is clear from the New Testament writings that with the resurrection Jesus' followers felt justified in giving to Jesus one of the names they gave to God, namely, Lord. Jesus' full divinity is secured, and he becomes an object of worship (see Phil. 2:11; Rev. 1:5-6; 5:13; 2 Pet. 3:18). Resurrection not only eternalizes Jesus in his saving mission but also in his divine identity.

Precisely how does Jesus as risen Lord continue his mission here in this penultimate world? How does Jesus speak the Word if he is no longer here in the flesh? These are the questions that will concern us in the next chapter.

SEVEN

The Risen Christ Continues the Mission

In the previous chapter, we examined the New Testament accounts of the appearances of the risen Jesus, the Lord, Christ, Messiah. It was important to the early Christians that Jesus had been resurrected bodily from the dead, and thus the Gospels tell of a Jesus who could be seen, heard, and touched. It was also important in all four of the Gospel narratives to show Jesus commissioning the disciples to carry on his mission. Matthew's Gospel ends with the Great Commission: "Go therefore and make disciples of all nations" (28:19), and this is repeated in the what is known as the longer ending of Mark (see 16:9-20). In John's Gospel, this commissioning is closely linked to Jesus' giving the Spirit: "'Peace be with you. As the Father has sent me, so I send you.' When he had said this, he breathed on them and said to them, 'Receive the Holy Spirit'" (John 20:21-22). Luke's account does not link the commissioning with the giving of the Spirit but with the *promise* to give the Spirit:

> Then he opened their minds to understand the scriptures, and he said to them, "Thus it is written, that the Messiah is to suffer and to rise from the dead on the third day, and that repentance and forgiveness of sins is to be proclaimed in his name to all nations, beginning from Jerusalem. You are witnesses of these

things. And see, I am sending upon you what my Father promised;
so stay here in the city until you have been clothed with power
from on high." (Luke 24:45-49)

The power that Jesus promises is of course a prediction of that great
event on Pentecost, when, as Luke tells it, "All of them were filled with the
Holy Spirit" (Acts 2:4). Then they immediately left the upper room and
went out and preached the forgiveness of sins, baptizing "in the name of
Jesus Christ" (2:38).

We see here not only the commissioning of individuals but also the
founding of the church, which is the work of God through the risen Christ
in the power of the Spirit.[1] I do not mean a church of pope, bishops,
priests, ministers, deacons, and deaconesses. Nor do I mean a church of
synods, creeds, councils, polity, and canon law. All that came later. I
mean, rather, a small group of women and men convinced that Jesus had
chosen them to continue his mission of drawing people into the reign of
God's love and mercy.

The Risen Christ and the Mission of Individuals

The risen Christ continues to communicate the Word in the power of the
Spirit. But he does not do so by producing an outer word, unless, of course,
he intervenes in the physical world and miraculously creates an outer
word, which over the centuries has been reported only rarely. Visions and
voices of Jesus from heaven are reported, like those experienced by
Stephen (Acts 7:55) and Paul (Acts 9:1-8), but these do not, strictly speaking, take place in this space and time as do outer words. Yet Christians
believe that the risen Christ still communicates to us here within the
penultimate world the Word in the power of the Spirit.

How, then, does the risen Christ speak to human beings if not through
outer word? First of all, Christians believe that the Word and Spirit of the
risen Jesus is in direct communication with human beings, without any
tangible medium, much as God was in direct communication with the
earthly Jesus. Through prayer and silent communion, they believe that
the risen Jesus can be heard, as it were, communicating God's unconditional love. They can, therefore, put themselves in the presence of the
risen Christ and feel the informative, emotive, and directive power of the
Word of Jesus spoken in the power of the Spirit. This is not simply a communication by way of Jesus' Spirit, but by way of Spirit and Word, power

and meaning.[2] In prayerful communion with the risen Christ,[3] a person therefore directly receives both Word and Spirit. God, through the risen Christ, thereby communicates the same identity-forming Word that God directly communicated to the earthly Jesus. God has the same aim for us through the risen Christ that God had with the earthly Jesus: to shape the very center of our spiritual selves according to the supreme value of love, so that we might, like Jesus, address God as our spiritual parent: "God has sent the Spirit of his Son into our hearts, crying, 'Abba! Father!'" (Gal. 4:6).

In responding to the Word and Spirit of the risen Christ, individuals thus come to identify themselves with the universal value of love. They carry an identity that persuades them to identify with the universal love of God in Christ. They love those whom God in Christ loves—all human beings. They then communicate that love to others in outer words, verbal and nonverbal. As soon as that occurs, the risen Christ, who does not have a body that is present in the flesh, finds bodies to speak the outer word of his Word in the power of Spirit. The risen Christ thus speaks not only through what we might call a direct vertical connection with discrete individuals but also through these individuals to other individuals, forming thereby a vast horizontal web of human intercommunication. This horizontal web is indispensable, for we human beings are intrinsically social, dependent on other human beings for life in all its dimensions—biological, psychological, and spiritual. Despite all of God's power, which God now communicates to the risen Christ, God and Christ are dependent on us human beings to give humanity to one another. Unless we human beings provide fundamental human receptivity to one another, God in Christ cannot fully communicate God's identity to us in Word and Spirit.

Individuals, then, can become bodies of the risen Christ through whom the Word and Spirit find expression in outer word. As such, they participate not only in the identity of Jesus but also his mission.[4] This participation in his mission, however, comes to full consciousness only insofar as individuals come together as a community, as church, "so we, who are many, are one body in Christ, and individually we are members one of another" (Rom. 12:5).

The Church as the Body of the Risen Christ

When the followers of Jesus as the risen Christ band together to continue in full consciousness the mission of Christ, they form the church. The church is a society whose purpose is to speak the outer word of the risen

Christ to human beings inside and outside the church. Followers of the risen Christ become members of the church through sacraments of initiation: Baptism, Confirmation, and Eucharist.

We are mistaken if we regard the church primarily as the society of those who are loved and saved by God in Christ. God's love in Christ is universal; no human being is excluded. One of the most pernicious, indeed terrifying, ideas to be enshrined by the Christian tradition is that God's saving love in Christ is effective only in the relatively few persons who have been elected and now make up the true church. But the church is not an enclave where the elect huddle in the smug satisfaction that only they have been given the gift of saving faith. The church is the body of Christ on earth; it is meant to do for the risen Christ what the earthly Jesus did for God: communicate in public the outer word of God's unconditional love, spread the rule of God's justice, draw people into identifying with God's values, help others find authentic meaning. The question for Christians in community should not be, Who is in or who is out, but What is being done to spread the meaning and power, the Word and Spirit.

The mission on earth, therefore, has moved from the earthly Jesus to the church.[5] This introduces complications, for a community on a mission is different from Jesus on a mission. What made Jesus so effective was the unity between his identity and mission. What he spoke publicly in outer word arose out of an identity that was in full spiritual possession of the meaning and power animating his outer word. Jesus was not a mere messenger. The church, however, is composed of individuals who more or less identify with the meaning and power of God. Some have deep faith and love; some do not. When they all band together in community, these varying degrees of faith and love affect the overall communal faith and love. Not only that, just as all politics is local,[6] so too are all churches. The quality of local churches varies, and for this reason the quality of the community's mission varies. Some local churches are so lacking in genuine Christian identity that whatever they do publicly to speak the Word is more hypocrisy than mission.

Over the centuries, the church has tried to overcome these difficulties through ingenious strategies. One strategy undertaken from the earliest days was the subdivision of mission.[7] That is, not every outer word spoken by the community was spoken literally by the whole community. Instead, the church commissioned individuals whose combination of deep piety and special gifts (called charisms) made them especially adapted to certain missions or ministries. And thus those gifted with piety and verbal skills became ministers of the word: preachers, teachers, and prophets. Others gifted in the ritualized word of sacrament presided over worship and liturgy. Others had a special capacity in the area of service, and they became those who distributed money to the poor, food to the hungry, and care to the sick. Others were charged with administration and jurisdiction.[8] In this way, the whole community, a mix of the worst and best, could speak through representatives, drawn from the best.

A second strategy was to formalize the outer word, especially the word of preaching and sacrament, in order to ensure that it would be reasonably well communicated even by those whose love and faith were less than the ideal. For despite continued efforts to find the most pious and gifted ministers, the church came to realize that its prophets and prophetesses, teachers and administrators, deacons and deaconesses, and presbyters and bishops did not always live out in their own spirit the outer word they spoke in their public mission. Left on their own, their lack of genuine piety led to outer words unclear in meaning and deficient in power. To some degree, therefore, the outer word became more formulaic, a set of protocols that each minister had to conform to in order to ensure that the Word and Spirit came through to the hearer even though mediated by an ineffective agent. Remember Anne, whose friend Kate had suffered a stroke and was in a New York hospital? Anne's first outer word was through a mere messenger: a person was commissioned to deliver flowers. The flower courier is not deeply identified with Anne's values nor therefore with Anne's love for Kate. For this reason, Anne cannot leave to his freedom the choice of outer word. She chooses the words that go on the accompanying card. Using protocols established by the flower service in cooperation with the symbolic codes given flowers by the surrounding culture, she chooses the quality and quantity of the flowers. Consequently, even if the flower courier halfheartedly goes through the motions when delivering the flowers to Kate, the outer word can still get through. For this outer word has been formalized. Not much has been left to chance. In somewhat the same way, the church formalizes the outer words it speaks.

This formalization sometimes went too far in the history of the church, to the neglect of the inner faith of both the minister of the outer word and the recipient.[9] Fortunately, prophets rose up, for example, during the Reformation and blasted away at the low level of faith and love in the church's members and ministers. These prophets were in effect telling the church never to accept being a mere messenger of the outer word, following preset protocols. Yet there is a delicate balance that the church must struggle to maintain. On one side of the balance is the certainty that the church's mission will be all the more effective if church members grow into their Christian identity as sons and daughters with Jesus the Son.

If all grow into their full stature, then the church can become a pure and powerful medium of the risen Christ. On the other side of the balance is the certainty that this has not happened. For this reason, the Word that in mission is supposed to come through the church must always simultaneously be directed to the church. The church, then, is both the speaker and needy recipient of the Word. The contrast between the church and Jesus is instructive here. The emotive and directive power of the Word was so successful in Jesus that he does become a pure medium of the Word. God's Word to him did not need to be turned on his own sinful self before it could radiate outwards to others. The church, by contrast, has to constantly turn the Word back on itself in judgment and forgiveness. The goal, however, is finally the transformation of self and community so that the community of persons that is church might be more effective as the body of Christ.[10]

The Church Preaches the Word

The earthly Jesus spoke the verbal word. He was a preacher. So also does the church as the body of Christ on earth preach the verbal word. To insure that its preaching reflects the mind of Christ and comes through relatively undistorted, the church formalizes preaching by insisting that its preachers follow Scripture and tradition. The church gives special authority to Scripture, for there can be found the original preaching of Jesus and his earliest followers.[11]

As the church encountered new historical situations, especially situations in which certain preachers were departing from the mind of Christ and the traditions of the community, the church found itself reformulating the message of Scripture into official statements of belief variously called symbols, creeds, or confessions. Almost all Christian denominations give authority to these statements produced by the tradition, but only the Roman Catholics and the Orthodox elevate them to a level of authority virtually equal to that of Scripture.

Preaching can be done at various levels of formality. A Christian can give verbal witness to his or her faith in the most casual person-to-person encounters. Evangelical street preachers, often with no formal training or certification, preach in public to passersby. But most Christian churches train and certify their preachers and try to insure that they adhere to the meaning of the good news or gospel of Jesus and do not take flight into idiosyncratic fantasy. Nevertheless, there are preachers with great rhetorical skills who manipulate their listeners for their own selfish purposes rather than persuade them to align themselves with God's purposes. Such preachers will typically call themselves good, often sincerely, after having deceived themselves. Some claim to be Christ or to speak directly for Christ without the need to measure their preaching against Scripture and tradition or to subject themselves to any guidance from the wider Christian community. The United States has been a fertile bed for spawning unscrupulous preachers: Jim Jones, Jim Bakker, Jimmy Swaggart, and David Koresh are recent examples. Some of them can scare you to death.

Effective preachers, those who are truly carrying out the mission of Christ, will do so in great humility, knowing that they are judged by the same Word they are preaching. The best preachers have that extraordinary spiritual combination of goodness and modesty. In being good, they have that spiritual identity communicated by the Word and Spirit that makes the mission effective; in being modest, they eagerly admit their fragile hold on goodness and thus convince their listeners that they not only speak the Word but listen to it. They convince their audience that they, as much as their listeners, need the informative, emotive, and directive power of the Word that judges, forgives, and transforms. They also are not dazzled by their own rhetoric and are zealous in their loyalty to the Word as formalized (not fossilized!) in Scripture and tradition.

A special place exists for the preaching of the prophetic word. The prophetic word is directed to sinful social structures, whether they be inside or outside the church. Sometimes, the prophetic word singles out individuals who are particularly venal architects and beneficiaries of these structures.[12] Not infrequently, preachers of the prophetic word are not officially approved preachers. Approved preachers often benefit too much from the current structure to subject it to thoroughgoing critique. As in ancient Israel, prophets make people uncomfortable. Today, Catholics who speak for full equality of women in the church are, in my view, prophetic voices. Virtually none of these voices can be heard from the American bishops, who are the official guardians of the preached word for Catholics in this country. Yet the prophetic word is directed not just to unjust structures in the church. It is directed to the surrounding culture, especially in our day, when the work of justice is so much in the hands of persons working in structures that are private or governmental, not under direct control of the church. Indeed, there are situations in which social injustice is so pervasive and the suffering caused so immense, that the prophetic word is or should be the dominant mode of preaching.[13] The main purpose of the prophetic word is critique. Preachers of the prophetic word should not be required to come up with a detailed proposal for the shape of new, more just structures. And they on their part should resist the temptation to provide such proposals, unless they also have the gifts of social analysis and policy formation.

Preaching is difficult. I have preached on a few occasions. I would much rather give a one-hour lecture than a ten-minute sermon. The person preaching must aim very explicitly at combining the informative, emotive, and directive functions. He or she must find that felicitous blend of thought and feeling. Some sermons are models of crystalline thought but devoid of feeling. Others are full of emotion but vacant of intellect. When thought and feeling come together, a sermon can be a revelatory and empowering experience for speaker and hearer. At that moment, the church as the body of the risen Christ flowers out into unexcelled performance of mission.

The Church Speaks the Ritualized Word

Certain words spoken by the risen Christ through the church reach a very high degree of formalization. These are ritualized words. Preaching is improvisational by comparison. In a ritualized word, two or more people decide to take an outer word and repeat it again and again, often at a set time, often in a designated space, as a way of binding themselves to the word's meaning from the past, in the present, and toward the future.[14]

Let me give an example from ordinary life. A couple speaks the word of married love at the wedding ceremony and then completes it later that day at the hotel. But prior to their lovemaking at the hotel that night, they have a wonderful meal in the hotel restaurant. Three days later, in the car on the way out of town, one says to the other, "Let's do this every year on our anniversary!" The other agrees, and precisely at that moment, they have agreed to ritualize an outer word. The outer word here is complex, for it consists of a whole series of verbal and nonverbal actions by which they communicate their love for each other at that restaurant and hotel. Note how the machinery of ritualization goes into motion. They talk about how they will preserve the formal elements of this word to ensure that the same word is spoken again. Months ahead of the anniversary date, they call and reserve a table in the restaurant and make an explicit request for the same table near the window overlooking the river. When they arrive that evening for dinner, they make every effort to order the same dishes along with the same wine they ordered the first time. With the first sip of wine, they repeat the verbal toast they made to one another the first time. They ask the musical group to play "our song" while they take their annual spin on the dance floor. They even escalate their ritualizing ambitions into the hope that the same waitstaff will be on duty. And, naturally, they reserve the same hotel room.

Ritualization always shows this exactitude about preserving the form of the outer word because human beings wish to keep the meaning of the original word alive by repeating its form over time. Couples and groups are bound together by the meaning they share. At one point, a couple or group or community has a beginning, and typically in this founding moment, they express the meaning that binds them in an outer word. They then keep the meaning alive by speaking this meaning again and again, with almost obsessive insistence on maintaining the form of the original outer word. It is an elaborate memory device. Without memory, there is no continuous identity. Memory is kept alive by ritual.[15]

Christians are a community with a founding meaning that, infused with power, binds them together.[16] That meaning is the unconditional love of God in Christ communicated through the Word and Spirit. Right from the beginning, the church ritualized this meaning.[17] At least one of these rituals, the Eucharist (also called mass, Holy Communion, Lord's Supper), was performed in imitation of the ritualized word Jesus spoke at the last supper. Over the centuries, the church has ritualized many words, both verbal and nonverbal: prayers, litanies, processions, songs, dances, pealing bells, pilgrimages, genuflections, blessings, and sprinklings with water. Some of these, however, achieve particularly high importance and form the heart of Christian ritual. These are called sacraments.[18]

Sacraments are a mix of the verbal and nonverbal. Often they make use of things, natural or human-made: water, oil, salt, bread, wine.[19] Things have material properties that open them up to natural or cultural functions on which a human speaker can then build in order to communicate meaning. These properties and functions also limit the range of meanings in which these things can participate. If we wish to communicate love, we do it with flowers, not a box of cow dung. If we wish to communicate our concern for someone who is thirsty, we offer them fresh water, not a bottle of badly vinegarized wine. If we wish to communicate our compassion for a wounded person, we do not rub salt in the wound but rather a healing balm.

Baptism

Water, for example, is rich in properties that allow it an astonishing range of functions. One is to promote life: without it, life is impossible. All life thirsts for water in one form or another. Water produces not only life but also beauty: much of the exuberant color of the natural world is the result of water. Water is life-giving and life-enhancing.

But water is also death-dealing. In huge amounts, it destroys all in its path. The roiling waters of a storm-tossed sea awe but also terrify because they cause terrible things. The dark, swirling depths of a lake or river have a fatal attraction: have you ever stood on a high bridge over a swollen river in early spring and felt both attracted and scared? People are afraid of water and will not go out in a boat. My mother, who almost drowned as a teenager, once told me about it in vivid detail. Ever since, I have had moments when, just briefly, I have empathetically relived that awful, deep-down tug of water that almost took her away forever.

In the sacrament of Baptism, the Christian community, acting as the body of Christ, builds on water in both its death-dealing and life-giving functions. When the early church performed adult baptism, this dual meaning of water was put to especially powerful use. The person being baptized first had to "die" by going down naked into the dark waters of a cistern or font located in or near the place of worship. Then the person would be "resurrected," would "come to life," when he or she came up out of the waters.[20] Baptism, then and now, was the sacrament of initiation whereby the person became a member of the Christian community bound by the meaning that shaped the identity and mission of Jesus.[21] When Jesus accepted this meaning, he took on a love that transformed him into a person who loved God and others. This love does not cling narcissistically to the self but gives the self away to God and others. This love directs one to die to the selfish self that the loving self might live. In the last word of his life, in his last supper and death, Jesus gave the culminating and most dramatic expression of this love. This final word was answered by God's word of resurrection: Jesus went down into the waters of death and came up into the risen life as the climax of a lifelong pattern of dying and rising.[22]

To become a member of the Christian community is to share in Jesus' meaning, which is to accept a love that deals death to the selfish self so that the loving self might rise up. The membership may even require, as it often did in the early church, when martyrdom was a real possibility, that a follower of Christ express that meaning in death for God and for others.[23] Baptism, as a sacrament of initiation, uses water with its complex dual meaning of death and life and calls the new member to a love that means life out of death. Water proves itself a wonderfully apt thing to use for this sacrament.

Baptism is performed by the church carrying out its mission as the body of the risen Christ. The new member being baptized commits to the meaning of that community. The community also commits itself to communicating the Word and Spirit to the new member so that she or he might be fully transformed into a daughter or son of God. When an infant is baptized, the church's commitment is particularly prominent because the infant is not able to consciously accept the membership she or he is being given. In infant baptism, then, the community, especially family, friends, and local church members, does all the choosing and all the talking. They say, in effect, "We will shape this child in the meaning of Christ, which is a love that dies to self that the loving self might live." In saying this, the community pledges itself to shape the infant into a good person instead of a sinner. It pledges to subject the infant to a set of redemptive social influences that counteract corrupting social forces. These corrupting forces have been active since the first human beings, mythically named Adam and Eve in the Hebrew Bible, committed the first sin, the original sin.

Sin as a social reality is more than the sum of individual sinful acts. Sin becomes social when it becomes pervasive in social structures, lending social power and normality to behavior that is unloving and unjust. Right from the moment a child comes into the world, these structures begin to work their corrupting effect, bending her or him in the direction of selfishness and indifference to others. The first human beings, the mythical Adam and Eve, started the history of sin, but then each succeeding generation makes its own contribution to the social weight of sin, and original sin snowballs down the centuries. The Christian community, in baptizing an infant or young child, publicly pledges to offer its own counterweight. It dedicates the child to a set of social forces that transform rather than corrupt. In this sense, baptismal waters can be said to wash away the effects of original sin, or better, introduce the child into a community pledged to shape the child into a spiritual identity that chooses authentic rather than inauthentic meanings. In the past, Christians tended to emphasize that Baptism accomplished this cleansing of original sin once and for all with one dip in the baptismal water. Were it that easy! Theologians today emphasize that Baptism is the initiation into a process whereby the effect of sin is gradually counteracted by God's self-communication through Christ and the church. For the process to have any chance of success assumes that the community, especially the family, has the capacity and willingness to live out consistently the identity and mission of Christ in relation to this child.[24]

Confirmation

In the early church, most baptisms were of adults. Scholars know that by 200 C.E. infant baptism was common practice, but prior to that, the evidence is ambiguous. Luke in Acts 16:25-33 tells of a prison guard who, moved by the example of Paul and Silas, asked how he might be saved. He and his household were instructed in "the word of the Lord" and "then he and his entire family were baptized without delay" (16:33). Probably the smallest children were included, but we cannot be certain. In the Eastern Church, infants were (and still are) initiated through one ceremony that has three phases: water immersion (or sprinkling), anointing, and Eucharist. In the Western Church, a different practice developed. The three phases came to be administered at two different times in the child's life: first, as soon as possible after birth, water immersion (Baptism); and second, at least seven years later, the anointing (Confirmation) and the Eucharist. In the contemporary Catholic Church, the custom is to administer the three phases of initiation at three different times: first, Baptism to an infant or young child; second, Eucharist (First Communion) to a child at least seven years old; and third, Confirmation (which now includes both anointing and laying on of hands) to an early adolescent. Protestant churches that practice infant baptism administer Confirmation in early adolescence and then immediately complete the initiation by admitting the confirmands to the Eucharist, the Lord's Supper. Among contemporary Catholics, lively debate about the timing of Confirmation is common. Some want to return to the original order and place it after Baptism and before Eucharist, but only a few want to adopt the Orthodox practice of administering all three to an infant.[25]

I slightly favor placing Eucharist after Confirmation, but I am open to either before or after. I feel quite strongly, however, that Confirmation should be delayed to adolescence. Confirmation is an opportunity for children to make an informed decision on whether to confirm or disconfirm their baptismal initiation into the church.[26] They were baptized without their choice. It was their fate. True, fate is a large part of life. Much of our identities are formed by fate, and we should not be scandalized that church membership begins as baptismal fate. But somehow, children must learn along the way that they live not only by fate but also by freedom, that the Christian identity that began as their fate can only become their possession by free choice. Confirmation is the rite that allows persons making the passage from childhood to adulthood to transform their imposed Christian fate into their chosen Christian destiny. Adolescence is as good a time as any to offer our youth the opportunity to accept publicly their baptism. They should be told that it is their free choice: if they choose not to be confirmed, that choice should be fully respected. Parents can, I believe, require that they go through the pre-Confirmation classes. Young people cannot choose to accept or reject membership in a community whose binding meaning they do not understand—they need to be instructed in the word of the Lord. The final decision to be confirmed, however, should be entirely theirs. I also like the ancient practice of having the bishop be present as the one who confirms the adolescent's confirmation of baptism. The bishop mediates between the local churches and the worldwide church. The confirmands should be aware that they are completing their initiation into the worldwide Christian community, not just into the local parish or congregational community. If it is a church that does not have bishops, then some other person who can convincingly symbolize a connection between the church local and the church universal should visibly participate in the ceremony.

After the sacrament of Confirmation was separated from Baptism, questions arose about exactly what distinguishes it from Baptism. Some authorities said that only in Confirmation does one receive the Holy Spirit. But the risen Christ never communicates without that Spirit that marks or seals (see Eph. 1:13; 2 Cor. 1:21) the recipient as a son or daughter of God, and thus this Spirit is necessarily present in baptism. We cannot in good theological conscience limit the Spirit to Confirmation. Yet the sacrament is rightly called the sacrament of the Holy Spirit, for it offers an excellent opportunity for the Spirit to arouse feeling and will. The sacrament should therefore be administered so that those being confirmed have a vivid experience of the emotive and directive power of the Spirit. In becoming a full member of the church in freedom, those being confirmed commit themselves to living out the identity and mission of Christ. This is an authentic meaning and, as with Jesus himself, a meaning that can be realized only with the power and energy of the Holy Spirit.

Eucharist

The climax of the formation of Jesus' identity and the completion of his earthly mission occurred in the final word of the last supper and death. In this final word, he gave himself over to humanity and to God in the fullest way possible. In the Epistle to the Hebrews, a neglected and underrated New Testament writing, the writer speaks of the death as the climax of Jesus' earthly high-priestly office: "For it was fitting that we should have such a high priest, holy, blameless, undefiled, separated from sinners, and exalted above the heavens. Unlike the other high priests, he has no need to offer sacrifices day after day, first for his own sins, and then for those of the people; this he did once for all when he offered himself" (Heb. 7:26-27). In the Jewish religion, the high priest at the temple mediated between God and human beings. First, he brought God to the people by officiating at ceremonial sacrifice that was regarded as God's gift to the people. Second, he brought the people to God by presenting their gifts to God for sacrifice. This two-directionality, from God to the people and from the people to God, is as we saw earlier the heart of Jesus' mission. Jesus' mission is therefore a priestly mission, and his last supper and death are his climactic priestly act. In this act, the downward movement of God and the upward movement of human being come into perfect unity.

As risen, Jesus continues his priestly mission.[27] He continues to communicate God's love by giving and offering himself to human beings, and he continues to draw human beings into his giving and offering of himself to God. The same meaning that he communicated at his last supper and death is now eternally active in the intention of the risen Christ. This same intention is now active in his body on earth, the church. Whenever the church communicates the outer word of its mission, it carries out the same two-directional priestly office of Jesus. Among the sacraments, this priestly office of two-directional self-giving and self-offering[28] reaches fullest and clearest expression in the Eucharist, which, fittingly enough, derives its ritualistic elements from the community's memory of the last supper. Because Jesus forges a link between his last supper and his death, Eucharist is the sacrament that is celebrated in most explicit unity with Jesus' death. Just as the last supper was the sacramental anticipation of the impending death, so now the Eucharist is the sacramental representation of the death and the communication of the continuing sacrificial intention of the risen Christ. It is not a question here of repeating the last supper or the death, but of communicating now in ritualized word the same two-directional meaning that was communicated then. A unity is forged among last supper, death, and Eucharist because all are animated by the communicative intention of Jesus to speak the definitive word of love to us and to God.[29]

A complex up and down movement is therefore the essence of the Eucharist. The sacrament opens with the confession of sin: in response to the downward movement of God's judging Word through the risen Christ, the community moves upward toward God in repentance. This confession is followed by forgiveness, which is the downward movement of God's forgiving Word through Christ and the Spirit. The rite continues with the offering of the bread and wine: inspired by the Spirit, the community offers itself up to God through Christ. This is followed by God's acceptance and blessing of the bread and wine: God descends through Christ, Spirit, and church upon the bread and wine and consecrates them, that is, transforms them into something sacred. The Eucharist concludes with the communal sharing of the consecrated bread and wine, whereby the community as Christ's body mediates the downward movement of God's self-gift through Christ and the Spirit, at the same time that the community moves up to accept this gift.[30] The community is simultaneously offering and receiving God's Word and Spirit. The interweaving of this double movement gives the Eucharist an inexhaustible richness and complexity. The Eucharist is the height and depth of the church's communication and reception of the ritualized word.[31]

I should like to focus for a moment on the consecration and sharing of the bread and wine. Bread and wine are things made by human beings, out of components derived from cultivated organic nature. They have material properties that allow them to function as nourishment for human beings. Human beings over the centuries have built on the function of nourishment to transform bread and wine into meaning communicated by outer word. By offering bread and wine, a person can say something to someone. Since food and drink do fulfill a human biological need and appeal to the senses, they are open to the communication of very positive meanings. Caught up in an outer word, food and drink can even carry the meaning of self-communication—of love, caring, and compassion.

For example, imagine that your dearest friend has just returned from a yearlong stay in France. You have missed her terribly, and you wish to speak a loving word of welcome. You go out and buy a bottle of the best French wine. You stop by an upscale deli and purchase some French cheese and a baguette. You invite her over, e-mailing her a fancy invitation you found on a postcard Web site. She accepts, and that evening she arrives. After expressing your welcoming love verbally, you shift into that special time and space where rituals unfold. With some solemnity, you bring out the wine, bread, and cheese. You break the bread, slice the cheese, and open the wine—and then with ceremonial flair you offer some to your friend.[32]

What are you doing here? Nourishing your friend biologically? Yes—yet more than that. You are communicating yourself in outer word. In handing over that bread, wine, and cheese to your friend, you are handing over your deepest psychological and spiritual self. The food and drink are no longer simply food and drink, they are . . . you! The proof lies in the kind of response that you desire in return. How would you feel if she wolfed down the bread and cheese, then chugalugged the wine, all in one voracious sweep, and concluded by exclaiming, "Wow, was I hungry! Anything else in the fridge?" You would rightly feel disappointed, even hurt. She would have treated your solemn word simply as an attempt to fill her stomach. You could just as well have been someone slinging hash at the local greasy spoon! She would have missed the presence of you in that food and drink. She would have been oblivious of the self-communicative depth of this nonverbal action. She would have failed to understand that you had dedicated—dare I say consecrated?—the bread, wine, and cheese to a purpose higher than that of simply filling her gullet.

If, however, she was able to understand that you were engaged in self-communicative speech, in an outer word whereby you were aiming to be informative (you wanted her to know that you were speaking a loving welcome back), emotive (you wished her to feel your love and to feel love for you in return), and directive (you were hoping for some kind of word from her showing appreciation and love in return), then she would move with you to the communicative level. She would see that you had transformed this food and drink into a sensory vehicle of love, that you had made this food and drink extensions of your body. You would not, of course, have transformed the wine, bread, and cheese in their physicochemical structure; rather, you would have caught them up into your self-communication. They really would become you in your action of loving your friend. You would be really present in this food and drink, not in the sense that you had physically crawled inside them, but in the sense that your spiritual self would enliven them with the motion of your self-giving.

The sacrament of the Eucharist builds on this openness of food and drink to the meaning of self-communication. Indeed, the bread and wine find their deepest purpose, their deepest meaning, when their human purposes of biological nourishment and spiritual self-communication are caught up in the purpose of God's self-communication through Christ in the church.[33] In imitation of Jesus at the last supper, the Christian community, now communicating in the name of the risen Christ, adds this meaning to the sharing of bread and wine when, in the eucharistic celebration, it solemnly consecrates them to this purpose and then eats and drinks. The wine and bread are hereby transformed into vehicles of the self-communication of God in Christ through the church.[34] The earthly Jesus at the last supper transformed the bread and wine into his body and blood, that is, into extensions of himself in his self-giving. The church now as the body of the risen Christ transforms the bread and wine into his body and blood, that is, into extensions of Christ in his self-giving.[35] God in Christ is really present in this bread and wine, not in the sense of having physically crawled inside them, but in the sense of spiritually enlivening them with the Word and Spirit.[36]

The Church Speaks through Service to Humankind

No matter how stirringly the church speaks the Word and Spirit of Christ through preaching and sacrament, this Word will not be consistently successful in the minds and hearts of hearers unless Christians as a community practice the Word they preach and ritualize. To be sure, the outer words of the church are formalized and thus can be spoken accurately and effectively even though a Christian group or minister is defective in virtue. But merely formal communication of the preached and ritualized Word should not be regarded as the pinnacle of Christian mission. This mission reaches its pinnacle when it breathes the life of genuine Christian identity.

If a hearer of the Word hears the Word primarily through the best individuals the community produces, then he or she may have little difficulty feeling the power of the Spirit that infuses this Word. Indeed, one very saintly and charismatic individual, particularly one who has been given an influential position, can carry a whole Christian community into very effective communication of the Word of preaching and sacrament. Even individual Christians who have not been granted a position of official importance, can, insofar as they are interpreted by others as giving Christian witness, become for hearers of the Word representative of the whole community, and, therefore, through that one individual, the whole church becomes more effective in its mission.

The church, however, is always more than a few outstanding individuals, and the church will always be judged as a community, not just as it is represented in its best individuals. As a community, the church is more than the total of all its individuals, which is as true for the local churches as for the national and international churches. Just as the emotive and directive power of the Spirit aims to dwell in the hearer and become the moving principle of his or her feeling and action, so also does the Spirit dwell in the community lending to it particular élan and esprit. The Spirit then becomes a collective power, greater than the total of all its indwellings in individuals. One can feel the level of Spirit in any Christian community, and it varies greatly from one to another. When the level is high, the Spirit flows into the preaching, enlivening both speaker and hearer. It animates the rituals, giving them not just beauty but power. Finally, the Spirit spills over into service, into those verbal and nonverbal words that meet the biological, psychological, and spiritual needs of people, both inside and outside the community. For service in love and justice is important: indeed, it is the final proof of the presence of Jesus and the Spirit.

I am talking here of the church as servant to humankind.[37] Service to humankind means the communal organization of good works that lead to the salvation of people, not just in their spiritual dimension, but in their biological and psychological dimensions. In an era of specialization, Christians are tempted to limit the church to the purely spiritual and to leave the other dimensions to individual Christians acting as laypersons in the secular world. That is a mistake, one that leads people to justifiably criticize the church as hypocritical, as more interested in spending large sums of money to house its preaching and ritual than to put love and justice into action.

Love and justice need to be directed both inward and outward. The church must be loving and just in relation to its own members. This is largely a matter of its social structures, which are those habitual ways of acting, thinking, imagining, and feeling that a community codifies in its customs, laws, and policies. When these structures are unloving and unjust, and when no prophetic voices rise up to condemn them, then a great scandal has occurred that will have a deleterious effect on the church's overall mission. For example, the way the contemporary Catholic Church is structured to invest so much power in the male, celibate priesthood has caused a great loss of credibility and effectiveness in the church's mission as communicator of the Word and Spirit. And I know from my experience of teaching thousands of young adults that their disgust with organized religion is usually traceable to what they perceive as Christian hypocrisy, on both an individual and communal scale. They see the church preaching and sacramentalizing the Word but not being moved by the Spirit of that Word to practice love and justice among its own members.

Yet we dare not overlook the complexity of the issue. Sometimes I become impatient with my younger students and their constant harangue about hypocrisy. I remind them that the church does not want to exclude sinners from membership. Not only would this result in a moralistic rigorism that would empty the churches of all but the most fanatically pious, but it would mean forgetting that the Word of God's unconditional love is a Word that judges and forgives. It is also a Word that transforms but not in one fell swoop. The church has always had a few perfectionistic holiness groups who believe in and insist on this instantaneous and complete transformation, but their membership is small and often forbidding. I prefer a community of believers who let themselves continually be judged and reconciled by the Word, but this is a community of sinners. This means that their behavior, both individually and communally, will often be far short of the highest standards of love and justice, and yes, this will reduce the effectiveness of the church's mission.

Nevertheless, the awareness of sin and sinners in the church is no excuse for complacency. The church should be ever vigilant for moral transformation in its individual members and social structures. Effectiveness in Christian mission is partly dependent on growth in Christian identity. To communicate the Word in power is done best by those who have surrendered as individuals to the transformational power of the Spirit.

The church directs its deeds of love and justice not only to those within, but to all human beings. In centuries past, almost all works of love and justice done in Western society were carried out by the church. The church through its structures provided for the poor, housed the homeless, fed the hungry, healed the sick, helped the widow, sheltered the orphan, and educated the uneducated. The church should continue to do this as part of its mission. But nowadays a so-called secular sphere has emerged, where people create social structures that specialize in meeting the various biological and psychological needs of individuals and groups. These structures are nongovernmental or governmental and, in our complex, highly interdependent societies, often pervasive and powerful. Frequently, individual Christians will find themselves choosing to work for justice within these structures rather than within the churches, and for this they should receive vigorous support from the church. And church structures should be on the alert for opportunities to enter into alliances with nonchurch structures.

And there is always the preaching of the prophetic word, which exercises vigilance over structures both inside and outside the church, spurring, sometimes lashing, them on to work more effectively for the oppressed, the suffering, the poor, and the powerless. In a world where vast and complex structures insinuate their influence into every corner of the globe, into even the most isolated tribal community, the church as a community cannot be indifferent to the humanizing and dehumanizing effects of such structures. It must be willing to exert institutional weight and pressure. In today's world, the hungry will not be fed, the naked will not be clothed, the captives will not be freed, the sick will not be healed, unless massive social structures operate efficiently and humanely.

EIGHT

The Human Response of Faith and Love

In the previous chapter, we examined the resurrection of Jesus as God's response to Jesus' final word of last supper and death. The resurrection establishes Jesus forever in his identity as the Son whose mission is to communicate the Word in the power of the Spirit. The risen Christ continues his mission through the outer words of human beings. These outer words reach full explicitness in the community called church, the body of Christ on earth. And thus the Word of God that begins in the mysterious interior grasping of God's self as love becomes outer Word in the mission of Christ and the church. To hear this outer Word in the power of the Spirit requires, then, that one hear the words of Jesus and his followers.

The Word as outer Word is a deeply personal word. It is God's self-communication. Such a Word is never purely informative. To self-communicate successfully, the self must go over to the other and dwell within the other and then evoke a self-communication in return. To dwell in another is to dwell not only in the other's intellect but also in the other's feeling and will. Something must happen not only informatively but also emotively and directively. To put it in more traditional theological language, the Word in the Spirit must evoke both faith and love in the hearer.

Informative Success: Faith

Christians believe that God is a self-communicating God. Since God is giving God's very self, God intends not only to inform but also to evoke feeling and arouse action. When God's Word is successfully informative, it evokes the response of faith; when this Word is successfully emotive, it evokes love as feeling; when this Word is successfully directive, it arouses love as action. Faith, then, is part of the human response to God's Word. It is distinct from love, but it cannot be separated from love. Indeed, it blurs into love. The distinction is there, but it is sharp only in theory, not in practice.

Faith occurs when the Word of God is informatively successful in the hearer. This faith has three steps. First, we must understand the Word of God. What does it mean to say that God loves us? Second, we must believe that the reality referred to by God's Word fits within our horizon of what we believe to be real or possibly real. Can we believe that there is a God and that this God is self-communicating, is loving? And third, we must trust that God in fact loves us, that God is not self-deceived or, more important, is not deceiving us. Can we believe in God; can we lean upon this love and know that it is real and unwavering? Can we trust that this God is in fact well-disposed to us?

Faith and Understanding

Understanding the Word of God is in part a cognitive act: to understand we must use our heads; we must use our reason. The man who murdered Alberta Williams King, the mother of Martin Luther King Jr., said that he was told by God to commit the murder. Did he understand God's Word correctly? Is it reasonable to think that God would have told him such a thing?

For a Christian, the Word of God comes through mediators, supremely through Jesus, as earthly and as resurrected, and through his followers, both as individuals and as bonded together in church. Understanding the meaning of that Word thus entails understanding the meaning as it has been communicated through the words of Jesus and his followers.

As we have seen, the words of the earthly Jesus were both verbal and nonverbal: he not only spoke in parables, which are verbal words, but performed miracles, shared bread and wine, and suffered and died, which are all nonverbal words. As resurrected, Jesus continues to communicate the Word through his earthly followers, whose formulation of the Word changes over the centuries, both in metaphor and concept, to meet new situations. Even Jesus' own words on earth, originally spoken in Aramaic, a dialect of Hebrew, were often reformulated by the New Testament writers to speak more directly to situations faced by their readers. The church that formed around the belief that Jesus was risen then formulated and reformulated its preaching as it encountered each new audience. It spoke first to a mostly Jewish audience, then to an audience of Jews and potential converts to Judaism, the so-called God-fearers and proselytes. And it spoke then to Greek-speaking Gentiles, and then to the Latin-speaking citizens of the Western Roman Empire, and then out to the Franks, the Anglo-Saxons, the Germans, and ever outward. The original preaching was not only retranslated but reconceptualized. In the early fourth century, Greek-speaking Christians in the Eastern Empire decided to formulate the relation of Jesus the Son to God the "Father" as "of the same essence," that is *homoousios.*[1] By this Greek term, they hoped to capture the original preaching of "The Father and I are one" (John 10:30). All these external words, beginning with Jesus and then undergoing reformulation in history, must not only be understood but also connected to the one fundamental Word of God's love as spoken through Jesus, the earthly mediator of God's Word, and through his followers, the earthly mediators of the resurrected Jesus. This understanding is in part a task of human reason. Even when these words as expression of God's Word are summed up rather simply in a creed or a catechism, they must be first understood before they can be believed and trusted.

The task of understanding the Word is complicated by the peculiar nature of religious language, which is not clean and conceptual like the language of the natural and social sciences. The Word contains information, yes, but information about very rich and complex realities that exist deep within the interior selves of Jesus and his followers, and these interior realities are in turn linked to the transcendent reality of God's self-communication in love. The language of Jesus and his followers is therefore often metaphorical rather than neatly conceptual. Jesus says that the rule of God is "like a mustard seed" (Matt. 13:31; Mark 4:31; Luke 13:17). John's Gospel has Jesus referring to himself as the "bread of life" (John 6:35) and the "vine" (15:5). Even the language of Christian creed and confession is rife with metaphor. According to the Nicene Creed,[2] the Son of God "came down from heaven" to save human beings and now as risen sits "at the right hand of the Father." This is highly metaphorical language!

The important point is that faith as informative success begins with understanding the meaning of the Word. To be informed by this Word, the hearer must have some cognitive grasp of what is meant by God's Word, not only in its original mediation through Jesus but also in its translation by his followers to meet new situations in history. This entails further a grasp of how the Word is mediated through human beings, and who can make a credible claim to be a mediator. What is Jesus saying when he communicates God's Word in his parables, at the last supper, in death? Who is this Jesus who is the prime mediator or speaker of God's Word and Spirit? And who are these followers who call themselves church through whom the Word and Spirit continue to be communicated? Reason in its theological exercise attempts to construct answers to these questions and then show how all these answers cohere in a harmonious and noncontradictory manner. Answering these questions is a mental exercise, a cognitive discipline, which requires the use of what I should like to call constructive reason. Constructive reason tries to understand the Word of God in its what, how, and who. Everyone who tries to understand the Word of God will use his or her constructive reason to at least some extent.

Understanding God's Word can never, however, be merely a matter of reason alone. I know from experience that many students can fairly easily acquire what the Canadian philosopher of religion Donald Evans calls a "lexical [dictionary] understanding" of the Word of God. Many write superb essays on what Christians mean by *God, Word, Spirit, Jesus, mission, reign of God*, and *unconditional love*. But full understanding of such words, says Evans, can only come with what he calls an "existential understanding,"[3] or perhaps better, an "experiential understanding." Helen Keller, who was deaf, mute, and blind, had a lexical, even perhaps scientifically precise, understanding of the color blue, but could she have fully understood the color blue without having experienced it? And how can one truly understand God's Word of love unless one to some extent has already experienced that love?[4] But to experience love takes us beyond reason to feeling and will, beyond the merely informative, into the emotive and directive. Reason has its limits.

Faith and Belief

The second step to faith is belief. If we are to believe that corresponding to the Word of God's self-communicating love there is a reality, we must first believe that God exists. Can reason help us here? The Catholic tradition has in the past said an emphatic yes. The bishops at the First Vatican Council in 1869–70 proclaimed that the reasonable person, properly disposed and open-minded, would find the various arguments for God's existence rationally compelling. Indeed, these arguments have the right to carry the banner of *proofs*.

In the last few decades, Roman Catholic thinkers have backed off somewhat for this strong view of reason's arguments for God's existence. Most would now agree with Hans Küng that none of the classical arguments is rationally compelling, or to use an expression much favored by philosophers and theologians, none of the arguments can claim to be a knockdown proof. Küng thus drops all use of the word *proof*.[5] These arguments do, however, point to God's existence and as such assure believers that their belief is not absurd but reasonable.

One argument that is enjoying quite a revival is the argument from design, also called the teleological argument. It is not the argument in its old form, which saw the world as an incredibly complex and wondrous machine, like a stupendously complex watch, and concluded that there must exist an extraordinarily intelligent designer called God. God in this view is a design engineer, directly fashioning every detail of every part of the vast cosmic machine. In the new form of the argument, very much influenced by Darwinism and contemporary physics, we are asked to look on the cosmos as a vast, sweeping process, steadily moving forward but without mechanical precision, with fits and starts and bursts, but gradually creating ever more complex forms of being, finally creating the most complex beings, namely, us human beings, who then look at that whole process, who are awestruck, and who raise the question: are we merely lucky accidents, the result of a totally unpredictable toss of the cosmic dice? One could certainly say yes; after all, the cosmic process does show a looseness, a blind and groping quality, that has led a whole generation of cosmologists and evolutionary theorists (Richard Dawkins, Stephen Jay Gould, Jacques Monod) to believe that we are sheer accidents, absurd occurrences; indeed, the cosmos itself is a surreal eruption out of a singularity indistinguishable from nothingness.

Yet believers in God, theists, many of them practicing scientists, have taken a closer look, and they see evidence of intelligent guidance. They have pointed out that for a life form like us to appear presupposes the prior occurrence of an immense number (more than fifty by the latest count) of physical constants that have to be constituted within very precise tolerances, all working together in the most harmonious way. Concerning just one of those constants, the force of gravity, let us hear from the U.S. philosopher of science Errol E. Harris:

> The currently accepted theory of the universe is that it began some eighteen thousand million years ago with a vast explosion. Its present age, size, and rate of expansion all depend upon the relation between the forces of gravity and [the forces] of the initial

propulsive outburst. Had the latter been weaker, the cosmos would rapidly have fallen back upon itself and contracted to a point. Had it been stronger, the cosmic matter would have dispersed at such speed that galaxies could not have formed. A difference of one part in 1060 would have been sufficient to bring either of these results. The precision of the actual balance of forces, therefore, necessary for the presently observed universe to exist matches that required to aim a rifle bullet at a one-inch target twenty billion light years away.[6]

To say that this stupendous improbability called human life happened by the purest chance seems to theists, well, absurd. It is better, theists say, to move into the belief that the cosmos gives evidence of intelligent guidance. In a word, God creates and draws primitive matter into life and consciousness, not unilaterally and neatly, for the universe is not a machine but an organism shot through with free play and chance, but persistently and finally successfully, with the result that there are now human beings (and perhaps other beings like ourselves in other parts of the universe), capable of knowing that God exists and responding to God in faith.

Reason thus can help us believe that it is reasonable to believe that God exists. Again, this new argument from design is not a knockdown proof, but it is reasonable to believe that God exists. But a belief that God exists is far from a belief that God is communicating a deeply personal Word of Love. To have belief in such a Word, we have to be disposed to believe that God the cosmic designer is also God the loving self-communicator. But to believe that God is speaking a Word of love, we must first believe in love as a general possibility and at least inchoately experience God as loving. This experience is not an experience of reason alone. At this point, reason must enter into a complex participation of the whole self, the self that not only reasons but also feels, desires, and wills. Reason can bring us to believe that believing in God's existence is reasonable, but reason alone cannot bring us to believing that this God is speaking a Word of Love to us. Again, we see that reason has its limits.

Faith and Trust

The third step to faith is trust. If someone says, "I love you," you must trust that she is not self-deceived or deceiving you. You must trust that she truly loves you, that she is on your side, that she is favorably disposed to you, that she wishes your flourishing. Reason has a role to play here. You can listen closely to her words. You can watch her closely to see whether her verbal declarations of love match her nonverbal actions. Reason should pause if she were to say "I love you" while throwing sand in your face. But reasoned judgment, however favorable, will not compel trust. You have to feel her feeling for you. You have to feel that her deepest interior is in movement toward a loving union with you. But her interior self is not directly available to you. You see only the bodily mediation of that interior in her verbal and nonverbal actions as they affect your external senses. You must move through her external word into an empathetic identification with the deepest feelings of her invisible interior. But even if your feelings tell you she is indeed feeling love for you, you can choose to deny your feelings and thus hers. You can flee them, shut them down, to the point of ceasing to feel her feeling for you. Thus, you have to *choose* to trust, which is always somewhat of a leap into the unknown. Trust leads beyond reason into feeling and will.

The great sociologist of religion and religious thinker Peter Berger says that reasoned reflection on the primal human experience of trust can help us trust that this world is anchored in a God who is trustworthy. He recounts the paradigmatic scene of a mother comforting her child who awakens in the night, terrorized by a nightmare: "She will turn on a lamp, perhaps, which will encircle the scene with a warm glow of reassuring light. She will speak or sing to the child, and the content of this communication will invariably be the same—'Don't be afraid—everything is in order, everything is all right.' If all goes well the child will be reassured, his trust in reality restored, and in this trust he will return to sleep."[7] Berger says that with these words, the mother is offering a consolation that, by implication, goes beyond the worldly to the transworldly, to the transcendent, to God. "*Everything* is in order, everything is all right." If she is not lying, if she is not offering false consolation, she must be pointing to God as the One who makes everything all right.

Hans Küng has reflected on this question with the thoroughness characteristic of a German theologian.[8] He grants that the world does not provide unambiguous support for fundamental trust. Yes, we have experiences of order, goodness, and consolation, but we also have experiences of disorder, evil, and disconsolation. If we cast the light of reason on such a world, we see evidence both for and against fundamental trust. But it would not be unreasonable, says Küng, to choose in favor of fundamental trust and to anchor this fundamental trust in God. Enough good things are going on in this world to point to God as the world's trustworthy creator, who in the end will secure order. Yet reason does not clinch the matter. Reason must team up with broader feeling, with a deeper cosmic sensitivity, and finally, to free surrender, if we are to secure fundamental trust in a

God who loves us enough to ensure that everything will be all right. The trust that is required for faith can therefore be secured only by a trust that God does indeed love us. But love involves more than reason; it involves feeling and will.

Here, the Catholic tradition needs the counterbalance of the classical Protestant emphasis on trust as an experience that takes one well beyond reason into feeling and will. Luther had it right when he said, "Faith is under the left nipple,"[9] in the feeling heart, a feeling evoked by God's Holy Spirit. Søren Kierkegaard had it right when he spoke of the "leap of faith,"[10] in the choice to surrender to God's Word, a choice moved by God's choice of us, which is grace. The Catholic tradition, of course, has never denied the role of choice (though until recently it paid scant attention to feeling), but it would want to weigh in here and warn against fideism, against setting trust against reason. The Catholic tradition stresses that trust is not a blind leap into pure paradox. There is evidence in the world pointing to God as the ground of trust. But to trust God demands that we feel God and choose God, in response to God's feeling for and choice of us, and feeling and choice, though not in opposition to reason, take us beyond reason.

But we are asked to trust not only God but those through whom God speaks the Word in the power of the Spirit. If all hearing of God's Word took place in direct, mystical communion with God, then perhaps trust would not be such an important element, though even in this case, trust could not be completely avoided, because the hearer or the responder in mystical communion must still ask if she trusts her own response. But such mystical communion is quite rare. Most human beings first hear the Word through the outer words of other human beings, and then the question of trust becomes particularly complex. Can Jesus and his followers be trusted?

I have already explored this question with respect to Jesus and concluded that it is reasonable to believe that he sincerely lived out in feeling and action the Word and Spirit he preached. Breakdown of the communication of the Word on the level of trust usually occurs when the speaker of the Word is a follower of Jesus, rather than Jesus himself. Potential hearers of the Word often will accuse his followers of both self-deception and insincerity. Skeptics accuse the church of self-deception about the mission of Jesus, about Jesus' relationship with God, about the meaning of the last supper and death, and about the resurrection. But I think that most people who distrust Christians think Christians are not so much self-deceived as insincere. They doubt the reality of what Christians refer to when they speak the Word because they are scandalized by how little Christians live out the reality of that Word in their own lives. They see

Christians speaking the Word informatively through preaching and sacrament, but not responding to the Spirit of the Word emotively and directively, and thus they do not trust Christians when Christians try to inform them about the meaning and the reality referred by that meaning.

Trusting the human speaker of the Word is partly an intellectual act. To the extent this is possible, the potential hearer of the Word must gather information about Jesus and his followers and critically evaluate it.[11] But trust is always more than a purely intellectual judgment. Trust is also a matter of empathetic intuition, what used to be called vibes when I was a student in the sixties. How does the hearer feel in the presence of Jesus and his followers? But even if the intellectual judgment and the intuition are very positive, trust does not come automatically. At the deepest level the hearer freely chooses whether to surrender in trust to the informative truth of the Word.[12] And the truth of this Word is that God is unconditionally loving, and one fully surrenders one's feeling and will to that truth only if one lets the power of the Word have its effect. But the power of the Word is the power of the Spirit, who is the power of love.

Note how in each step in my analysis of faith as understanding, belief, and trust, I slide from reason into an experience that goes beyond reason into feeling and will.[13] When talking about trust as the third step to faith, we found that to trust God is to feel God's love for us. But what is the feeling of someone's feeling for us but the first stage of love? Feeling God's feeling for us means already that we have been opened up enough by God's initiating love to feel God. This opening up to the other's love is the first stage of loving the other. Suddenly, we realize that in order to make sense of the response of faith to God's Word we have to move into the response of love to God's Spirit.[14]

Emotive Success: Love as Feeling

Emotive success begins with the hearer's feeling the influx of divine feeling as it comes through Jesus and his followers. From the side of the hearer, this is a more passive moment in response to the Spirit of the Word.[15] Here, the hearer is being moved more than moving—not that the hearer is completely passive. Simply to let the power of the Word in requires the active willingness of the hearer.[16]

If the hearer chooses not to let the love of God in, that love is still felt by the hearer but as judgment. This happens between human beings as well. Imagine that someone loves you with full emotive and directive power, urging you to respond in kind. If for no defensible reason you choose not to let this love in, and if you have any conscience at all, you will then feel that love as a reproach, as a judgment. Indeed, you may find yourself avoiding the presence of the person who loves you in order to avoid the nagging feeling of reproach. At times, Jesus and his followers bring this judging moment of the Word and Spirit to full explicitness in the outer Word of their verbal preaching. Scripture and tradition are therefore full of judgments, warnings, and admonitions, urging people not to remain in a state of refusal.

The Spirit who is refused is felt as a judge, but this same Spirit brings the power of unconditional love, which always forgives and accepts, and thus, if the power of the Spirit is allowed to have its emotive effect, the hearer feels forgiven and accepted, liberated from all the sin and guilt that has accumulated because of past refusals.[17] This, too, is a more passive moment. It cannot occur without the hearer's willingness, but it is more a willingness to let something happen than to make something happen. And it can be an experience of extraordinary power. It was at the heart of Martin Luther's experience of God in Christ. As a young man in the late Middle Ages, he was very earnest in his religion. How hard he labored to live up to the demands to love God and neighbor, and to obey all the rules that specified how this love should be carried out! But all he could see was how much he was failing to live up to these demands. He experienced the Spirit of the Word more as judgment than acceptance. But then, partly in response to reading some key passages from the outer Word of Scripture, he experienced the Spirit as mercy and forgiveness. His sense of liberation was palpable. It became the defining experience of his life.[18] The great Protestant theologian Paul Tillich evokes a similar experience when he speaks in one of his sermons of the "acceptance of acceptance": the hearer simply accepts that God loves the hearer no matter what his or her prior failures.[19]

The two moments of feeling judged and then forgiven are more passive. Luther stressed the passivity of this moment so strongly that he denied the free participation of the will of the hearer. When he first felt the forgiving moment of God's love, Luther appears to have felt as much *over*powered as *em*powered. This is understandable in light of both his psychological development and the theology of divine power, for this moment is in fact more passive. More important, the response of feeling, whether in its more passive or active moments, is always evoked by the Spirit and therefore comes as a gift that the human person in sin feels is undeserved. The Spirit is not a power that the hearer first moves toward and then demands, but a power that the hearer reacts to and is drawn by.

And so Luther's stress on passivity was understandable, though as a Catholic I become a little uneasy when I see how he brought his experience of grace to theological expression.[20] Against classical Lutheranism, I tend to favor the Catholic, Orthodox, and Methodist traditions in insisting that, even in the passive moment of accepting acceptance, the human being is freely and actively participating.[21]

The third moment of feeling on the part of the hearer is more active. Feeling flows back toward the speaker of the Word, back toward the community, toward Jesus, but finally back to the ultimate source of Word and Spirit, God. The hearer is thus moved from feeling loved to feeling love in return.[22] It is the completion of the circle of feeling. This is the transformative moment of love. The hearer has been transformed from a more passive recipient of judging and forgiving love to a more active subject who feels love in return.

Hearers of the Word experience this third, more active moment as a feeling of joyful gratitude toward the God who initiated the vast movement of the world toward the point where humble beings like themselves can be loved. But in feeling love for God, they also feel love for all those others whom God loves, all beings, all life, but especially their fellow human beings, beginning with those who have brought them the Word and Spirit, namely, the risen Christ and his followers, and flowing out to include all their brothers and sisters in the human family. One of the marks of emotive response to the Spirit is an overflow of feeling toward cosmos and humanity. For the God to whom one returns love is the God whose core value is universal love.

The hearer of the Word must have the capacity and willingness to let the emotive power of the Spirit have its effect, in both the more passive and more active moments. The capacity to feel love in response to the self-communicative Spirit of God in Christ cannot be assumed as a given. Such a capacity can atrophy, virtually dry up, though I do not think it can disappear to the point that the person remains forever incapable of feeling loved or feeling loving.[23] But it is frightening to see how much this capacity to love can be diminished, often because of the vicious work of other human persons who in their inability and unwillingness to love, kill in those charged to their nurturing the ability to love. Long before some persons have any chance to make their own free and conscious choice about love, the unloving actions on them by others have had this terrible effect.

Yet we dare not absolve the individual of all responsibility. The response of feeling is a matter of not only capacity but also will.[24] To some extent, a particular feeling is under the control of will, even in its more passive moments. Indeed, so too is feeling in general, for continual choices against feeling love can lead to a diminished capacity for that feeling. Choices have a way of turning into habit. Habit is character, and character is the ongoing disposition or the capacity to feel and act in a certain way. The feeling of love for God and others can be avoided. We can develop the habit of fleeing the movement of the Spirit as it approaches us and knocks on the chambers of our hearts. Admittedly, this flight is difficult to sustain. The fundamental tendency of our human nature is toward feeling love toward God and all of God's creatures. The will has to work hard to deny the thrust of this tendency. To utter a radical no to this tendency is to reject not only God's Spirit but also our own better nature. Is uttering this radical no possible? To protect human freedom, I think we have to say it is, though of course we do not know if anyone has ever uttered a radical no to love and sustained it. But we dare not fall into sentimentality and underestimate the abysmal reach of our freedom.[25] The emotive flow of our love is partly a consequence of our free yes.

Directive Success: Love as Action

The Spirit of the Word is not only emotive but also directive: it urges action. The Spirit infuses the Word with an urgent insistence on doing, not just feeling. Jesus was nurtured by a religion that was very activistic. To say that we are saved by faith and not by works would have made no sense to the one who said: "Let your light shine before others, so that they may see your good works and give glory to your Father in heaven" (Matt. 5:16). We are saved, therefore, by the one whole complex response to God's self-communicative Word and Spirit, which means understanding, believing, trusting, feeling, and acting. Without that final step of action, salvation is not complete; the Word has not achieved full success.[26] The movement of God toward human beings in the Word and Spirit completes itself only in the movement of human beings back to God and out to others. From the human side, this movement is feeling that proves itself in action. It is beyond me how anyone can read the stories of Jesus' verbal and nonverbal words, which are actions expressive of his identity and mission, and not see the indispensable role of action in our saving response to the Word—and not just any action, but appropriate action, that is, authentic meanings expressive of the universal value of love.

Appropriate action from the hearer of the Word assumes a willingness and capacity. First, we as the human hearers must choose to act on our feeling of love for God and neighbor. In the New Testament, this love is called agapē.[27]As directed to the neighbor, it is directed to all human beings, for all in principle are our neighbors. Second, we must have the capacity to act appropriately, to choose the authentic meanings and know how to carry them out. This is a skill, a set of powers, a savoir faire that is acquired through long training. Learning the verbal and nonverbal language of love requires experience and practice. Fortunately, in the great ethical traditions of humankind, we have centuries of accumulated wisdom about how one acts appropriately. It is important to stress that all acts of love are self-communicative; the spiritual self that is constituted by inner meanings and values is not just expressed in these actions but communicated. Works of love are, therefore, always words that carry the self toward the other.

We show love to God in Christ through worship, which finally is nothing but communication from human beings, individually or collectively, to God. Worship begins, however, with a more fundamental action, or better an inaction, and that is the avoidance of idolatry, which is the worship of gods other than the one true God of Jesus Christ. Obedience to the First Commandment is therefore the presupposition to all genuine worship: "I am the Lord your God. . . . you shall have no other gods before me" (Exod. 20:2-3). We human beings have this insistent hunger, nay, craving, for God, but we are corrupted by others and are free to corrupt ourselves, and thus we continually yield to the temptation to settle on the wrong object of worship. Instead of loving and worshiping the unlimited and uncreated God, we love and worship an idol, something limited and created. Only God is absolute, but we make absolutes of things or persons that are not God and bow down before them. In creating idols, human beings have exhibited a wild and promiscuous imagination. We have made gods out of virtually anything or anyone or any cause: money, sex, political power, an ethnic group, a nation, a mountaintop, a golden calf, Madonna, Elvis, Hitler, a particular religious group, communism, fascism, the boyfriend or girlfriend inflated into perfection itself.[28] According to Paul Tillich, any one of these can and has become an object of "ultimate concern," the center of a person's whole life, the object of uncritical devotion.[29] But only God is absolute. Only God can receive the full discharge of religious feeling without manipulating it for selfish purposes, for God is unconditional love and wishes only our good.[30]

Letting God be God is, then, the first step to showing love for God in Christ. Then proper worship, which is prayer, can flourish. Prayer is regular communication with God through and with Christ, who draws us into his prayer. Prayer and worship are especially powerful in community, where prayer is fully ritualized, where the community both speaks God's love to us and we answer God through and with the community in prayer with and through Christ, our brother. But not all prayer is communal, though it lives off the community, often borrowing its ritualized words. In the past, some theologians of the spiritual life ranked prayers in order of importance. At the bottom were prayers of petition where one asked God for things. At the top were prayers of thanksgiving and gratitude, where one asked for nothing but simply expressed gratitude for all that God was already doing. Spiritual writers today shy away from such rankings.[31] After all, they say, Jesus made no such rankings. I must confess to a certain preference for the old ranking. It seems to me that the most important thing we ought to be requesting, God is already giving, namely, God's very own self in love, truth, and beauty. And most of the other things that we ask God for are either outside God's direct power (for example, a life free of disease, a sunny day) or are particular meanings that we are asked by God to carry out (for example, a more harmonious relationship with the natural environment, world peace). In theory, then, I prefer simple prayers of gratitude for the love that God is already offering us. In such prayer, we open up so that more love pours in, not because God rewards each such prayer with more love, but because in prayer we become more open. Yet in practice, I do not follow my own ranking. I send out very specific requests to God, without knowing precisely how such prayers work with God. After all, what could God do for someone that God is not already doing? But if God is already doing everything, should not my prayers be of gratitude and not petition? So then I start saying prayers of gratitude again. But within hours, I am once more sending off prayers of petition. About only one thing am I certain: we show love to God directly through prayer.

We cannot show love in action to God and not show love in action to those whom God loves, which is everyone. First, we show love to those who have spoken the Word as outer Word to us, namely, Jesus and his body, the church. Love means loving those Christians who have nurtured us in the Word and Spirit, and shaped our spiritual identities around the universal value of love. It may come as a surprise to the reader to know that many of the scriptural injunctions to love are urging Christians to love only fellow Christians. Indeed, in the writings attributed to John, that great theologian of love, this reached a form of communal introversion: in virtually all of those beautiful passages urging "love for one another," John means other Christians.[32]

But Christian love, agapē, is universal. All human beings, not just fellow Christians, are objects of love. This love is directed toward others in all three dimensions of their humanity: biological, psychological, and spiritual. It aims at the whole person. The spiritual enjoys a *primacy*, but the biological and psychological often enjoy *priority:* the bodily and psychic suffering of others makes an immediate claim on agapē that cannot be evaded with pious talk about spiritual needs. And the ultimate desire and hope of love is to evoke love, to see the other become loving toward others and God. For finally, love desires mutuality and community. Christian love, as unconditional, does not depend on mutuality for its continuance, but it nevertheless passionately desires it. This is God's desire as well. God desires friendship with us and among us. We can even imagine a divine sorrow and disappointment when this mutuality does not occur,[33] yet its occurrence does not condition the existence of God's love. God continues to love all and hope for a response from all even when this does not occur from and among human beings.

There is a difference, however, between God and us. God has the capacity for universal relationality.[34] If every human being were to respond to God's self-communication in Word and Spirit, God could sustain the extraordinary range and depth of the mutuality that would ensue. Human beings, by contrast, at least within the limits of this world, are restricted in the number of intense and deep relationships that they can sustain. This has led some to conclude that the Christian command to agapic love is totally unrealistic. How can we love everyone? How can we desire mutuality in every instance of agapic love? And when agapic love achieves full success and evokes a response in return, does it continue to be agapic love? Is married love still agapic love?

There is very little guidance in the New Testament on these questions, though it is clear that Jesus and his followers were well aware that while agapē is in principle universal, mutuality is limited. Jesus loved everyone but was not friends with everyone. Clearly, he enjoyed a mutuality with his friends Lazarus, Martha, Mary, and the beloved disciple that he could not enjoy with all those he brought under the rule of God's love. He also undoubtedly enjoyed a mutuality with some members of his immediate and extended family, and especially, with his mother.[35]

Agapic love in its universal and unconditional outreach to all human beings is purely agapic, but when it evokes genuine mutuality, then it begins to co-inhere with other loves: love between friends (in Greek, *philia*), love between romantic lovers (in Greek, *eros*) and love between family members (familial love).[36] These other loves are partly conditional; they are conditioned on certain attractive features of the other *(philia* and *eros)* or on biological or legal kinship ties (familial love), and above all they are conditioned on the capacity and willingness of the other to stay in that particular kind of love relationship. This does not mean that agapē is fully absorbed into these other loves. It co-inheres with them, initiating them, inspiring them, preventing them from degenerating into selfish interest, and giving them staying power when the other is struggling through a period when he or she is having difficulty responding.

Yet it is important to insist that although agapic love finds fulfillment in these mutual loves, agapic love remains distinct from these loves. Christians can become very confused on this point. Convinced rightly that agapic love is unconditional, they uncritically import this unconditionality into *philia* and *eros*. In my office, I have heard from students many a woeful story of unrequited or unsuccessful romantic love. At the end of her story, with heroic determination, she will say, "But I will always love him. It is the Christian thing to do." Well, no! Not if you mean by love, romantic love. Love him always in his basic humanity, yes. Wish him well; respect his freedom and autonomy; alleviate his suffering (unless you think that he will interpret it as yet another bid on your part for his romantic response), but it is masochism, not unconditional love, to hang on forever, desperate for a romantic mutuality that this fellow cannot or will not deliver. The same is true of friendship. Even familial love, which is perhaps the most unconditional of the various loves, has its limits. Sometimes, a parent or a child must pull back from the intensity of familial love simply to spare himself the misery of constant rejection. Not every member of the family wants to enter into the full mutuality of familial love. When a romance, friendship, or family relationship fails to blossom into complete mutuality, this does not mean that the Christian ceases loving that person. But the love becomes more purely agapic, more like the love that should be shown everyone.

How does one show agapic love to everyone? Must every human encounter be an occasion for a compassionate outpouring of agapic love? How, when many if not most encounters day to day are superficial and fleeting? And how about those whom we do not directly encounter? How do we love them? Can we love them? What kinds of authentic meanings are open to us in a world where sheer human limits, both physical (we cannot be everywhere at once) and psychological (surely, our emotional economy prohibits every encounter from being intensely agapic), limit in practice the reach of love? We cannot give the maximum to everyone, can we? If not, what then is the minimum that we owe everyone? When we raise these questions, we are anticipating the need for a translation of agapic love into its more feasible public form, which is justice. To illustrate the translation of Christian love into justice, with its twin forms of interpersonal justice and social justice, I shall in the next chapter revisit a famous New Testament parable.

Christian Faith and Non-Christians

When the Word evokes faith, the Word has informative success. When the Spirit evokes love, the Word has emotive and directive success. With faith, the mind is informed; with love, the heart is moved, and the will is activated. But we cannot neatly distinguish faith and love: they blur into each other. Nor can we smartly arrange them in chronological order. Faith does indeed precede love, yet love also precedes faith. Love not only precedes but crowns faith. No one has stressed the preeminence of love more eloquently than Paul: "If I have all faith, so as to remove mountains, but do not have love, I am nothing" (1 Cor. 13:2). "Faith, hope, and love abide, these three; and the greatest of these is love (13:13).

How important is informative success of the Word? How indispensable is faith as full and conscious understanding, belief, and trust? Theologians today have raised this question in the face of the widespread loss of faith among residents of the Christian world and as a reaction to the enormous number of people in the world who live outside the world of Christian faith. The Catholic theologian Karl Rahner thought long and hard on this question. In his answer, he starts from the assumption that God loves everyone and, therefore, is universally present to all human beings in the Word and Spirit. He looks around him and sees many persons living lives of selfless love and justice, but who interpret the meaning of their lives in atheistic or agnostic terms. They do not have full, explicit, conscious faith, but, says Rahner, God is affecting them on the levels of feeling and action. In a certain sense, they *are* being informed, the meaning of God's Word is getting through and shaping their lives in a certain direction, but they do not interpret the meaning with full and explicit understanding. Their faith, he would say, is "pre-thematic." And now, because the Word and Spirit have been fully invested in the risen Christ, these same people are being shaped and moved not by God alone, but by God in the risen Christ. They simply are not aware of it. They are, he says, "anonymous Christians."[37] The meaning of what is happening to them is not fully understood as a Christian meaning, but on the deeper levels of feeling and will the Word and Spirit of God in Christ are having success. And what is true for atheists and agnostics is true for devout practitioners of other religions: they will interpret their experiences with the explicit meanings of their religious tradition, and thus it will be the word of Mohammed or the spirit of the Buddha, but on the deepest level it is God acting through the risen Christ and *his* Word and Spirit.

Rahner's view is that of a Christian *inclusivist;* he believes that the Word and Spirit invested in Christ are poured out over all persons whether or not they have conscious faith in Christian meaning. Rahner of course prefers that a response on the level of feeling and action be accompanied by explicit, conscious Christian faith, but he does not require it in order for the person to be in positive relationship to the God who is communicating through Word and Spirit in Christ. His views are then to be distinguished from *exclusivists* on the one hand and *pluralists* on the other.

The Christian exclusivist insists that the only genuine response to the Word and Spirit of God in Christ is the one that occurs with full consciousness on the informative, emotive, and directive levels. It is not just a matter of such a response being better than a less than fully conscious response, but of being absolutely indispensable if a person is to be saved now and for eternity. For the exclusivist, the only way to come into saving relation with God is through conscious faith in Christ followed by baptism. That millions, if not billions, of people have never had the opportunity to come to such a faith is a mystery, perhaps a sorrowful mystery, but the exclusivist dares not question God or the teaching of Scripture that "no one comes to the Father except through me" (John 14:6).[38] We find exclusivists in other religions as well.

The Christian pluralist believes that ultimate reality, the really real, the sacred dimension, the mystery, whatever one may want to call it so long as one does not let the term be defined solely by Christian meaning, is accessible to all human beings. And each system of belief and practice is an equally valid way to enter into relationship with the ultimate.

Does this mean that all religious believers are experiencing the same ultimate reality and simply giving it a different name? Here, there is a division of opinion among the pluralists. One group, let us call them the *soft pluralists*, says yes, all are basically experiencing the same ultimate. These soft pluralists are saying that religious experience is to some degree generic and that despite different ways of describing this experience religious people, when they sit down to talk about their experiences, will intuitively recognize some basic similarities.[39] Another group, more radical in their pluralism, let us call them the *hard pluralists*, says no: not only the terms are different but the experience is different, radically so. Buddhist experience and theory cannot therefore be compared to Christian experience and theory. Christianity and Buddhism are two radically different worlds of religious meaning and experience. Hard pluralism necessarily entails these views: that the ultimate is itself plural,[40] or that the ultimate lies fully beyond human experience and understanding, or that there is no ultimate reality and, therefore, each religious system is a purely human construct enclosed upon itself.[41]

On the question of exclusivism, inclusivism, or pluralism, I have been torn between inclusivism and soft pluralism. The key issue is the role of the risen Christ. Have the Word and Spirit been fully invested in him so that he now is *the* universal mediator of God's meaning and power? Is Christ's mission now universal in scope? I cannot escape the conclusion that the logic of the Christian Scripture and tradition moves unmistakably toward a yes to these questions. Yet I shrink back from saying that those who respond to the meaning and power of God are de facto "in Christ," even if they do not interpret their experience in Christian terms. To say this may be more than just impolitic and condescending, it may be wrong. Are the meaning and power of God unsurpassingly understood in terms of the Word and Spirit of Christ? Is not the mystery of God larger than all our systems of meaning? Cannot one believe in Christ and yet exercise some modesty in the face of the cosmic mystery? Yet I cannot go over to a hard pluralism, which has each system of religious meaning strictly incomparable to any other. Pushed to an extreme, hard pluralism pushes one back toward exclusivism (only one of these systems can be true), or toward a plurality of ultimates, or to the view that each religion is closed in on itself, mediating no encounter with ultimate reality. But I believe that religious systems of meaning do get outside themselves and speak meaningfully of the ultimate, which in turn forms the basis for a dialogue that can lead to comparison and yes, even evaluation. I am assuming, then, that the ultimate is basically one (though perhaps more mysterious and multidimensional than I have yet imagined) and universally accessible. I freely admit that out of this dialogue may come a greater feeling on my part for the limitations of the Christian meaning.[42]

Nevertheless, I cannot be shaken from the meaning and value of love. To me, in some mysterious way, love and ultimate reality are convertible. I believe this because I have explicit, conscious faith in the Christian Word. Let me go back to Helen Keller. She became not only blind in infancy but deaf and mute. She was rescued by the discovery of language. Long before she could name water she had a sensuous experience of water. But what happened when she named it? Water came alive in a way never before experienced. Something happened to the experience when she was able to name it accurately. I cannot get away from believing that naming the ultimate reality with the language of unconditional self-communicating love truly speaks out of and to an authentic experience of the ultimate and that in Jesus this self-giving love achieves a definitive expression, and that knowing all this in explicit faith leads to a deepening of the experience of the ultimate. This conviction moves me back toward inclusivism. Yet at the same time I very much want to affirm all the religious tolerance, respect, humility, and nontriumphalism that are the strengths of plural-ism. Indeed, I applaud and expect believers from other traditions to speak with the same passionate conviction about their meanings as I have just spoken about mine. In a word, I feel at this point an unresolved tension between inclusivism and pluralism. For now I shall just have to live with it.

NINE

Love into Justice: The Good Samaritan Revisited

Most Christians would say that the foundation of social justice is love, especially love of neighbor, agapē. But how do we get from agapē to an active commitment to social justice? We do not answer this question well if we say simply that agapic love and social justice are the same thing. They are not. Yet I want to argue that work for social justice is a necessary expression of agapic love.

In the New Testament, the epitome of agapic love is the Good Samaritan. We do not ordinarily think of the Good Samaritan as practicing social justice. We see him as practicing compassion, performing an act of charity, carrying out a mission of mercy, not, surely, working for social justice. What the Good Samaritan did and what a social reformer like Martin Luther King Jr. did are clearly very different things.

But is social justice so sharply different from agapic love? In this chapter, I shall argue that there is indeed a distinction between agapic love and social justice, but it is a distinction within a unity.

Luke's Parable of the Good Samaritan

Here is the parable of the Good Samaritan as told in Luke's Gospel:

> Just then a lawyer stood up to test Jesus. "Teacher," he said, "what must I do to inherit eternal life?" He said to him, "What is written in the law? What do you read there?" He answered, "You shall love the Lord your God with all your heart, and with all your soul, and with all your strength, and with all your mind; and your neighbor as yourself." And he said to him, "You have given the right answer; do this, and you will live."

> But wanting to justify himself, he asked Jesus, "And who is my neighbor?" Jesus replied, "A man was going down from Jerusalem to Jericho, and fell into the hands of robbers, who stripped him, beat him, and went away, leaving him half dead. Now by chance a priest was going down the road; and when he saw him, he passed by on the other side. So likewise a Levite, when he came to the place and saw him, passed by on the other side. But a Samaritan while traveling came near him; and when he saw him, he was moved with pity. He went to him and bandaged his wounds, having poured oil and wine on them. Then he put him on his own animal, brought him to an inn, and took care of him. The next day he took out two denarii, gave them to the innkeeper, and said, "Take care of him; and when I come back, I will repay you whatever more you spend." (10:25-35)

Luke situates the parable of the Good Samaritan within what is known as the travel narrative (Luke 9:51—19:27) that follows Jesus' journey from Galilee to Jerusalem.[1] During the journey, Jesus frequently pauses to instruct his followers in the way of discipleship. The Good Samaritan parable is classified by Joachim Jeremias as a "parable of realized discipleship,"[2] though it is not a parable in the narrow or typical sense. Rather, it is an *example story,* not an extended metaphor or simile where the figures and events symbolize something else, as when the mustard seed symbolizes the reign of God (Matt. 13:31-32) or the generous vineyard owner (Matt. 20:1-16) symbolizes God's unconditional love.[3] The Good Samaritan parable does not refer beyond itself in this way. Jesus is not saying that God acts like the Good Samaritan but rather that *you* should act like the Good Samaritan.

The Good Samaritan story does, however, display other elements typical of a parable, most obviously the element of surprise. The surprise is not that the priest and the Levite (a temple official subordinate to the priests) pass by the injured man. Out in the countryside, "anticlericalism" was widespread among Jews. That Jesus would portray temple officials as morally callous would evoke a knowing murmur from his Jewish audience. His audience would then expect Jesus to finish off his story by having an Israelite layperson like themselves stop and do the right thing.[4] Instead, a Samaritan stops, and, "moved with pity," does the right thing. This is the major surprise to Jesus' Jewish audience. John Donahue reminds us: "Centuries of pious reflection have dulled our sensibilities to the hatred that existed between Jews and Samaritans." Jews regarded Samaritans not only as a mongrel people who had intermarried with pagan invaders, but as deserters of the Jewish religion.[5] That a Jew could love the Samaritan as a neighbor, and that a Samaritan could love the Jew as a neighbor, well, it's a scandal, it's out of the question. When the lawyer asked, "Who is my neighbor?" he was being serious. There was genuine debate among Jews at this time about who was included under the heading *neighbor*. According to Jeremias, "It was generally agreed that the term connoted fellow countrymen, including full proselytes."[6] It did not include Samaritans. Jesus defines *neighbor* to include the hated Samaritan, depicting the Samaritan as one who is a neighbor precisely by treating the injured Jew as a neighbor. This is a surprise. This is a shock.

In the parable of the Good Samaritan, Jesus offers an example of agapic love in action. Such love imitates the love shown by Jesus, and Jesus' love is in turn an imitation of God's love. Such is the nature of Jesus' radical moral demand on those called to the mission of bringing people into the reign of God. In the parable, apapic love shows the following qualities:

- *It is unconditional.* The Samaritan does not demand that the person injured fulfill any conditions before the Samaritan is willing to give help.

- *It is universal.* The Samaritan does not care to which gender, race, class, religion, or ethnic group the injured person belongs. A human being is hurt. This Samaritan would have reached out to any human being who was suffering.

- *It is unconcerned with merit or just deserts.* The Samaritan does not say to himself: This half-dead person in the ditch does not deserve my help because he had it coming. He did not take sufficient care to avoid the threat of robbery. The

Samaritan does not say to himself: There is probably some past sin in the victim's life. God through this violent assault and robbery is punishing him.

- *It is love moved by compassion.* The Samaritan is moved by feeling. Indeed, one can imagine him seized by feeling and impelled to the ditch beside the road.

- *It is a love that is spontaneous and uncalculating.* The Samaritan is moved to act quickly. He is not shown pondering the pros and cons. He is not shown engaging in subtle calculations about precisely what he should do. He spends no time in rational analysis.

- *It is a love that goes beyond the minimum one would expect of even the most decent person.* That is, it is supererogatory; it goes beyond what is asked. He does not just bandage the injured man's wounds and get him to the next town, but he stays with him, takes care of him, pays his lodging, and then— and here is the special touch—says to the innkeeper: "If it comes to more than this, I'll pay the difference on my way back." Here the Samaritan shows himself to be a virtuoso of the supererogatory.[7]

These qualities constitute agapic, that is, Christian, love in action, in the public sphere, among strangers, who through love become neighbors and friends.

Now, if the Christian moral life were simply a matter of letting oneself be moved to uncalculating love toward any human being in special need, we would have no need for lengthy books on Christian morality and justice. But the Christian moral life often requires us to go beyond spontaneous acts of agapic love. Morality then becomes more complex, and when it does, it begins to move from agapic love pure and simple to agapic love that expresses itself in the work of justice.

Love into Interpersonal Justice

The great U.S. theologian Reinhold Niebuhr said that Christian love becomes justice when there are three or more people in the room.[8] Expanding on the story of the Good Samaritan, let us imagine that the

Samaritan, instead of discovering one robbery victim in the ditch, discovers three. The Samaritan is moved by compassion to go over to the three victims, but as soon as he arrives, he finds himself having to step back from the situation and from his feeling in order to engage in some rational analysis and calculation. He finds himself engaged in what we today call triage. *Triage* is a system of principles and rules by which one judges how one can best treat victims like these, given one's resources. Whenever my family calls our health maintenance organization (HMO) after hours, we talk first to the triage nurse; using a complex system of principles and rules, she decides what the HMO can and should do for us given our ailments and given their resources.

Coming upon the three victims, the Good Samaritan must also practice triage. The principles and rules of triage he uses will be much less explicit and formalized than those of the HMO triage nurse; nevertheless, if he is to do justice to these three victims, he will have to turn his thoughtful attention to some principles and rules, however rudimentary they might be.

In practicing triage, the Samaritan does not completely turn from feeling to thought, but he does distance himself enough to allow a rational analysis of the situation. If he lets himself be ruled only by feeling, he might spontaneously attend first to the victim who is screaming and moaning the loudest, but to do so would be unjust. One of the first principles of triage is that one should attend first to the victim who is most seriously injured and then make a judgment about whether one has the resources to help him or her. With a cool head, the Samaritan turns his attention very self-consciously toward this principle and sets about putting it into practice. He first gathers empirical data about the condition of the victims. He discovers that the victim screaming the loudest is a teenage boy holding his ankle. A second victim is very quiet, not bleeding, but he has a weak pulse. A third victim is bleeding profusely from the neck. He decides to help her first, bandages her wounds, and stops the bleeding. On her, he decides to concentrate his maximum effort. He has acted justly.

Yet it would be unfair, it would be unjust, if he were to cease thinking about the other two. They, after all, are human beings, with their inherent dignity and worth. He cannot give them his maximum effort in this situation, but he feels bound to give them at least a minimum of attention. But what precisely is the minimum he owes them in this situation? The answer requires another calculation on his part. Observing the boy holding his ankle, the Samaritan decides that the injury is not that serious, and he limits himself to wrapping the ankle and uttering words of comfort. And he double-checks the person with the weak pulse to make sure that he is still alive.

At this point, the Samaritan is now expressing his love in the form of justice, and specifically, *interpersonal justice*. Interpersonal justice is practiced by one individual to another in a situation in which the person practicing the justice has to distance himself somewhat from his feelings, consult a set of principles and rules, gather data about this situation, and make a rational decision about what should be done. Interpersonal justice requires attention to the questions of what is equal treatment, what is fair treatment, what is the minimum one owes each individual who is present, and what is the maximum one can offer, given one's resources. This kind of analysis tells the Samaritan that it would be wrong, it would violate the principles of interpersonal justice, if he were to spend himself totally in selfless and supererogatory love on only one of the victims that now confront him. He must therefore carefully and rationally distribute his efforts in an equal yet fair manner, giving the most he can give to one without at the same time totally neglecting the others.

Interpersonal justice is practiced not only in the kind of extraordinary situation in which the Samaritan finds himself. It is, in fact, the stuff of ordinary daily life, in a way that heedless agapic love can never be. Every day, we have many encounters with our fellow human beings. Not every encounter is, or should be, an occasion for agapic love in the pure form. Rather, we should treat those individuals we encounter every day with a simple, interpersonal justice, with a basic respect for their worth, dignity, and autonomy.[9] There is a minimum that we owe everyone. Some might require more than the minimum from us. We must weigh matters and decide what we can give. Knowing how this is done takes much training and learning. Some people take to this very well and show an acute ethical intelligence.

Let us return to our story. The Samaritan has bound the wounds of the woman bleeding, attended to the man with the weak pulse, and calmed the boy with the injured ankle. Somehow, after making a whole series of further decisions, all accompanied by considerable rational analysis, he gets them to the nearest town and arranges for their care, though, this time, a check of his financial resources precludes an offer to pay the innkeeper and the local physician. He has done justice to these people.

But the whole experience has left him angry. For the fourth time this month, he has encountered victims of brutal robberies left to die in the ditch. What would have happened to these poor people had he not happened along? The Samaritan thinks on the many others who were passed by and left to suffer and die. This tragic situation is more than he as an individual can manage. He is moved to conclude that one-to-one agapic love and interpersonal justice are not enough. He decides to move into social justice.

Love into Social Justice

The Good Samaritan decides to involve the larger community and attempt a more systematic solution to this terrible problem of assault and robbery.[10] He decides thereby to make the move from interpersonal justice to the work of *social justice*. Social justice is justice practiced by a group or community toward individuals or other groups or communities. It is a social endeavor, which involves the creation of social structures.

Social structures have two elements: the mental and the institutional. The *mental* element is concerned with the consciousness, the mind, the attitude, the ethos of the community. It is obvious to the Samaritan that many people are passing by these victims in the ditch and not doing anything to help. There is a deeply faulty ethos in these parts, he says to himself. People around here are indifferent to this kind of human misery.

The Good Samaritan resolves to change the ethos, to raise consciousness, to change the mentality. On his next trip down this road, he stops at each village and gives a little talk to the villagers, alerting them to the suffering of the victims of these robberies and urging them not to pass by the victims. He talks about the basic dignity and equality of all human beings. All human beings, he insists, have a claim on our love and justice, especially those who are suffering. He even includes in his talk a rudimentary introduction to triage. In his efforts to create a new social mentality, the Samaritan enjoys some success. People become more sensitized. More people than before are reaching out with agapic love and interpersonal justice.

In one village, this new consciousness becomes so pervasive that helping robbery victims becomes what sociologists call an *institution,* that is, an established pattern of behavior, which is the second element of a social structure.[11] Helping victims is something that villagers practice without hesitation. The institution in this case is a *custom,* a pattern of behavior that establishes itself spontaneously and lacks formal organization.

Nevertheless, this proves to be not enough. There are still many victims, and many people are passing them by. The ethos of reaching out to help is indeed deeper and more widespread, but it is far from pervasive. Human beings, after all, are free to defy ethos and custom and are especially prone to do so when they are asked to go outside themselves for someone else's sake. And so the Samaritan decides to move beyond custom and create a more formal institution.

He decides to create an institution in which groups of volunteers will patrol the road in shifts in search of victims.[12] To ensure that these volunteers will be skilled in applying triage, he arranges for training sessions. He rents several buildings in the villages in which to hold these sessions. Since those who conduct the sessions will be engaged in virtually full-time work, he decides to pay them. Realizing that he does not have enough money for rent and salaries, he sets out to raise money, trusting that the ethos he created earlier is wide and deep enough to produce people willing to contribute. He organizes a fund drive, to occur on a regular basis. His institution comes thereby to depend on both the willingness of people to volunteer their time to work on the patrols and their willingness to contribute money on a regular basis. And since the contributions of time and money depend on the continued vitality of the ethos, the Samaritan must continue to give talks to raise ethical consciousness; that is, he must continue to be concerned with the element of mentality.

The Samaritan has thus created not only a new mentality but also new institutions. And many robbery victims are helped. Yet many victims continue to die in the ditch unhelped. The crime rate is up. Also, there are difficulties with the Samaritan's institutional structure. The patrols are staffed largely by unpaid volunteers, who are free to cease volunteering, and quite regularly one or more will suddenly and unpredictably pull out. On nights before holidays, the most dangerous nights, whole patrols have to be canceled for lack of volunteers.

Funding is a continuing problem. The regional economy fluctuates wildly and along with that, financial contributions fluctuate wildly. The Samaritan sometimes has the funds to do the training, sometimes not. A fickleness and unpredictability pervade the institution, making for a fickle and unpredictable service to the victims along the road. One of the principles of justice is universality of coverage: all persons will receive the minimum due them. This institution is failing to provide that coverage, which causes acute pangs of conscience in the Samaritan. The pity or compassion that moved him to that first act of agapic love has now moved him toward the work of justice that aims to reach all those suffering, but he is not reaching them all in any consistent way.

For a while, the Samaritan considers going to what we now call the free market approach. In order to guarantee more predictable and reliable staff, he could staff the patrols with paid professionals. To pay for them, he could market their services by charging the victims—with some provision for their ability to pay—or by selling their services to villages along the road or to groups of travelers. To raise the initial capital outlay for this service, he could sell shares to the enterprise and then pay the shareholders out of the profits.

But he decides against going into the market. He is not opposed to the market as such. He is in fact a businessperson and believes firmly that some goods and services are best delivered to people through the market. But he has come to believe that a robbery victim in the ditch has not just a *need* for help but also a *right* to help. A right means that the victim has an absolute claim on the community for a consistent, predictable, and skilled response to his or her suffering. The free market approach introduces the profit motive and, with that, the inevitable tendency to provide the best service to those who have the most money to pay for it. But this is the kind of service that every human being has a right to, irrespective of wealth or social position.

So the Samaritan chooses another step, namely, he decides to go to the state, to the institutions of government. This road is in a province under the jurisdiction of Rome. He decides to go to the Roman governor and ask that a new social structure be created. While talking with the governor and his aides, he learns that the problems occurring along this road are occurring on roads throughout the province. The governor is responsive. He petitions Rome for permission to create a new structure and collect a tax to pay for it. The Roman senate passes a law; the emperor approves it; and the governor's bureaucrats work out detailed policies, that is, principles and rules, to guide the new institution in its service. Paid governmental patrols are put in place along the roads. They deliver medical help more quickly and predictably and thus provide coverage that approaches universal. Because the government owns the means of legalized violence, it equips the patrols with the physical means to pursue, subdue, and arrest the violent robbers who are causing so much human suffering.[13] And since the taxes are set and levied by law, funding is more predictable year to year.

The Good Samaritan is quite satisfied with his work. He has moved from agapic love to interpersonal justice, and finally, to social justice. To be sure, he has not ceased practicing agapic love—indeed, just the other night, an opportunity again presented itself, and he reached out to help a victim—but he has spent most of his time these past several years on the long march through social structures.

Despite his general satisfaction, the Samaritan has frequently found the work of social justice tedious and boring. Giving ethical pep talks, finding buildings to rent, training volunteers, writing up detailed policy suggestions for the governor—more than once during all this, he has felt a slackening in his original agapic motivation. Indeed, there have been moments when he has become wistful for the spontaneous purity of that original act of agapic love. He recalls the deep joy and peace he felt after he had paid the innkeeper, knowing that he had done the right thing.

In addition, he is no naive reformer. He has seen the negative side of this movement from agapic love to social justice. He worries, for example, about the impersonality of the new government structure. He has talked with some members of the patrols and found that quite a few are not motivated by the desire to help their neighbors but by the desire to advance their careers. Some government administrators appear less interested in providing a good service than in protecting their turf and increasing their budgets. He worries that with the movement to a government structure, the community ethos will decline. There is already much grumbling about the new taxes. Taxes, after all, are coercive. They are extracted by law and backed by the organized violence of the state. The other day, he heard someone say, "They're confiscating my hard-earned money to pay for these patrols—I never even take those roads. It's not fair!" He fears that giving this work of social justice over to the state will diminish the motivating energy of agapic love to the point where individuals will pass by victims in the ditch with the excuse that a patrol will take care of the problem for them. He has even heard rumors that some patrols are abusing their power and using their instruments of violence not to protect the victims but to blackmail them. Social justice, when it is carried out by the structures of government, has its dark side.

But all in all, despite these concerns, the Samaritan remains cautiously proud of his work. He is convinced that this new social structure has reduced the total amount of human suffering. Social justice has accomplished more than his individual acts of agapic love ever could.

As we watch the Samaritan move from agapic love to social justice from our perspective in the twenty-first century, we notice something missing from his vision and practice. At no time does the Samaritan engage in an in-depth social, political, and economic analysis of his society. He does not ask himself why there are so many robberies. He does not link the rise in the crime rate with the high concentration of wealth in the hands of a few large absentee landowners. He fails to bring into view the many tenant farmers who live in virtual slavery.[14] Many are so poor that they are drawn to lives of crime. As he journeys to see the governor, he does not wonder if perhaps his work of social justice would not be more effective if this region were not under imperial rule and if Jews and Samaritans were independent peoples with grassroots, egalitarian political structures more immediately responsive to crime and its victims. This kind of analysis might very well have led the Samaritan to a vision of radical and sweeping change in the social, economic, and political structures of his day. But this kind of analysis, and the political vision that often goes with it, is a relatively recent development in the history of ethical intelligence.

Jesus did not undertake this kind of analysis,[15] nor did the early church. And the Catholic Church was indifferent, sometimes even hostile, to this kind of analysis until late in the nineteenth century. In our day, however, virtually all Christians engaged in the work of social justice are aware of the need for complex social analysis.

I hope that my revisit of the Good Samaritan story has shown that the distinctions among agapic love, interpersonal justice, and social justice are real, but not hard and fast. Agapic love, Christian love, is not replaced by interpersonal and social justice, but continues to accompany both as their motivational fount, energizing both,[16] preventing each from becoming impersonal and bloodless. Justice has been described as the public expression of love, a definition that strikes me as particularly apt. The movement from agapic love to social justice is continuous and necessary. Any theology that draws too sharp a separation between love and justice, that sees them as belonging to utterly different spheres, or that sees them in opposition is a deeply flawed theology.

Just as there is a natural movement from agapic love to social justice, so too is there a natural movement from social justice to agapic love. Even the most intense, one-to-one expression of agapic love does not occur in a social vacuum. Social structures—mentality, ethos, custom, laws, institutions—all preshape even the most private actions. The Good Samaritan, after all, is a member of a schismatic Jewish sect whose members followed the Torah, the Jewish law found in the first five books of the Hebrew Bible. The heart of this law is the twofold commandment to love God and love your neighbor as yourself. This twofold law was part of the Samaritan ethos and passed on to the Good Samaritan through the institutions of religious learning and instruction. The religious and ethical logic of the twofold law led him to oppose a mentality that would forbid him to help an injured Jew. And, therefore, his spontaneous act of agapic love as told in Jesus' story did not arise solely out of his own spontaneity, it was not utterly his own, sui generis, but in part the consequence of a social structure. Indeed, the very spontaneity of his action is partly a sign of how thoroughly he was socialized by the redemptive elements of this structure.[17] And we must not forget that the parable of the Good Samaritan was told by Jesus, who was raised a Jew and was taught the same twofold law of love.

We must, therefore, be wary of drawing overprecise distinctions among agapic love, interpersonal justice, and social justice. The distinctions are real, but within an unfolding unity. In his story of the Good Samaritan, Jesus beautifully captured the first and decisive moment of agapic love. Yet we can well imagine that the logic of love carried the Good Samaritan, as it should carry us, into the work of justice.

But with all this talk of social justice we dare not forget that the direction of agapic love is not only out into the public sphere of social structures.[18] There is the other direction, toward the intimacy of full mutuality, toward friendship, romantic love, and family. What is the final purpose of just social structures if not a world where mutuality can flourish? It is mutuality with God and mutuality with others. The full terror of a corrupt social structure is the way its destructive power makes even the intimacy of mutuality impossible. Agapic love achieves public expression in justice but finds fulfillment in mutual self-giving.[19]

TEN

The Human Response of Hope

Throughout this book, I have referred to three functions of human words: informative, emotive, and directive. These three functions come together in deeply personal words, which are the words of human self-communication. By analogy, they come together in the Word of God's self-communication in the power of the Spirit. But there is another function of words that often accompanies words of self-communication, and that is the promissory function.

We are talking here about the function of promise. When a person promises, she commits herself to the future in one of the following three ways: first, to continue a state of affairs into the future ("I promise to continue making the payments"); second, to discontinue a state of affairs in the future ("Beginning tomorrow, I promise to stop calling you so early in the morning"); or third, to create a new state of affairs in the future ("I will make the first payment tomorrow").[1] When the speaker makes a promise, she intends to evoke confident hope in the hearer. The speaker wants the hearer to trust her and to believe that she will be able and willing to carry out her promise. Trust, of course, cannot be forced on the hearer. The hearer must take himself through the steps to trust, similar to the steps he went through to arrive at informative success, and free choice is one of those steps. Moreover, it is up to the hearer to judge whether or not the speaker will be able and willing to make good on her promise.

170

In the case of a deeply personal word of love, the lover promises to continue a state of affairs into the future. The lover feels and wills a movement of her deepest self out toward the deepest self of the beloved. This is the state of affairs she promises to continue. Let us take a closer look.

Self-Communication and the
Promissory Function

The language of self-communication is the language of love. Love is animated by the speaker's desire for a response. When a speaker utters the words I love you, she infuses them with emotive and directive power, a power that receives much of its urgency from the speaker's desire that the hearer will respond with the appropriate feeling and action. The speaker may feel this love with such power that she is moved to give her whole future over to the one she loves.[2] Thus, she says, "I love you—and always will." She says that the love she feels now will continue into the future. She has made a promise and hopes to arouse in the beloved hearer the confident hope that she will continue to love into the future. In other words, she as the lover not only desires a response of love from the beloved, but also hopes to arouse the beloved to hope.

Before the hearer can respond with confident hope, he must go through the same steps required for informative success of the word, namely, understanding, belief, and trust. The hearer must understand the words of love, must believe in general that such love can endure into the future, and above all must trust that the speaker is not lying (does the speaker truly intend to carry out this promise to love?) or deceiving herself (has the speaker deceived herself into thinking that she has the capacity and willingness to carry this love into the future?).

But other elements must enter into the hearer's response if he is to have confident and well-founded hope. In promising to love the hearer into the future, the speaker has promised to carry out a particular meaning. But as we saw in chapter 1, not every particular meaning chosen by someone is possible. Everyone is limited by his or her internal and external situation. In chapter 1, I spoke of my desire to spend a year in a French-speaking country, but my external situation of modest salary prevents me from carrying out this meaning, and therefore I cannot promise myself or anyone else that I will soon carry it out. One of my student advisees promises me, "I am going to get straight A's next term." I try not to discourage her, but I know her internal situation quite well. She has intelligence but lacks drive and discipline. Consequently, she fails to evoke confident hope in me. In fact, I am feeling more despair than hope because, once again, as in past semesters, she has promised a meaning that she cannot deliver!

If the hearer is to have confident hope in the speaker's promise to love him into the future, he needs to know her internal situation. He needs to know the quality and intensity of her love for him, but he knows this only if he feels her feeling. Is her feeling of love charged with power and energy? Does her feeling run strong and deep? In order to judge this, he must allow her feeling to come into him enough so that he can feel it. She must, therefore, have emotive success with him, at least to the extent of evoking in him a feeling of her feeling. We see here the close link between emotive success and promissory success: to convince him of her promise, she must convince him of her love, a love he must feel.

He must also feel and evaluate the constancy of her will. Feeling is not a surge that overpowers the person who is feeling. In the earlier stages of love, the sense of being overpowered by feeling is indeed strong, but persons experienced in the ways of love know that feelings need the focus of will. A person who relies only on the rush of feeling will fall out of love, sometimes with alarming quickness. And constancy of will is expressed and reinforced by action. The lover does not every second feel in love, but if she has a constant will, she focuses her will and carries out loving actions, verbal and nonverbal. Thus, the hearer, in order to judge whether to surrender in confident hope to the speaker, must not only feel her feelings but observe her actions. We see how closely linked the decision to hope is to the decision to trust. Both trust and hope require the hearer to attend to the speaker's feeling and action. We could indeed argue that confident hope in someone's promise is nothing but trust extended to the future.[3] Hope, then, is the twin to trust, and both together form a bridge between the cognitive (understanding and belief) and the affective-volitional (feeling and acting) aspects of the spiritual self.

Hope can never be compelled. The hearer is free to abort the process of understanding, belief, trust, feeling, and evaluation that leads to hope. Freedom plays a particularly strong role in hope because hope refers to a future reality that is not yet there.[4] Hope is directed toward things unseen and is therefore free and risky. This is doubly true when the things unseen exist in the ultimate dimension, beyond the limits of the penultimate world. About such things, we can have confident hope but never absolute certainty.

God's Word of self-communication is a promissory word that intends to arouse not only faith and love in the human hearer, but also confident hope. God through Christ communicates love to humankind and promises to continue communicating love in the future. God will not revoke this Word. God will not turn God's face from us. God's love is therefore unconditional with respect to both present and future. Nothing we are doing now in the present or later in the future can condition God's love for us: it abides and will abide no matter what we do from our side. This is God's promise, and if it has promissory success in us, we will have a fully confident hope in the future of that love.

God's promise for the future is pledged in the resurrection of Jesus. We are mistaken if we understand the resurrection as an event solely between God and the crucified Jesus. The resurrection also establishes an ongoing event between God and us, because in the resurrection God has established Jesus forever in his identity and mission. In the risen Christ, we have God's pledge that the divine self-communication in the Word and Spirit will continue through Christ. Not only that, God promises by the resurrection that God's love for human beings will continue beyond death. If in death we are in relationship with God, we shall share in Christ's resurrection and, like Christ, will share in his eternal relationship with God. Not even death will break our loving relationship with God.[5]

Individual Penultimate Hope

We have hope for ourselves as individuals in this penultimate world. We hope to find our meanings, and we hope to experience the joy that comes with meanings found and meanings carried out. We hope for meanings that are compatible with universal values. But we are restless beings, always on the move. Because the meanings we have found and fulfill do not exhaust our hope for meaning, we are always stretching out beyond the meanings fulfilled toward meanings that are not yet fulfilled. We are always in tension toward a future, and therefore the tendency toward meaning, which is at the core of who we are, is intrinsically linked to hope, which connects us toward the promised future.[6]

When the hope for meaning focuses on a particular meaning, hope in the general sense becomes a particular hope. A particular hope charged with the urgency for its fulfillment is a *desire*. We desire to carry out this particular meaning, and we desire the joy that comes with carrying out this meaning.[7]

Are not desires selfish? Not if we desire an authentic meaning. A desire for an authentic meaning is a desire for a universal value. It is the desire to give the self over to larger purposes. Furthermore, carrying out an authentic meaning requires attention, discipline, and skill. It usually extracts a measure of pain and suffering proportionate to the nobility and size of the meaning. Our desire, then, must focus on the meaning to be achieved and the universal value to be expressed, and not on the joy that will come with the meaning achieved. Meanings in the service of truth, love, and beauty require a selfless immersion in the meaning. Our desire for joy thus must not be the focus, precisely for the sake of dedicated attention to the meaning itself. This is particularly true when our meaning is in the service of the value of love. Love cannot flourish if we are preoccupied with what we shall receive in return. Such preoccupation converts the desire for response into a compulsive need, into an obsessive alertness for signals from the other, and finally into the refusal to make the first move, to take the plunge, unless first convinced that our desire for response will be satisfied.[8] At this point, our legitimate desire for a response, and for the joy such a response will bring, begins to be transformed into narcissistic self-absorption, which of course prevents true self-giving. As a result, the desire for response has overwhelmed the meaning and made it impossible.

Even eros, romantic love, works best if it is motivated by an initial rush of selfless generosity toward, and focus on, the other. In a word, romantic love needs the infusion of agapic love. This does not mean that in loving someone we are prohibited from having a lively desire that the person we love respond in kind. All love is animated by the desire for mutuality.[9] But we must not let this desire for mutuality eclipse the moment of agapic heedlessness.

Penultimate hope is more likely to be fulfilled if it is realistic. Belief in God's existence and love can be an enormous help in making hope realistic. This is particularly true with respect to the meaning and value of love. The human appetite for love is infinite because it aims ultimately to be in love with God. We wish to love perfectly and to be loved perfectly. And if we have faith in a God in whom love receives its universal anchorage, then we wish to see all our loves as an expression of God's love; indeed, when we love others, we are carrying out the mission of God's agents of love in the world. In loving, we are therefore involved with God, the absolute. This is all well and good, but it can lead to problems when the person loved is a limited human being. We have this fatal tendency to ask the limited other to satisfy our hunger for the absolute. When injected into penultimate hope, this absolutizing energy, which finds rest only in the true absolute that is God, can inflate the objects of our hope and desire to unmanageable proportions, turning them into idols. Instead of desiring this person as a friend, we desire that this person be the perfect friend.

Instead of desiring this woman as lover and mate, we desire that she be the perfect woman. Unless we live in a dream world where no reality is allowed to intrude, these absolutized hopes are inevitably dashed, and we are not only disappointed but also devastated. The more we have absolutized the finite object of hope and desire, the steeper we fall. Sometimes the disenchantment at seeing our idol reveal itself as fallible and limited turns us from creator of the idol to its destroyer, and we strike out in a frenzy of grief-stricken anger.

The absolutization of penultimate hope is the destroyer of penultimate hope. There is only one perfect lover, and that is God. Only in God does our hunger for the absolute find satisfaction.[10] A love relationship with God liberates us to turn toward others and invest in them a realistic hope, unburdening them of idolatrous inflation. This same realistic hope unburdens other penultimate meanings as well—those meanings that express not the value of love but the values of truth and beauty. A research project is a meaning that participates in the universal value of truth and is an excellent thing, but beware of researchers who transform such a project into the absolute project. Their fanatical energy makes them persons to be feared. Artists who absolutize their work in the pursuit of beauty can become monstrous creatures. Instead of serving God, they begin to fancy themselves gods, and their latest creation ceases to be a participation in divine meaning and power, but the primordial instance thereof. The penultimate hopes of art and science, wonderful as they are, cannot bear the weight of such absolutizing energy. Only in God do we find the perfect fulfillment of truth, beauty, and love.

Individual Ultimate Hope for Resurrection of the Body

Human hope is directed not only toward the penultimate future but toward the ultimate future, beyond death.[11] Christian hope is for resurrection with Christ and thus for an eternal life of truth, love, and beauty.[12] The usual teaching of the New Testament, following Jewish belief, is that our ultimate hope is for the resurrection of the body rather than the immortality of the soul, the eschatological symbol generally favored by the Greek philosophical tradition.[13] It is true that the Christian tradition has believed that those who die after Jesus' bodily resurrection and before the universal bodily resurrection at the end of time exist as souls separated from the body. But this same tradition has always affirmed that after this interim or intermediate state, the ultimate state of the individual is not that of an immortal soul but a resurrected body. Indeed, many contemporary theologians, in reaction against the mind-body dualism of Greek thought, favor a return to the holism of Jewish thought and urge therefore an eschatology that sees the resurrection as occurring immediately after the individual's death.[14] These theologians are inclined to believe that the soul is never separated from the body, even during the interim state.

The body resurrected is not to be taken as if the literal flesh and bones of our bodies were to be resurrected. That view of the resurrection is called the physicalist view and was common in the earlier centuries of the church, forming the theological background to the long-standing opposition to cremation.[15] Physicalism has been abandoned by mainstream Christianity; nevertheless, theologians continue to use the term *body* in reference to the next life. How can we make sense of this? I think the best way to answer this question is to examine the purposes of our bodies in this life and then by analogy apply what we have learned to the next life. These purposes are the following two.

First, our bodies root the human spirit in the material cosmos. Our bodies are made of bits of inorganic matter that originally shot through space after the initial big bang, the cosmic explosion that marked the beginning of the universe. These bits eventually struck the earth and became part of the nourishing substrate of all life. This life evolved toward greater complexity until it produced the most complex constellation of organic matter, the human brain, which is the organic presupposition for human psyche and spirit. We are then the culmination of a long inorganic and organic evolution to which we are forever linked through our bodies. We continue to be dependent on the cosmos for our very survival. To be sure, as spirit, we transcend the material world to some degree and can therefore stand back from it and make it an object of human knowledge and action, yet we remain profoundly linked in ways that contemporary ecological science is only beginning to grasp fully.[16] Resurrection of the body should therefore resonate in those whose ecological sensitivities have been sharpened, for it says that the promise of resurrection includes a continued connection between us and the material world. The bond between us and the cosmos out of which we emerged is forever.

Second, our bodies link us with other human beings. It is through the communication and reception of the outer word that our identities are constituted and sustained. All relationships with others are continuously dependent on the body as the vehicle of the word. Without the body, there is no sociality. The resurrection of the body means, therefore, the continuance of our connection with other human beings. Our risen bodies will continue the function of communicating ourselves with others. But our hope for a risen body as our vehicle of self-communication conflicts with the long-standing belief, well-founded in Scripture and tradition, that the body of the risen Jesus has burst the limits of space and time. But we conceive of the body as a vehicle of self-communication only if that body is located in a space and time producing outer words. How could the body lose its space-time coordinates and still be a principle of communication? The theologian Karl Rahner tries to solve the problem by imagining that in the risen state the individual human spirit enters into a deep connection with the whole material cosmos.[17] The whole cosmos becomes our body. But how could the whole cosmos be a vehicle of self-communication if it were our common possession? How would we distinguish my body from yours?[18] Perhaps the risen body is a mysterious combination of boundedness and openness that would allow it to be at once individual and cosmic. But how is this possible? Frankly, I am stumped. It may be best to keep it simple and leave it at that: in the risen life, we shall continue through our bodies to be in self-communicative relationship with one another and with the material cosmos. Therefore, the whole self—biological, psychological, spiritual—will be transformed in unity with the physical world. To say more is to go beyond the limits of the eschatological imagination, which leads me to the next point.

When thinking about the next life, we should continually keep in tense union the categories of continuity and discontinuity. If we give too much emphasis to continuity between the penultimate and ultimate, then the latter becomes a simple extrapolation of the former. Heaven then is merely more of this life, without the pain, irritation, and suffering. Not long ago, a member of a religious group came to my front door with a leaflet illustrating the next life. The pictures made heaven look just like Edina, a wealthy suburb of Minneapolis. It struck me as a comical extrapolation. On the other hand, if we give too much stress to discontinuity, we risk seeing the ultimate as an absolute break with the penultimate. The result would be complete silence about the risen life, for no language, however symbolic or metaphoric, could even begin to point us in the direction of the ultimate content if the discontinuity between penultimate and ultimate were absolute. At the very least, it would seem to me, there must be enough continuity to assure that in the next life we have a memory of this life, for memory is one of the requirements of continued self-identity. If there is enough continuity to assure memory, then the discontinuity is not absolute. Furthermore, if we take seriously the symbol of the risen body, I should think we can expect some continuity of gender identity and other individualizing attributes.[19]

I am, however, more inclined to reticence than verbosity about the exact shape of the next life. If one is going to err in this balancing act between continuity and discontinuity, I would therefore recommend erring toward discontinuity. We must, it appears to me, be prepared for a big surprise. We should therefore resist the temptation to be precise about the furnishings of heaven. It is perfectly legitimate to desire to live with God in the next life and to share in Christ's resurrection because such a desire is fueled by the love and promise of God, but the content of that life remains largely beyond our ken. "What no eye has seen, nor ear heard, nor the human heart conceived, what God has prepared for those who love him" (1 Cor. 2:9).

Ultimate Consequences of Human Choice: Heaven, Hell, Purgatory

God's love is offered unconditionally to all human beings. This love is persuasive, not coercive. Human beings are free to say yes or no to it. Our choice of yes or no has ultimate consequences. Heaven is that eschatological symbol that points to the ultimate consequence of our saying yes to relationship with God, others, and cosmos. Heaven is the resurrection of the body, with the body as the principle of union with others and the material world. As such, heaven is the consummation of the universal value of love, though this does not exclude the values of truth and beauty, neither of which is absorbed by love but rather preserves its distinctiveness within a unity cemented by the value of love.

Simply because the participation of human freedom is required to reach heaven does not mean that heaven is solely our achievement. Heaven begins as God's gift because it is motivated and effected persuasively by God's Word and Spirit. Human beings cannot demand this gift from God without its ceasing to be a gift. Yet the divine gift does not override human freedom but inspires it, and thus our share in the risen life is also our achievement, understood as our yes in response to the initiating divine yes. Heaven then is really the natural consequence of a yes that we begin to say here in the penultimate world. Indeed, in our yes, we begin to live our heaven here insofar as we choose meanings that deepen love, expand truth, and create beauty.

Hell, by contrast, is the ultimate consequence of a radical no to God's offer of love.[20] Hell is the utter refusal to enter into relationship with God and others, the no to God's unconditional yes. In the past, hell has been conceived as a person's no to the divine yes that elicits, in turn, a divine no if the person persists in his or her no through death. In this view, human beings not only send themselves to hell with their absolute refusal, but God, at their death, exercises divine "wrath" and "sends them to everlasting hell." Both the human no and the divine no are then eternalized at death. God and the person then stand in an eternal relation of mutual hatred and hostility. But clearly, then, God's love is not unconditional, for it cannot survive the condition of a person's saying no up through death. God ceases loving those who are in hell. This makes God's love conditional. But God's love is unconditional. Something is wrong here.

I was raised in the Roman Catholic Church and still find in it my spiritual and theological home. As a boy, I became confused and frightened by the eschatological symbol of hell. I swallowed whole the idea that God's love had turned to enmity toward those who in their radical refusal were now in hell (and even though I was taught not to assume that any one particular person was in hell, it was a widespread assumption that there were millions). I thus had a lively fear that if at death I should be caught in what the catechism called a state of mortal sin, outside the state of grace, I would be cast into the pit by a God without mercy. Combined with my Catholic conviction that it was quite easy for me to commit a mortal sin, hell became a preoccupation that drove me to weekly visits to the confessional box. I worried a lot as a young boy that I might be killed on my way to confession. Obviously, I believed that in my sin I had said a no to God that caused God to say a no to me and that God's no would have eternal validity if I died before I could undo it with confession. God's love for me was shot through with conditionality.

Young Catholics are no longer taught this way. Most theologians today within Catholicism and other mainstream Christian groups would say that God's love is absolutely unconditional and that therefore God never ceases to say yes to human beings, even those who at death are in a state of radical refusal of that love. God loves all human beings, including those whose refusal has put them in a state of total estrangement from God and others.[21] They are estranged from God, but God is not estranged from them. Indeed, their no to God has no meaning unless it is a no to God's continuing yes.

But this deeply consoling view raises new questions. My students, whose interest in eschatological questions is unexpectedly lively and persistent, invariably ask, "Can anyone say a radical no to God's love? How can anyone refuse all offers of love?" My own view is that a human can, though such a no is enormously difficult to sustain; in addition, I do not know if anyone has ever said such a no and sustained it through death.

Yet I think we should insist on the possibility of such a radical refusal, lest we underestimate the power of human freedom. We must avoid sentimentalism and face unflinchingly the terrifying willingness of human beings to choose what is worst for them and for others, namely, hatred, hostility, destruction, cruelty, fear, self-withdrawal, and self-absorption. Next to the mystery of God, there is no greater mystery than the human choice against universal values, especially the values of love and justice. This freedom of choice is the source of radical evil. In our freedom, we take God's cosmic power of love and twist it into a demonic power that not only chooses inauthentic meaning but also smashes authentic meaning. And when our individual choices for disvalue coalesce with the similar choices of others, when individual evil becomes collective, then the demonic can reach a frenzy of merciless destruction.

That we human beings choose to crucify our best selves defies rational explanation.[22] True, we can point to some social and psychological benefits that help to explain evil. The understandable desire to get along with the group explains in part how decent German people could let a sinful social structure like Nazism incline them toward evil. Also comprehensible to some degree is the proud and defiant individual who enjoys securing himself at the expense of another or who, in a thrilling exercise of manipulative intelligence, elicits abject service from another by insisting that she can secure her own vital self only through him.[23] I confess to a perverse fascination for those whose ruthless vitality enables them to sustain their freedom and life at all costs, even at the cost of the freedom and life of others. Indeed, I can imagine a strange self-satisfaction in those who have pushed their freedom to the point of a grand refusal of all love.[24] Yet all this does not fully explain the mysterious movement of freedom into a destructive commitment to disvalues. The question raised by my students thus remains: has anyone ever been able to press freedom to the radical no of complete lovelessness and sustained this no through death, choosing hell instead of heaven? I tell them again that I do not know the answer.

This raises another, perhaps more interesting question. Let us grant for the sake of argument that someone who has sustained the radical refusal through death is in the state of ultimate estrangement called hell. Since God's love of this person continues, this person is forever saying no against God's eternal yes. But how is it possible to sustain forever a no under the persuasive pressure of the divine yes? Without denying the power of human freedom, how can it not finally yield to God's love? According to long-standing Christian teaching, a human being is given only one chance to accept or reject God, and that chance is only as long as this penultimate life. But how can a radical rejection of love become eternally definitive unless God makes it so?[25] And how can God make it so unless God ratifies it with God's own no to the human no? That makes God's love conditional again. But God's love is unconditional. And thus the decision for hell is the individual's, not God's. But how can any human decision be eternally definitive, especially given the asymmetry of divine power and human freedom? Even though the Christian tradition insists on the power of human freedom, this same tradition denies that divine and human powers are equally responsible for the achievement of heaven, as if each were an equally powerful horse pulling the carriage of the self toward its ultimate end. And thus though the divine power is not coercive, it is nonetheless very powerful and difficult to resist, and is pressing down even on the person in hell. How could one resist it forever?

Furthermore, the radical refusal of love is a negation of the being who is the source of all being and value. Saying no to being makes this a choice for nonbeing; indeed, evil has been defined as the "privation of being."[26] The no of hell is thus the energy of freedom directed toward a purely negative resisting of all that is positive. Not only is there an interpersonal imbalance between the power of God's loving yes and our unloving no but also a metaphysical imbalance between being and nonbeing. How can a human being sustain this continuous plunge into the abyss of nonbeing, this everlasting flight from the self-communicative source of all being and love?[27]

Does God not eventually win the day with everyone? Is hell necessarily eternal for anyone who might die in a state of radical refusal? Christians, who profess their faith in a God who loves everyone unconditionally, should be first among those not to wish hell on anyone. Christian agapic love requires that we always hope that God's love finds emotive and directive success in everyone, even those who appear unyielding in their refusal to love and in their enmity toward those who love them.[28] Yet we have to be careful here. We must, it seems to me, take human freedom with utter seriousness. My hope is that God wins everyone. Yet I do not wish to banish the eschatological symbol of hell from the Christian imagination. The symbol belongs as a warning against sentimentality and as a protection of human freedom.

But surely if there are those who say a radical no to love and sustain it through death, their number must be relatively small. This leads naturally to the next question: how about those, surely the majority, who say a partial yes to love? It is difficult to imagine anyone saying a radical no, but it is easy to imagine a halfway yes. How many of us die full of sanctifying grace, to use the Catholic terminology, or fully sanctified, to use Protestant terminology? Catholics, Methodists, and some holiness groups have affirmed the possibility of reaching such a state of perfection before death. Indeed, the Catholic Church officially designates as saints those whose perfection in love is a communal certainty. But most Christians, including Catholics, are pessimistic about reaching a perfect yes to love in this life. Traditional Lutheran theology denies the possibility altogether, reserving complete sanctification for the heavenly state of full glorification.

How does one get from the partial yes said in this life to the perfect yes of the heavenly life? Most Protestant Christians would say that this transition is effected by the power of God in Christ who through the Word and Spirit instantaneously transforms the partial yes at death into a perfect yes after death. Catholics, however, have the eschatological symbol of purgatory: all those who die short of perfect love will have to undergo a purgation, a cleansing of selfishness so the fully loving self might emerge. The symbol of purgatory, however, has become a much less lively part of Catholic belief and piety in the last decades of the twentieth century and into the twenty-first century. In my Catholic boyhood, by contrast, it was very lively, and I was constantly scrambling to reduce my time in purgatory by making satisfaction for my sins through good works, self-sacrifice, prayer, and worship.[29] The way I went about all this was not spiritually healthy, and in my late teens, I cast off most of my purgatorial belief and piety.

Yet I have found myself unable to expunge completely the symbol of purgatory from my Christian imagination. I cannot shake the idea that everything I do or fail to do with respect to my moral growth has consequences. The notion that I can live a lukewarm Christian life, die in a state of half-committed love for God and my fellow human beings, and then in the twinkling of an eye be transformed into the full glory of perfect love strikes me as more than a little preposterous. I firmly believe that God in Christ intends this transformation for us and, in fact, is working now through the Word and Spirit to effect such a transformation. But if God cannot unilaterally effect such a transformation now in this penultimate life, how can God unilaterally effect it at death? The weight of human sin—my own sin and the sin of others in their corrupting effect upon me—stands in the way of God's intention. I am not always able or willing to let the Word and Spirit have the informative, emotive, and directive success that God desires. I resist the transformative power of God's love because I do not want the pain of having to repent of long-established and cherished habits that serve my short-term selfish needs. I am slothful. What is worse, I do not even like to admit any of this. After all, I'm okay, and you're okay, right? Are we not all quite wonderful? Well, in our moments of honesty, we know the truth: we are only partly okay. Why is it so painful to admit this? Dying to the old self, giving up inauthentic meanings, is difficult, and inevitably brings suffering. Suffering is no fun.

I do not believe that we can get away forever with our spiritual half-heartedness. Either we are willing to let the transformation occur within the penultimate, with all the suffering that comes from dying to the old self, or it will occur later, in the transition to ultimate fulfillment. This transition is symbolized by purgatory. If at the moment of death we have accumulated deferred spiritual growth, then we shall have to go through a purgatorial painful growth proportionate to the amount deferred. God does not inflict purgatory on us: it is simple obedience to the facts of our human nature. It would be in utter defiance of these facts for us to expect that at death we could move from tepid love to the ecstasy of perfect love without a spiritual pain proportionate to the distance we would have to travel.[30] How could we possibly avoid at death the sorrow, the repentance, and the remorse that we have so assiduously avoided in this life? How could we avoid purgatory without exempting ourselves from our human nature?

Imagine for a moment that someone has loved you for many years and you have been indifferent and ungrateful in response. But this person stood by you and was patient, pulling back perhaps a little to protect herself but never ceasing to love you. Suddenly one day, it dawns on you that she has always been there. In a flash, you understand and feel her love in its full meaning and power. You feel all the acceptance and transformative power of her love as never before, and you are joyful. But mixed in with this joy is a deep stab of remorse, regret, and repentance. It is a stab that runs as deep as your previous indifference and ingratitude. You move through this pain, yes, into the full glory of love gratefully received and eagerly given, but you cannot bypass this pain. Indeed, your willingness to endure the pain will be the one reliable sign that you are now truly ready to enter into the full mutuality she has been offering. This pain need not last for more than an instant, but it will cut with proportionate depth, and you must allow the cut to occur and the pain to exact its price. Yes, the pain will not overwhelm you, partly because the one who loves you will not let you spiral down into masochistic self-reproach and groveling unworthiness, for she continues to offer forgiveness and transformative energy. And so your joy in having finally accepted her love will take you through the pain. Yet there is something deeply necessary about your pain. Grace does not come cheap.

I imagine purgatory occurring in a timeless instant. Purgatory here in the penultimate usually has temporal duration—it lasts for seconds, minutes, hours, days—but time as we know it does not occur in the ultimate dimension or in the transition thereto. Our purgatory in the ultimate will, however, be proportionate to the amount of repentance and transformation that we have refused to undergo in the penultimate. It will be painful, but the pain will commingle with the more intense joy of forgiveness accepted and transformation effected. Fear of the pain of this purgatorial transition should not become self-preoccupying, for such fear is not the best motivation to become more loving; true love requires that we leave the closed circle of self-preoccupation. It is therefore a fear that can only be overcome by love, by resurrection made possible now, in the penultimate, by death to the selfish self. People who are loving do not go around fearing purgatory or hell, for "love casts out fear" (1 John 4:18). But this does not mean that purgatory is a superfluous eschatological symbol to be tossed into the dustbin of an obsolete theology. Our choices have consequences. Pain deferred is pain that cannot be avoided, even with the release of death.

Penultimate History and Ultimate Hope

As individuals have hope for themselves, humanity has hope for itself. Our individual life histories are embedded in society and its structures. The drama of our little lives is part of a larger drama of humanity as a whole. We are who we are partly because of who our families are; our families are who they are because of who the surrounding communities are; and those communities are shaped by clan, tribe, ethnic group, nation, region, and finally that whole collectivity that is humanity. Christians are called to translate agapic love into the work of social justice, and this work takes place in these larger communities. How much do we dare hope that this larger work of justice will be successful in the future of humanity? Will we make progress toward ever more just social structures? And what is the connection between this work of global justice within penultimate history and the ultimate fulfillment at the end of history?

Through the centuries, Christians have varied greatly in their view of the relationship between penultimate history and ultimate fulfillment. On one end of the spectrum are *apocalyptic pessimists,* who draw heavily on the mood and content of apocalyptic writings that were very popular during the time of Jesus. The apocalyptic genre had a definite, though not pervasive, influence on the New Testament writers. One thoroughly apocalyptic book found its way into the New Testament, the Book of Revelation. This book is not optimistic about human history. Before Christ comes again to save only those who have endured in the faith, things will get much worse in the world. The apocalyptic genre has had enormous influence on evangelical Christianity in the United States. Billy Graham is an apocalyptic pessimist. He and many of his fellow evangelicals believe that the end of history will be preceded by a host of collective woes: war, famine, conflagration, totalitarianism, anarchy, and persecution of the faithful. These woes will lead many Christians to doubt their faith and to lapse into apostasy, falling thereby into the clutches of the Antichrist. The stout believer, however, will read these woes as signs of the end of history that is coming soon "like a thief in the night" (1 Thess. 5:2). Those who persist in the faith will be "caught up in the clouds . . . to meet the Lord in the air" (1 Thess. 4:17).[31] Apocalyptic pessimists have, therefore. little hope for penultimate history. History for them is decidedly not the collective forward march of humanity into greater sisterhood and brotherhood. The Scriptures tell them of the virtual certainty that the march will not be forward but backward, and that history will culminate not in social justice but in unspeakable horror. Apocalyptic pessimism leads them to penultimate despair, but only as a way of inciting them to place their hopes in the merciful Christ, who will intervene at the end of time and bring this whole penultimate mess to an end.[32] Penultimate despair is supposed to strengthen ultimate hope.

I am not saying that apocalyptic pessimists are opposed on principle to working for justice. I have not heard Billy Graham say that Christians should cease to do good, even in the public sphere. But insofar as doing good becomes the positive work of reforming social structures, the apocalyptic pessimist has to undertake such work utterly without illusions, indeed without any confident penultimate hope. The practical consequence of such pessimism is to undercut the work of justice or to reduce it to the more negative task of restraining the forces of anarchy, which are always threatening to overpower human communities. This pessimism encourages the privatization of agapic love, tending to reduce it to one-to-one acts of compassion or to interpersonal justice. It tends also to spiritualize the doing of good toward others, aiming primarily at their spiritual redemption and only instrumentally at their biological or psychological healing.[33] Spiritual redemption means converting them to Christian faith, or at least strengthening their Christian faith, so that when Christ does come—and he could be coming soon because there is war in Kosovo, killing in East Timor, uneasy peace in the Middle East, and holes in the ozone layer—they will be among those faithful whom Christ will greet as his own. For this reason, apocalyptic pessimists engaged in doing good, even the most practical good, tend to see it primarily as giving witness to the faith, and thus as an extension of preaching Jesus Christ as one's personal savior.

For apocalyptic pessimists, then, there is a sharp discontinuity between penultimate history and ultimate fulfillment. There is the virtual certainty, based on a rather literal interpretation of the Book of Revelation, that humanity will fail miserably in the collective work of social justice.

At the other end of the spectrum are the *progressive optimists*. I am referring to those Christians who have great hope for collective progress, indeed harbor a virtual certainty that the combination of God's power in Christ and human effort will in the penultimate future achieve great success. They believe that within penultimate history the ultimate fulfillment can be progressively approximated.[34] In the late nineteenth and early twentieth centuries, this optimism became widespread among Protestant thinkers like Albrecht Ritschl and Walter Rauschenbusch and later seized the imaginations of Catholics like Pierre Teilhard de Chardin and Emmanuel Mounier.[35] There even developed a kind of Christian utopianism that was extraordinarily confident in the attainment of a just world virtually coincident with ultimate fulfillment. The distinction between the penultimate and the ultimate became blurred, and, in some instances, totally lost in favor of a vision of worldly utopia, usually of a socialist or communitarian variety.

Progressive optimists have a confident hope in the collective transformation of humankind and are typically very dedicated to the penultimate work of social justice. They believe that humanity, with God's help, can make it a better world. In contrast to the apocalyptic pessimists, they focus more on public good than on personal conversion. Sheltering the homeless, feeding the hungry, insuring good medical care, combating racism and sexism, ending warfare, working for ecological harmony, and empowering the poor tend to be their preoccupations. They talk less of giving witness, preaching the gospel, converting the sinner, waiting for Christ to come; they talk more of transforming social structures.

With World War I and all the subsequent horrors of collective life in the twentieth century, Christian progressivism, especially in its utopian variants, has been in retreat. There are few unbridled optimists among Christians today. Even the liberation theology movement, the most potent incarnation of progressivism in recent times, is careful to distinguish penultimate achievement from ultimate fulfillment.[36]

Somewhere between the apocalyptic pessimists and the progressive optimists are perhaps the majority of Christians, usually leaning slightly more in one direction or the other. I find myself muddling around somewhere in this middle. The apocalypticists are all too confident that things will get worse; the progressivists are all too confident things will get better. It seems to me that the penultimate is an arena of open possibilities. Things could become better *or* worse. I really do not know how tenacious the sin of injustice will prove to be, though I do not believe that injustice can be fully eradicated in the penultimate. God is luring and empowering people toward love and justice, about that I am confident, but God's power is not unilateral. How many individuals and groups will be able and willing in the future to respond to God and commit themselves to the most arduous work of social justice? I am always astonished when I meet people who have a quick answer to this question and betray no self-doubt. What could be more unpredictable than human freedom? I do not think even God knows for sure whether human beings, in the collective work of social justice, will be up to the task that God has set them.

Penultimate history could end in the ruins of a global war or ecological catastrophe. Or with the power of of God's Spirit we could move history toward a genuine approximation of ultimate justice and thereby narrow the gap between penultimate achievement and ultimate fulfillment. But neither of these developments can be guaranteed. I do share with the progressivists the conviction that the work for global justice has a positive connection with the ultimate fulfillment. I do not think we are building here a utopia that will coincide with the ultimate. But I do believe that those social structures that genuinely make the world a more truthful, a more loving, a more just, and a more beautiful place are not eternally lost, even if, at the end, all collapses in a rubble. Somehow, and I do not know how, God has the wisdom and power to blend the best of collective penultimate achievement into the ultimate content.[37] I said earlier that individual human choices have ultimate consequences; by analogy, I believe that collective human choices for or against social justice have ultimate consequences. I trust that God will work all this out so that our work for justice is neither pretentious nor in vain.

Taking a middle position between apocalyptic pessimism and progressive optimism opens up the penultimate future to a wide range of possibility, which is more compatible with the uncertainties of human freedom. Furthermore, it helps ensure a balance between personal conversion and the work of social justice. The two are not in conflict. Personal conversion is the God-empowered movement of the self into Christian faith, love, and hope, the greatest of which is love. The public expression of love is justice. Individuals converted by the Word and Spirit of God in Christ are not only engaged in reforming social structures but also unwilling to corrupt those structures from within by their own individual greed and selfishness. Thus, they are aware of the continued need for personal conversion. But they also know that just social structures reach deep into the lives of individuals, healing their bodies and minds, and readying them for that love and justice that is the chief work of personal conversion. Transform individuals or transform social structures? Christians try to do both, in light of their internal and external situations. Some might specialize in one direction or the other, but they should not exclude one or the other from the overall aim of Christian mission.

Cosmic Hope

Earlier in this chapter, we examined the resurrection of the body as an eschatological symbol of our continued connection with the material cosmos. Yet this is not just an individual hope but also a collective hope. Our harmonious relationship with the earth and all its creatures, with the atmosphere surrounding the earth, and, as we human beings continue to probe space, with the planetary system and beyond, is the ecological aim of all humanity, not just of committed environmentalists.[38] And building this harmony and ensuring its sustainability for future generations is now clearly a collective responsibility and thus a task of social justice. In theory, this responsibility extends out into the galaxies to include extraterrestrial life in whatever form.

Christians have hope for this cosmos, both penultimate and ultimate. The New Testament, assimilating one of the most fruitful ideas from apocalyptic literature, hopes not only for an ultimate fulfillment of human beings both individually and collectively, but also for "new heavens and a new earth" (2 Pet. 3:13; Rev. 21:1), when God in Christ will be "all in all" (1 Cor. 15:28). Through Christ "God was pleased to reconcile to himself all things, whether on earth or in heaven" (Col. 1:20). The "whole creation has been groaning in labor pains" (Rom. 8:22) in hope that it "will be set free from its bondage to decay" (8:21). With ultimate hope comes penultimate responsibility. Justice is no longer merely a work among and for human beings, because human destiny is tied up with the destiny of the air, the water, the plants, and the animals. We are bound together with these things and they with us. How far we shall be able to move toward harmony with the inorganic and organic cosmos is impossible to predict. But we must let ourselves be motivated by the Spirit: justice is also the work of environmental justice. Hope is cosmic hope.

Notes

1. The Quest for Meaning

1. The current *Books in Print* lists 267 books with the word *meaning* in the title, and the majority are about the quest for meaning and the meaning of life.

2. Viktor E. Frankl, *Man's Search for Meaning*, 3rd ed. (New York: Pocket Books, 1984). The first German edition (1946), entitled *Ein Psycholog erlebt das Konzentrationslager* ("A Psychologist Experiences the Concentration Camp"), was an autobiography of Frankl's time in the camps, with not much theory. It was first published in English as *From Death-Camp to Existentialism: A Psychiatrist's Path to a New Therapy*, trans. Ilse Lasch (Boston: Beacon Press, 1959). To this first English edition Frankl added a second, more theoretical part, which he enlarged and rewrote for the second edition, which carried the title *Man's Search for Meaning: An Introduction to Logotherapy*, part one trans. by Ilse Lasch (New York: Washington Square Press, 1963). For the third edition (1984), the publisher dropped the subtitle, and Frankl revised part two and added a postscript. Part one has remained unchanged throughout the three editions, though unaccountably the translator's name has been dropped from the third edition. In the United States alone, the book in its various editions has sold five million copies.

3. Viktor Frankl, *Recollections: An Autobiography*, trans. Joseph and Judith Fabray (New York: Plenum Press, 1997), 100.

4. Frankl, *Recollections*, 121. Another extraordinary witness to the importance of the quest for meaning can be found in the life and work of Václav Havel, the former dissident and current president of the Czech Republic. In *Letters to Olga: July 1979–September 1982*, (trans. Paul Wilson [New York: Henry Holt and Company,

1989]), Havel writes: "Perhaps it could be said that the 'I' is, in fact, the search for meaning—the meaning of things, events, its own life, itself" (332).

5. See Frankl, *Man's Search for Meaning*, 40, 55, 58, 70, 155. In his understanding of the biological, psychological, and spiritual dimensions of the human self, Frankl was dependent on the work of the German phenomenologist Max Scheler. In *Recollections*, Frankl writes: "At that time I finally saw through my own psychologism. My ultimate shakeup came from Max Scheler, whose *Der Formalismus in der Ethik und die materiale Wertethik* I carried with me like a bible" (62). See for example, Max Scheler, *Man's Place in Nature*, trans. Hans Meyerhoff (New York: Farrar, Straus and Cudahy, Noonday Press, 1961), chap. 3, "The Essence of Spirit," 35ff. Also see Herbert Spiegelberg, *Phenomenology in Psychology and Psychiatry: A Historical Introduction* (Evanston, Ill.: Northwestern University Press, 1972): "Frankl's major guide to phenomenology was clearly Max Scheler. . . . In fact, at one time Scheler's central work on ethics became something of a Bible to Frankl" (346). Also see Joseph B. Fabry, *The Pursuit of Meaning: Viktor Frankl, Logotherapy, and Life*, 2nd rev. ed. (New York: Harper and Row, 1980), 17–18.

6. Frankl, *Man's Search for Meaning*, 48.

7. For a recent account of the human capacity in drastic situations to sustain the spiritual dimension, see Tzvetan Todorow, *Facing the Extreme: Moral Life in the Concentration Camps* (New York: Henry Holt and Company, 1996).

8. For a fascinating look at the pressures on contemporary people searching for meaning in a world that demands "continuous psychic re-creation" (5), see Robert Jay Lifton, *The Protean Self: Human Resilience in an Age of Fragmentation* (New York: Basic Books, 1993). Lifton is, by and large, confident of our ability to handle such proteanism, but he warns against "negative proteanism," which is a "fluidity so lacking in moral content and sustainable inner form that it is likely to result in fragmentation (or near fragmentation) of the self, harm to others, or both" (190–91).

9. See Jean-Paul Sartre, *Being and Nothingness: An Essay on Phenomenological Ontology*, trans. Hazel E. Barnes (New York: Washington Square Press, 1966), 653. It is, however, a caricature of Sartre's position to say that he regards human beings as completely free of situational limits. See the subtle analysis by David Detmer in his *Freedom as Value: A Critique of the Ethical Theory of Jean-Paul Sartre* (La Salle, Ill.: Open Court, 1986), 40–51.

10. See B. F. Skinner, *Beyond Freedom and Dignity* (New York: Alfred Knopf, 1971), where he attacks the notion of the "autonomous man," his code word for the human being who thinks him or herself free. This notion "depends on ignorance" (14) of the environmental forces that govern human behavior: "As a science of behavior adopts the strategy of physics and biology, the autonomous agent is replaced by the environment—the environment in which species evolved and in which the behavior of the individual is shaped and maintained" (184).

11. Frankl, *Man's Search for Meaning* (1963), 156. Although these words cannot be found in the 1984 edition, the thought behind them is consistent with the 1984 edition, where it reads: "The true meaning of life is to be discovered in the world rather than within man and his own psyche" (133).

12. Frankl, *Man's Search for Meaning* (1984), 98.

13. William Lynch, *Images of Hope: Imagination as the Healer of the Hopeless* (Notre Dame, Ind.: University of Notre Dame, 1965), 193. Lynch first introduces the term *realistic imagination* on page 37; for his use of the term *gnostic*, see page 215. His view is well summed up: "But reality is a better producer of dreams and visions than nonreality. Satisfactory fantasy has to feed on reality and keep returning to it. The further it would soar, the deeper it must plunge into the facts" (243). The British philosopher Iris Murdoch echoes Lynch's distinction with her contrast between "vision," which is attentive to the reality of one's situation, and "personal fantasy," which provides the false consolation of unrealistic wishes and dreams. See *The Sovereignty of the Good* (New York: Schocken Books, 1971), 59. Herbert Fingarette, a practicing psychotherapist, writes: "I think there are good reasons to suppose that it is usually better to present insight psychotherapy as an attempt to *discover* what is present but hidden in one's life rather than as a task of *making* a new world for oneself by 'creative choice,' by the mobilization of will and purpose" (*The Self in Transformation: Psychoanalysis, Philosophy and the Life of the Spirit* [New York: Harper Torchbooks, 1965], 57).

14. See Karl Rahner, *Foundations of Christian Faith: An Introduction to the Idea of Christianity,* trans. William V. Dych (New York: Seabury Press, A Crossroad Book, 1978), where he speaks of human actions that are "a synthesis of original freedom and imposed necessity, a synthesis which cannot be resolved completely in reflection" (97).

15. Frankl, *Man's Search for Meaning* (1984), 98.

16. Frankl, *Man's Search for Meaning* (1984), 112.

17. Frankl, *Man's Search for Meaning* (1984), 112–13. Frankl also praises "high moral behavior" (88), speaks confidently of "right action and right conduct" (122), distinguishes between the "decent and indecent" (108), demarcates "swine" from "saints" (157), and praises someone for living up to "the highest standard of moral behavior" (155). He also does not hesitate to call some meanings "pseudo" or "false" (11). It is not my impression, however, that when Frankl makes these judgments he always, or even usually, intends to judge the subjective culpability of any individual; rather, he is focused on the objective morality of the action.

18. Frankl, *Man's Search for Meaning* (1984), 57.

19. Viktor Frankl, *The Unconscious God: Psychotherapy and Theology* (New York: Simon and Schuster, Touchstone Books, 1975), 119–20. See also Fabry, *The Pursuit of Meaning,* chap. 4, "The Value of Values." Generally, it must be said that Frankl puts far more emphasis on the unique meanings and on the unique situations that give rise to them than on the universal values. Furthermore, as we shall see later, he tends to root the universal values in humanity's biological nature.

20. Frankl, *Man's Search for Meaning* (1984), 59: "As the inner life of the prisoner tended to become more intense, he also experienced the beauty of art and nature as never before."

21. Frankl, *Man's Search for Meaning* (1984), 137, for his reference to the lost manuscript, which he then tried to reconstruct during his years in the camp by jotting shorthand notes on scraps of paper. See Frankl, *Recollections,* 99.

22. Patrick Sherry, *Spirit and Beauty: An Introduction to Theological Aesthetics* (Oxford: Clarendon Press, 1992): "The claim that beauty is an analogical concept has often gone together with the claim that it is a transcendental one, that is, a concept, like 'one' or 'good,' which may be applied to things in different categories and indeed, some say, to all being. . . . [T]his claim was not made explicitly by Aquinas himself, for he does not include beauty in his lists of transcendentals (e.g., in *On Truth* i, I and xxi, 3), but some of the things which he says have led his followers to make the claim on his behalf (also some other medieval thinkers regarded beauty as a transcendental, because all things have form)" (44–45). Also see 69–79, where Sherry offers the names of a host of thinkers who ascribe beauty to God or identify God with beauty.

23. Frankl, *Man's Search for Meaning* (1984), 128–30.

24. Modern literature is distinguished by characters that perform acts of gratuitous cruelty without ideological mystification. I am thinking of Raskolnikov in Fyodor Dostoyevsky's *Crime and Punishment* (New York: Modern Library, 1950) and Lafcadio in André Gide's *The Vatican Swindles* (New York: Alfred Knopf, 1925). The modern loss of belief in transcendent values is so complete in some individuals that even sublime self-justification becomes impossible for them.

25. Frankl says that when the existential vacuum and its painful symptoms are not acknowledged, the symptoms get displaced from the spiritual to the psychological or physical. He does not thereby deny that much suffering is physical or psychological in origin and must be treated as such; he simply maintains that some of it comes from disturbances in the dimension of spirit. See *Man's Search for Meaning* (1984), 96, 123, 124, 129.

26. Frankl, *Man's Search for Meaning* (1984), 176.

27. Martin Buber says: "[Fate] is not [a person's] limit but his completion; freedom and fate embrace each other to form meaning; and given meaning, fate—with its eyes, hitherto severe, suddenly full of light—looks like grace itself." *I and Thou*, trans. Walter Kaufmann (New York: Charles Scribner's Sons, 1970), 102. Beethoven seized his fate over a long period, for his deafness only gradually progressed. See Maynard Solomon, *Beethoven*, 2nd rev. ed. (New York: Schirmer Books, 1999), 151–62.

28. Our response to fateful suffering need not take the shape of heroic action. In circumstances like those in the death camps, where the range of free action is very limited, we transform our fate simply by a change in attitude. Frankl says: "There is also purpose in that life which is almost barren of both creation and enjoyment and which admits of but one possibility of high *moral* behavior: namely in man's attitude to his existence, an existence restricted by external forces" (*Man's Search for Meaning* [1984], 88). This freedom is for Frankl the last freedom, the freedom to suffer our fate with dignity, courage, honor, and generosity.

29. See Albert Camus, *The Myth of Sisyphus and Other Essays*, trans. Justin O'Brien (New York: Random House, Vintage Books, 1955), especially 3–48.

30. Frankl, *Man's Search for Meaning* (1984), 60, 141.

31. See Leon Wieseltier on Spielberg's film in *The New Republic*, 210, no. 4 (1994): 42. The enormity of the evil strikes Wieseltier as too much for this "glib" film. His essay implies that art necessarily fails in the face of such "radical evil."

32. Frankl, *Man's Search for Meaning* (1984), 141.

33. On the virtues of faith, love, and hope, see Thomas Aquinas, *Theological Texts*, selected and trans. Thomas Gilby (Durham, N.C.: Labyrinth Press, 1982), 180, 184, 203. For Aquinas, love or charity enjoys preeminence among these three virtues: "Eternal life consists in enjoying God. The motion of the human spirit to this end is the proper act of charity, which sets in order all acts of the other virtues, since all are summoned by charity" (180).

34. The limited scope of this book prohibits me from entering into the extraordinarily complex debate among contemporary philosophers and theologians about foundationalism. I will say that my own very modest argument for a universal foundation of values does not claim the infallible certainty characteristic of a strong foundationalism, nor does it claim to rest on reason apart from the activity of the whole feeling and willing self. For a good introduction to this debate see John E. Thiel, *Nonfoundationalism* (Minneapolis: Fortress Press, 1994), 1–37. And for an excellent general introduction to the "postmodern sensibility," see Paul Lakeland, *Postmodernity: Christian Identity in a Fragmented Age* (Minneapolis: Fortress Press, 1997), 1–38.

35. For the role of discourse theory in postmodernism see Chip Sills and George H. Jensen, eds., *The Philosophy of Discourse: The Rhetorical Turn in Twentieth-Century Thought*, 2 vols. (Portsmouth, N.H.: Boyton/Cook, 1992). This anthology provides an excellent introduction to the whole range of postmodern thought. Most of the major figures (Rorty, Lacan, Derrida, Foucault, Lyotard) are introduced in clear prose.

36. The best entry into Richard Rorty's work is his early pioneering work, *Philosophy and the Mirror of Nature* (Princeton: Princeton University Press, 1979) and the later volumes of essays, *Consequences of Pragmatism: Essays, 1972–1980* (Minneapolis: University of Minnesota Press, 1982), *Contingency, Irony, and Solidarity* (Cambridge: Cambridge University Press, 1989), and *Objectivity, Relativism, and Truth: Philosophical Papers*, vol. 1 (Cambridge: Cambridge University Press, 1991), especially the essay "Postmodernist Bourgeois Liberalism," 197–202.

37. According to Rorty, the anti-foundationalist is necessarily the ironist: "The ironist . . . is a nominalist and a historicist. She thinks that nothing has an intrinsic nature, a real essence. . . . The ironist spends her time worrying about the possibility that she has been initiated into the wrong tribe, taught to play the wrong language game. She worries that the process of socialization which turned her into a human being by giving her a language may have given her the wrong language, and so turned her into the wrong kind of human being. But she cannot give a criterion of wrongdoing." See "Private Irony and Liberal Hope," in *Contingency, Irony, and Solidarity*, 73–95, here 74–75. For a convincing philosophical critique of Rorty, see Charles Taylor, "Rorty in the Epistemological Tradition," *Reading Rorty: Critical Responses to "Philosophy and the Mirror of Nature" (and Beyond)*, ed. Alan R.

Malachowski (Oxford: Basil Blackwell, 1990), 257–75. In fairness to Rorty, I must note that he vigorously opposes cruelty. He indeed is a humane and civilized liberal in his politics. And he tries to persuade others to his liberalism. But his reasons for liberalism do not go beyond the discourse of those who agree with him. His claims therefore are mere conventions, with no anchorage in the real. And thus his pervasive irony and the difficulty of taking him with full philosophical seriousness.

38. Frankl, *Man's Search for Meaning* (1963), 164.

39. Frankl, *Man's Search for Meaning* (1963), 156.

40. See Frankl, *The Doctor and the Soul: From Psychotherapy to Logotherapy* (New York: Random House, Vintage Books, 1973), 55, 58.

41. Frankl, *The Unheard Cry for Meaning: Psychotherapy and Humanism* (New York: Simon and Schuster, Touchstone Books, 1978), 38.

42. Frankl, *Man's Search for Meaning* (1984), 169–70.

43. Opposition to "biologism" was one of the reasons for Frankl's attraction to Scheler's thought. See Spiegelberg, *Phenomenology in Psychology and Psychiatry*, 346. See also note 3 above.

44. Robert Wright, *Moral Animal: Evolutionary Psychology and Everyday Life* (New York: Vintage Books, 1995). The new biologism found its first impetus in Edward O. Wilson's *Sociobiology: The New Synthesis* (Cambridge: Harvard University Press, 1975). It does not yet have an agreed-upon label: I have heard it referred to as sociobiology, evolutionary psychology, evolutionary psychiatry, behavioral ecology, Darwinian anthropology, and neo-Darwinism. Some very heavy hitters (Stephen Jay Gould, Richard Lewontin) have lined up against evolutionary psychology. See the informative piece by Melvin Konner, "Darwin's Truth, Jefferson's Vision: Sociobiology and the Politics of Human Nature," *The American Prospect*, July–August 1999, 30–38. For a subtle appropriation of the insights of evolutionary biology that avoids its reductionism, see Stephen J. Pope, *The Evolution of Altruism and the Ordering of Love* (Washington, D.C.: Georgetown University Press, 1994).

45. For the expression "*sacred canopy,*" I am indebted to Peter L. Berger, *The Sacred Canopy: Elements of a Sociological Theory of Religion* (Garden City, N.Y.: Doubleday Anchor Books, 1969).

46. No one has explored this phenomenon of cloaking one's inauthentic meanings in universal values in more depth than U.S. theologian Reinhold Niebuhr: "Man touches the fringes of the eternal and universal. Only because he has this dignity can he be tempted to exceed his bounds and claim a universality which they can never possess" (*Beyond Tragedy: Essays on the Christian Interpretation of History* [New York: Charles Scribner's Sons, 1937], 43).

47. Ernst Bloch, *The Principle of Hope*, 2 vols., trans. by Neville Plaice and Paul Knight (Cambridge, Mass.: MIT Press, 1986), 1:184–89. For an analysis, see Thomas H. West, *Ultimate Hope without God: The Atheistic Eschatology of Ernst Bloch* (New York: Peter Lang Publishing, Inc., 1991), 143–46.

48. Yet despite these variations I cannot accept the view of extreme postmodernists that meanings and values are so embedded in the culture that no transcul-

tural appeal can be made when morally judging how values and meanings are constructed and carried out in a given culture, even one that is very much other. The debate about transcultural appeal to values has become heated among Western feminists who want both to practice a postmodern, multicultural tolerance and yet also stand in solidarity with their oppressed sisters in non-Western cultures. I am in decided agreement with a feminist like Lisa Cahill, who, while rejecting an "abstract universalism" arrived at by way of a narrow rationality, insists that "to abandon any ideal of reasonableness and shared values would be morally disastrous" (*Sex, Gender, and Christian Ethics* [New York: Cambridge University Press, 1996], 34). Inspired to some degree by Martha Nussbaum's neo-Aristotelianism and nourished by her own Catholic philosophical and theological roots, Cahill argues that "human reason, as a deliberative and evaluative power, can work within, between, and among cultures, looking for common ground and moving inductively but defensibly toward social and moral consensus" (236). Nussbaum herself is unequivocal: "[T]here are universal obligations to protect human functioning and its dignity, and . . . the dignity of women is equal to that of men. If that involves assault on many local traditions, both Western and non-Western, so be it" (*Sex and Social Justice* [New York: Oxford University Press, 1999], 30).

49. For a penetrating analysis of Plato's views, see John M. Rist, *Human Value: A Study in Ancient Philosophical Ethics* (Leiden: E. J. Brill, 1982), especially chap. 3.

50. On James K. Feibleman, see Andrew J. Reck, *The New American Philosophers: An Exploration of Thought since World War II* (New York: Delta Books, 1970), 221–54.

51. See René Le Senne, *Obstacle and Value,* trans. Bernard Dauenhauer (Evanston, Ill.: Northwestern University Press, 1972). Le Senne belongs to a French philosophy movement known as the "philosophy of the spirit," a movement that is indebted to Max Scheler's work on values.

52. See Murdoch, *Sovereignty of the Good.*

53. Schubert Ogden, in a brilliant essay entitled "The Strange Witness of Unbelief," has pointed out that Jean-Paul Sartre of all people has given testimony to the coordination of universal values and universal consciousness. Sartre rejects God precisely because he rejects universal values. Ogden quotes Sartre: "There can no longer be any good *a priori,* since there is no infinite and perfect consciousness to think it." And precisely from this standpoint Ogden shows that Sartre despite himself believes in a universal value, which is freedom. There is then in Sartre's atheism an implicit theism. Ogden's essay can be found in *The Reality of God and Other Essays* (New York: Harper and Row, 1966), 120–43, here 132. The quote from Sartre is from his *Existentialism and Human Emotions* (New York: Philosophical Library, 1957), 22.

54. Václav Havel says it well: "The Being of the universe, at moments when we encounter it on this level, suddenly assumes a personal face and turns this, as it were toward us. . . . But however it is, one thing seems certain to me, that our 'I'—to the extent that it has not been entirely successful in suppressing its orientation toward Being, and becoming completely absorbed in its existence-in-the-world—

has a sense of responsibility purely and simply because it relates intrinsically to Being as that in which it feels the only coherence, meaning and the somehow inevitable clarification of everything that exists, because it relates and aspires toward Being with all its being, because it hears within and around itself the 'voice' in which this Being addresses and calls out to it, because in that voice it recognizes its own origin and its purpose, its true relevance and its true responsibility, and because it takes this voice more seriously than anything else" (*Letters to Olga*, 346–47).

55. In a number of places in *Man's Search for Meaning* (1984), Frankl refers to his religious beliefs. For example: "I called to the Lord from my narrow prison and He answered me in the freedom of space" (111).

56. Viktor Frankl, *The Will to Meaning: Foundations and Applications of Logotherapy* (New York: New American Library, Plume Books, 1969), 154.

57. God, however, is not simply reducible to the universal values of truth, love, and beauty with which God is identified. This has led many thinkers, among them Max Scheler, to postulate a realm of values called the "religious" or "sacred." It is here that one experiences the awesome majesty, remoteness, and mystery of God. My own preference is not to postulate a separate realm of religious values apart from the aesthetic, intellectual, and moral, but rather to locate the awesome mystery of God in God's infinite and inexhaustible freedom. As free, God can never be reduced to necessity, and thus to exhaustive comprehensibility, even in terms of universal values. This whole issue was argued out by H. Richard Niebuhr and Douglas C. Macintosh. Niebuhr criticized Macintosh for understanding God too simply in terms of universal values. See H. Richard Niebuhr, "Value-Theory and Theology," in *The Nature of Religious Experience: Essays in Honor of Douglas Clyde Macintosh* (New York: Harper and Brothers, 1937), 93–116. On Scheler's "sacred values," see Alfred Schutz, "Max Scheler's Philosophy," *Collected Papers* (The Hague: Martinus Nijhoff, 1966), 3.138–39. For a bracing contemporary argument for God's continued hiddenness, see David Tracy, "The Hidden God: The Divine Other of Liberation," *Cross Currents*, 46 (1996): 5–16.

58. Here, perhaps, the reader can see why I have throughout this chapter defined the universal ethical value not simply as the good, but as love and justice. Like Plato, one can regard the good as a nonpersonal transcendent value, but as soon as one asks, "What makes the good good?" and then receives an answer that gives real content to the good, as in "The good is love" or "The good is compassion," it becomes hard to avoid sliding into anchoring the good in some kind of personal being. It is therefore difficult to define the good in terms of love and justice without implying that there is personal, conscious being that is loving and just. Christian theologians have therefore agreed with Plato that human beings desire and love the good, but their faith has led them to further define the good as loving personhood. God is the highest good precisely because God is loving and just.

59. Frankl, *Man's Search for Meaning* (1984), 132.

60. Frankl, *Man's Search for Meaning* (1984), 133: "The more one forgets himself—by giving himself to a cause to serve or another person to love—the more human he is and the more he actualizes himself. What is called self-actualization

is not an attainable aim at all, for the simple reason that the more one would strive for it, the more he would miss it. In other words, self-actualization is possible only as a side effect of self-transcendence [toward meaning]." This more philosophical view has led Frankl to a very practical therapeutic technique that he labels "para-doxical intention." See *The Will to Meaning*, 99–116. For a very clear explication of Frankl's views on paradoxical intention, see Marvin C. Shaw, *The Paradox of Intention: Reaching the Goal by Giving up the Attempt to Reach It* (Atlanta: Scholars Press, 1988), 61–76. See also Herbert Fingarette, *The Self in Transformation* (New York: Harper, 1965), 26: "Meaning may be used to maximize pleasure and may itself provide gratification (as is especially clear in the arts). Yet the drive toward meaning is autonomous and distinct from the pleasure-aim." I do not think Frankl and Fingarette should be understood here as narrowly anti-eudaemonistic, that is, against a healthy, self-affirming desire for self-actualization and for the pleasure, happiness, joy, and satisfaction that it brings. Nor do I think Abraham Maslow, who popularized the term *self-actualization,* should be held responsible for the fre-quently unnuanced use of the term by his epigones. Indeed, he came to regret the term, urging the switch to "full humaneness" and linking this humaneness intrin-sically to the realization of meaning and value: "[The] human being is so con-structed that he presses toward fuller and fuller being and this means pressing toward what most people would call good values, toward serenity, kindness, courage, honesty, love, unselfishness, and goodness" (*Toward a Psychology of Being* [Princeton, N.J.: D. Van Nostrand Company, Inc., 1962], 147).

61. See Reinhold Niebuhr, *The Children of Light and the Children of Darkness: A Vindication of Democracy and a Critique of Its Traditional Defense* (New York: Charles Scribner's Sons, 1944): "Man is the kind of animal who cannot merely live. If he lives at all he is bound to seek the realization of his true nature; and to his true nature belongs his fulfillment in the lives of others. The will to live is thus trans-muted into the will to self-realization; and self-realization involves self-giving in relations to others. When this desire for self-realization is fully explored it becomes apparent that it is subject to the paradox that the highest form of self-realization is the consequence of self-giving, but that it cannot be the intended consequence without being prematurely limited" (19).

62. I first heard this line from Donne quoted by Reinhold Niebuhr in a talk that he gave in the early 1950s. He did not give the source, and, so far, I have not been able to find it in Donne's poems or sermons. The title of the talk is "Christian Faith and Humanism," published in 1979 by the Audio Tape Collection of Union Theo-logical Seminary in Virginia.

63. The leitmotif of Iris Murdoch's *The Sovereignty of the Good* is that there is a self-forgetfulness common to great art, great morality, and great science. She is particularly intent on making this point with reference to art and morals: "Great art teaches us how real things can be looked at and loved without being seized and used; without being appropriated by the greedy organization of the self" (63). Morality also thrives when the greedy self does not intrude, and thus art and morals are "two aspects of the same struggle" (41).

64. Later in a discussion of Barbara McClintock, we shall see that the anticipated joy can in part be experienced in the very movement toward the full achievement of the meaning. Our point here is that this joy should become not the primary focus but the meaning itself.

65. Frankl, *Man's Search for Meaning* (1984), 129.

66. The correlation of feeling and value is at the heart of Max Scheler's philosophy. For Scheler, not only are the ideas of the mind intentional, but also the feelings of the heart (he frequently refers to Pascal's "*logique du coeur*"), and the object of feeling's intentions are values. See the excellent anthology edited by Harold J. Bershady, *Max Scheler: On Feeling, Knowing, and Valuing: Selected Writings* (Chicago: University of Chicago Press, 1992). It is precisely in giving feeling its role in the discovery and realization of value that, Scheler believes, distinguishes his "non-formal" ethics from Kant's ethics. On this point, see Manfred S. Frings, *Max Scheler: A Concise Introduction into the World of a Great Thinker* (Pittsburgh: Duquesne University Press, 1965), 49, and Schutz, "Max Scheler's Philosophy," 3.133–44, especially 137–38. To Scheler, one must give a good deal of the credit for the contemporary revival of what Andrew Tallon calls the "heart tradition." Scheler influenced Dietrich von Hildebrand who then influenced Bernard Lonergan. The most active bearer of the heart tradition right now is Tallon. His *Head and Heart: Affection, Cognition, Volition as Triune Consciousness* (New York: Fordham University Press, 1997) is rich in historical reference and systematic reflection. I have found it a great help in clarifying my own ideas. See also Dietrich von Hildebrand, *Christian Ethics* (New York: David McKay, 1953), where the "affective response to value" is the dominant motif of the book. See also Bernard Lonergan, *Method in Theology* (New York: Herder and Herder, 1972), 30–31, where he explicitly shows his indebtedness to von Hildebrand. Also contributing to the revival of the heart tradition are feminist thinkers, who rightly see in rationalism an example of patriarchal one-sidedness, and historians of spirituality, who have alerted us to the great mystics and spiritual writers, who put great stress on feeling. A somewhat less important influence in general but a strong influence on me in particular is the work of those U.S. thinkers who represent the empirical wing of Whiteheadian process thought. I am thinking here of people like Bernard Loomer and Bernard Meland, but above all, Nancy K. Frankenberry, who combines strong feminism with the stress on feeling that is characteristic of those on the empirical wing. Her emphasis on the "felt quality of experience" is found throughout her *Religion and Radical Empiricism* (Albany: SUNY Press, 1987).

67. G. W. F. Hegel, *Lectures on the Philosophy of World History: Introduction*, trans. H. B. Nisbet (Cambridge: Cambridge University Press, 1975), 73.

68. With Andrew Tallon, I see head, heart, and will not as three separate faculties but as three distinct operations that nevertheless interrelate and interconnect. One operation may predominate, but the other two are always copresent and coactive. See Tallon, *Head and Heart*, throughout.

69. I am indebted to von Hildebrand, *Christian Ethics*, 320, for the language of avowal and disavowal, and to Tallon, *Head and Heart*, 169, for the reference to von Hildebrand.

70. See Tallon, *Head and Heart,* 232–33, for the way a predisposition to habitual "connatural" feeling becomes a virtue.

71. W. Jay Wood, *Epistemology: Becoming Intellectually Virtuous* (Downers Grove, Ill.: InterVarsity Press, 1998), 49. For this illustration, including the quotation from Evelyn Wilken, I am indebted to Wood. The Wilken quotation is from a chapter devoted to McClintock in Sharon Bertsch McGrayen's *Nobel Prize Women in Science* (New York: Birch Lane, 1993), 167. Wood is very persuasive on the connection between emotion and intellectual virtue (see especially 175–96).

2. Meaning and the Formation of Human Identity

1. See Mortimer Adler, *Some Questions about Language* (La Salle, Ill.: Open Court, 1976), for a deeper analysis of how the mind abstracts meanings from things in the outside world. We do not generate the concept of a thing immediately. First, we have it in the mind as a sensory image or percept. Conceptualization, however, is impossible without the words that we have learned from our native language. There is then, to use Emile Benveniste's term, a "consubstantiality" between thought and language. See Emile Benveniste, *Problems in General Linguistics* (Coral Gables, Fla.: University of Miami Press, 1971), 56. See also Mikel Dufrenne, *Language and Philosophy* (Bloomington: Indiana University Press, 1963), 78: "[B]etween intelligence and speech, between thought and language, there is a complete and total solidarity."

2. See Walker Percy, *The Message in the Bottle* (New York: Farrar, Straus, and Giroux, 1975), 173, where he speaks of the present world, past world, future world, fictional past world, fictional joke world, dream world, hypothetical world, and abstract world.

3. Percy, *The Message in the Bottle,* 254: "To give something a name, at first sight the most commonplace of events, is in reality a most mysterious act, which is quite unprecedented in animal behavior and imponderable in its consequences."

4. See Herbert Fingarette, *The Self in Transformation: Psychoanalysis, Philosophy and the Life of the Spirit* (New York: Harper Torchbooks, 1965), 15–70, for an elucidation of how the active subject creates "meaning schemes" that mediate between it and reality. With Fingarette, I adopt a critical realism, which is midway between a naive realism and a subjective idealism. Critical realists differ with postmoderns like Richard Rorty and Stanley Fish, for whom the individual mind is captive to the social mind (that is, the discourse) and the social mind captive to itself, unable to get outside itself and make genuine contact with the real. For Rorty, see chap. 1, 16ff. The best way into Fish's work is his collection of essays, *Doing What Comes Naturally: Change, Rhetoric, and the Practice of Theory in Literary and Legal*

Studies (Oxford: Clarendon Press, 1989). A persuasive critique of Fish from some-
one who is in many ways very sympathetic to postmodern thought can be found in
Christopher Norris, *What's Wrong with Postmodernism: Critical Theory and the
Ends of Philosophy* (Baltimore: Johns Hopkins University Press, 1990), 77–133.

5. The systematic examination of language as one more way of acting or doing
is usually regarded as the pioneering achievement of the British ordinary language
philosopher J. L. Austin, though he was to some degree influenced by Ludwig
Wittgenstein. See J. L. Austin, *How to Do Things with Words,* 2nd ed. (Cambridge,
Mass.: Harvard University Press, 1975). Austin's ideas became widely known as
speech-act theory. I am heavily indebted to speech-act theory, especially the version worked out by Austin's American student, John Searle. See his *Speech Acts: An
Essay in the Philosophy of Language* (Cambridge: Cambridge University Press,
1969) and *Expression and Meaning: Studies in the Theory of Speech Acts* (Cambridge: Cambridge University Press, 1979). Recently it has been argued that the
true founder of speech-act theory is not Austin but Anton Reinach, a member of
the Munich school of phenomenology in the early decades of this century. See
Barry Smith, "Towards a History of Speech Act Theory," in *Speech Acts, Meaning
and Intentions,* ed. Armin Burkhardt (Berlin: Walter de Gruyter, 1990), 29–61. However, it has not yet been proven that Austin was familiar with Reinach's ideas,
which were applied primarily to the philosophy of law. Reinach and Austin could
very well have arrived at their ideas independently.

6. Pragmatics is a subspecialty within the discipline of linguistics, though
occasionally it is incorporated into another linguistic subspecialty, semantics.
Some of the subject matter considered by pragmatics overlaps the subject matter
of speech-act theory, and thus the work of ordinary language philosophers like
Austin and Searle is often referred to in books about pragmatics. For my understanding of pragmatics as a subspecialty of linguistics, I am most indebted to the
following works: John Lyons, *Semantics,* 2 vols. (Cambridge: Cambridge University
Press, 1977); Keith Allan, *Linguistic Meaning,* 2 vols. (New York: Routledge and
Kegan Paul, 1986); and Stephen Levinson, *Pragmatics* (Cambridge: Cambridge
University Press, 1983). I have also learned much from German philosophers who
have been working on a transcendental pragmatics. See the seminal, programmatic
essay by Jürgen Habermas, "What Is Universal Pragmatics," chap. 1 in *Communication and the Evolution of Society* (Boston: Beacon Press, 1979), 1–68.

7. *Function* is one of the terms used by pragmaticists and speech-act theorists when they analyze what a speaker is doing with words. Thus an utterance has
not only a sentence-meaning, but a function. The Viennese psychologist Karl
Bühler is usually given credit for first analyzing speech in terms of functions. He
distinguished among the representative function, the expressive function, and
the conative function. Searle, partly dependent on Austin, uses the term *illocutionary point* to denote an utterance's function and distinguishes it from the
perlocutionary act that the speaker aims to effect in the hearer. For example, the
illocutionary point of the utterance "It is raining" is to assert something, but it
may also have the perlocutionary aim of informing someone. I find the distinc-

tion between the illocutionary and the perlocutionary difficult to apply in many communicative situations. I am in agreement with Eckhard Rolf, who stresses the overall communicative purpose of the speech act, rather than the precise line that separates the illocutionary from the perlocutionary. See his "On the Concept of Action in Illocutionary Logic," in *Speech Acts, Meanings and Intentions,* ed. Burkhardt, 147–65. Habermas also emphasizes the overall communicative purpose and judges the success of the utterance in terms of the perlocutionary effect. He writes: "I shall speak of the success of a speech act only when the hearer not only understands the meaning of the sentence but also actually enters into the relationship intended by the speaker" ("What Is Universal Pragmatics," 39). For a contrasting view, see Searle, *Expression and Meaning,* 1–29.

8.   I have taken the term *directive* from Searle, *Expression and Meaning,* 13–14.

9.   It is a question here then of the mother's finding the tone appropriate to the emotion that she wishes to arouse in Daniel. Tone is provided not only by word choice, but by the paralingual devices, which are subdivided into the vocalic and nonvocalic. As vocalic, they are prosodic components, that is, those vocalizations that are part of an utterance but which are not themselves words. Keith Allan has identified seven prosodic components: stress, intonation (pitch and melody), disjuncture (pause), intensity (loudness), rhythm, duration, and phonation (husky, breathy, nasal, etc.). As nonvocalic, they are nonverbal cues (gesture, grimace, distance, posture, etc.) which accompany an utterance. The paralingual devices are particularly important when the function of a word goes beyond the merely informative into the emotive and directive. Paralingual devices become ways of infusing the power of feeling into the meaning of a word. See Keith Allan, *Linguistic Meaning* (New York: Routledge and Kegan Paul, 1986), vol. 2, 1–58, and Stephen Levinson, *Pragmatics* (Cambridge: Cambridge University Press, 1983), 36, 255, 296, 302, and 313. A pioneering essay on the paralinguistic is that of G. L. Trager, "Paralanguage: A First Approximation," *Studies in Linguistics* 13 (1958): 1–12. The other day, I saw a wonderful example of an utterance whose double meaning and function were completely dependent on differing vocalic stress: it was a sign at a local bakery store that read, "Get your buns in here!"

10. Although one can doubt that any utterance ever has one and only one function. To some degree, other functions are always copresent, however minimally. Roger Fowler in *Understanding Language* (London: Routledge and Kegan Paul, 1974) writes: "It would be difficult to discover a piece of language in which all the functions could not be detected, even though some might be severely diminished." (257). The communication theorist J. L. Aranguren has a very subtle statement about the copresence of the emotive function: "But *all* language, including the most 'coldly' objective and scientific, has an emotive as well as a cognitive dimension: that is to say it transmits an emotional 'significance,' (in the widest acceptation of the words 'emotive' and 'emotional'). Sometimes this 'significance' may be a mere 'halo' or 'aura' of agreement, something 'extra' added to the description. The presence of a 'disposition' or the expression of an 'attitude,' in conjunction with or based upon the descriptive meaning, may establish an equilibrium

between both functions which is destroyed when what we call 'prejudice' weighs down the non-cognitive side. At other times the emotive or expressive aspect may be obviously dominant under a disguise of pseudo-rationalism. In every case of communication, each word, however purely descriptive it sets out to be, carries a certain load of emotion" (*Human Communication,* trans. Frances Partridge [New York: McGraw-Hill, 1967], 67). Aranguren's point strikes me as correct and reminds me of the views of Andrew Tallon, who defines the human spirit as a "triune consciousness," that is, an integration of the operations of cognition, emotion, and volition (will). These operations are not separate faculties operating autonomously. Each can become primary in a given speech function, but never solitary. On Tallon's work, see chap. 1, n. 66.

11. The informative, emotive, and directive functions do not exhaust the functions of language. Other functions are, for example, the declarational ("We the Congress declare war"; "I pronounce you husband and wife") and the commissive, or promissory. Chapter ten of this book is given over to the promissory function. For more on these other functions, see Searle, *Expression and Meaning,* 12ff.

12. See Searle, *Expression and Meaning,* 14–15, 19–20, 44–45, 54–56, for his ideas on the "sincerity condition."

13. My use here of the language of I and Thou is a deliberate evocation of Martin Buber, whose *I and Thou* (New York: Charles Scribner's Sons, 1970) has much to say about the language of interpersonal communion. His "basic word," which "can be spoken only with one's whole being" (62), overlaps my "deeply personal word." I find further affinity with Yves Congar, who says in *The Word and the Spirit,* trans. David Smith (San Francisco: Harper and Row, 1984): "These [informative words] are words which offer purely objective information, but there are others in which we hand over something or even the whole of ourselves and which expect an equally personal response in return" (10).

14. The relation between feeling and the will is intimate and very complex. Medieval philosophy in the Aristotelian tradition tended to collapse affectivity or feeling into the will and gave affectivity a distinct function only in the lower sensitive soul rather than in the higher rational soul. This tradition contrasted with the Platonic-Augustinian tradition that believed in a tripartite division of the soul, giving a distinct role to the affective and elevating it to the highest level of the soul, though even in this tradition affectivity was often placed in a position subordinate to intellect. The Catholic theologian Karl Rahner also linked feeling closely to will, though how closely is a matter of dispute. I am indebted here to Andrew Tallon, "The Heart in Rahner's Philosophy of Mysticism," *Theological Studies* 53 (1992): 700–728, for the historical background and for Rahner's views. I want here to argue against assimilating feeling to will, or subordinating feeling to intellect.

15. The terms *persuasive* and *coercive* are frequently used by process philosophers and theologians to describe divine power. Process thinkers distinguish their neoclassical theism, which sees God's power in the world as always persuasive, from classical theism, which sees God's power as too often coercive. See John B. Cobb Jr. and David Ray Griffin, *Process Theology: An Introductory Exposition*

(Philadelphia: Westminster Press, 1976), 52–54. The contrast that process thinkers make between the two theisms is, I think, overdrawn, but not without historical foundation. While not labeling myself a process theist, I do believe that all love, if it is genuine love, whether it be divine or human, is persuasive and never coercive.

16. My understanding of temperament is partly dependent on the work of C.G. Jung. See his *Psychological Types*, rev. by F. C. Hull (Princeton: Princeton University Press, 1971). Jung's work was taken up and put to more practical use by Katharine Briggs and her daughter Isabel Myers, who constructed a psychometric device called the Myers-Briggs Type Indicator, which is much used today, though not always with proper discrimination and qualification. For a brief history of this use of Jung's work, see "Appendix I: A Brief History of Typewatching," in Otto Kroeger and Janet M. Thuesen, *Type Talk: The 16 Personality Types That Determine How We Live, Love, and Work* (New York: Delta, Tilden Press, 1988), 280–84. For a more academic treatment, see Arnold H. Buss and Robert Plomin, *A Temperament Theory of Personality Development* (New York: John Wiley & Sons, 1975) and *Temperament: Early Developing Personality Traits* (Hillsdale, N.J.: Lawrence Erlbaum Associates, 1984). The reader should take note that I am defining the psychological identity rather narrowly and in doing so countering the contemporary habit of giving the broadest elasticity to the psychological self, often to the point of including all those aspects that I attribute to the spiritual self. This indeed is where I part company with Jung's use of the word *psyche*, which is too broad for my taste.

17. More than a little resemblance exists between what I call the spiritual identity and what Amélie Rorty and David Wong call the "ideal self." It is this ideal self, they write, that "defines a set of general rules and values." See Rorty and Wong, "Aspects of Identity and Agency," in *Identity, Character, and Morality: Essays in Moral Psychology*, ed. Amélie Rorty and Owen Flanagan (Cambridge, Mass.: MIT Press, 1990), 24.

18. The relation between genetics and environment is enormously complex and not much is known with scientific certainty. Buss and Plomin insist on the role of each but admit that not much is known about the relationship between the developing temperament and what they call the "post-natal environment." See their *Temperament: Early Developing Personality Traits*, 153.

19. I obtained the figure of 75 percent from Kroeger and Thuesen, *Type Talk*, 286.

20. In our individualistic culture, where "I gotta be me" and do it "my way," it is easy to overlook the degree to which the self is the work of others' influence. The individual self is not solely a self-made self, but a social self. For my own understanding of this social self, I am greatly indebted to the theologian Horace Bushnell, the sociologist Peter Berger, and the philosopher Charles Taylor. See Horace Bushnell, *On Christian Nurture* (1861, reprint Grand Rapids, Mich.: Baker Book House, 1971); and Peter L. Berger and Thomas Luckmann, *The Social Construction of Reality: A Treatise on the Sociology of Knowledge* (New York: Doubleday, Anchor Books, 1967). A good introduction to Charles Taylor's ideas on the social self can be found in his essay, "The Nature and Scope of Distributive Justice," in *Justice and*

Equality Here and Now, ed. Frank S. Lucash (Ithaca, N.Y.: Cornell University Press, 1986), 34–67. I have also been influenced by "symbolic interactionism," a school of thought within the discipline of social psychology. This school traces its roots back to George Herbert Mead, who was the first great American proponent of the social self. See the informative book by Paul Rock, *The Making of Symbolic Interactionism* (Totowa, N.J.: Rowman and Littlefield, 1979). Berger and Luckmann acknowledge their debt to Mead in their *Social Construction*, 17. I follow Mead in stressing the importance of language in the formation of the self. A very helpful summary of Mead's understanding of the role of language in the formation of the social self can be found in Ian Burkitt, *Social Selves: Theories of the Social Formation of Personality* (London: Sage Publications, 1991). See chap. 2, "Language and the Social Self," 28–54. The self-in-relation is given great emphasis by feminist thinkers: "The embodied self lives in a context of relationships. As with the category of embodiment, feminist theologians are critical of conceptions of the self which abstract from physical and social context" (Susan A. Ross, "Feminist Theology: A Review of the Literature," *Theological Studies* 56 [1995]: 327–41, here, 335).

21. This mysterious process of doubling the self through a self-mediation, whereby the I grasps itself as a me, as its own other, has been the object of much philosophical and theological reflection. Probably the first to carry out such a reflection systematically was Augustine in his speculations on the analogy between the human soul and God's inner trinitarian life. See Augustine, *The Trinity*, trans. Edmund Hill, O. P. (Brooklyn: New City Press, 1990), Books VIII–XV. Thomas Aquinas continued this tradition with his ideas on the divine and human production of the inner word or "*verbum interius.*" See the famous series of articles by Bernard J. Lonergan published in the journal *Theological Studies*, 7 (1946), 8 (1947), and 10 (1949), and republished as *Verbum: Word and Idea in Aquinas* (Notre Dame, Ind.: University of Notre Dame Press, 1967). The tradition continues into our time. Eugene Fontinell describes it in the thought of William James: "The self as 'I' does not possess an *additional* part called 'me,' or vice versa. It is one and the same self, whether grasped as 'I' or 'me.' When it experiences itself as object or as the receptor of other activities, it says 'me.' When it feels itself as subject or as the initiator of activities, it says 'I'" (*Self, God, and Immortality: A Jamesian Investigation* [Philadelphia: Temple University Press, 1986], 95). See also this testimony from the modern French phenomenological tradition in the words of Mikel Dufrenne: "At the same time that language permits thought, it permits consciousness itself. That is to say, it permits it by introducing the . . . interval, this film of nothingness, as Sartre called it, which separates me from myself and makes me into a *pour-soi*, a for-itself. Moreover, it does this by shattering the opaque identity that defines the *en-soi* or the in-itself. The 'I' is another, Rimbaud said." *Language and Philosophy* (Bloomington: Indiana University Press, 1963), 73. Sartre's language of *en-soi* and *pour-soi* finds its roots in the work of the German philosopher G. W. F. Hegel, who in turn is dependent on the Western tradition of trinitarian speculation. Many would argue, and I with them, that this doubling and grasping of oneself in inner word is the presupposition for a self-communication in a way most full, free, and

conscious. A contemporary theologian says it well: "A rational being through experience and reflection attempts to form an image or expression of self. In knowing itself it fully possesses itself and only then is able to give itself completely." Seely Beggiani, "A Case for Logocentric Theology," *Theological Studies* 32 (1971): 377. I do, however, want to stress that this process of self-mediation is mysterious and for human beings dynamic and elusive. We never gain an absolutely secure grasp of ourselves through the inner word. I am sensible of the following (somewhat hyperbolic) warning from Walker Percy: "The one thing in the world which by its very nature is not susceptible of a static symbolization is *myself!* I, who symbolize the world in order to know it, am destined to remain forever unknown to myself" (*The Message in the Bottle*, 283).

22. Because the child soon knows that his parents are not only loving, but communicating identity, the child quickly begins to see the whole range of parental activity as giving example, that is, as offering an identity for the child to follow. The child becomes particularly adept at spotting contradictions between what the parent says verbally and yet does nonverbally.

23. I am in agreement with Rollo May when he says that fate accepted and transformed in freedom becomes our destiny, our "vital design" (*Freedom and Destiny* [New York: Norton, 1981], 93). May on his part is dependent on Paul Tillich. "Fate," Tillich writes, is the "opposite of freedom, but when fate is seen as conditioning freedom rather than contradicting it, and when in freedom we use our fate as material out of which we decide who we are and want to be, then fate has become destiny, which is not in contradiction to freedom: My destiny is the basis of my freedom; formed by nature, history, and myself. My destiny is the basis of my freedom; my freedom participates in shaping my destiny" (*Systematic Theology*, 3 vols. [New York: Harper and Row, University of Chicago Press, 1967], 1:185).

24. See Karl Rahner, "Concerning the Relationship between Nature and Grace," *Theological Investigations*, vol. 1, trans. Cornelius Ernst (Baltimore: Helicon Press, 1961), 297–317; "Anonymous Christians," *Theological Investigations*, vol. 6, trans. Karl-H. and Boniface Kruger (New York: Seabury Press, 1974), 98; "Observations on the Problem of the 'Anonymous Christian'," *Theological Investigations*, vol. 14, trans. David Bourke (New York: Crossroad Books, 1976), 280–94; "The One Christ and the Universality of Salvation," *Theological Investigations*, vol. 16, trans. David Morland (New York: Seabury, 1979), 199–224.

25. Heidegger laid out his views on the existentials of human being in his early pioneering work *Being and Time*, trans. John MacQuarrie and Edward Robinson (London: SCM Press, 1962). He writes: "Because *Dasein's* [human being's] characters of Being are defined in terms of existentiality, we call them 'existentials.' These are to be sharply distinguished from what we call 'categories'—characteristics of Being for entities whose character is not that of *Dasein*" (68). Besides possibility, some other existentials that emerge out of Heidegger's "existential analytic" are care, discourse, understanding (interpretation), worldhood, de-severance (bringing things closer that are categorically distant, for example, via radio), the impersonal Other (*das Man*), anxiety, guilt, and being-unto-death.

26. In the words of Rahner: "We are presupposing then that the goal of the world is God's self-communication to it, and that the entire dynamism which God has implanted in the process by which the world comes to be in self-transcendence . . . is already directed towards this self-communication and its acceptance by the world" (*Foundations of Christian Faith. An Introduction to the Idea of Christianity*, trans. William V. Dych [New York: Seabury Press, A Crossroad Book, 1978], 192).

27. Although Rahner says that the supernatural existential is not a natural right, he does insist that the supernatural existential belongs to the human essence. For Rahner, the human essence is a mixture of natural and supernatural elements. These elements are so intermixed that there is no way intellectual reflection can neatly separate them. He states: "Thus 'dignity' is, in the last analysis, objectively identical with the being of an entity—understood as that which is necessarily given its 'essential structure.' . . . And in the present context 'essential structure' means everything man necessarily is and must be, whether the entity—regarded in itself—be a natural essence [*Natur*] or whether it be—with reference to the basic structure—a free gift of God, a grace and hence supernatural." See Karl Rahner, "The Dignity and Freedom of Man," *Theological Investigations*, vol. 2., trans. Cornelius Ernst (Baltimore: Helicon Press, 1963), 235–63, here 236. He goes on to say: "The dignity of man's nature embraces the following [natural and supernatural] moments which mutually determine each other" (239). And further: "The supernatural is related to what we have called the personal nature of man, as a gratuitous gift of God, as grace. In this way man exists in nature and 'supernature.' This does not, however, mean that it is left to his free choice whether he intends to understand himself as a purely natural person or as a person called to direct communion with God by grace" (240).

28. I come down on the side of classical theism instead of the neoclassical theism of process thought. For a process thinker like Alfred North Whitehead, God's "envisagement" of value is necessarily linked with what God is everlastingly doing in the world. God cannot be God as the center of value without a world. We can, he says, speak of a "primordial envisagement" of value, but that is an abstraction. In fact, God is always necessarily envisaging values for the world. According to classical theism, by contrast, God envisages and affirms values in an eternal act of envisaging and affirming God's own nature. It is not a metaphysical requirement of God's nature that God have a world into which to feed values. For Whitehead's view, see *Process and Reality: An Essay in Cosmology*, corrected edition by David Ray Griffin and Donald W. Sherburne (New York: Free Press, 1967), 34, 44, 189, and all of part v, chap. 2, 342–52. On the question of necessity and freedom in God, I find myself in sympathy with the revisionist classical theism of the great nineteenth-century German theologian, Isaak Dorner. See his "The Dogmatic Concept of the Immutability of God," in *God and Incarnation in Mid-Nineteenth-Century German Theology*, ed. and trans. Claude Welch (New York: Oxford University Press, 1965), 115–179. A contemporary British philosopher of religion, Keith Ward, proposes ideas that are in continuity with Dorner's. Both Dorner and Ward reject the

idea that God in order to be God must have a world. See Ward, *Rational Theology and the Creativity of God* (New York: Pilgrim Press, 1982), 85: "One cannot say that God must necessarily create some world, on pain of failure to be God." Yet both Dorner and Ward are intent on allowing temporality and contingency into God's dynamic relationship to the world. In opposition to the classical theism of E. L. Mascall, Ward says in *The Concept of God* (New York: St. Martin's Press, 1974): "If one maintains that God is beyond temporal change, one is neither committed to the view that he is imprisoned, as it were, in a condition of static immobility, nor to the view that God cannot change in any aspect of his being" (154). It is a question of finding a middle position between a neoclassical theism that involves God so much in the world that the world becomes metaphysically necessary to God, and a classical theism that makes God so free over against the world that God becomes sovereignly aloof from the world without any real relation to it.

3. The Identity of Jesus

1. I have borrowed the terms *fidelity* and *plausibility* from Wesley J. Wildman, *Fidelity and Plausibility: Modest Christologies in the Twentieth Century* (Albany: SUNY Press, 1998), xxviii. They are paralleled by Schubert Ogden's criteria of appropriateness and credibility. See Ogden, *The Point of Christology* (San Francisco: Harper and Row, 1982), 4.

2. For the formation of the New Testament canon, see Raymond E. Brown, and Raymond F. Collins, "Canonicity," in *The New Jerome Biblical Commentary,* Brown et al., eds. (Englewood Cliffs, N.J.: Prentice Hall, 1990), 66:5–86, pp. 1034–54. It was not until the end of the fourth century that "there was general acceptance of the 27-book canon of the New Testament" (66:81, p. 1050), and during the Reformation differences about the canon broke out again. To this day, the so-called oriental churches (Syrian and Coptic) have a different New Testament canon (66:85, p. 1051).

3. It is easy to forget that before there were the canonical scripture called the New Testament there was a tradition of faith passed on orally. The first Christian writing (most likely, Paul's first letter to the Thessalonians) was written about twenty years after Jesus' death.

4. When I say Jesus had a theology of himself and his work, I do not of course mean a conceptual, systematic theology of the kind found in the work of someone like the great medieval theologian Thomas Aquinas. Systematic theology came with the influx of Greek philosophical conceptuality into Christian culture. Jesus understands himself in the language of a narrative theology, that is, he tells the story of God's action in history. Most of the theology found in the Bible is narrative theology.

5. It became the role of the church to judge whether or not a theology was faithful to the tradition. This role came to be exercised by the bishops, especially when they all met in the great ecumenical councils.

6. The rise of modern critical history and its effect on Christian faith is well summarized by Hans Schwarz, *Christology* (Grand Rapids, Mich.: Eerdmans, 1998), 8–16, and by Gerd Theissen and Annette Merz, *The Historical Jesus: A Comprehensive Guide* (Minneapolis: Fortress Press, 1998), 1–16. The first great telling of this story was by Albert Schweitzer in his *The Quest of the Historical Jesus: A Critical Telling of Its Progress from Reimarus to Wrede* (1906; Baltimore: Johns Hopkins, 1998).

7. In other words, when a modern historian does history, she does so as a methodological atheist. In her explanation of historical events she cannot point to God's causal power, but only to other worldly events. If she does bring God's power into her explanation, she is exceeding the reach of historical method and moving into theology, or at least into a metaphysical theism. She cannot do that and still claim she is only practicing the historical method. For the term *methodological atheism,* I am indebted to Peter L. Berger, *The Sacred Canopy: Elements of a Sociological Theory of Religion* (Garden City, N.Y.: Doubleday Anchor Books, 1969), 100. It is equally mistaken for someone to practice the historical method as a metaphysical atheist, namely, to practice the historical method as if it committed him or her to the belief that worldly events are in fact a closed continuum. Such a belief is a metaphysical or ontological belief, which cannot be justified on purely historical or scientific grounds. In the words of the Dutch Catholic theologian Edward Schillebeeckx: "As an epistemological category, that is, *qua* method, historical abstraction is totally justifiable, provided one does not turn it into an ontological category" (*Jesus: An Experiment in Christology,* trans. by Hubert Hoskins [New York: Crossroad Books, 1979], 68). Schillebeeckx's *Jesus* has been of decisive help to me in thinking through the issues of history and faith.

8. On the need to demythologize the mythology of the New Testament, see Bultmann's extraordinarily influential essay, "New Testament and Mythology," in *Kerygma and Myth: Rudolf Bultmann and Five Critics,* ed. Hans Werner Bartsch (New York: Harper Torchbooks, 1961), 1-44.

9. See Ben F. Meyer, *The Aims of Jesus* (London: SCM Press, 1979), 49–51, for a summary and critique of Bultmann's views on the relationship between history and faith. Meyer's book is a brilliant programmatic essay that anticipates some of the most recent historical reconstructions of Jesus' life. N. T. Wright, for example, frequently acknowledges his debt to Meyer in his *Jesus and the Victory of God* (Minneapolis: Fortress Press, 1996).

10. One must be careful to give Bultmann his due. He is not saying that reconstructing the history of Jesus is impossible. He himself undertook such a reconstruction, even though he thought the amount of reliable material was quite meager. He was convinced as a historian that Jesus lived, preached, and was crucified. See his *Jesus and the Word* (1926; New York: Charles Scribner's Sons, 1958), where he reconstructs the preaching and acknowledges that Jesus lived and was crucified. In reaction, however, against earlier "lives of Jesus," which gave exhaustive descriptions of Jesus' inner psychology, he was very skeptical about saying anything about the "personality of Jesus" (8ff.). And, frankly, when I read

a nineteenth-century "life" like Ernst Renan's *Vie de Jesus* (Paris, 1963), an enormously popular book in its day that is rife with seminovelistic psychologizing, I can fully understand his reaction, indeed, his overreaction. I found myself sympathizing with Bultmann recently while reading the heavily psychologized life of Jesus by Raymund Schwager, *Jesus of Nazareth: How He Understood His Life* (New York: Crossroad, 1998). I also continue to find bracing truth in Bultmann's stress on the decisive importance of the faith-decision in gaining access to the ultimate significance of Jesus' life. Yet, in my view, he too sharply separated this decision from the historical reconstruction.

11. The start of the new quest is traced to Ernst Käsemann's famous Marburg lecture of 1953, published as "The Problem of the Historical Jesus," in *Essays on New Testament Themes* (London: SCM Press, 1964), 15–47. Käsemann influenced even his teacher Bultmann and to the point that the scholarship of Bultmann's last years affirmed more continuity between the Jesus of history and the Christ of faith preached by the earliest Christian community. On this point and for references see James H. Charlesworth, *Jesus Within Judaism: New Light from Exciting Archeological Discoveries* (New York: Doubleday, 1988), 167.

12. Schillebeeckx, *Jesus*, 74: "Historical study of Jesus is extremely important, it gives a concrete content to faith; but it can never be a verification of faith. A historically reconstructed picture of Jesus can never do more than allow for or keep a place for the Christian interpretation; it cannot from its own standpoint make this obligatory." When he says "allow for," that is what I mean by "compatible or consistent with." I should also stress here that all historical reconstruction is an interpretation of the available evidence on the part of the individual historian. There are no such things as the bare facts that speak for themselves. And when the historian reconstructs the history of Jesus, the room for interpretation is especially wide because the evidence is relatively sparse compared to, for example, the amount of evidence available for a historian reconstructing the history of Martin Luther King Jr.

13. Jesus' eschatological hope is often referred to as his apocalyptic hope, for he lived at a time when devout Jews often expressed their hope for the messiah and the final reign of God in the language of apocalypse, a genre of writing that recounts visions purporting to reveal (the Greek for revelation is *apocalypsis*) what God has in store for Israel's future. The last book of the New Testament, Revelation, is an apocalyptic writing. Apocalyptic language is highly symbolic and metaphorical, often allegorical and enigmatic, full of cataclysmic events on a cosmic scale. Recent historical reconstructions of Jesus display a new appreciation for the degree to which Jesus' self-understanding was indebted to the apocalyptic worldview. See, for example, Dale Allison, *Jesus of Nazareth: Millenarian Prophet* (Minneapolis: Fortress Press, 1998).

14. I find myself most drawn to the work of those historians whom N. T. Wright classifies as "Third Questors." See his list with bibliographical references in *Jesus and the Victory of God*, 84. Wright excludes Crossan from his list because of Crossan's continued Bultmannian tendencies, especially his noneschatological and nonapocalyptic Jesus and his suspicion of the New Testament as a historical

source, a suspicion, says Wright, that borders on "paranoia" (see Wright, in Marcus J. Borg and N. T. Wright, *The Meaning of Jesus: Two Visions* [San Francisco: Harper-SanFrancisco, 1998], 18). And thus Crossan is a part of the "new wave of the New Quest," not the Third Quest (Wright, *Jesus and the Victory of God*, 29–84). On the list, Wright includes himself, and I have learned a great deal from him, despite reservations on certain points and some nervousness about the ease with which he reconstructs the theology from his very confident and "strong" reconstruction of the history. Wright sees Marcus J. Borg as straddling the "revived 'New Quest' and the 'Third Quest'" (84). Borg indeed is a special case. I found him less convincing on the earthly Jesus and more convincing on the resurrection experience of Jesus' followers. On the earthly Jesus, or what he calls the "pre-Easter Jesus," see his *Jesus: A New Vision* (San Francisco: Harper & Row, 1988). On the "post-Easter Jesus," see Borg and Wright, *The Meaning of Jesus: Two Visions*, 129–42.

15. For much more extensive theological reconstructions with whose aims I am in considerable agreement, see Roger Haight, *Jesus Symbol of God* (Maryknoll, N.Y.: Orbis Books, 1999), and Keith Ward, *Religion and Revelation: A Theology of Revelation in the World's Religions* (Oxford: Clarendon Press, 1994), 193–282, and *Religion and Human Nature* (Oxford: Clarendon Press, 1998), 186–254, 271–330. An ongoing feminist reconstruction of the greatest interest and importance is that of Elizabeth Johnson. See her *Consider Jesus: Waves of Renewal in Christology* (New York: Crossroad, 1990), and *She Who Is: The Mystery of God in Feminist Theological Discourse* (New York: Crossroad, 1992).

16. I prefer the term *virginal conception* because the term *virgin birth* has come to connote for some Christians not just Jesus' conception but the actual passage of the infant through the birth canal. Indeed, some Christians did come to understand the virginal *conception* as necessarily entailing a birth that left Mary's hymen intact, the so-called *virginitas in partu*. This understanding linked up with the developing tradition that Mary retained her *virginitas post partum*, a perpetual virgin, *semper virgo*. Karl Rahner finds the notion "problematic," and laments that it has distracted people from the essence of the doctrine of the virgin birth, which was that it was a virginal conception. See Karl Rahner, "Virginitas in Partu," *Theological Investigations*, vol. 4, trans. Kevin Smyth (Baltimore: Helicon Press, 1966), 134–62. See also Raymond E. Brown, *The Birth of the Messiah: A Commentary on the Infancy Narratives in Matthew and Luke*, new updated ed. (New York: Doubleday, 1993), 517–18.

17. To use a more archaic term, the man to whom she was betrothed, though neither *engaged* nor *betrothed* is perhaps strong enough to capture in full the seriousness of Jewish betrothal at the time of Jesus. According to Raymond Brown, it would be more accurate to say that the matrimonial process was carried out in two stages: (1) "a formal exchange of consent before witnesses" and (2) "the subsequent taking of the bride to the groom's family home" (*The Birth of the Messiah*, 123). Mary had already been through stage one.

18. The literal sense of *miracle* must be distinguished from the figurative sense. Nowadays when people say "It's a miracle," they often do not wish to be understood as saying literally that the laws of nature were suspended by a supernatural

power. The understanding of miracle as the interruption of the normal operation of natural law is classical, since it is derived from a view of nature that can be traced back to the Greeks. The discussion of miracle in the eighteenth century used these classical categories. These categories are not biblical, which has led the biblical scholar John P. Meier to offer this definition of miracle: "A miracle is (1) an unusual, startling, or extraordinary event that is in principle perceivable by any interested and fair-minded observer, (2) an event that finds no reasonable explanation in our world of space and time, and (3) an event that is the result of a special act of God, doing what no human power can do" (*A Marginal Jew: Rethinking the Historical Jesus,* 2 vols. [New York: Doubleday, 1991, 1994], 2.512). His definition is helpful, although it does not really contradict the classical definition, for whenever one talks of "perceptible events" and "known forces," one inevitably is talking of events that are open to an explanation that refers to the regularities of nature. True, insofar as human powers are activated by human free choice, they escape a deterministic rule of nature's laws. Yet insofar as human powers cause perceptible events in this space and time, they work with and assume the regular operations of nature's laws. And since miraculous events are special acts of God that suspend the normal operation of precisely those laws, or enable human power to suspend their normal operation, we are right back more or less into the framework of the classical definition. It is of course true that contemporary science has revealed to us that the natural world does not operate deterministically, that is, as if every perceivable effect were reducible solely to its causes. A certain amount of free play lurks within the flow of cause and effect, and thus the laws of nature are better understood as generalizations about the high probability of certain causes leading to certain effects than as rigid formulas showing the strict predictability of nature's activity. Yet contemporary science does not interpret this to mean that the perceptible events in the macrocosmic world can occur *without* worldly causes. If such an event does occur, it can only occur because a cause beyond this world has provided a power that interrupts, suspends, or exceeds the normal operation of cause and effect. For a more general account of contemporary science and its implications for religion, see Ian G. Barbour, *Religion in an Age of Science: The Gifford Lectures,* vol. 1 (San Francisco: Harper and Row, 1990).

19. For the feminist theological implications of God's being beyond gender, see Rosemary Radford Ruether, *Sexism and God-Talk: Toward a Feminist Theology* (Boston: Beacon Press, 1983); Sallie McFague, *Metaphorical Theology: Models of God in Religious Language* (Philadelphia: Fortress Press, 1982); and Johnson, *She Who Is.* These three books are peak achievements in contemporary feminist theology.

20. As far as I can ascertain, the first major Christian thinker to raise doubts about the traditional understanding of the virginal conception was Friedrich Schleiermacher (1768–1834). For him, no worldly event occurred without a worldly cause. There are no "phenomena that have a less immediate relation to nature or to the finite than other phenomena," although he also believed that God was causally involved in all events and for this reason, "every event, even the most ordinary and natural, is to be seen as a miracle as soon as it permits the religious view of it to become the predominant one" (*On Religion: Addresses in Response to Its*

Cultured Critics, trans. and ed. Terrence M. Tice [1799; Richmond, Va.: John Knox Press, 1969], 141). In a later work, *The Christian Faith* (1821; Edinburgh: T. & T. Clark, 1928), he does not explicitly deny a literal virginal conception, but questions its "dogmatic value" (404), insisting that Jesus could be the sinless Son of God and redeemer of the world without such a conception. One can sense his general attitude in this passage: "Anyone who takes the stories of a Virgin Birth as literally exact has of course one more miracle to stand for" (403).

21. Raymond E. Brown, *The Birth of the Messiah*, 142–43, 150, 530, 534–42. Brown writes that a "too early birth may be implied in the tradition as far back as we can trace it" (530). I should note that Brown, a committed Roman Catholic, has religious faith in the literal virginal conception as it is officially taught in the church's tradition.

22. For Mackey's views, see James P. Mackey, "Christian Faith and Critical History," in *Critical History and Biblical Faith: New Testament Perspectives*, ed. Thomas J. Ryan (Villanova, Pa.: College Theology Society, 1979), 59–90, and *Jesus, the Man and the Myth* (New York: Paulist Press, 1979), 268–80. For Schaberg's views, see *The Illegitimacy of Jesus: A Feminist Theological Interpretation of the Infancy Narratives* (New York: Harper and Row, 1987). Mackey's speculations are the more modest; Schaberg's require a strained and often unconvincing exegesis. The German feminist scholar Luise Schottroff rejects Schaberg's thesis and argues instead that "the legend of Mary tells that Mary brought a child into the world through the creative power of the *pneuma* . . . without the procreation of a man or a male divinity. In light of the pivotal veneration of men's procreative prowess in patriarchal ideology and biology . . . the legend of a fatherless pregnancy is critical of patriarchy at a decisive point" (Luise Schottroff, Silvia Schoer, and Marie-Theres Wacker, *Feminist Interpretation: The Bible in Women's Perspective* [Minneapolis: Fortress Press, 1998], 224).

23. Article 11 of the *Decree on Ecumenism* reads: "When comparing doctrines [with their separated brethren], [Catholic theologians] should remember that in Catholic teaching there exists an order or 'hierarchy' of truths, since they vary in their relationship to the foundation of the Christian faith" (Walter Abbott, ed., *Documents of Vatican II* [New York: America Press, 1966], 354). For interpretation see Herbert Vorgrimler, ed., *Commentary on the Documents of Vatican II*, vol. 2 (New York: Herder and Herder, 1968), 114–21. See also Thomas Bokenkotter, *A Concise History of the Catholic Church*, rev. ed. (New York: Doubleday Image Books, 1990), 384.

24. Scholars like Dan Otto Via Jr. examine the parables not only as communications of existential religious truth but also as "real aesthetic objects," as literary works created by a highly artistic temperament. See *The Parables: Their Literary and Existential Dimension* (Philadelphia: Fortress Press, 1979).

25. The Jewish background of Jesus has received enormous attention during the past ten to fifteen years. For my own understanding of this background, I am most indebted to Leonard Swidler, *Yeshua: A Model for Moderns* (Kansas City, Mo.: Sheed and Ward, 1988); E. P. Sanders, *Jesus and Judaism* (Philadelphia: Fortress

Press, 1985), and *The Historical Figure of Jesus* (London: Allan Lane Penguin Press, 1993); N. T. Wright, *The New Testament and People of God* (Minneapolis: Fortress Press, 1992), and *Jesus and the Victory of God;* and the books by Geza Vermes, *Jesus and the World of Judaism* (Philadelphia: Fortress Press, 1984), and *The Religion of Jesus the Jew* (Minneapolis: Fortress Press, 1993).

26. In the words of the British theologian Keith Ward: "For incarnation [of the Word in Jesus] is not just a matter of God picking out some human being, any human being, and uniting that being to the Divine Word in a unique way. Human persons are to be understood in terms of their historical and cultural context, as parts of larger processes in the light of which we can interpret the meaning of their lives" (*Religion and Revelation*, 194).

27. In comparing the Righteous Teacher of the Qumran community with Jesus, James H. Charlesworth is struck by the differences in social support. The former had a fiercely loyal band of supporters who appear to have understood and supported him in his self-understanding. It was different for Jesus: "Jesus never obtained such support from his little band of Jews. The disciples failed to comprehend his message and did not follow him to the end. He died alone and deserted. According to [the Gospels of] Mark and Thomas, Jesus' only source for self-understanding was God, his Father" ("The Righteous Teacher and the Historical Jesus," in *Earthing Christologies: From Jesus' Parables to Jesus the Parable*, ed. James H. Charlesworth and Walter P. Weaver [Valley Forge, Pa.: Trinity Press International, 1995], 46–61, here 58).

28. It is true that in the Gospels of Mark, Matthew, and Luke, Jesus is depicted more as the proclaimer of the Word than the incarnation of the Word. But Paul, in letters written before these Gospels, is already identifying Jesus not just as the proclaimer but the proclaimed. By the time the Gospel of John is written late in the first century, the emphasis has shifted very much to the person of Jesus: it becomes almost more important to believe in Jesus than in the Word that Jesus proclaims. Nevertheless, I do not see as illegitimate a theological development that comes to see Jesus not only as the communicator of the Word but as the one identified with the Word in the most intimate way possible. In the words of Nils A. Dahl: "Even before Easter, however, the religious attention of the apostles must have been focused upon Jesus. For them, the call to repentance was virtually identical with the call to listen to Jesus and follow him. Before any explicit Christology emerged, sayings and actions of Jesus had identified him in terms of the coming kingdom of God" (*Jesus the Christ: The Historical Origins of Christological Doctrine* [Minneapolis: Fortress Press, 1991], 131).

29. See chap. 2, note 20, for more on human self-mediation through inner word.

30. In using the process of human self-mediation as an analogy for understanding God's self-mediation in Word and Spirit, I show my preference for the psychological analogy rather than the social analogy when trying to make some dim sense of God as Trinity. I ally myself then with a tradition going back at least as far as Augustine, further developed by Thomas Aquinas, and reaffirmed in our time by Karl Barth and Karl Rahner (see Karl Rahner, *The Trinity*, trans. Joseph

Donceel [New York: Herder and Herder, 1970]). Therefore, when I think on the Trinity, I think more in terms of one personal I who differentiates herself into three modes of subsistence, rather than on three personal I's who are perfectly united into a mutual, three-way I-Thou relationship. I share the view of Piet Schoonenberg that God does not stand in a perfectly mutual I-Thou relationship until God finds the perfect Son in Jesus, though I part company with him when he insists that this requires that we be totally silent about the "immanent" Trinity before its "economic" relationship with the earthly Son. See Piet Schoonenberg, "Trinity—The Consummated Covenant: Theses on the Doctrine of the Trinitarian God," *Studies in Religion*, 5 (1975-76): 111–16, and *Der Geist, Das Wort und Der Sohn: Eine Geist-Christologie* (Regensburg: Friedrich Pustet, 1991), 182–89. Schoonenberg's views are shared by Catherine Mowry LaCugna, *God for Us: The Trinity and Christian Life* (San Francisco: HarperSanFrancisco, 1993), 209–42. Liberationist theologians like Leonardo Boff (*Trinity and Society* [Maryknoll, N.Y.: Orbis Books, 1993]) and feminist theologians like Elizabeth Johnson (*She Who Is*) favor the social analogy (though on 207 Johnson shows awareness of the weaknesses of the social model) because they want to make egalitarian sociality and relationality intrinsic to the Godhead. I appreciate their aims, but I think they have neglected another key element in relationality, freedom. To say that God has by eternal nature full I-Thou inner-trinitarian relationships is to say that God has such relationships by metaphysical necessity. I should prefer to say that a true I-Thou relationship occurs when one I freely gives itself over to another Thou who freely responds to that gift. God finds this Thou not within the Trinity but within the world which God has freely created. Free relationality is at the heart of God's relationship with the created world. And thus to be freely relational, God needs the world, but this does not mean that the world is necessary. For help in untangling the philosophical issues, I relied on Keith Ward, *Rational Theology and the Creativity of God* (New York: Pilgrim Press, 1982), 86f and 138–42.

31. "God's 'relativity' is in the first instance vis-a-vis himself; but precisely because of that he is able to enter into relations with the *world* in unparalleled *freedom*" (Peter C. Hodgson, *Jesus—Word and Presence: An Essay in Christology* [Philadelphia: Fortress Press, 1971], 125). Earlier in his book, Hodgson informs the reader that he understood this relativity of God to Godself in terms of the divine Word: "God is the one who has the word absolutely and in this sense is the primordial word-event; the event of being" (116).

32. With virtual unanimity, Biblical scholars agree that a preexistent Word Christology like that of John's Gospel has for its background Jewish Wisdom theology. See, for example, the Old Testament book of Proverbs and the apocryphal book of Sirach, where Wisdom is depicted as a personified female figure who preexists the world (see Prov. 8:22-31; Sir. 24:1-12). There are clear traces of a Wisdom Christology in the Gospels (see Matt. 11:19; 11:42; Luke 11:31; 21:15). But this incipient Wisdom Christology was eventually transposed into the Christologies of the preexistent Word, which in turn became interchangeable with christologies of the preexistent Son, who eventually in later centuries is defined as the second person of the Trinity. Feminists rightly protest this development as a defeminiza-

tion of divine imagery for God and in reaction have been arguing strongly for a Wisdom or Sophia Christology (*Sophia* is the Greek word for Wisdom). See Elizabeth A. Johnson, "Jesus, Wisdom of God: A Biblical Basis for Non-Androcentric Christology," *Emphemerides Theologicae Lovanienses*, 61 (1985): 261–94 and *She Who Is*, 124–87; and Elisabeth Schüssler Fiorenza, "Wisdom Mythology and the Christological Hymns of the New Testament," in *Aspects of Wisdom in Judaism and Early Christianity*, ed. Robert L. Wilken (Notre Dame, Ind.: Notre Dame University Press, 1975), 17–41. For a very clear summary of Johnson's Sophia Christology, see Shannon Schrein, *Quilting and Braiding: The Feminist Christologies of Sallie McFague and Elizabeth A. Johnson in Conversation* (Collegeville, Minn.: Liturgical Press, 1998), 48–64.

33. That trinitarian theology developed partly as a way of explaining how God could be simultaneously fully within the economy of salvation and yet still be fully transcendent is, I think, what Rahner is trying to say in the following passage from *The Trinity:* "[T]he Father (God as such) is there [in the world as the Word]; yet he is the unoriginate, who keeps to himself, who remains the incomprehensible; . . . this distinction [between Father and Word] 'pre-exists' to the free gratuitous self-communication of God [in the world] . . . as its possibility" (64). But perhaps Isaak Dorner said it more clearly more than a century earlier: "Because God is distinguished in himself, he can maintain himself in self-impartation without self loss," ("System of Christian Doctrine, part 2, Special Doctrines: The Doctrine of Christ," in *God and Incarnation in Mid-Nineteenth Century German Theology*, trans. and ed. C. Welch [New York: Oxford University Press, 1965], 215).

34. Seely Beggiani, "A Case for Logocentric Theology," *Theological Studies* 32 (1971): 371–406: "Our stress on Logos is not intended to diminish the role of the Holy Spirit, who is the energizing force of love in the Trinity" (371, n. 1). Or "The Father is the unoriginated personal principle who forms a perfect self-expression, namely, the Word or Logos, and in accepting Self gives of Himself with full energy as Spirit" (378). The association of the Word (Hebrew *dabhar*, Greek *logos*) with meaning and the Spirit (Hebrew *ruach*, Greek *pneuma*) with power has a secure scriptural foundation (see Acts 1:8; 10:38; Rom. 15:13), though there is considerable overlap. Both meaning and power are combined in the metaphor of God as Wisdom (Greek *sophia*, which in the Old Testament is personified as a female figure), though the tilt is toward power (and specifically the power of feeling). I am indebted here to Bernard J. Lee, *Jesus and the Metaphors of God: The Christs of the New Testament* (New York: Paulist Press, 1993). Feminist theologians, who have done much to restore feeling to its rightful place in theological reflection, are especially attracted to an image of God as Wisdom and Christ as the human embodiment of Wisdom (see above, n. 32, for sources). I am attracted to using Wisdom as a metaphor that embraces the meanings of Word and Spirit, and I have tried it in my classes, most of which are comprised entirely of women, but I have found that the students usually give it a more cognitive or *Word* meaning when they use it. And thus Jesus becomes the embodiment of a higher knowledge or wisdom. So I have gone back to using Word and Spirit, pairing them as often as possible.

35. The baptism of Jesus by John is widely accepted as historical. It is of course very different with the voice and the dove that accompany the baptism. This is a *theophany*, a self-manifestation of God, that exceeds the reach of historical explanation. My discussion of it is motivated by the theological question of how God acts in the world to shape human identity, not with the historical question of the meaning of the baptism in the history of Jesus. For a strictly historical analysis, see John P. Meier, *A Marginal Jew*, 1.100–16. Another biblical story in which God is depicted as speaking is that of Jesus' transfiguration (see Mark 9:7; Matt. 17:5-6; Luke 9:34-35).

36. See Fyodor Dostoyevsky, *The Brothers Karamazov*, trans. by Constance Garnett (New York: Random House, Modern Library, 1950), 287ff. There is something fiercely right about Ivan's argumentation. For him, not the amount of innocent suffering is significant, but the sheer fact of its existence. Innocent suffering for Ivan does not have to reach a critical mass before the question of God's existence presses for an answer. Psychologically, it is understandable that an enormous evil like the Holocaust is what finally compels one to raise the question and give an atheistic answer, but philosophically, the question cries out for a response in the face of any innocent suffering, especially when this suffering is followed by death.

37. Harold Kushner, *When Bad Things Happen to Good People* (New York: Avon Books, 1981).

38. See Kushner, chapter 3, "Sometimes There is No Reason." In this chapter, he suggests that when the God of the book of Genesis hovered over the "formless void" (Gen. 1:2) and then imposed order on this chaos, God did not finish the work. There may then be "residual chaos, chance and mischance" (55) that escape the rule of natural law or the control of human freedom. Perhaps God's work is not yet finished or God has "left the rest [of the creative work] to us." Kushner may indeed be correct on this point, but his argument as presented in this chapter is marred by his failure to distinguish mere unlucky coincidence from random events that are pure chance, that have no cause. He gives the example (47) of an army veteran who, suffering from nightmarish memories of war, goes on a shooting rampage. An innocent woman walking along is struck by a bullet and killed. This surely is an example of unlucky coincidence, not a chaotic event that has completely escaped natural law or human freedom. For a positive view of "randomness" as that "free play" in nature that opens nature up to divine influence and human freedom, see John Polkinghorne, *Quarks, Chaos and Christianity: Questions to Science and Religion* (New York: Crossroad, 1997), 36–50.

39. Kushner, *When Bad Things Happen to Good People*, 43: "God would like people to get what they deserve in life, but cannot always arrange it." And on 148: "Can you learn to love and forgive [God] despite His limitations?" These passages suggest that God has limitations built into God's nature. Some things God cannot do, and that is all there is to it. And yet there are passages that suggest God's free self-limitation (see n. 41 below).

40. On Rabbi Kushner and process theism, see David Ray Griffin, *Evil Revisited:*

Responses and Reconsideration (Albany: SUNY Press, 1991), 229, n. 2. Griffin's first study of evil resulted in a very fine account in his *God, Power, and Evil: A Process Theodicy* (Lanham, Md.: University Press of America, 1990).

41. Kushner, *When Bad Things Happen to Good People*, 81: "God has set Himself the limit that He will not intervene to take away our freedom."

42. The whole question of how God acts in the world finally turns on the question of necessity and freedom in God's relation to the world. In one respect, neoclassical process theism comes down stronger on necessity, insisting that the world exists of necessity and that the metaphysical principles governing the relationship between God and the world exist of necessity. God thus at best can only choose how the world is in its general structure and never that the world is. Classical theism on its part is very intent on preserving divine freedom, believing that both how the world is and that it is are the result of free divine choice. According to classical theism, God can be God even if the world does not exist. I have enormous respect for process theism, but if pushed I find myself inclined more to protect divine freedom than to insist on the eternal rule of metaphysical principle with respect to God's relationship to the world. And yet a part of me doubts that God intervenes miraculously in natural laws or human freedom, and in some dim way I am inclined to believe that God cannot do so. But this "cannot" is a consequence of divine choice rather than prior to divine choice. My intuition is that the choice of God to create a relatively autonomous world with its own life carries with it the requirement that God respect the logic of God's own choices. I cannot argue this point in a rationally compelling way; I can only offer it as an intuition. This does not answer all the questions. One still cries out, "Why not at least an occasional intervention?" and I feel the force of the question, and unlike the process theists, I have no neat philosophical argument against the possibility of such an intervention.

I have a second reason for leaning toward classical theism: to do justice to an emotion that along with Kushner I believe is usually unjustified, yet sometimes is justified, namely, anger at God. As far as I can tell, process thought permits no anger at God, no lamentations as recorded in the Old Testament, for God is in the same grip of metaphysical principles as we are. But if God is freer than that, then in some deeply mysterious way this world is more God's "fault." And sometimes a kind of rage wells up in us, and we shake our fist at God and scream, "Why create such a mess? Could you not have done better?" For the process theist, an expression of such anger is purely cathartic: it has no metaphysical justification. Without believing for a second that God directly causes suffering or requires it as part of an overarching plan, I nevertheless sense that some kind of anger is strangely appropriate and that it is precipitated by a deep intuition about the extent of divine freedom.

I offer all this in a spirit of speculative modesty. For all that God has revealed of God's loving self, God remains hidden and incomprehensible, and in the face of evil, awesome and unsettling. I take with great seriousness David Tracy's warning: "It is self-destructively sentimental for Christians to allow their understanding of the God who is Love to be separated from the Hidden God" ("The Hidden God: The Divine Other of Liberation," *Cross Currents*, 46 [1996]: 13).

43. No one has spoken with greater eloquence, or with more sorrow and anger, about God's silence in the concentration camps than Elie Wiesel: "The barbed-wire kingdom will forever remain an immense question mark on the scale of both humanity and its Creator. Faced with unprecedented suffering and agony, He should have intervened, or at least expressed Himself. Whose side was He on?" (*All Rivers Run to the Sea: Memoirs* [New York: Schocken Books, 1995], 105). For a searingly honest Christian response to Wiesel's work, see Robert McAfee Brown, *Elie Wiesel: Messenger to All Humanity* (Notre Dame, Ind.: University of Notre Dame Press, 1983), especially chap. 5, "The Silence of God, and the Necessity of Contention," 139–65.

44. Without claiming to be privy to the details of Jesus' inner consciousness, I think what Jesus said and did historically is consistent with concluding theologically that he possessed the "Abba-experience." With Edward Schillebeeckx, I agree that while this alone is not enough to sustain a full-blown trinitarian Christology, it does nevertheless point to "a religious experience of deep intimacy with God, in terms of which Jesus would seem to be conscious of a distinction between his experience and of God and that of his disciples" (*Jesus: An Experiment in Christology*, 263). Support for Schillebeeckx's position can be found in James H. Charlesworth, *Jesus Within Judaism*, 132–36. See also Bernard Cooke, *God's Beloved: Jesus' Experience of the Transcendent* (Philadelphia: Trinity Press International, 1992), 1–24. Cooke writes: "I think the evidence points very strongly to Jesus' use of the term 'Abba,' but even more strongly to the kind of experience that has been associated with it" (7). Cooke points out further that though "Abba" is a male metaphor, Jesus' words and actions as the obedient servant of the divine Abba show him to be a Jewish male who offered a "radical challenge to the image of God as superpatriarch" (57). See also the very insightful remarks by Sandra M. Schneiders, *Women and the Word* (New York: Paulist Press, 1986), 37–49.

45. A few decades later, the power that energized this Word was fully personified as the Holy Spirit, the "third person." At the Council of Nicaea (325 C.E.), the Holy Spirit is scarcely mentioned, but by the Council of Constantinople (381 C.E.), the Holy Spirit is elevated into the Trinity of divine persons. See Leo Donald Davis, *The First Seven Ecumenical Councils (325–787): Their History and Theology* (Wilmington, Del.: Michael Glazier, Inc., 1987), 81–133.

46. See, for example, Keith Ward, *A Vision to Pursue: Beyond the Crisis in Christianity* (London: SCM Press, 1991), 100–101.; Frans Jozef van Beeck, *Christ Proclaimed: Christology as Rhetoric* (New York: Paulist Press, 1978), 390; and Roger Haight, *Jesus Symbol of God* (Maryknoll, N.Y.: Orbis Books, 1999), 274–85.

47. If we regard the incarnation as an accomplished fact that merely is *revealed* in Jesus' life and death (and of which Jesus merely becomes increasingly conscious), then we devalue Jesus' *developing* personhood. We forget that Jesus as an infant is not just a person in fact but a person in potential. He lies there open to receiving the identity-forming words from human persons and the identity-forming Word from a divine person. As an infant he cannot receive much, but he is already on his way toward a greater capacity to receive more. The confluence of

divine and human influences in interaction with his developing freedom will produce the personal center that we call the one divine-human Son. Nels F. S. Ferré says it well: "Incarnation must be conceived of as an *event in history,* not as a descent on humanity from outside without need for historic time and decision" (*Christ and the Christians* [New York: Harper and Brothers, 1958], 104). I find attractive the view of Piet Schoonenberg who speaks of a mutual "enhypostasis" by which the Word becomes fully personalized in the human history of Jesus and Jesus becomes fully personalized by the Word (in the power of the Spirit) (*Der Geist, Das Wort und Der Sohn,* 193, n. 37). Even those who out of loyalty to a particular interpretation of classical Christology would insist against Schoonenberg that the Word is already fully personalized as the second Person of the Trinity, must grant, I believe, that the full personalization of Jesus' human nature by that Word requires "historic time and decision." Otherwise, the full humanity of Jesus is compromised. Growing freely into personhood is an essential mark of human nature.

48. In the words of Peter C. Hodgson: "The cross is the event by which Jesus' being as presence is fully realized, since it is the final . . . enactment of the word of faith" *Jesus—Word and Presence,* 55.

49. I was first alerted to the determinism of the apocalyptic worldview while reading Jürgen Moltmann, *Theology of Hope: On the Ground and the Implications of a Christian Eschatology,* trans. James W. Leitch (New York: Harper and Row, 1967), 133–38. I should stress here that I am not using the word *determinism* in a pandeterminist sense, as if all were determined and human freedom were nonexistent. I have been alerted by the Jesuit theologian John H. Wright in private communication that *determinism* is a later Stoic and Neo-Platonic idea that should not be read into the Bible. Perhaps *determinism* is not the best word here, yet I do not think it can be denied that with respect to the overall unfolding of the events of salvation history, the apocalyptic view is more deterministic than the earlier prophetic view. The prophets saw God as able and willing to revise plans in response to human repentance (see Ezek. 18:30, Mal. 3:6-12). Granted, apocalyptic does not deny the human freedom, but it is more a freedom to trust or not trust in the divine plan than it is a freedom to influence it in any significant way.

50. Benedict Viviano, "The Gospel according to Matthew," in *The New Jerome Biblical Commentary,* Raymond E. Brown et al., eds., 42:19, pp. 630–74, here, 638, says that the "historicity of the [temptation of Jesus] need not be doubted." Robert A. Karris, "The Gospel according to Luke," (ibid.) says: "But since 4:1-13 contains such a mythological way of thinking, it is difficult to assess its historicity. It is somewhat plausible to [think] that Jesus himself used these apocalyptic thought patterns of his day to tell his disciples about the testings of his faith engendered by the conflicts he encountered when he preached the kingdom" (43:52, pp. 675–721, here, 688). E. P. Sanders concludes his discussion of the temptation stories by saying that "it is reasonable . . . to think that Jesus really did fast and pray before beginning his active ministry and that he was subject to temptation" (*The Historical Figure of Jesus,* 117). N. T. Wright, *Jesus and the Victory of God,* argues that the success of Jesus' mission necessarily entailed a victory over Satan, and that the "hypothesis" (458)

that such a victory began with a "struggle that he had undergone immediately after the baptism" (457) is a "likely one" (458).

51. I am thinking here of Jesus' agony in the Garden of Gethsemane (see Mark 14:32-42 and parallels in Matt. 26:36-46; Luke 22:39-46). Wright, *Jesus and the Victory of God*, 606, rightly sees this agony as Jesus' final battle not only with his own doubts and fears, but with Satan as the "power of darkness" (see Luke 22:53). This scene of agony, which is "hard to comprehend as a later Christian invention," recalls Jesus' earlier temptations.

4. The Mission of Jesus

1.   John F. O'Grady writes: "Jesus lived by transferring the epicenter of his life to God, to *Abba*, and thus the externals always expressed the internal principle. This does not mean that he found his center of existence outside himself; rather he discovered that his center was his relationship to God and thus he could live a harmonious life in which the outward expression flowed from an inner conviction" (*Models of Jesus Revisited* [New York: Paulist Press, 1993], 181).

2.   I align myself therefore with the theological view that the full incarnation of the Word in the power of the Spirit is God's intention for creation from the beginning and not an intention that emerges in the divine consciousness only because Adam and Eve as the first human beings sinned. The former view is known as the Scotist view after Duns Scotus (1266–1308); the latter view is known as the Thomistic view after Thomas Aquinas (1224–1274). Yet I would not want my Scotism to be interpreted to mean that before the world and before sin God had predetermined the incarnation of Word in precisely the man Jesus in first-century Palestine. Rather, the divine intentionality is more general than that and therefore open to the contingencies of natural accident and human freedom. I reject therefore the kind of strict Scotist Christocentrism that can be found in a theologian like Karl Barth. Here, I am indebted to the ideas put forward by Eugene TeSelle, *Christ in Context: Divine Purpose and Human Possibility* (Philadelphia: Fortress Press, 1975), who argues for a general "covenantal commitment" on God's part that is present to creation from the beginning and yet open to greater precision in response to the contingencies of nature and history. On the differences between Scotus and Thomas, see the references supplied by O'Grady, *Models of Jesus Revisited*, 93.

3.   If the love of God leads necessarily to the love of other human beings, is not the reverse true? Does not love of other human beings mean necessarily that one is loving God because in loving others one has allied oneself completely with God's intention for the world? Karl Rahner has worked out a complicated yes to this question, even to the point of asserting that one can love God in loving the other even without being consciously aware that one indeed is also loving God. He writes: "In the original act which precedes all reflex systematisations, God is always

given as the subjectively all-bearing *ground* of experience, a ground which is beyond this world; he is therefore given indirectly in a kind of boundary experience as the origin and destination of an act which is objectively directed towards the world and which, therefore, . . . is a loving communication with . . . the Thou [the neighbor] in the world." God therefore is the unconscious "destination" of the act of neighbor love. Quoted from Karl Rahner, "Reflections on the Unity of Love of Neighbor and Love of God," *Theological Investigations*, vol. 6, trans. Karl-H. and Boniface Kruger (New York: Crossroad, 1974), 244–45.

4.   In New Testament Greek, the word for end or final or last is *eschaton*, and thus Jesus is the eschatological prophet: "Long ago God spoke to our ancestors in many and various ways by the prophets, but in these last [*eschatou*] days he has spoken to us by a Son" (Heb. 1:1-2). Edward Schillebeeckx has argued persuasively that the first confessional utterances of Jesus' followers identified him as the eschatological prophet. See his *Jesus: An Experiment in Christology*, trans. by Hubert Hoskins (New York: Crossroad Books, 1979), 441–49. Also see Bernard Cooke, *God's Beloved: Jesus' Experience of the Transcendent* (Philadelphia: Trinity Press International, 1992), chap. 4, "Jesus' Experience as an Israelite Prophet." Cooke argues that one of the modes of Jesus' self-identification is that of prophet and shows in detail the continuity between Jesus and earlier prophets. No Israelite prophet therefore is a mere messenger; all show an immediate "awareness of the divine" (76), though Jesus' awareness was "beyond anything granted his predecessors" (81). See also the monumentally erudite and in large part convincing depiction of Jesus as an eschatological prophet by N. T. Wright, *Jesus and the Victory of God* (Minneapolis: Fortress Press, 1996), especially 145–243.

5.   These words from Matthew (paralleled in Luke 10:21-22) are part of a longer passage: "At that time Jesus said, 'I thank you, Father, Lord of heaven and earth, because you have hidden these things from the wise and the intelligent and have revealed them to infants; yes, Father, for such was your gracious will. All things have been handed over to me by my Father, and no one knows the Son except the Father, and no one knows the Father except the Son and anyone to whom the Son chooses to reveal him.'" For decades, biblical scholars have tended to dismiss Matt. 11:25-27 as a later creation of the Hellenized Christian church, but there is now more willingness to trace it back to Jesus and to his Jewish wisdom heritage. See, for example, the careful argumentation of Ben Witherington III, *The Christology of Jesus* (Minneapolis: Fortress Press, 1990), 215–22.

6.   The Greek word is *exousia* and can, depending on the context, be translated as authority, in the sense of being authorized, or power, in the sense of being able to effect something. Not infrequently, it is difficult to decide which of the two senses applies. What is clear to me is that Jesus, and gradually his followers, understand him as both authorized and empowered by God. The other important New Testament word for power is *dynamis*, and this too is a power that comes from God and is closely associated with God's Spirit, as in Luke 4:14: "Then Jesus, filled with the power [*dynamei*] of the Spirit, returned to Galilee." On the various meanings of *dynamis* and *exousia*, see William F. Arndt and F. Wilbur Gingrich, *A Greek-English*

Lexicon of the New Testament (Chicago: University of Chicago Press, 1957), 206–7, 278–79. E. P. Sanders, *The Historical Figure of Jesus* (London: Allan Lane Penguin Press, 1993), 238–39, sees Jesus' authority exercised in the "follow me" passages, most extraordinarily in Matt. 8:21-22: "'Lord, first let me go and bury my father.' But Jesus said to him, 'Follow me, and let the dead bury their own dead.'" Here Jesus' authority overrides filial piety. Also in play here is Jesus' eschatological urgency: the reign of God is at hand; time is short!

7. At this point the analogy between God-Jesus and Anne-Sarah reaches its outer limits. The identity-sharing between God and Jesus has a depth and completeness that has no exact parallel in human life.

8. Numerous passages in the New Testament show that the reign of God was dawning in and through what Jesus was saying and doing: "But if it is by the finger of God that I cast out the demons, then the kingdom of God has come to you" (Luke 11:20); "The kingdom of God is among you" (Luke 17:21); "'The time is fulfilled, and the kingdom of God has come near'" (Mark 1:15); and when John the Baptizer's followers ask Jesus if he is the one to come, Jesus responds, "Go and tell John what you have seen and heard: the blind receive their sight, the lame walk, the lepers are cleansed, the deaf hear, the dead are raised, the poor have good news brought to them" (Luke 7:22). Jesus' strong claim to be embodying the reign of God in his actions distinguishes him from the Baptizer and most likely from all other Jews who preached the coming of the final age. In the words of the great Jewish scholar David Flusser: "[Jesus] is the only Jew of ancient times known to us who preached that the new age of salvation had already begun" (*Jesus,* 2nd ed. [Jerusalem: Magnes Press, 1998]), 110.

9. Matt. 10:40. We see here connection between the subspecialty of theology called Christology, which is concerned with Jesus' person or identity, and the subspecialty called soteriology, which is concerned with Jesus as the one called to the mission of saving by making the Word and Spirit of God present to Israel. It is precisely the intimacy of shared identity that gives Jesus the authority to make the welcoming of him during his mission tantamount to the welcoming of the God who sent him on this mission.

10. Keith Ward, *Religion and Revelation: A Theology of Revelation in the World's Religions* (Oxford: Clarendon Press, 1994), 272.

11. See Mark 6:46; 14:32; Matt. 14:23; 26:36-44; Luke 3:21; 5:16; 6:12; 9:18; 9:28-29; 11:1; John 17; and Heb. 5:7.

12. See his prayer in the Garden of Gethsemane: Matt. 26:36-46; Mark 14:32-42; Luke 22:39-46.

13. In the previous chapter, I offered a Christology that sees Jesus' Sonship as an identity that he does not possess in eternity but which is the result of God's self-communication in Word that only becomes Jesus' full possession over time. This "over time" includes the mission. Indeed, I should want to say that Jesus fully proves and secures his identity in and through his mission. It is then a unique identity not the least because it is a unique mission. It is therefore abstract and misleading to discuss Jesus' uniqueness solely in terms of his identity, especially

an eternal identity, neglecting the unfolding, earthly, dialectical union between identity and mission. According to Brian Hebblethwaite, in his *The Incarnation: Collected Essays in Christology* (Cambridge: Cambridge University Press, 1987), "the main point of the incarnation is not a matter of relation at all. It is a matter of identity. Jesus *is* God incarnate" (52). Precisely here is the rub. Hebblethwaite means here a preexistent, eternal identity, whereas I mean an identity that God communicates to Jesus from the beginning but that is fully secured only through a relation between God's Word and Jesus that unfolds in time and culminates in death.

14. I share with Third Questors a confidence that Jesus' teaching is generally accessible to historical research. See N. T. Wright, *Jesus and the Victory of God*, 83–91.

15. The Hebrew for *anointed one* is *messiah*, whose Greek translation in turn is *Christ*.

16. The term *proto-rabbi* is taken from Leonard Swidler, *Yeshua: A Model for Moderns* (Kansas City, Mo.: Sheed and Ward, 1988), 49, who in turn is dependent on Phillip Sigal, *The Halakhah of Jesus of Nazareth according to the Gospel of Matthew* (Lanham, Md.: University Press of America, 1987), 6.

17. Matt. 5:17: "Do not think that I have come to abolish the law or the prophets; I have come not to abolish but to fulfill."

18. Swidler, *Yeshua*, 82–83: "What was most special about Yeshua [Jesus] was that he *lived* not only according to the Torah, but also according to his supererogatory kenotic ideal, *lifnim meshurat hadin*—even to the point of agonizingly dying for the sake of his friends."

19. Jesus' summons to repentance was not just to individual persons but to corporate entities in Israel and the corporate entity of Israel. Jesus could upbraid whole cities that failed to repent (see Matt. 11:20-24), lament over Jerusalem's rejection of his message (Matt. 23:37-39), and weep over the fate of a Jerusalem that failed to hear his word (Luke 19:41-43). See Wright, *Jesus and the Victory of God*, 248, 256.

20. The contrast between the judgmental John the Baptizer and the merciful Jesus has been overdrawn: both teach judgment and salvation, punishment and forgiveness. But a difference in emphasis is clearly discernible. In the words of Marius Reiser, *Jesus and Judgment: The Eschatological Proclamation in Its Jewish Context* (Minneapolis: Fortress Press, 1997): "Jesus' preaching was sustained by the conviction that the repentance of the individual and of the whole nation should not so much aim at avoiding catastrophe as at gaining God's salvation. Thus, for him, in contrast to the Baptizer, the offer of salvation stands in the foreground of his preaching. The central focus of his speech and action is not judgment and the way to avoid it, but the reign of God and how to gain it; it is not fear of judgment that should move Israel to repentance, but the fascination of the reign of God. Therefore the message could not be better summarized than in Mark 1:15 ['The time is fulfilled, and the kingdom of God has come near; repent, and believe in the good news.']. But when it met with rejection, Jesus had to point to the reverse of the medal" (255; also see 315).

21. I am using the word *moment* here not in the sense of chronological priority but in the sense of logical priority.

22. For the woman and the lost coin as a neglected female metaphor for the reign of God, I am indebted to Rachel Wahlberg, *Jesus according to a Woman*, 2nd rev. ed. (New York: Paulist Press, 1986), 27–34.

23. See Luke 7:36-50. John F. Haught in his *What Is God: How to Think about the Divine* (New York: Paulist Press, 1986) has some wonderful things to say about the way unconditional acceptance provides the context for eliciting honesty from the recipient of such acceptance: "The only alternative to a religious vision of ultimate unconditional acceptance is the view that reality offers us merely conditional acceptance at best. But can this latter option conceivably be a truthful interpretation of our situation? Our settling for merely conditional love, a love whose other side is always fear of rejection if one does not fulfill the conditions, lies in opposition to a desire for the truth about ourselves. For in such a case we shall inevitably devise illusory conceptions of ourselves in order to combat the fear of rejection by others who place conditions on their acceptance of us" (105–6). "The name for this truth that coincides with unconditional love is God" (109). This honesty that a forgiving God enables us to embrace is of course an honesty about our guilt. But we cannot know how guilty we are until we know the full goodness of the God we have sinned against. And this goodness is revealed precisely in God's love. Karl Rahner says it well: "The ultimate and radical nature of guilt itself lies in the fact that it takes place in the face of a loving and self-communicating God, and only when a person knows this and makes this truth his own can he understand the depths of guilt" (*Foundations of Christian Faith: An Introduction to the Idea of Christianity*, trans. William V. Dych [New York: Seabury Press, A Crossroad Book, 1978], 93).

24. On the importance of the heart, understood in the Scriptures as the deepest dimension of the feeling and willing self, see Matt. 15:18-20; 18:35; 19:8; Mark 6:51; 7:21; 10:5; Luke 8:15. See also Wright, *Jesus and the Victory of God*, 282–87, where he shows how Jesus' call for a "renewed heart" can only be understood as one of the characteristics of the "renewed covenant," which is dawning in the present age but coming to full fruition in the eschatological age to come. Jesus' ethics are not therefore an abstract system but a call to live in conformity to the reign that is coming.

25. Further nuancing is in order. A careful reading of the Gospels reveals, I believe, an earthly Jesus more intent on challenging people to carry out the ethical ideal than a Jesus supplying people with the power to carry out the ideal. To be sure, Jesus is "filled with the power of the Spirit" (Luke 4:14), but this Spirit is more engaged in leading Jesus to mission and enabling him to perform deeds of power such as exorcisms and miracles, than empowering the hearers of his word to meet the ethical challenge. In the New Testament, the full transformative power of Jesus' Spirit is given more emphasis after Jesus' death. As the risen Lord, Jesus can unleash the Spirit in a way that he could not while on his earthly mission. And thus it is especially Paul (though see John 3:33; 7:39), who has encountered Jesus only as the risen Christ, who emphasizes the power of Christ's Spirit to transform human beings into loving people. See Rom. 1:4; 5:5; 6:4; 8:9; 2 Cor. 1:21-22; Gal. 1:4; 2:19; 4:6; Phil. 3:10; 2 Thess. 3:5;12:13.

26. See John Donahue, *The Gospel in Parable: Metaphor, Narrative, and Theology in the Synoptic Gospels* (Philadelphia: Fortress Press, 1988), 10: "For the most part, parables are extended similes, since they have an introductory 'like' or 'it may be compared to.'"

27. Donahue, *The Gospel in Parable*, 75. I am reliant on Donahue, 72–79, at crucial points in my analysis of this parable.

28. Reiser, in his *Jesus and Judgment*, throughout, offers a sobering corrective to all attempts to expurgate Jesus' teaching of the moment of judgment. The note of eschatological judgment is unmistakably sounded in Jesus' teaching about the reign of God, sometimes in terms that will strike the contemporary person as over-harsh. We must not forget that Jesus is a person of his time and in some respects a stranger to us. He is sharply either-or. The reign of God is not something one can negotiate or finesse. Either yes, and the consequent joy of dining at the eschatological banquet, or no, and the self-imposed agony of exclusion from the reign of God. And again, this judgment is directed toward not only individuals but also towns, cities, the whole nation.

29. So demanding is the lifestyle of those who enter the reign of God that the American theologian Reinhold Niebuhr calls it an "ideal" that is both "relevant" and yet "impossible." See his *An Interpretation of Christian Ethics* (1935; reprint, New York: Crossroad, 1979), 5, 19, 22–38, 62–83, 141. Albert Schweitzer found Jesus' moral demands so difficult that he was convinced that Jesus could only have meant them to apply to the short "interim period" between Jesus' announcement of the reign and its final coming at the end of the present age. On Schweitzer's idea of the "interim ethic," see Hans Schwarz, *Christology* (Grand Rapids, Mich.: Eerdmans, 1998), 32–33. It is precisely because Niebuhr sees Jesus' ethic as still "relevant" that he rejects Schweitzer's relegation of that ethic to a brief interim period.

30. The communicative importance of food and table fellowship in Jewish culture is examined by Gillian Feeley-Harnik in *The Lord's Table: Eucharist and Passover in Early Christianity* (Philadelphia: University of Pennsylvania Press, 1981): see especially chap. 4, "Food Symbolism in the Judaic Tradition," 71–106. Jesus' table fellowship was, to use the words of the social ethicist Stephen C. Mott, one of the ways Jesus crossed "status boundaries" and thereby attacked one of "the most basic elements of the social system" ("The Use of the New Testament for Social Ethics," *The Journal of Religious Ethics*, 15 [1987]: 225–59; here, 236). John Dominic Crossan sees in Jesus' "open commensality" (that is, open-table fellowship) one of the dominant motifs of Jesus' teaching and action. *The Historical Jesus: The Life of a Mediterranean Jewish Peasant* (San Francisco: HarperSanFrancisco, 1991), 261–64. Crossan, however, eliminates entirely any connection between these meals and the eschatological banquet, the banquet that was for Jesus a symbol of the new age to come. In the words of N. T. Wright: "Most writers now agree that eating and drinking with 'sinners' was one of the most characteristic and striking marks of Jesus' regular activity. This would not have been of any significance, of course, if Jesus were acting simply as a private individual. But when

it is allied with the claim, made in practice and story, that Jesus was inaugurating the long-awaited kingdom, it becomes deeply symbolic. That is why . . . it aroused controversy. Jesus was, as it were, celebrating the messianic banquet, and doing so with the wrong people" (*Jesus and the Victory of God,* 431).The key biblical passages are Mark 2:13-17; Matt. 9:10-13; 22:1-13; Luke 5:29-32; 7:34;14:13-24; 15:1-2; 19:1-10.

31. For an excellent introduction (along with lists of biblical passages and secondary sources) to the question of Jesus' relationship to women see Gerd Theissen and Annette Merz, *The Historical Jesus: A Comprehensive Guide* (Minneapolis: Fortress Press, 1998), 219–25. In Jesus' teaching about the coming reign of God, we can hear a strong note of radical social egalitarianism, which has led some contemporary feminists to believe that the reign of God demands equality between the sexes. They point to Jesus' rejection of the patriarchal family in favor of the family of God (see Mark 3:35; 10:28-30; Matt. 23:8–10) as inspiring to a feminist today. Many of my women students do not hesitate to call Jesus a feminist. I believe firmly that equality between the sexes is a necessary theological retrieval of Jesus' teaching, but to call him a feminist strikes me as somewhat anachronistic and misleading. It makes him stand out too dramatically from his time and can lead to a new form of anti-Judaism: "Under the title 'Jesus and women' it is the historical uniqueness of Jesus that is frequently presented. This means that a good deal of energy is expended in presenting Jesus in opposition to Judaism. . . . There is an anti-Judaism that is [therefore] related to the subject 'Jesus and women" (Luise Schottroff, Silvia Schoer, and Marie-Theres Wacker, *Feminist Interpretation: The Bible in Women's Perspective* [Minneapolis: Fortress Press, 1998], 222. This is not to deny the feminist implications of Jesus' egalitarianism, which already began to yield fruit in the earliest Christian communities, but it is an egalitarianism that has its roots in Jewish eschatology. For the egalitarian tendencies in Jewish eschatology, see Dale Allison, *Jesus of Nazareth: Millenarian Prophet* (Minneapolis: Fortress Press, 1998), 63, 108–9. For evidence of early (sadly short-lived) Christian egalitarianism between the sexes, see Elisabeth Schüssler Fiorenza, *In Memory of Her: A Feminist Theological Reconstruction of Christian Origins* (New York: Crossroad, 1983), 160–204.

32. John P. Meier places the exorcisms in a separate category (*A Marginal Jew: Rethinking the Historical Jesus,* 2 vols. [New York: Doubleday, 1991, 1994], 2.646–61). Meier also has a separate category for the miracles of raising the dead. Only three such miracles are recounted, and each belongs to a separate tradition: the raising of the daughter of Jairus (Mark 5:21-43), the raising the son of the widow of Nain (Luke 7:11-17), and the raising of Lazarus (John 11:1-45). All of them, says Meier, probably go back to "some incident" in Jesus' ministry that led his followers to believe that Jesus could indeed raise people from the dead. The raising that has the greatest claim to historicity, raising of Jairus' daughter, could in fact be a "miracle of healing" (2.787). In general, Meier is very reluctant as a historian to say more than that "some incident" lies behind these stories. He is especially cautious about the other two: "I can understand well why others would prefer to

assign it [son of the widow of Nain] entirely to the early church. The same can be said for John's story of the raising of Lazarus" (2.970).

33. Meier is not saying that he as a historian has judged that these incidents were indeed miracles in the theological sense. He warns throughout his analysis that he cannot as a historian say that Jesus did indeed perform a miracle through the power of God. This is a theological judgment that can only be made in faith. All he concludes as a historian is that some of the miracle stories (especially those of exorcism and healing) go back to incidents that make it plausible that some witnesses believed that Jesus performed a miracle.

34. Meier, *A Marginal Jew*, 2.970. The one exception is the feeding of the multitude: "[T]he multiple attestation of sources and the coherence of the story with Jesus' habit of holding joyful meals fraught with eschatological significance argue for a historical basis to the feeding of the multitude. The story must go back to an especially memorable and symbolic meal Jesus celebrated with a large crowd by the Sea of Galilee" (2.970).

35. Wright, *Jesus and the Victory of God*, 191. Wright explains in his *The New Testament and People of God* (Minneapolis: Fortress Press, 1992), xv, why he does not capitalize the word *god*.

36. Sanders, *The Historical Figure of Jesus*, 168.

37. This transformation is not only of the self, but of the physical world in which that self is embedded. Unlike Meier, Wright does not judge the nature miracles on their historicity but draws out their theological significance: "Thus it is not surprising that we find echoes in the gospels of strange events in which Jesus exercises power over the natural order, bringing it into a new harmony with itself and with the divine saving purpose only previously seen at odd moments such as the crossing of the Red Sea. The extraordinary catch of fish, the stilling of the storms, the desert feedings, and, negatively, the cursing of the fig tree, must all be included here. . . . In all of these, as in the 'might works' as a whole, what was 'seen' within the first-century Jewish worldview would be the restoration of creation, which Israel had expected to happen when her god became her king and she was vindicated by him" (*Jesus and the Victory of God*, 193–94).

38. This assumes that the spiritual cannot be reduced to the psychological, and the psychological cannot be reduced to the physical. The physical is thus not a closed system operating solely according to its own laws of cause and effect, but is a system open to psychological and spiritual power, especially when placed within a complex unity like that of a human person where the spiritual, psychological, and physical dimensions interact in extraordinarily subtle and complex ways. I am not offering a purely psychosomatic explanation whereby through autosuggestion, hypnosis, or exaggerated placebo effect the person is cured. This would be a natural explanation. Rather, I am talking here of the power of God's Spirit working through Jesus on the spirit of the person healed by faith. This power from God may indeed be continuously present to and in the creative process that is the world. Charismatic healers like Jesus are able to open up to this power and use it for the good. Thus a healing miracle does not require a unilateral, abrupt intervention on

God's part, but the full utilization of a power that God is always feeding into the world. It is faith as openness to this power that allows Jesus to effect the healing. In connection with this whole discussion, there is that remarkable passage in Mark 6:1-6 (see also Matt. 13:58) where Jesus comes to his hometown and the townspeople take "offense at him." It goes on: "And he could do no deed of power there, except that he laid his hands on a few sick people and cured them. And he was amazed at their unbelief." Perhaps here we see an indication that Jesus' miracle working may have depended in part on the spiritual flow between him and others, and not only on the spiritual flow between him and God.

39. According to Wright, the "evidence from Qumran suggests that, in some Jewish circles at least, a maimed Jew could not be a full member of the community. In addition to the physical burden of being blind, or lame, or deaf, or dumb, such a Jew was blemished, and unable to be a full Israelite. How far this was taken by Jewish society in Jesus' day is difficult to assess. But we know that at least in Qumran it was a very serious matter. This means that Jesus' healing miracles must be seen clearly as bestowing the gift of *shalom*, wholeness, to those who lacked it, bringing not only physical health but renewed membership in the people of Yahweh" (*Jesus and the Victory of God*, 191–92).

40. In the words of Wright, *Jesus and the Victory of God*, 193: "They [the healing miracles] were linked with the great blessing of the renewed covenant, namely the forgiveness of sins." The healing of the paralytic brings together in a particularly dramatic way the faith that accepts God's forgiving love and the faith that allows the healing power of Jesus to have its effect. See Matt. 9:2-7; Mark 2:1-10; Luke 5:17-26.

41. It is striking how frequently Jesus performs a healing miracle and then asks the person healed to keep it quiet. See Matt. 12:16; Mark 1:43-44; 5:43; 7:36; Luke 5:14. Then there are passages like Mark 8:11-13: "The Pharisees came and began to argue with him, asking him for a sign from heaven, to test him. And he sighed deeply in his spirit and said, 'Why does this generation ask for a sign?'" And we can sense his frustration when the Gospel of John has him say: "Unless you see signs and wonders you will not believe" (John 4:48). All this makes it understandable that "Jesus did not want to rest his case on miracles" (Sanders, *The Historical Figure of Jesus*, 167).

42. When the liberation theologian Jon Sobrino, in his *Jesus the Liberator: A Historical-Theological Reading of Jesus of Nazareth* (Maryknoll, N.Y.: Orbis Books: 1993), discusses Jesus' miracles he places the emphasis on Jesus' compassion for suffering people and on the liberation of the whole self, not just the spiritual self. Precisely here, we see how in his miracles Jesus applies what Sobrino calls the "principle of partiality for the poor" (18), for it is the poor who lack the means to achieve bodily and psychological health. See his discussion of miracles, 88–95; on Jesus' compassion, see 90.

43. An excellent illustration of the primacy of the spiritual is Luke's story of Jesus' healing of the ten lepers. Only one of the ten healed shows gratitude and praise to Jesus and God. And he is a Samaritan. It is only to him that Jesus says, "Your faith has made you well," that is, completely well, physically and spiritually. See Luke 17:11-19.

5. The Death of Jesus as the Final Word of Mission

1. Peter C. Hodgson says it well: "The saving significance of this particular death can be understood only from the significance of the particular life that preceded it" (*Jesus—Word and Presence: An Essay in Christology* [Philadelphia: Fortress Press, 1971], 204).

2. The reader will recall that *soteriology* means a theory of how Jesus the *soter*, the savior, saves human beings.

3. In the words of N. T. Wright: "[Jesus'] ministry and his death are thus loosely connected. . . . If the main purpose of Jesus' ministry was to die on the cross, as the outworking of an abstracted atonement-theology, it starts to look as though he simply took on the establishment in order to get himself crucified, so that the abstract sacrificial theology could be put into effect. This makes both the ministry and death look like sheer contrivance" (*Jesus and the Victory of God* [Minneapolis: Fortress Press, 1996], 14).

4. On the tension between the reign (kingdom, rule, dominion) of God as already present and realizing itself through Jesus' ministry and this reign as the object of Jesus' eschatological hope, see John P. Meier's magisterially detailed and convincing exposition in *A Marginal Jew: Rethinking the Historical Jesus,* 2 vols. (New York: Doubleday, 1991, 1994), 2.287–397 (kingdom as present) and 2.398–500 (kingdom as future).

5. From the very beginning of the modern search for the historical Jesus, historical reconstructions of Jesus' mission have interpreted it as motivated primarily by the intention to instigate a social, political, or economic revolution. See the work of Herman Samuel Reimarus in the eighteenth century (*Fragments*, ed. Charles H. Talbot [1778; Philadelphia: Fortress Press, 1970]), and quite recently that of S. G. F. Brandon (*Jesus and the Zealots: A Study of the Political Factor in Primitive Christianity* [Manchester, England: Manchester University Press, 1967]).

6. I thus cannot agree with Geza Vermes and Ellis Rivkin, who argue that those ultimately responsible for the death of Jesus, namely, certain members of the Jewish and Roman establishment, were motivated solely to prevent civil unrest and protect their own political power. According to Rivkin, the agents of Jesus' death were not the least bit concerned with the "religious issue" (*What Crucified Jesus?* [Nashville: Abingdon Press, 1984], 102). It is strictly a case, then, of mistaken identity. Vermes takes a similar view: "[Jesus] died on the cross for having done the wrong thing (caused a commotion) in the wrong place (the Temple) at the wrong time (just before Passover)" (*The Religion of Jesus the Jew* [Minneapolis: Fortress Press, 1993], x). I am not denying that political motives existed (and undoubtedly motives of pure self-interest), nor am I denying that Jesus' message had political, even revolutionary, implications, but the Word Jesus spoke and the authority with which he spoke it went beyond the political and aroused opposition motivated by interests that were religious, and these interests played an important role in his

death. My view here is quite close to that of Raymond Brown, who writes that "the way [Jesus] was treated was certainly motivated by religious issues." Brown is also fully alert to other contributing factors, such as "the distrust on the part of the Jerusalem authorities for outside or country religious figures, the economic dependence of a good portion of the Jerusalem populace on the Temple, and the past relations between the Herodian kings of the Palestine area and the Roman prefect of Judea, as well as the interplay between the Pharisees and the Saducees" (*The Death of the Messiah: From Gethsemane to the Grave, a Commentary on the Passion Narratives in the Four Gospels,* 2 vols. [New York: Doubleday, 1994], here vol. 1, 21–22. Also see vol. 2, 383–97, where Brown summarizes the sad and terrifying history of later Christian efforts to impute guilt for Jesus' death to the whole Jewish people. Some Jews were involved in Jesus' death, and some were involved in part out of a religious interest, and that is the extent of it. And we must not forget that it was a cowardly and cruel Roman, Pontius Pilate, who sentenced Jesus to death. For more on the religious issues, see Wright, *Jesus and the Victory of God,* 547–52.

7.   On the historical minimum required for theological reconstruction of Jesus' death, see the clear and insightful articles by John Galvin, "The Death of Jesus in Contemporary Theology: Systematic Perspectives and Historical Issues," *Horizons* 13 (1986): 239–52, and "From the Humanity of Christ to the Jesus of History: A Paradigm Shift in Catholic Christology," *Theological Studies* 55 (1994): 252–73. I agree completely with Galvin when he writes in the latter article: "Soteriological reflection . . . of Jesus' crucifixion is . . . dependent on access to historical information about his life" and "questions concerning Jesus' personal stance when confronted with his death are inescapable" (267). Galvin stands in contrast to a contemporary theologian like Schubert Ogden who argues that the quest for the historical Jesus is "theologically unnecessary" (*The Point of Christology* [San Francisco: Harper and Row, 1982], 55). I find it incomprehensible that this quest is irrelevant to theology. Here, I would defer to the biblical scholar Nils A. Dahl: "If the interpretation were correct that Jesus was a political insurgent and was rightly executed as such, and that the end of his life broke in upon him as a completely unforeseen catastrophe, that would, in fact, be fatal for faith in the Christ proclaimed in the New Testament" (*Jesus the Christ: The Historical Origins of Christological Doctrine* [Minneapolis: Fortress Press, 1991], 32).

8.   There is good historical evidence that during Jesus' time there were two main tendencies within the Pharisees, that inspired by Hillel, more liberal in Torah observance and less zealously anti-Roman in eschatological politics, and that inspired by Shammai, stricter in Torah observance and more revolutionary in anti-Roman sentiment. See N. T. Wright, *The New Testament and People of God* (Minneapolis: Fortress Press, 1992), 164, 183–84, and Daniel J. Harrington, "The Jewishness of Jesus: Facing Some Problems," in *Jesus' Jewishness: Exploring the Place of Jesus within Early Judaism,* ed. James H. Charlesworth (New York: Crossroad, 1991), 123–52, especially 111, 126, 127, 130, 134. But we must not forget that in general the religious views of the Pharisees were not far from those of Jesus. Even Matthew, who has Jesus pronouncing the fiercest woes on the Pharisees, has Jesus

saying: "The scribes and the Pharisees sit on Moses' seat; therefore, do whatever they teach you and follow it" (Matt. 23:2-3), and Luke has Pharisees warning Jesus that Herod wants to kill him (Luke 13:31).

9. See Matt. 11:20-24 where Jesus predicts judgment for the towns of Chorazin, Bethsaida, Tyre, Sidon, and Capernaum for not accepting his message. This passage, says Marius Reiser, "can be associated with a clearly discernible situation in the life of Jesus: namely, the time shortly before his departure for his last Passover in Jerusalem. Jesus probably knew that the decisive event would happen there; he could regard his activity in Galilee as finished, and for the most part unsuccessful" (*Jesus and Judgment: The Eschatological Proclamation in Its Jewish Context* [Minneapolis: Fortress Press, 1997], 229).

10. The Gospels have Jesus predicting in some detail his death in Jerusalem before going up to Jerusalem (for example, Mark 8:31). It is difficult to decide to what degree these predictions are a retrojection of the post-Easter community (that is, *vaticinia ex eventu*, prophecies after the event), and to what degree they come from Jesus, who was realistically assessing his situation and beginning to interpret it theologically. For the theologian, the important point is that Jesus did come to see his death as inevitable and thus was faced with the question of how his death might fit into his mission. As someone influenced by Jewish apocalyptic, Jesus expected that the reign of God would not come before a period of trial and suffering. It is not unthinkable that he could have begun quite early to expect that the trial and suffering would first fall on him. See Wright, *Jesus and the Victory of God*, 574ff.

11. This riddling appears most often in Mark's Gospel and is the source for the famous "messianic secret" proposed by William Wrede (see *The Messianic Secret* [1901; Greenwood, S.C.: Attic Press, 1971]). For Wrede, Jesus is "Messiah" only as a retrojection of the post-Easter community. By contrast, E. P. Sanders, *The Historical Figure of Jesus* (London: Allan Lane Penguin Press, 1993), allows that Jesus avoided the title of *Messiah* as a self-designation but that "in a very general sense it corresponded to his own view of himself; he would be the leader in the coming kingdom" (242).

12. On the Temple incident see Mark 11:15-17; Matt. 21:12-13; Luke 19:45-48; and John 2:13-17. For analysis, see Sanders, *The Historical Figure of Jesus*, 255–62, and *Jesus and Judaism* (Philadelphia: Fortress Press, 1985), 61–90.

13. For Jesus' predictions of the destruction of the Temple, see Matt. 24:1-2; Mark 13:1-2; Luke 19:43-44; John 2:19. One of Jesus' followers, Stephen, was stoned to death for predicting the destruction of the Temple (Acts 6:14).

14. One of the charges leveled by the chief priest against Jesus was that of blasphemy. Christians like to think that this meant that Jesus, because he was the second person of the eternal trinitarian God, provoked the charge of blasphemy by acting as the One he had been from eternity, the metaphysical Son of God. A close reading of the relevant passages (Mark 2:7: 14: 61-63; Matt. 26:62-65; John 10:33-38) shows that it was Jesus' claim to be acting as God's anointed one, the Messiah, that provoked the charge of blasphemy, not his claim to be God. To the priests, Jesus' claim was false and therefore dangerous: Jesus was leading the Israelite people astray (see Luke 23:2) and deserved death (see Deut. 13:1-11 and 21:22-23).

15. For more information on other messianic movements and claimants within Judaism just before and after Jesus, see Gerd Theissen and Annette Merz, *The Historical Jesus: A Comprehensive Guide* (Minneapolis: Fortress Press, 1998), 141–46.

16. Jesus' ethical teaching is epitomized in the Sermon on the Mount (see Matthew 5–7), in which Jesus brought together Jewish teachings and his own insights to shape a radical kingdom ethic, which, if followed, would inaugurate but not force the coming of God's reign. For the mixture of old and new in Jesus' very Jewish ethical teaching, see David Flusser, *Jesus,* 2nd ed. (Jerusalem: Magnes Press, 1998), 81–102.

17. See Sanders, *The Historical Figure of Jesus*, 254–61, 270–73.

18. See, for example, Marcus Borg (with T. H. Wright), *The Meaning of Jesus: Two Visions* (San Francisco: HarperSanFrancisco, 1998), 87.

19. John's account of the last supper lacks the symbolic word of sharing bread and wine, but it has Jesus washing the feet of the disciples with an explicit link to Jesus' death. This then is John's way of expressing the theological meaning of the impending death: the death is a final word of loving service.

20. Ben F. Meyer, *The Aims of Jesus* (London: SCM Press, 1979), 218.

21. In connecting the last supper with the word of marriage, I follow Bernard Cooke, who made this connection in lectures I heard in the fall of 1966. He has continued to make the connection: "In his symbolic use of bread at the last supper, Jesus crystallized the link between Christian marriage and Christian eucharist, a link so close that neither can be understood adequately without the other." *Sacraments and Sacramentality,* 2nd rev. ed. (Mystic, Conn.: Twenty-Third Publications, 1994), 100. Cooke, however, is not responsible for the way I elucidate this connection in detail here.

22. This word is of course renewed through countless words throughout the marriage, for the word of marriage ceremony is not only a word of love but a word of promise, whereby the couple commit themselves to speak the word of love into the future. See chap. 10, where I elucidate the promissory function of language.

23. For the connection between the last supper and the covenant between God and the Israelites, see Bernard Cooke, "Synoptic Presentation of the Eucharist as Covenant Sacrifice," *Theological Studies* 21 (1960): 1–44. Also see Wright, *Jesus and the Victory of God*, 555–65.

24. In great detail, Wright, *Jesus and the Victory of God*, shows that Jesus had Jewish material to draw on when shaping the theology of his own suffering and death: the suffering and death of prophets, Isaiah's notion of the "suffering servant" (Isa. 52–53), the suffering of the righteous person (see Wis. 2:12-20), the sufferings of the Teacher of Righteousness in the Qumran community, the theology of the Maccabean martyrs (see 2 Macc. 7:36-38; 4 Macc. 6:27-29; 9:23-24; 17:20-22; 19:3-4), and the suffering of the people of Israel (Dan. 12:1-10; Zech. 9-14). In the words of Wright: "[W]e are here in touch with a tradition that was reasonably widespread and well known in the period of the second Temple. According to this tradition, the suffering and perhaps the death of certain Jews could function with

YHWH's plan to redeem his people from pagan oppression: to win for them . . . rescue from wrath, forgiveness of sins, and covenant renewal. This by itself, I suggest, would be enough to give us some substantial clues as to the world of thought within which a prophet and would-be Messiah, in the first third of the first century, might find his own vocation being decisively shaped" (583–84). Granted, a messiah who dies for the nation does not appear to have become an explicit Jewish idea, but Jesus' own theological creativity shaped the idea and then embodied it in practice.

25. Feminist theologians, critical of any theology that might encourage passive victimhood, have been particularly sensitive to the way the sacrificial imagery around Jesus can be harmful to women. Anne E. Carr, in *Transforming Grace: Christian Tradition and Women's Experience* (San Francisco: Harper and Row, 1988), writes: "For women, the sacrificial love of Jesus on the cross requires reinterpretation in which Jesus' act is clearly seen as a free and active choice in the face of an evil that has been resisted. It is not passive victimization. Nor did God require a sacrificial death. Jesus died because of the way he lived, because of the pattern of fidelity and commitment of his life and his liberating message" (174). Also see Julie M. Hopkins, *Towards a Feminist Christology: Jesus of Nazareth, European Women, and the Christological Crisis* (Grand Rapids, Mich.: Eerdmans, 1994), 50–55.

26. Two of the more harmful ideas approved by strains of the Christian tradition are (1) that God is all powerful and that this means everything occurs because of God's will and plan, and (2) that God directly willed and planned the suffering and death of Jesus as the means of completing his saving mission. Beginning in the Enlightenment, these ideas have been the object of a relentless and fully justified critique. See the stinging remarks by Matthew Tindall (1657–1733) in his influential work "Christianity as Old as Creation," in *Deism and Natural Religion: A Source Book*, ed. E. Graham Waring (1730; New York: Ungar, 1967), 107–70, especially 134–35. In these critiques, Christianity has been rightly accused of indifference to human suffering, because it said everything was God's will, and enthusiasm about suffering, because it said that it was the means God chose to save humanity. Name any one of the major historical sins committed by Christendom down through the centuries—approval of slavery, dehumanization of women, persecution of the Jews, killing of the infidel, oppression of the poor and powerless—and at the ideological base of these crimes will be found the appeal to the all-powerful God and the privilege God has given to suffering and death by the sacrifice of God's Son. Also see, Dorothee Sölle, *Christ the Representative: An Essay in Theology after Auschwitz* (London: SCM Press, 1967).

27. One of my women students reminded me that men deserted Jesus at the end, not women. True, the Synoptic Gospels (Matt. 27:55-56; Mark 15:40-41; Luke 23:49) have women followers (Luke also has some male "acquaintances") witnessing the crucifixion; however, they do so "from a distance." John 19:25-27 has his mother, his aunt, Mary (wife of Clopas), Mary Magdalene, and the " [male] disciple whom he loved" standing near the cross. Raymond E. Brown, in *The Death of the Messiah: From Gethsemane to the Grave, a Commentary on the Passion Narratives*

in the Four Gospels, 2 vols. (New York: Doubleday, 1994), argues that the "Marcan presentation of them [which is paralleled in Matthew and Luke] after the death observing from a distance is closer to the ancient tradition" (2.1019). The historicity of the presence of the beloved disciple is rejected by most scholars, though Brown holds out a slim possibility (2.1019–20). He gives his attention, however, to John's theological point, which is to bring his mother and the beloved disciple into the same spiritual family (2.1024ff.) The presence of the three other women may also have been staged by John to make a theological point, namely, to show "the Son of Man lifted up on the cross has begun drawing all to himself [see John 12:32-34]" (2.1019). We must also recall that earlier in his Gospel John has Jesus make this prediction: "The hour is coming, indeed has come, when you will be scattered, each one to his own home, and you will leave me alone" (John 16:32). And this is probably how it happened: Jesus on the cross was alone, abandoned by friends and followers.

28. Some of these concepts and images go back to the New Testament, but only later in the history of theology did they become bases for fully developed soteriologies. Some of the most vivid imagery comes from the apostle Paul. For example: "For our sake he made him to be sin who knew no sin, so that in him we might become the righteousness of God" (2 Cor. 5:21); "Christ redeemed us from the curse of the law by becoming a curse for us—for it is written, 'Cursed is everyone who hangs on a tree'" (Gal. 3:13). The word *for* in "for our sake" and "curse for us" is a translation of the Greek *hyper,* which carries some of the same ambiguity of the English *for,* which can mean "for the sake of" or "in the place of." Contemporary scholars argue that in the New Testament, *hyper* usually means "for the sake of" rather than "in the place of" (see William F. Arndt and F. Wilbur Gingrich, *A Greek-English Lexicon of the New Testament* [Chicago: University of Chicago Press, 1957], 846). It is clear, then, that some of the classical substitutional soteriologies have not been sufficiently attentive to the nuances of the original Greek. Perhaps the underlying problem here lies in the tendency of theological reconstruction to convert the a posteriori fact of Jesus' death into an a priori necessity. We see the beginnings of this already in the New Testament. When, for example, the Epistle to the Hebrews says that "without the shedding of blood there is no forgiveness of sins" (5:22) the theologian is tempted to turn that into a tight theological necessity for Jesus' death. This necessity is then lodged in God's reasoning, who of necessity "gave [Jesus the Son] up for [*hyper*] all of us"(Rom. 8:32). Both Anselm (1033–1109) in his theory of satisfaction and Calvin (1509–1564) in his theory of penal substitution succumbed to this temptation to construct overtight arguments for the necessity of Jesus' death.

29. For an explanation of Calvin's theory of penal substitution and references to Calvin's works, see Paul S. Fiddes, *Past Event and Present Salvation: The Christian Idea of the Atonement* (Louisville: Westminster/John Knox Press, 1989), 97–104.

30. Note that the Epistle to the Hebrews, despite strong objectivistic tendencies, provides a balancing subjective emphasis in a passage like the following: "For if we willfully persist in sin after having received the knowledge of the truth, there no longer

remains a sacrifice for sins, but a fearful prospect of judgment" (Heb. 10:26-27).

31. The ideas that I present here and on the following pages are the result of my own thinking and my dialogue with the ideas of Fiddes, *Past Event and Present Salvation,* especially chaps. 8 and 10.

32. In seeing the death of Jesus as a Word of forgiving love I am taking an Abelardian position on the saving efficacy of Jesus' death. Abelard (1079–1142) is associated with the so-called subjective theory of atonement whereby the emphasis is on what happens in the human subject instead of what has already happened objectively in the death of Jesus, though this should not be understood to mean that Abelard thought nothing objective happened in Christ. See the detailed study by Richard E. Weingart, *The Logic of Divine Love: A Critical Analysis of the Soteriology of Peter Abelard* (Oxford: Oxford University Press, 1970), which demonstrates that in fact Abelard keeps in balance the objective and subjective elements and cannot be regarded simply as a precursor of modern liberal Protestant subjectivism. For centuries, Abelard's approach was overshadowed by the satisfaction theory of Anselm, but since 1800 it has slowly been pulling even, to the point where it now enjoys considerable favor, especially among feminist theologians, who are understandably uneasy with theories that place the accent on passive, self-sacrificial suffering as Jesus' contribution in death to the divine plan (Anne Carr, for example, shows an appreciative view of Abelard in *Transforming Grace,* 182–86). In the history of modern theology since 1800, I find the contribution of Friedrich Schleiermacher on this matter (and so many others) pioneering. He vigorously rejected highly objectivistic theories in favor of a view that gave ample room for the human subjective response: the act of Christ does not "set us free from the necessity of pursuing this spiritual life by our own endeavor in fellowship with Him" (*The Christian Faith* [1821; Edinburgh: T. & T. Clark, 1928], 461). It is my guess that Schleiermacher's Pietist heritage, which acted in felicitous complement to his Calvinist heritage, spurred him to move beyond purely objectivist, substitutionary theories. This theme has been taken up with great vigor and brilliance by the contemporary German feminist theologian Dorothee Sölle in her *Christ the Representative.* She writes: "He died for us—namely in our place—but we too must learn to die" (106). By death she means not just physical death but also death to the sinful self.

33. Here are only a few passages from the New Testament that refer to evil cosmic powers: 2 Thess. 2:1-12; Rom. 8:38; 16:3; 1 Cor. 15:25-27; Eph. 3:10; 6:12; Col. 1:16; 2:15; 1 Pet. 3:22; Rev. 2:10; 12:9; 20:2-7.

34. The modern reader of the New Testament carefully will be amazed at the number of references to these cosmic powers. See, for example, Matt. 4:1-11; 8:16; 12:28; Luke 8:48; 2 Cor. 11:14; Eph. 6:12; Col. 2:8; 2:15; 1 Pet. 3:22; 1 John 2:13; 3:8. Both Jesus and his followers perform exorcisms. For the Jewish mind at that time, the drawing near of God's reign would have to prove its power by defeating these powers. Indeed, Jesus' public ministry opens with a major struggle with Satan (see Matt. 4:1-11; Mark 1:12-13; Luke 4:1-13) and closes with his encounter with the "power of darkness" (Luke 22:53).

35. The soteriological theme of *Christus victor* that was prominent in the New Testament and in the early church enjoyed a revival with Luther but went into slow decline until the work of the Swedish theologian Gustav Aulén, whose *Christus Victor: An Historical Study of the Three Main Types of the Ideas of the Atonement*, trans. A. G. Herbert (1931; New York: MacMillan, 1969) made the theme prominent again in theological conversation.

36. See Fiddes, *Past Event and Present Salvation,* 118ff., 190ff.

37. For my understanding of the cosmic powers, I am indebted in part to Walter Wink, whose trilogy on the powers has been pioneering: *Naming the Powers: The Language of Power in the New Testament* (Philadelphia: Fortress Press, 1984); *Unmasking the Powers: The Invisible Forces That Determine Human Existence* (Philadelphia: Fortress Press, 1986); and *Engaging the Powers: Discernment and Resistance in a World of Domination* (Minneapolis: Fortress Press, 1992). Recently, Wink took the ideas presented in his trilogy and summed them up for a wider audience in his book *The Powers That Be: Theology for a New Millennium* (New York: Galilee Doubleday, 1998). Wink points out that the early Christians saw the powers as personalized beings who, while "inextricably united" with corrupt institutions, had an existence independent of these institutions and of human history itself. Wink believes that we must now "regard them as the impersonal spiritual realities at the center of institutional life" that have no independent existence apart from these institutions (*The Powers That Be,* 28).

38. Raymond Brown writes: "To the accumulated teaching of his era Jesus at times offers a sovereign challenge, the sole authority for which seems to be his claim that he can speak for God. If one takes the Gospels at face value (and even if one examines them through the microscope of historical criticism), there emerges a Jesus capable of generating intense dislike. Indeed, that is the usual result of asking self-consciously religious people to change their minds (which is literally what is meant by *metanoia*). Those Christians who see Jesus as offensive only in the context of (what they think of as) legalistic Judaism fail to grasp that mutatis mutandis, he would be offensive on any religious scene if he told people that God wants something different from what they know and have long striven to do, and if he challenged established sacred teaching on his own authority as self-designated spokesman for God" (*The Death of the Messiah,* 1.392–93).

39. The apostle Paul, that great dialectician, believes that Christ has defeated the powers and yet insists that the eschatological kingdom will not come until Christ "has put all his enemies under his feet" (1 Cor. 15:25). Clearly he believes that the powers have been defeated in principle but not in fact.

40. Liberation theology, a contemporary movement that began in Latin America but has spread to other countries, can be given credit for insisting that salvation means not only liberation of the individual from sin but also liberation of the society from sinful social structures. The seminal theological work is by Gustavo Gutierrez, *A Theology of Liberation: History, Politics and Salvation* (Maryknoll, N.Y.: Orbis Books, 1973). A more exegetically informed work is that of Jon Sobrino, *Jesus the Liberator: A Historical-Theological Reading of Jesus of Nazareth* (Maryknoll,

N.Y.: Orbis Books, 1993). See 93–95 where Sobrino links Jesus' victory over Satan with liberation of the poor from the "powers of this world" (94). Feminist theologians are inspired by liberation theology; indeed, it would not be inaccurate to say that a feminist theologian like Rosemary Radford Ruether is really doing liberation theology from a feminist perspective. See her *To Change the World: Christology and Cultural Criticism* (New York: Crossroad, 1983), especially 45–56, and *Women and Redemption: A Theological History* (Minneapolis: Fortress Press, 1998), 241–81.

6. The Resurrection of Jesus

1. See Mark 10:35-45; Matt. 20:20-28; Luke 22:24-27. In Mark, the disciples are squabbling even after Jesus has told them for the third time that he must suffer and die. Matthew and Luke place the squabble at the last supper just after Jesus has shared with them the bread and wine as a symbolic preenactment of the self-gift that would occur in his impending suffering and death.

2. Luke's resurrection narrative (Luke 24:13-35) of the two disciples on the road to Emmaus places the recognition scene in the context of Jesus' blessing and breaking bread (Luke 24:30). Luke, of course, is fond of placing Gospel scenes within meals, but the reader cannot help but think of the last supper, at which the disciples did not comprehend Jesus' nonverbal word of breaking bread. They were not able to see that Jesus had incorporated his impending death into his mission of redeeming Israel. They tell the stranger walking with them, who is the risen Jesus unrecognized, that the one that they had hoped would "redeem Israel" (Luke 24:21) had been crucified, that is, had failed in his mission. They invite the stranger in for a meal and as soon as he breaks the bread, they recognize him as the risen Jesus: "their eyes were opened" (Luke 24:31). This time, disciples of Jesus understood and believed. Jesus' death becomes clarified as part of his mission only in the light of resurrection.

3. Gerd Theissen and Annette Merz, in *The Historical Jesus: A Comprehensive Guide* (Minneapolis: Fortress Press, 1998), review all the arguments for and against the historicity of the empty tomb and conclude that the "balance would tilt towards the possibility that the tradition of the empty tomb has a historical nucleus" (502). N. T. Wright is much more certain of the empty tomb; he has not the slightest doubt that a videotape would have shown a body there and then shown a body suddenly not there. See his remarks in the book he wrote with Marcus J. Borg, *The Meaning of Jesus: Two Visions* (San Francisco: HarperSanFrancisco, 1998), 125. I prefer Theissen and Merz's more tentative view.

4. On the empty tomb, see Peter Carnley, *The Structure of Resurrection Belief* (Oxford: Oxford University Press, 1987), especially 60–62. See also Raymond E. Brown, John R. Donahue, Donald Senior, Adela Yarbro Collins, "The Resurrection of Jesus," in *The New Jerome Biblical Commentary*, Raymond E. Brown et al., eds. (Englewood Cliffs, N.J.: Prentice Hall, 1990), 81:121; pp. 1373–77, here p. 1374.

5. In not classifying the resurrection as a miracle, I am agreeing with most

contemporary theologians and biblical scholars like John P. Meier. See his *A Marginal Jew: Rethinking the Historical Jesus,* 2 vols. (New York: Doubleday, 1991, 1994), 2.525, n. 7.

6.   Theissen and Merz, *The Historical Jesus,* 496ff., review the disputed first appearance: was it to Mary Magdalene or Peter? Generally, it is granted to Peter on the basis of the list in 1 Cor. 15:3-8, "but equally good arguments can be advanced for the rival tradition of the first appearance to Mary Magdalene" (497). They review the evidence for and against and conclude: "[I]t is more probable that an original protophany [that is, a first appearance to Mary Magdalene] has been suppressed than that it first came into being at a later date" (498). Much has been made of the advancement of women in early Christianity as shown by their role as witnesses to the resurrection. No one, of course, witnessed the resurrection, only the effects thereof, and the New Testament accounts of the women's role are mixed. Luke, for example, in whose Gospel women are very prominent, excludes Mary Magdalene altogether from the list of those to whom Jesus appeared. Recent feminist scholarship has emphasized the complexities, even the contradictions, in the early Christian view of women and of their role in the nascent church. Undoubtedly, strong liberating and egalitarian forces were at work in women's favor, but opposing forces were also there from the beginning. There was no initial feminist egalitarian utopia from which the community later fell into patriarchy. Contradictory tendencies could be exhibited in one person, in Paul, for example. See Luise Schottroff, Silvia Schoer, and Marie-Theres Wacker, *Feminist Interpretation: The Bible in Women's Perspective* (Minneapolis: Fortress Press, 1998), especially 190–96. What does all this say to the question of whether it was Mary Magdalene or Peter to whom Jesus first appeared? With Theissen and Merz, I am inclined to believe that it was Mary Magdalene, but later tradition gave it to Peter, because the stories of the appearances served in part as legitimations of male leadership positions in the early church. Yet it is a remarkable testimony to persisting egalitarian impulses in the New Testament church that the witness of women to the appearances of Jesus was not completely suppressed.

7.   Wright's argument in detail can be found in two articles published in the *Sewanee Theological Review* 41, no. 2 (1998): 107–23: "Christian Origins and the Resurrection of Jesus as a Historical Problem" (107–23) and "Early Tradition and the Origins of Christianity" (125–40). See also, Borg and Wright, *The Meaning of Jesus,* 111–27.

8.   Wright accepts that other elements of Jewish eschatological hope could be negotiated and redefined. Jesus' followers could, for example, see the enemy not as the Roman occupation forces, but as all those who refused Jesus' offer of the reign of God; they could relocate the newly restored Israel in the nascent church; they could accept the continued existence of the physical Temple but transfer the supreme locus of God's presence to Jesus; and they could acknowledge the continued existence of worldly evil while insisting that the demons had been in principle defeated by Jesus. But bodily resurrection was not negotiable, not redefinable. See Wright, "Christian Origins and the Resurrection of Jesus," 113.

9. In the words of Wright, "Christian Origins and the Resurrection of Jesus": "You see, it would have been very natural for first-century Jews, especially if they had belonged to a kingdom-of-God movement already, to say of a leader who had paid the ultimate penalty at the hands of the authorities, that his soul was in the hand of God, that he was alive to God, that he had been exalted to paradise, and that he was therefore among the righteous who had been unjustly put to death but who would rise again to rule the world in God's good time. . . . And if Jesus' followers had indeed a sense that he was alive in a nonphysical way they would have expressed it. But in doing so they would *not* have been claiming . . . that the *eschaton*, the longed-for kingdom of God, had now arrived; they would not have been saying that their crucified leader was the Messiah; and above all they would not have been saying that he had been raised from the dead or that the 'resurrection from the dead' had now occurred" (122). For a detailed survey of first-century Jewish conceptions of the afterlife, see Pheme Perkins, *Resurrection: New Testament Witness and Contemporary Reflection* (Garden City, N.Y.: Doubleday, 1984), 37–66. I should like to add that this very Jewish belief in the coincidence of the coming of the kingdom and the resurrection of the dead required the early Christians, once they had come to believe that Jesus had been raised from the dead, to expect that quite soon the present world would come to an end and that they and the already dead would soon join Jesus in his resurrection. Those who had died would be resurrected, those still living would "be caught up in the clouds together with them to meet the Lord in the air" (1 Thess. 4:17). But the world continued, and the end did not come, and thus the final coming or *parousia* of Christ had been delayed. This required yet another adjustment in the inherited Jewish eschatology, an adjustment that the early followers of Jesus appear to have made without much of a fret. The big fret has been made by German scholars, who have built up a whole industry around the *Parousieverzögerung* (the delay of the parousia).

10. The German biblical scholar Gerd Lüdemann makes use of bereavement theory in *What Really Happened to Jesus: A Historical Approach to the Resurrection* (Louisville: Westminster John Knox Press, 1995). He argues that the belief of Peter and Paul that Jesus was raised occurred when they felt forgiven by Jesus for their sin of denial (Peter) and persecution (Paul). Lüdemann does believe that Jesus is "with God" (137), but in a way utterly hidden from human beings, including Peter and Paul. He does not, therefore, see a causal link between Jesus' resurrection and Peter and Paul's reconciliation to Jesus. Only reflecting on the way Jesus died brings Peter and Paul to this point. For Lüdemann, there is a resurrection of sorts, but it is theologically and psychologically irrelevant to the rise of the resurrection faith of Peter and Paul. Their faith arose simply as a stage of their bereavement process. I have some sympathy with Lüdemann's use of bereavement theory, but I am unconvinced by his effort to disconnect the resurrection faith completely from the resurrection itself. Wright, "Early Tradition and the Origins of Christianity," 121, has a stronger reaction: he says that Lüdemann's hypothesis is "at best unprovable and at worst wildly fantastic."

11. See N. T. Wright (with Marcus Borg), *The Meaning of Jesus,* 125.

12. See Stephen T. Davis, "'Seeing' the Risen Jesus," in *The Resurrection: An Interdisciplinary Symposium on the Resurrection of Jesus*, ed. Stephen T. Davis, Daniel Kendall, S.J., and Gerald O'Collins, S.J. (New York: Oxford University Press, 1997), 142. Davis uses another scene for his photo opportunity, that of the raised Jesus feeding the seven disciples at the Sea of Tiberias (see John 21:1-14), but it is clear that he would allow any appearance scene to serve his point.

13. Davis, "'Seeing' the Risen Jesus," 147: "Were enhanced powers of perception . . . necessary to have seen the risen Christ? I am arguing that the answer to that question is no. But was a special grace necessary to see the risen Christ in such a way as to recognize him as Lord and to grasp what he was calling one to be and do? Of course."

14. See Kenan B. Osborne, *The Resurrection of Jesus: New Considerations for Its Theological Interpretation* (Mahwah, N.J.: Paulist Press, 1997), especially 116–20, where he stresses that faith is required to see the appearances as the appearances of the resurrected Jesus. Karl Rahner, in his *Foundations of Christian Faith: An Introduction to the Idea of Christianity*, trans. William V. Dych (New York: Seabury Press, A Crossroad Book, 1978), puts it nicely when he says that the Easter experience "is given only in faith and yet it grounds and justifies this faith" (277).

15. Some, of course, were more ready than others. See Matt. 28:17; Luke 24:38; and John 20:24-28.

16. Paul tried to get at the mystery by saying that Jesus as risen was no longer a "physical body," but a "spiritual body" (1 Cor. 15:44).

17. With Peter Carnley, I am intrigued by bereavement theory, not as a reductionistic explanation that explains away the resurrection, but as an explanation that suggests possible analogs to the resurrection appearances. I have talked to a number of persons who have experienced what they considered visitations from recently deceased beloved ones, and they frequently insist that the deceased appeared in a strangely visible way. For some of those who already had a belief in the resurrection, or an openness to the possibility of resurrection, this experience of the visiting loved one led them to a new appreciation of the resurrection as somehow bodily. See Carnley's very careful remarks in his "Response to Gerald O'Collins," *The Resurrection: An Interdisciplinary Symposium on the Resurrection of Jesus*, 38ff. I agree with Carnley that even if we were to find the bereavement visitations analogous, we would still have to move to a faith level to counter the reductionistic explanation that they are purely subjective and psychological.

18. I am using language characteristic of Karl Rahner's work: "In the unity of this triplicity of faith, hope, and love, Jesus himself surrendered himself in his death unconditionally to the absolute mystery that he called his Father, into whose hands he committed his existence" Karl Rahner, "Following the Crucified," *Theological Investigations*, vol. 18, trans. Edward Quinn (New York: Crossroad Books, 1983), 165.

19. See Mark 12:26-27, where Jesus is quoted: "And as for the dead being raised, have you not read in the book of Moses, in the story about the bush, how God said to him, 'I am the God of Abraham, the God of Isaac, and the God of Jacob'? He is God not of the dead, but of the living; you are quite wrong."

20. For the Pharisees' belief in the resurrection, see Ellis Rivkin, *A Hidden Revolution: The Pharisees' Search for the Kingdom Within* (Nashville: Abingdon Press, 1978), 96–97, 110–11, 303–11. The Sadducees, by contrast, did not believe in the resurrection.

21. In many contemporary theologies of the resurrection, we find a concerted effort to forge a strong link between the risen Jesus and the earthly Jesus, and, with that, a link between the God who raises to life and those innocent ones who have suffered and died because of a cruel and oppressive social structure. Liberation theologians in particular have been alert to this link. See, for example, Jon Sobrino, *Christology at the Crossroads* (Maryknoll, N.Y.: Orbis Books, 1978). Roger Haight continues this line of thought in *Jesus Symbol of God* (Maryknoll, N.Y.: Orbis Books, 1999), especially 148ff.

22. No one has elucidated better how we experience resurrection now than H. A. Williams in *True Resurrection* (Springfield, Ill: Templegate Publishers, 1972). This book is an extraordinary look at ordinary human existence to see how life rises out of death. Unless, he says, we can experience the "impact [of the resurrection] on the present" (5), what happened in the past to Jesus and what might happen in the future to us after death will be of no real interest to us.

23. The Gospel of John has the risen Jesus who appears to the disciples bestowing on them the Spirit: "When he had said this, he breathed on them and said to them, 'Receive the Holy Spirit'" (John 20:22). Luke spreads out the events flowing out of resurrection over an extended period: the resurrection, the bodily appearances of the risen Jesus (Luke 24:1-50), the exaltation or ascension of Jesus to the risen state (Luke 24:50-53; Acts 2:6-11), and finally the sending of the Holy Spirit at Pentecost (Acts 2:1-4). The writings of John and Paul, by contrast, do not separate resurrection, exaltation, and the sending of the Spirit into discrete phases. Contemporary theologians follow them in this respect.

24. See Willi Marxsen, *The Resurrection of Jesus of Nazareth* (Philadelphia: Fortress Press, 1970).

25. In the words of Michael Cook: "In a sense, God can tell us no more about the divine intention than that at the moment of death divine love will embrace us" (*Responses to 101 Questions about Jesus* [New York: Paulist Press, 1993], 86).

26. See Karl Rahner, *Foundations of Christian Faith*, 266: "The death and resurrection of Jesus can be understood only if the intrinsic relationship of the two realities and their unity are kept clearly in view. . . . The death of Jesus is such that by its very nature it is subsumed into resurrection. It is death into the resurrection. . . . It means . . . precisely the permanent, redeemed, final and definitive validity of the single and unique life of Jesus who achieved the permanent and final validity of his life precisely in freedom and obedience." The older Catholic apologetics also saw the resurrection as caused by Jesus but as the effect of the divine power that was his as the eternal Son, the second person of the Trinity. In contrast, Rahner stresses what Jesus in death achieves by his human freedom (in response to God's initiative): he gives himself freely over to the divine mystery in love and acceptance, and in that sense and that sense alone he is the "cause" of

God's response that "raises him from the dead." It is John's Gospel (see John 2:19; 10:15-18; 20:17) that gives the most attention to the resurrection as Jesus' achievement. For an elegant essay on the older Catholic apologetics in contrast with the newer, see Avery Dulles, S.J., *Apologetics and the Biblical Christ* (Baltimore: Newman Press, 1966), especially 45ff.

27. We see once again how difficult it is to draw a sharp distinction between the Word-function and the Spirit-function of God's self-communication through Christ, which always comes as both meaningful and powerful, cognitive and affective, instructive and inspirational. The Word is powerful, which implies the Spirit; the Spirit is instructive, which implies the Word. In the Johannine writings, the Word-function of the Spirit often becomes very explicit, which is not the case in the Pauline writings, where Spirit is most often explicitly linked with transformative power (though see 1 Cor. 2:12-13).

28. The Gospel of John shows the tension between the earthly and the heavenly sending of the Spirit. In clear reference to the earthly Jesus, read 3:34: "He whom God has sent speaks the words of God, for he gives the Spirit without measure." But now read 7:38-39: "As the scripture has said, 'Out of the believer's heart shall flow rivers of living water' [see Num. 20:2-13; Isa. 12:3]. Now [Jesus] said this about the Spirit, which believers in him were to receive; for as yet there was no Spirit, because Jesus was not yet glorified." But in general, in the New Testament, while allowing that the earthly Jesus is a bearer of the Holy Spirit, Jesus becomes a general distributor of the Spirit only with the resurrection. Passing through death into risen life opens Jesus up to the universe and thus universalizes the range of the Spirit. This, of course, is part of Jesus' role as the Messiah who ushers in the final reign of God, which in Jewish eschatology includes a new outpouring of the Spirit. The classic text here is Joel 2:28-42.

7. The Risen Christ Continues the Mission

1. On the connection between the founding of the church and the commissioning of the disciples, see Kenan B. Osborne, *The Resurrection of Jesus: New Considerations for Its Theological Interpretation* (Mahwah, N.J.: Paulist Press, 1997), 135–36.

2. Let me again stress that the Spirit never comes without the Word, and vice versa. A balanced theology holds fast to a God in Christ who provides both meaning and power, ideal and energy, shape and movement, thought and feeling, wisdom and push, Word and Spirit. Unable to tolerate a pluralism of pieties and theologies, Christianity has unfortunately split into many denominations. Along with this split has occurred a splitting into "Word churches" and "Spirit churches." The former, in their stress on the meaning of the Word, emphasize doctrine and theology; the latter, in their stress on the power of the Spirit, emphasize experience and emotion. In churches of the Word, people listen attentively to precise sermons; in churches of Spirit, people dance and shout. In Word churches, meaning is poured into neat doc-

trinal channels, and everything is clear but often lifeless; in Spirit churches, power is allowed free rein, and everything is full of life but often unclear. Mainstream churches have in general erred more on the side of doctrinal clarity than of free-wheeling emotion. Robert W. Jenson, who, as a Lutheran, is a member of a Word church, says it well: "In the theological tradition, a recurrent disaster has been that Christ's presence as embodied word, as audible and visible address, and the coming of the Spirit, have been separated and even played off against each other" (*Visible Words: The Interpretation and Practice of Christian Sacraments* [Philadelphia: Fortress Press, 1978], 57). An example of a very balanced understanding of the relation between the "rational, articulate" Word and the "nonrational, numinous" Spirit can be found in John Macquarrie, *Thinking about God* (New York: Harper and Row, 1975), especially 125–26.

3.   Despite the exaltation of the risen Christ, we still pray *with* him to God, not just *to* him, for all begins with God and ends with the God whom Jesus called Father, and whom we can also call Mother, Parent, Wisdom, Friend, Lover, and, yes, Father. The key is that everything begins and ends with this first person of the Trinity. And thus it is not our worship of Jesus as the second person that is the aim of Jesus' mission, but worship of God the Mother-Father. Jesus, our brother, calls us to solidarity with him to share the relationship he has with God, the first person. Prayerful communion with the risen Jesus must not end with Jesus but lead through him to the One with whom he is in prayerful communion. Even as risen, exalted Lord, Jesus remains the mediator, the person through whom we enter into relation with God the Mother-Father.

4.   For more detail on how individuals carry out the work of Christ through the practice of love and justice, see chaps. 8 and 9.

5.   This is not to say that the mission shifts exclusively to the church. Individuals not affiliated with the church can still carry out the mission. Theologians like Karl Rahner who are proponents of the inclusivist theory of Christ's saving Word argue that the work of Christ can continue in individuals who are not even aware that they are instruments of the risen Christ. In Rahner's famous expression, these persons are "anonymous Christians," that is, they are doing the work of Christ but they do not consciously know they are doing so. See Karl Rahner, "Anonymous Christians," *Theological Investigations,* vol. 6, trans. Karl-H. Kruger and Boniface Kruger (Hew York: Seabury Press, 1969), 390–98; and "Observations on the Problem of the 'Anonymous Christian,'" *Theological Investigations,* vol. 14, trans. David Bourke (New York: Crossroad Books, 1976), 280–94.

6.   "All politics is local" was made famous by Tip O'Neill, former Speaker of the House, who learned it from his father. See Tip O'Neill, *All Politics Is Local: And Other Rules of the Game* (New York: Times Books, 1994). For a theological reflection on the importance of the local church, see Alexandre Ganoczy, *An Introduction to Catholic Sacramental Theology* (New York: Paulist Press, 1984), 153ff.

7.   This subdivision of mission and ministry began very early. The early Christians interpreted this as the work of the Holy Spirit dispersing various charisms or gifts. See Acts 6:1-10; Rom. 12:4-8; 1 Cor. 12:4-11; and Eph. 4:7-13.

8. Still unsurpassed on the development of the many ministries in the church is Bernard Cooke's *Ministry to Word and Sacraments: History and Theology* (Philadelphia: Fortress Press, 1976).

9. As Bernard Cooke puts it, "How can one give the Spirit if he himself does not possess the Spirit?" (*Ministry to Word and Sacraments*, 258). To say it in the terms used by this book, if a person speaking for the church in the name of Christ communicates only the formalized outer word without having been moved by its emotive and directive power, that is, by the Spirit, how can he or she be effective? This issue became particularly important with respect to the sacramental word. During the time of Augustine, a group known as the Donatists insisted that the person administering a sacrament must show perfection in the Christian life (in this case this person must never have disavowed the faith under the threat of torture and death). If he could not show this perfection, that sacrament (the sacrament under consideration here was Baptism) was to be regarded as invalid, indeed nonlicit in the juridical sense. Augustine attacked this position and said that the sacrament was valid and could be effective in the recipient even if the administer of the sacrament was an apostate or a heretic. Most Christians who have thought about the matter would say that he was correct, but in the late Middle Ages, ideas about the objective effectiveness (*ex opere operato*) of sacramental sign developed in a juridical direction, even to the point where the faith and love of the one receiving the sacrament (*ex opere operantis*) was given less and less attention, all of which led to a fairly widespread sacramental minimalism, in which the correct performance of a sacrament was deemed sufficient for fully effective sacramental ministry. This set the scene for the Protestant attack, which itself at times went to the other extreme (see Zwingli's tendency to reduce sacraments to signs of the recipients' faith). Nevertheless, formalization of the words of the church as Christ's body on earth would seem not only inevitable but also desirable given continued human sinfulness and lack of full growth in Christ. For a subtle account of the Donatist controversy, see Jaroslav Pelikan, *The Emergence of the Catholic Tradition (100–600)*, vol. 1 of *The Christian Tradition: A History of the Development of Doctrine* (Chicago: University of Chicago Press, 1971), 308–13. On sacramental minimalism in the late Middle Ages and the Protestant reaction, see Joseph Martos, *Doors to the Sacred: A Historical Introduction to Sacraments in the Catholic Church* (Tarrytown, N.Y.: Triumph Books, 1991), 65–102. I highly recommend Martos's book to all readers, whatever their denominational tradition. With great ecumenical sensitivity, the author gives detailed and fair accounts of the Reformational critique of Western sacramental theology.

10. I do not mean to say here that the moral transformation of the church is simply a matter of moral transformation of its individual members. It also means transforming its social structures so that they ever more approximate the ideal of justice. This has been particularly difficult for my own church to learn. Before the Second Vatican Council, the Catholic Church was fond of referring to itself with the biblical metaphor *the spotless bride of Christ* (see Eph. 5:27). It knew, of course, that it had sinners in its midst, even among its ordained priests, yet it believed that

whenever the church officially communicated the outer word, it did so as Christ's perfect instrument. It thought this in part because it was convinced that it alone among all the Christian communities had perfect possession of the outer word as formalized in doctrine and shaped in sacrament, and in part because it prided itself on a certain corporate holiness that put it above any prophetic criticism. Vatican II, with its talk of the "pilgrim church always in need of reform" (see Walter M. Abbott, ed. *Documents of Vatican II* [New York: American Press, 1966], 79, 358) signaled the beginning of a movement to counter this ecclesial triumphalism. This movement is far from finished with its work.

11. Deciding which writings belonged in the canon of Scripture took many years for the Christian community. The canon of the Old Testament was not fixed in the Western church until the sixteenth century, and even then Catholics and Protestants differed on which books to include. The canon of the New Testament was not fixed until the end of the fourth century. See Raymond E. Brown, and Raymond F. Collins, "Canonicity," in *The New Jerome Biblical Commentary*, Brown et al., eds. (Englewood Cliffs, N.J.: Prentice Hall, 1990), 1034–54. The precise relation of Scripture to tradition continues to be a vexing theological question. As a Catholic, I have a deep reverence for tradition, but I have become uneasy about saying simply, without qualification, that I am guided by Scripture and tradition, as if the two were precisely equal in function and authority. True, tradition is prior to Scripture (there were followers passing on the Jesus tradition years before there were the writings that became the New Testament), and tradition has determined which writings are canonical; nevertheless, I give Scripture a certain priority. In my view, the tradition is judged by Scripture in a way that Scripture is not judged by tradition. Indeed, by deciding on a canon, I think the church in effect acknowledged a degree of deference to scriptural authority.

12. The prophets of the Old Testament were more likely to strike out at individuals, especially those who abused their privilege and power within certain social structures (for example, in the monarchy) to exploit the poor and powerless. They were less interested in attacking social structures as such; indeed, according to Bruce Vawter, "with certain exceptions [see the opposition to animal sacrifice expressed in Amos 5:21-27; Hos. 6:6; Jer. 7:21-23; Isa. 1:1-12] the prophetic attitude . . . was to try to make the best use of existing institutions" (*The New Jerome Biblical Commentary*, 194). Yet we dare not forget that prophetic criticism in the Old Testament was often accompanied by soaring eschatological visions of the Day of the Lord, when not only individuals, but a whole people and its institutions, would be made new. In the spirit of that vision, and in a time when we are more aware of the pervasively corrupting power of structures, Christians today direct the prophetic word more toward these structures, though this does not rule out directing it to individuals who are particularly venal beneficiaries of a sinful structure.

13. I think for example of the case of Archbishop Romero of El Salvador. Apparently a modest and shy man intent on going about his business, he found himself propelled into prophetic preaching by the pervasive evil of the structures of his society. During the last few months of his life, he rarely passed up an opportunity

to speak the prophetic word. He was murdered for doing so. For profound libera-
tion-theological reflections on Romero and his message, see Jon Sobrino, *Jesus the
Liberator: A Historical-Theological Reading of Jesus of Nazareth* (Maryknoll, N.Y.:
Orbis Books: 1993), 184–85, 212–13, 216–17, 269–71.

14. On ritual as communication, see Ganoczy, *An Introduction to Catholic
Sacramental Theology.* It is not my intention, however, to define ritual solely in
terms of the communication of meaning. Ritual contains what we might call
meaningless elements, purely playful or ludic elements that are for aesthetic
pleasure. Rituals are festive and celebratory; they have color, music, dance, and
pageantry. Ronald L. Grimes, a noted scholar of ritual, says it well: "Unintentional,
nongoal-oriented actions such as playing and gamboling, as well as preconscious
habits and mannerisms, must not be excluded by definition from ritual, since they
are the seedbeds of ritualizing" ("Defining Nascent Ritual," *The Journal of the
American Academy of Religion* 50 [1982]: 539–55, here 545). Correct as he is, it is
also important to note that these other elements come into play partly because the
meanings communicated in ritual are invariably more than merely informative,
invariably more than the outer expression of precise concepts about concrete and
easily graspable realities. Rather these meanings are animated by emotive and
directive power and therefore aim to evoke, arouse, move, and excite people.
Human beings know preconsciously that such meanings will require a special kind
of outer word, and indeed many rituals simply rise up in a group without a great
deal of conscious forethought. For other critiques of the reduction of ritual to the
communication of referential meaning, see Frits Staal, "The Meaninglessness of
Ritual," *Numen* 26 (1979): 2–22, and Dan Sperber, *Rethinking Symbolism*, trans.
Alice L. Morton (Cambridge: Cambridge University Press, 1975).

15. For a very profound social philosophical study of the way societal memory
is sustained by ritual performances, see Paul Connerton, *How Societies Remember*
(Cambridge: Cambridge University Press, 1989). See also David N. Power, *Sacrament: The Language of God's Giving* (New York: Crossroad, 1999), 91–95.

16. Shared meaning without power is simply agreement in belief. But communal life at its deepest is shared emotion and not just shared belief. Emotion is what
gives the union its mysterious depth and intensity. This same emotion moves
Christians to act in a certain way. To put it another way, it is the emotive and directive power of God's Word that binds Christians into community. This power is the
Holy Spirit. It is no accident that through the centuries the Spirit has been closely
linked with the formation of community and church.

17. In the language of pragmatics and speech-act theory, sacraments are therefore words that are *institutionally bound,* in contrast to the informal *institutionally
unbound* words of everyday communication. See Jürgen Habermas, "What Is Universal Pragmatics," chap. 1 of *Communication and the Evolution of Society*
(Boston: Beacon Press, 1979), 1–68, here 40.

18. According to the Roman Catholic and Orthodox churches, seven of these
ritualized words carry the name of *sacrament.* These seven are Baptism, Confirmation, Eucharist (the mass, Lord's Supper), Reconciliation (Penance, Confession),

Holy Orders (Ordination), Marriage, and Anointing (Extreme Unction, sacrament of the sick and dying). Protestant churches give the name *sacrament* (some churches, for example, the Brethren, prefer the term *ordnance* to the term *sacrament*) only to Baptism and Eucharist, because only these two are unmistakably found in Scripture, but in fact these churches have rituals that are functional equivalents of the other five sacraments. It should be noted that it took the Western church until the twelfth century to isolate these seven and give them the exclusive designation of *sacrament.* Augustine in the fifth century had a much broader understanding of *sacramentum,* dividing sacraments into word-sacraments (sermons, prayers, Scripture readings, and so on) and action-sacraments (rite of initiation, Eucharist, sign of the cross, anointing, blessing, and so on). See Martos, *Doors to the Sacred,* 43 and 48ff. Throughout this section on sacraments, I am deeply indebted to Bernard Cooke, who for more than forty years now has been North America's premier sacramental theologian. All the strengths of his work are present in *Sacraments and Sacramentality,* 2nd rev. ed. (Mystic, Conn.: Twenty-Third Publications, 1994).

19. The Christian rite of initiation in Rome at the opening of the third century is described by Hippolytus as using water, oil, bread, wine, milk, and honey. See Michael G. Lawler, *Symbol and Sacrament: A Contemporary Sacramental Theology* (New York: Paulist Press, 1987), 85.

20. See William J. Bausch, *A New Look at Sacraments,* rev. ed. (Mystic, Conn.: Twenty-Third Publications, 1983), 50–60, for a stirring account of adult baptism in the early church.

21. The baptismal rite in the early church was seen as one sacramental action that included water immersion or sprinkling, an anointing or laying on of hands (or both), which later became a distinct sacrament called Confirmation, and the Eucharist. The Orthodox Church still performs all three as one initiation rite, even when it baptizes infants.

22. St. Paul weaves the theme of our baptismal death and resurrection into the theme of Jesus' death and resurrection: "Therefore we have been buried with him by baptism into death, so that, just as Christ was raised from the dead by the glory of the Father, so we too might walk in newness of life. For if we have been united with him in a death like his, we will certainly be united with him in a resurrection like his. We know that our old self was crucified with him so that the body of sin might be destroyed, and we might no longer be enslaved to sin. For whoever has died is freed from sin. But if we have died with Christ, we believe that we will also live with him. We know that Christ, being raised from the dead, will never die again; death no longer has dominion over him. The death he died, he died to sin, once for all; but the life he lives, he lives to God. So you also must consider yourselves dead to sin and alive to God in Christ Jesus" (Rom. 6:4-11).

23. It was common in the early church for adults to wait years before submitting to Baptism because of the morally rigorous demands of full membership in the church. Many were very devout proselytes who, though prebaptismal, died for their faith in one of the many Roman persecutions. Some theologians taught that

these martyrs were granted salvation despite not having been baptized. Theirs was a "baptism of blood" (Martos, *Doors to the Sacred*, 148). Others taught that any sincere proselyte who died before Baptism was saved by the "baptism of desire" (162). Roman Catholics in the modern period broadened this category to include any person who was living a moral life. Thus, the so-called "good pagan" could reach heaven (171–72).

24. My understanding of original sin as the social transmission of sin's corrupting influence and of Baptism as initiating the church's redemptive counterforce against this influence is heavily indebted to the work of Friedrich Schleiermacher (1768–1830) and Horace Bushnell (1802–1876), two nineteenth-century theologians. On original sin as "corporate solidarity," see Schleiermacher, *The Christian Faith* (1821; Edinburgh: T. & T. Clark, 1928), 286ff. His ideas on infant baptism are also suggestive. Baptism does not automatically produce saving faith in the infant being baptized, unless we want to ascribe "magical powers" (637) to it, but Baptism does bring infants into the church. "[It] is part of church order to bring them, as the outer circle most intimately entrusted to us, into direct relation to the Word of God, and to maintain them therein until faith awakens" (635). He fails, however, to link his ideas on original sin with his theology of baptism. This link is provided by Bushnell, known as the "American Schleiermacher" (see Sydney E. Ahlstrom, *A Religious History of the American People* [New Haven, Conn.: Yale University Press, 1972], chap. 37), in his masterpiece, *On Christian Nurture* (1861; reprint, Grand Rapids, Mich.: Baker Book House, 1971). Bushnell's approach (purged of theological Lamarckianism) has enjoyed revival today, even though Bushnell's achievement is not always acknowledged. For contemporary views, see Brian O. McDermott, "The Theology of Original Sin: Recent Developments," *Theological Studies* 38 (1977): 478–512; and Stephen Duffy, "Our Hearts of Darkness: Original Sin Revisited," *Theological Studies* 49 (1988): 597–622. Neither Duffy nor McDermott, however, tries to explain this "dark involuntary at the heart of the will" (Duffy, 620) solely as the effect of our "poisonous solidarity" (616) with our ancestors. Innate to human beings is an involuntary anxiety that tempts us all, even Adam and Eve, to sin. See also the penetrating analysis by Reinhold Niebuhr in *The Nature and Destiny of Man: A Christian Interpretation*, vol. 2, *Human Destiny* (New York: Charles Scribner's Sons, 1943), 182–86, 192–93, 250–52, 271–72, 290–91, and the profound meditations of Sebastian Moore, *The Crucified Jesus Is No Stranger* (New York: Seabury Press, 1977), xi, 106f, 113.

25. For the historical background on Confirmation, I am relying on Martos, *Doors to the Sacred*, 179–201.

26. See Schleiermacher, *The Christian Faith*, 636–37: "It is therefore unjust to infant baptism when confirmation—which for us is simply the depositing and acceptance of a personal profession of faith, and thus supplies the lack in baptism—is regarded as nonessential; for it is only as combined with Confirmation that infant baptism answers to Christ's institution." The church should therefore "give confirmation very close attention, in order that . . . the later rite may approve itself the true and worthy consummation of infant baptism." I have learned recently that some Lutheran churches are beginning to refer to Confirmation as the Affirmation of Baptism. Good idea!

27. It is clear in the Epistle to the Hebrews that with his resurrection Jesus has "become a high priest forever" (6:20) and thus continues his high-priestly mediation from God to humanity and from humanity to God (see 7:25). If the essence of sacrifice is his self-giving to God and to others, then Jesus as risen continues to sacrifice himself to God for us and to us for God. No contemporary theologian has stressed this continuing priestly ministry of the risen Christ more than Bernard Cooke. See his first book on sacraments, *Christian Sacraments and Christian Personality* (New York: Holt, Rinehart and Winston, 1965), especially 105–14, and his latest, *Sacraments and Sacramentality,* 2nd rev. ed. (Mystic, Conn.: Twenty-Third Publications, 1994), throughout.

28. As I explained in chap. 5, the self-offering of Jesus to God could be termed a self-sacrifice, not in the self-abnegating, masochistic sense of the word, but in the original etymological sense of making holy, of offering something to God who in accepting it makes it holy. In this latter sense, Jesus' last supper and death is a sacrifice, as is the Eucharist that represents sacramentally Jesus' continued self-offering. In the past, Catholics called the Eucharist the sacrifice of the mass. Unfortunately, the sacrifice of the mass came to be understood in the popular mind as a repeat of the cross, not its sacramental representation. This misunderstanding in combination with the negative connotations of the word *sacrifice* has led contemporary Catholic theologians to almost completely abandon the word in connection with the Eucharist. See, however, Bernard Cooke's rescue of the term in *Sacraments and Sacramentality,* 110–13.

29. The linchpin here is the continuing communicative intention of Jesus, which is not possible unless Jesus is risen and still carrying out his high-priestly mission. If Jesus is not risen, then Eucharist is simply a memorial meal wherein the community recalls the final word of Jesus. God may indeed be present in and through this memorial meal, but not Jesus, except in our vivid memory of him, and thus Jesus does not perform this sacrament through his body the church. That is the key point. Recent efforts by Hans Küng and his American follower Leonard Swidler to bring people into a livelier connection with the historical Jesus are to be applauded, but there is a danger that Christian theology and piety will be thrown out of balance in a way that will negatively affect the theology of church and sacraments. Bernard Cooke in his essay, "The Experiential 'Word of God'," in *Consensus in Theology? A Dialogue with Hans Küng and Edward Schillebeeckx,* ed. Leonard Swidler (Philadelphia: Westminster Press, 1980), 69–74, especially 70, makes the point that Jesus' risen state is as important as his earthly state.

30. That the Word and Spirit come from Christ through the church as a community and not simply from Christ through the clerical hierarchy to the church as a community is emphatically stressed by many contemporary Catholic theologians. See Edward Kilmartin, "Sacraments as Liturgy of the Church," *Theological Studies* 50 (1989): 527–47. This is not an abstract theological point but has burning practical import for the Catholic Church, as it discusses the matter of ordination of women to the priesthood. Does the priest primarily represent Christ *to* the church, or does the priest primarily represent the church and *through* the church, Christ?

Those who wish to retain the male priesthood tend to favor the former, arguing that only a male can properly represent Christ. For background, see Dennis Michael Ferrara, "Representation or Self-Effacement: The Axiom *in Persona Christi* in St. Thomas and the Magisterium," *Theological Studies* 55 (1994): 195–224. My own view is that it is perfectly possible for the church to interpret the will of the risen Christ so that one person, an ordained priest, for example, would, for the sake of sacramental effectiveness, act in the person of Christ. I would venture to say that in such a role the presider would be acting not simply as a representative of the community but in a certain sense as a direct representative of the risen Christ. But I find no scriptural or theological warrant for excluding women from playing such a role. Furthermore, I would stress that sacramental theory and practice are a living tradition, subject to development in response to changed historical circumstances and to the developing consciousness of the risen Christ. For a more in-depth look at women and sacraments, see the book by Susan Ross, *Extravagant Affections: A Feminist Sacramental Theology* (New York: Continuum, 1998). As far as I know, Ross's work is the first book-length presentation of a feminist sacramental theology (though it should be noted that she offers a fundamental sacramental theology, rather than a systematic theology of individual sacraments). Ross points out that Catholic sacraments have so excluded women that many have turned to "unofficial" liturgical celebrations and away from official sacramental ceremony. This may in part account for the relative neglect of sacramental theology by feminist theologians (24–28). Ross takes up the issue of women representing Christ at the Eucharist on pages 80–88.

31. There are suggestive parallels between the role of Eucharist in the church and the role of sexual self-giving in marriage. The purpose of each is to express in the most general way the meaning that binds the community or the couple together. All other sacraments address themselves to highly specific "transition situations" (see Martos, *Doors to the Sacred*, 6) in the community's life: birth and first initiation (Baptism), rite of passage into adult decision (Confirmation), choosing communal leaders (Holy Orders), reconciling the sinner (Reconciliation), making a couple two in one flesh (Marriage), and healing the sick (Anointing). Within marriage, there are many words, often ritualized, in which the couple speak their love into very particular transition situations: pregnancy, birth, adoption, guilt, hunger, sickness, thirst, need for conversation, child off to college, death of a parent, and so on. Love's meaning has to take on great particularity in order to speak to the situation. But in sexual lovemaking, the situation is the celebration of the relation itself, of the couple's love in its broadest and deepest meaning. The couple celebrates itself as couple. The situation here is not one of transition but of "intensification" (6). By analogy, so too with the Eucharist. The community celebrates itself as community. It speaks the meaning that binds it together in the most general sense, which is the meaning of two-directional self-giving with Christ.

32. Food has been used so much as part of an outer word that now any time a friend serves food to a friend, the whole act of serving takes on a ritualized quality. Both server and served adopt a more ritualistic and ceremonial manner. It is no

accident, therefore, that eating and drinking are so pervaded by rules of courtesy, protocols of good order, fixed gestures (for example, the toast), strict taboos, jealously guarded privileges, and fussy procedures. Already bound to special places and times, frequently repeated in the daily round of life, biologically indispensable to human flourishing, rich in sensory appeal, food lends itself very easily to becoming part of a ritualized word.

33. This transformation of the eucharistic bread and wine has been officially termed *transubstantiation* by the teaching office of the Roman Catholic Church. In the 1960s, a movement arose among Catholic theologians—a movement that began in the Netherlands—to use terms like *transfinalization, transignification,* or even *transymbolization* in order to get away from the physicalist associations of the term *transubstantiation.* In 1965, Pope Paul VI in his encyclical *Mysterium Fidei* reaffirmed the use of the term *transubstantiation* and the teaching of the Council of Trent, which had the intended effect of discouraging the use of the new terms and the unintended effect of causing the virtual disappearance of the old term from theological discourse. Furthermore, the work of these theologians had its effect anyway, and the thinking behind their use of the new terms—a thinking that is more phenomenological than Aristotelian and more sensitive to the real personal presence of Christ in the church as a whole and therefore analogously in all the sacraments—continues to dominate Catholic sacramental theology. For a history of the discussion of the 1960s, based on a thorough understanding of the Dutch sources, see Joseph Powers, *Eucharistic Theology* (New York: Herder and Herder, 1967), especially 111–83. See also Kenan B. Osborne, *The Christian Sacraments of Initiation: Baptism, Confirmation, Eucharist* (New York: Paulist Press, 1987), 190–211, and Lawler, *Symbol and Sacrament,* 142–52. As Catholic theologians move away from the language of transubstantiation to the language of real presence, they find themselves increasingly in basic agreement with those Protestant theologians who believe, along with Luther and Calvin, that Christ through the church is really present through the bread and wine. See Martos, *Doors to the Sacred,* 243–44. The Protestant theologian Horton Davies sees an ecumenical convergence on the eucharistic real presence. See his *Bread of Life and Cup of Joy: Newer Ecumenical Perspectives on the Eucharist* (Grand Rapids, Mich.: Eerdmans, 1993), especially 220–56.

34. *Through the church* means that the Eucharist, or any sacrament for that matter, cannot effectively occur without the binding faith of the community that is church. If a group of people with no faith in Christ come together and perform all the words and actions of a Eucharist, there is no sacrament and no communication from the risen Christ. It would be the equivalent of a group of actors performing a Eucharist onstage for the sole purpose of simulating it. This does not mean that everyone celebrating the Eucharist needs to be a holy person, or even that the bonds of love among the members need be perfect. Rather, there needs to be, minimally, a faith intention to make Christ present in and through the community ritual. To be sure, a community should aim for more than the minimum. Maximal sacramental effectiveness takes place in communities of love, where members

have responded to the Spirit and made a commitment to bond with one another. For this reason, Paul says that those members in the community estranged from one another should seek reconciliation before they celebrate the Eucharist (see 1 Cor. 11:17-18 for Paul's opposition to a Eucharist celebrated by a community of factions and discord). Those Christians who belong to the *believers churches,* that is, those who trace their origins to the Anabaptist (Anabaptists, that is "re-baptizers," were against baptizing infants and in favor of re-baptizing adults who had already been baptized as infants) wing of the "Radical Reformation," have consistently given more stress than have mainline churches to the Lord's Supper as a sign of the community's love and faith. See the essays in Dale R. Stoffer, *The Lord's Supper: Believers Church Perspective* (Scottdale, Pa.: Herald Press, 1997).

35. Christians who are entrusted with teaching the Christian faith must take great care when they tell their students that the bread and wine are transformed into Christ's body and blood. The terms *body* and *blood* are examples of metonymy, in which a part stands for the whole (e.g., *crown* in "lands belonging to the crown"). Thus *body* stands for the whole self in its tangible self-expression: only through our bodies can we, as whole selves, express ourselves. *Blood* stands for the whole self as a pulsating life force: only through our blood can we, whole selves, be alive and present in body. Catholic teaching has implicitly recognized these metonymies by insisting that the person of the risen Christ is wholly present in and through the bread as well as through the wine. For that reason, the Catholic Church has in the past believed itself theologically justified in restricting lay communion to only what it terms one species, namely, bread. Yet Catholics, with their language of "substance" and their anxiety about lapsing into "mere symbolism" must continue to take particular care to avoid the "physicalism" of "bread into body" and "wine into blood." The transformed bread is not literally Christ's body; the transformed wine is not literally Christ's blood. Communicants do not chew the bones and drink the blood. But Christ is really, personally, wholly, self-communicatively present in and through each. But, I must add, even though metonymy rescues us from physicalism by preventing us from reducing whole to part and makes comprehensible how Christ is wholly present through the bread as well as the wine, post–Vatican II Catholics have done right in following the Protestants in their practice (which is ancient church practice) of communion with both bread and wine. Under both species, the symbol of nourishment is enriched, for indeed we live by food *and* drink, not just by food or just by drink. And more of the symbolism of Jesus' death is present: the bread that is broken is the body that is broken; the wine poured out is the blood that is poured out; death comes when body and blood are separated. For an interesting discussion of metonymy, with special emphasis on the distinction between metonymy and metaphor, see George Lakoff and Mark Turner, *More Than Cool Reason: A Field Guide to Poetic Metaphor* (Chicago: University of Chicago Press, 1989), 100–106. On the meaning of Jesus' Aramaic words *body* and *blood* at the last supper, see Bernard Cooke, "Synoptic Presentation of the Eucharist as Covenant Sacrifice," *Theological Studies*, 21 (1960): 1–44; here 25–26.

36. There are four other sacraments (Catholic and Orthodox) or ritual equivalents (Protestant)—Reconciliation, Holy Orders, Marriage, and Anointing—that I shall not consider here. For these other sacraments, I highly recommend Cooke, *Sacraments and Sacramentality;* Bausch, *A New Look at Sacraments;* and Lawler, *Symbol and Sacrament.*

37. For the history of the church as servant see Cooke, *Ministry to Word and Sacraments,* 343–402. For a treatment concerning the contemporary church, see Avery Dulles, S.J., *Models of the Church* (New York: Doubleday Image Books, 1978), 95–108.

8. The Human Response of Faith and Love

1. When Christianity entered into full philosophical dialogue with Greek, that is, Hellenistic culture, there was a change in both Christian language and Christian thought. The first order language of biblical narration, myth, symbol, metaphor, and parable was in part translated into the second order language of logic, reason, metaphysics, and concept. Protestant theologians (for example, Adolph von Harnack) who have a special reverence for the language of Scripture, have lamented this "Hellenization of dogma," while Catholics and Orthodox in their loyalty to tradition have seen it as necessary to a living tradition. I think that reformulation is necessary and laudable, but in recent years, I have become more aware of the relative inadequacy of all language in the face of divine mystery and more insistent on the need to check any reformulation against Scripture and then to bow before a mystery that not even Scripture can fully capture. On the distinction between first order and second order language, see Gary L. Comstock, "Two Types of Narrative Theology," *Journal of the American Academy of Religion* 55 (1987): 687–717, here, 695, 701.

2. The so-called Nicene Creed is, in fact, the creed formulated at the Council of Constantinople in 381 C.E., though in formulating it, the delegates incorporated many phrases from the creed formulated at the Council of Nicaea in 325.

3. See Donald Evans, *Faith, Authenticity, and Morality* (Toronto: University of Toronto Press, 1980), 249–50.

4. In the words of the great U.S. theologian Jonathan Edwards: "If the great things of religion are rightly understood, they will affect the heart" (*Religious Affections: The Works of Jonathan Edwards*, vol. 2, ed. John E. Smith (New Haven, Conn.: Yale University Press, 1959), 120. In "religious matters," says the Catholic theologian Bernard Lonergan, "love precedes knowledge, and, as that love is God's gift, the very beginning of faith is due to God's grace" (*Method in Theology* [New York: Herder and Herder, 1972], 123). Later in the same book, Lonergan will identify this "gift of grace" with "God's love flooding our hearts through the Holy Spirit" (241).

5. See Hans Küng, *Does God Exist? An Answer for Today,* trans. Edward Quinn (New York: Random House, Vintage Books, 1981), 529–33.

6. Errol E. Harris, *Cosmos and Anthropos: A Philosophical Interpretation of the Anthropic Cosmological Principle* (Atlantic Highlands, N.J.: Humanities Press, 1996), 48.

7. Peter L. Berger, *A Rumor of Angels: Modern Society and the Rediscovery of the Supernatural*, 2nd expanded version (New York: Doubleday Anchor Books, 1990), 61–62. Berger joins many other contemporary religious thinkers by beginning his argument for God's existence with the anthropological rather than with the cosmological. Thomas Aquinas' five ways to God all begin with the external evidence of the cosmos. Berger begins with the internal human experience of trust. See also Schubert Ogden, in *The Reality of God and Other Essays* (New York: Harper and Row, 1966), 1–70, who begins with the experience of "basic confidence," that is, "existential faith"; and John E. Smith, in *The Analogy of Experience: An Approach to Understanding Religious Truth* (New York: Harper and Row, 1973), who begins with the human hunger for ultimate purpose. I have already cited Küng, who is a notable Catholic practitioner of the "anthropological approach." This anthropological approach began with Augustine, continued with Bonaventura, retreated with Aquinas, disappeared with the Protestant reformers (who did not believe that one could reason to God's existence, even if reason began with interior experience), and revived with Schleiermacher. It remains in ascendancy today, though one can sees signs of a resurgence of the cosmological approach, as exhibited in Harris, *Cosmos and Anthropos*.

8. See Küng, *Does God Exist?*, 568–75.

9. The Luther quotation can be found in the *Oxford Book of Aphorisms*, chosen by John Gross (New York: Oxford University Press, 1983), 11. Gross does not provide a source. Readers?

10. For a concise and subtle analysis of Kierkegaard's ideas, along with apt quotations from the relevant primary sources, see James Livingston, *The Enlightenment and the Nineteenth Century*, vol. 1 of *Modern Christian Thought*, 2nd ed. (Upper Saddle River, N.J.: Prentice Hall, 1997), 384–97, esp. 391–94.

11. Jürgen Habermas uses the felicitous expression "cognitive work" to denote the process by which the hearer decides on the sincerity and trustworthiness of the speaker. See "What Is Universal Pragmatics," chap. 1 of *Communication and the Evolution of Society* (Boston: Beacon Press, 1979), 1–68, esp. 62–65.

12. Choosing to trust is partly dependent upon the general level of basic trust or distrust the person brings to reality in general before hearing the Word in the outer words of Jesus and his followers. No one has more insightfully explored how this basic trust, which "pervades the whole personality" and affects "every individual one encounters," works than Donald Evans in his *Struggle and Fulfillment: The Inner Dynamics of Religion and Morality* (Philadelphia: Fortress Press, 1979), here, p. 2.

13. Reason thus can help faith, but reason has its limits, particularly as faith moves from understanding to belief, and then to trust, and finally spills over into love. These limits do not mean that reason abandons its role. Indeed, I would suggest that reason cannot truly know its limits unless it pushes itself to its limits.

Thomas Aquinas said it well: "To realize that God is far beyond anything we think, that is the mind's achievement" (*Theological Texts*, selected and trans. Thomas Gilby [Durham, N.C.: Labyrinth Press, 1982], 266). Thomas is giving voice to the *docta ignorantia*, variously translated as educated ignorance, or learned unknowing. *Docta ignorantia* with respect to the mystery of God is the ever-growing realization that God exceeds our intellectual reach, that God is unknowable, qualitatively, as inexhaustible mystery, as luminous darkness. Our reason can never fully wrap itself around the incomprehensible mystery of a God who freely creates the world and who freely self-communicates in love to this world. Even human love has about it an unaccountable mysteriousness. Surrender to the other, total abandonment of the self, is by definition mysterious because freedom is mysterious. All the more so with God's gift of self to us in Word and Spirit and our gift of self to God in faith and love. Reason falls short, conceptual language limps, and we are humbled and suddenly modest about our soaring intellectual efforts to understand. On the *docta ignorantia*, see Frans Jozef van Beeck, *The Revelation and the Glory*, vol. 2, pt. 1 of *God Encountered: A Contemporary Catholic Systematic Theology* (Collegeville, Minn.: Liturgical Press, 1993), 78–79, 87–88.

14. I think we can see here the deepest reason for the incredibly broad range of definitions that have attached to faith in both Scripture and tradition. Some, especially Catholics between Vatican I and Vatican II, have defined faith in largely cognitive terms, as if faith were simply a rational assent to some important information about God. Others, like Luther, define faith so much as the feeling of trust that faith begins to sound like love. Perhaps also we see the deepest reason for the way that the so-called missions of God as Word (or Son), the second person of the Trinity, and God as Holy Spirit, the third person, have been defined in Scripture and tradition. Yes, very generally one could say that the mission of the Word has been seen as having a more informative function, as intent first on moving the mind rather than the feeling and will; and faith has been correlated more with the response to this Word. Yes, very generally one could say that the mission of the Holy Spirit is more emotive and directive, as an energetic presence that moves feeling and will. Yet this same Scripture and tradition says that the Word is energizing, not only informing the mind but moving the heart and will; and this same Scripture and tradition sees the Spirit as illuminating, not only moving the heart and will, but illuminating the mind and bringing wisdom (see Acts 15:8; Rom. 5:5; 15:13; Eph. 3:16-17; 1 Thess. 1:5). This is not to say that the distinctions between the activity of God as Word and God as Spirit, between faith as the response to the Word and love as response to the Spirit, are invalid, but it is to say that if we are to do full justice to Word and faith, we shall have to also talk about Spirit and love.

15. In the words of Jonathan Edwards: "The Spirit of God in those that have sound and solid religion is a spirit of powerful holy affection" (*Religious Affections*, 100). Edwards is on very secure scriptural foundations: "[A]nd hope," writes Paul, "does not disappoint us, because God's love has been poured into our hearts through the Holy Spirit that has been given to us" (Rom. 5:5; see also 2 Cor. 1:21-22; Gal. 4:6; and Eph. 3:16-17).

16. See Margaret A. Farley, *Personal Commitments: Beginning, Keeping, Changing* (San Francisco: Harper & Row, 1986), 25–37, for an excellent analysis of the passive and active moments of love.

17. 1 John 3:18-20: "Little children, let us love, not in word or speech, but in truth and action. And by this we will know that we are from the truth and will reassure our hearts before him whenever our hearts condemn us; for God is greater than our hearts."

18. My entry into Martin Luther's experience was provided by Erik H. Erikson, *Young Man Luther: A Study in Psychoanalysis and History* (New York: W. W. Norton & Company, 1962). Of course, Luther labeled this experience as faith, in response to the Word, not love, in response to the Spirit, as I have done here. However, for Luther, the Word always came in power, and thus despite my differences with him in the way I use the terminology of faith and love, we may indeed agree in essence about the reality behind the terminology. For I am convinced that God's Word never comes without God's Spirit, and therefore God's meaning never comes without God's power, and therefore God's truth never comes without God's love. See note 14 of this chapter.

19. Paul Tillich, *The Shaking of the Foundations* (New York: Charles Scribner's Sons, 1948), 162: "It is as though a voice were saying, 'You are accepted. *You are accepted*, accepted by that which is greater than you, and the name of which you do not know. Do not ask for the name now; perhaps you will find it later. Do not try to do anything now; perhaps later you will do much. Do not seek for anything; do not perform anything; do not intend anything. *Simply accept the fact that you are accepted!*'" Note Tillich's emphasis on the passivity of this moment.

20. See Martin Luther, *The Bondage of the Will*, trans. J. I. Packer and A. R. Johnson (London: James Clarke and Co, 1957). One must conclude from reading this work that Luther denied free will to all human beings born after the sin of Adam and Eve. Luther's logic in this piece is tight—and a little scary. I must note, however, that on the question of grace and free will, there has been considerable rapprochement between contemporary Catholics and Lutherans. See George H. Anderson, T. Austin Murphy, and Joseph A. Burgess, *Justification by Faith: Lutherans and Catholics in Dialogue, VII* (Minneapolis: Augsburg, 1985), and *The Joint Declaration on the Doctrine of Justification* (1999), which can be found at http://www.elca.org/ea/ecumenical/romancatholic/jddj/index.html

21. I do not understand this free participation from the human side as synergistic with the power of the Spirit, as if the Spirit power and the human power were two ropes pulling with the same power. The Spirit is prior, initiatory, evocative, and drawing. It can almost be said to work fully the response it evokes, but only almost. It can be resisted and, therefore, there is genuine human participation when it is not resisted. This is a great mystery that cannot be fully resolved in rational theological concept. Indeed, denying that there is free participation from the human side in this so-called passive moment is unacceptable precisely because it is too rational. The tension of the mystery is lost when it is resolved in favor of unilateral divine power. Karl Rahner states the mystery in all its tension: "The Christian doc-

trine of faith, hope and love, of the union in grace with God and of the free reception of God's self-communication can well be understood in the sense of true self-redemption. The person who redeems himself in freedom, i.e., places God in the centre of his own free existence, is a creature who is constituted by the creative freedom of God and therefore given the capacity to accept God's self-communication. God, however, shares himself with man both through uncreated grace which forms his very being and through the supernatural capacity which arises from grace and belongs to man in his freedom. God is himself the condition of possibility of human salvation from which man freely realizes his salvation. Naturally, it is taken for granted in Christian theology, in contrast to any form of Pelagianism, that the free acceptance of salvation is a gift of God's grace and thus forms the very core of the human person and of human freedom" ("The One Christ and the Universality of Salvation," *Theological Investigations,* vol. 16, trans. David Morland [New York: Seabury, 1979], 199–224, here, 206–7).

22. "By coming *into* man the Holy Spirit opens him *out* for God" (T. F. Torrance, "The Relevance of the Doctrine of the Spirit for Ecumenical Theology," chap. 13 of *Theology in Reconstruction* [Grand Rapids, Mich.: Eerdmans, 1965], 229–39, here, 238).

23. For extraordinary cases of children who have surmounted an upbringing intent on murdering their souls, see Lillian B. Rubin, *The Transcendent Child: Tales of Triumph over the Past* (New York: HarperCollins, 1997).

24. Two eloquent witnesses to the effect of will on emotion are Thomas Aquinas and Jean-Paul Sartre. On Thomas, Judith Barad writes: "Aquinas explains that emotions are morally good or bad 'either from being commanded by the will, or from not being checked by the will' (*Summa Theologiae* I–II, 24, i)." See her article "Aquinas on the Role of Emotion in Moral Judgment and Activity," *Thomist* 55 (1991): 397–413, here, 404. And Sartre, that great apostle of freedom, says: "[The existentialist] thinks that man is responsible for his passion" (*Existentialism and Human Emotions* [New York: Philosophical Library, 1957], 23).

25. For more on freedom and its ultimate consequences, see chap. ten.

26. See James 1:22: "Be doers of the word, and not merely hearers who deceive themselves." See also James 2:22; 1 Thess. 1:11; 3:5.

27. I must take care to note that in New Testament Greek the words for *love* are more fluid and overlapping than we might be led to believe by contemporary theologians. Considerable semantic overlap exists between agapē and philia, particularly in their verb forms. I am not saying that the contemporary theological distinctions among agapē, philia, and eros are illegitimate, but only that the biblical basis for such distinctions is not as firm as often thought. I am indebted here to James Barr, "Words for Love in Biblical Greek," *The Glory of Christ in the New Testament,* ed. L. D. Hurt and N. T. Wright (New York: Oxford Clarendon, 1987), 3–18.

28. See William Lynch, *Images of Hope: Imagination as the Healer of the Hopeless* (Notre Dame, Ind.: University of Notre Dame Press, 1965), esp. 101–25, for a brilliant discussion of the idolatrizing power of the "absolutizing instinct."

29. See Paul Tillich, *Systematic Theology,* 3 vols. (New York: Harper and Row, University of Chicago Press, 1967), 1.216.

30. The idols really cannot deliver. They therefore cannot bear the weight of our absolute hopes. The absolutizing instinct, says Lynch, is thus the "creator of hopeless projects and hopeless idols" (*Images of Hope*, 106). When these idols come crashing down, we enter a salutary kind of hopelessness, for then we are prepared to place our absolute hope in the one absolute, God, and invest only a relative hope in finite persons and things. For more on hope, see chap. ten of this book.

31. For an outstanding contemporary theology of prayer, see John H. Wright, *A Theology of Christian Prayer* (New York: Pueblo Publishing, 1987). Wright takes up the subject of prayers of thanksgiving and petition on pp. 52–86.

32. Raymond Brown in his *The Community of the Beloved Disciple* (New York: Paulist Press, 1979) writes: "The Matthean Jesus says 'Love your enemies and pray for those who persecute you' (Matt. 5:44), but there is no such maxim in the Johannine tradition. The command to love is *not* in terms of love of neighbor (as in Matt. 19:19) but in terms of loving *one another* (John 13:34-35; 15:12,17); and John 15:13-15 allows that 'one another' to be interpreted in terms of those who are disciples of Christ and obey the commandments [and not those Christians who have apostatized from the Johannine community]" (133). For a more general elucidation of love according to the New Testament, see Pheme Perkins, *Love Commandments in the New Testament* (New York: Paulist Press, 1982).

33. On God's desire for mutuality and God's suffering, see Paul S. Fiddes, *The Creative Suffering of God* (Oxford: Oxford University Press, 1988): "[God] freely chooses covenant with man and the suffering that entails; suffering then is implicit in the very desire of God for fellowship"(254).

34. According to the process theist Charles Hartshorne, God's universal relativity to all, "surrelativity" to use his term, is the essence of divine perfection. He thus understands God's transcendence to mean not only that God is not simply identical with the world (as in pantheism) but also that God is everlastingly in process toward new relations with the world. See *The Divine Relativity: The Social Conception of God* (New Haven, Conn.: Yale University Press, 1948), throughout.

35. I do not deny that Jesus' relationships with his family could be problematic (see Mark 3:21). He believed that if loyalty to God came in conflict with loyalty to family, then loyalty to God had to prevail (see Mark 3:32-34; Luke 9:60; Matt. 10:37). Yet Jesus endorses marriage and family in general and never elevates celibacy, which he apparently practiced, to a state higher than marriage. On Jesus' desire for mutuality, Stephen Post writes: "The image of Jesus beyond all self-concern is really quite superficial. Granted, after the moral good of mutuality became an impossibility and even his closest followers deserted his love, a purposeful and radical act of self-abnegation occurred. Yet this does not imply that the initial goal of mutuality is no longer the highest ideal of love"(*A Theory of Agape: On the Meaning of Christian Love* [Lewisburg, Pa.: Bucknell University Press, 1990], 59).

36. For the meanings I attach to the terms agapē, philia, and eros, I am adopting contemporary theological conventions. I am not claiming that these are precisely the same meanings that were attached to these terms in classical and biblical Greek (see n. 27). I should also mention here that no agreement exists on these contem-

porary conventions. This is particularly true of the term *eros*, which can be used more broadly to denote the desire that seeks fulfillment in the union with any object, value, or person; or more narrowly to denote the desire that seeks fulfillment in the passionate and romantic union with a person. I am using *eros* in the narrower sense, though not so narrowly as to reduce it to the merely libidinal or sexual. Two thinkers who use the term more broadly are Paul Tillich and Daniel Day Williams. See Alexander C. Irwin, *Eros toward the World: Paul Tillich's Theology of the Erotic* (Minneapolis: Fortress Press, 1991), and Daniel Day Williams, *The Spirit and the Forms of Love* (New York: Harper and Row, 1968).

37. See Karl Rahner, "Anonymous Christians," *Theological Investigations*, vol. 6, trans. Karl-H and Boniface Kruger (New York: Seabury Press, 1969), 390–98; "Observations on the Problem of the 'Anonymous Christian'," *Theological Investigations*, vol. 14, trans. David Bourke (New York: Crossroad Books, 1976), 280–94; and "The One Christ and the Universality of Salvation," *Theological Investigations*, vol. 16, trans. David Marland (New York: Crossroad Books, 1983), 199–224. Rahner gradually used the term less and less (for example, he does not use it in *Foundations of Christian Faith: An Introduction to the Idea of Christianity*, trans. William V. Dych [New York: Seabury Press, 1978], 311–21, where one would have expected to see it). Yet he never disavowed the term. He tells this story: "Nishitani the well known Japanese philosopher, the head of the Kyoto school, who is familiar with the notion of the anonymous Christian, once asked me: What would you say to my treating you as an anonymous Zen Buddhist? I replied: certainly you may and should do so from your point of view; I feel myself honored by such an interpretation" ("The One Christ," *Theological Investigations*, vol. 16, 219).

38. This favorite exclusivist passage has been given an interesting interpretation by James D. G. Dunn, in *New Testament Theology in Dialogue: Christology and Ministry* (Philadelphia: Westminster Press, 1987), 77–79. The Gospel writer, says Dunn, has Jesus say this so uncompromisingly as "an evangelistic or paranetic strategy to force readers to recognize the either-or of faith in Christ which confronts them" (77). This seems "to be the primary thrust of the Johannine claim not the outright denial that God's spirit and word may well be experienced elsewhere in the world" (79).

39. The classic expression of this view can be found in Rudolf Otto, *The Idea of the Holy*, 2nd ed. (Oxford: Oxford University Press, 1950), though it must be said that his "generic experience" sounds more specifically Lutheran than generically universal. A more nuanced view is that of John Hick, who sees all religions as a response to "transcendent Being" (he warns the reader not to understand this in the narrowly Western theistic sense and later he will prefer the term "ultimate Reality"), but insists that in a genuinely "truth-seeking dialogue" each participant will be conscious that this being is "infinitely greater than his own limited vision of it" (*God Has Many Names* [Philadelphia: Westminster Press, 1982], 117). In this same group belongs Leonard Swidler, author of *After the Absolute: The Dialogical Future of Religious Reflection* (Minneapolis: Fortress Press, 1990).

40. See John B. Cobb Jr., "Toward a Christocentric Catholic Theology," in

Toward a Universal Theology of Religion, ed. Leonard Swidler (Maryknoll, N.Y.: Orbis Books, 1988), 86–101, where he says that interreligious dialogue should be open to the possibility of a pluralist metaphysics of the ultimate (97).

41. Among those who believe that religious symbols do not speak of the ultimate are those who see religion as positively harmful and those who see religion as more benign than harmful. In the former group, I would place Karl Marx, Friedrich Nietzsche, Sigmund Freud, Bertrand Russell, and Jean-Paul Sartre. In the latter group, Ludwig Feuerbach, Max Weber, George Santayana, John Dewey, and Erich Fromm. For an interesting analysis of four other thinkers who would belong to the second group (namely, R. B. Braithwaite, John Herman Randall Jr., D. Z. Phillips, and Don Cupitt) see John Hick, *An Interpretation of Religion: Human Responses to the Transcendent* (New Haven, Conn.: Yale University Press, 1989), 193–201.

42. Recently, a fourth option is emerging, which shies away from exclusivism and inclusivism, but warns against a precipitate embrace of pluralism. According to this option, we should not a priori embrace pluralism until we have entered into careful study of the other religious traditions. We may eventually come to accept pluralism, or, at least in theory, even exclusivism or inclusivism, but we should do so only a posteriori, after patient dialogue and study. A representative of this fourth option is Schubert Ogden, who suspects John Hick of committing himself too quickly to pluralism, though he holds out the hope that Hick may be convinced to proceed more carefully. In Ogden's words: "As for the question of pluralism, suffice it to say that in my view—even as, presumably, in Hick's—any answer to it must be a posteriori and at least in part be empirically justified. So far as my own experience in such matters goes, I am not yet at the point at which I can assert that there are in fact several ways of salvation of which the Christian way is but one" (*Doing Theology Today* [Valley Forge, Pa.: Trinity Press International, 1996], 166). An interesting variant on this fourth option is found in Keith Ward's "convergent pluralism," which allows that there may be a "unitary truth" toward which humankind through "dialogical interpenetration" may converge, though such convergence is "unlikely to destroy the diversity of traditions, rooted in diverse histories, cultures and temperaments." See his book, *A Vision to Pursue: Beyond the Crisis in Christianity* (London: SCM Press, 1991), 175–76. For an excellent anthology that offers a range of views, see Leonard Swidler and Paul Mojzes, eds., *The Uniqueness of Jesus: A Dialogue with Paul F. Knitter* (Maryknoll, N.Y.: Orbis Books, 1997).

9. Love into Justice:
The Good Samaritan Revisited

1. See John Donahue, *The Gospel in Parable: Metaphor, Narrative, and Theology in the Synoptic Gospels* (Philadelphia: Fortress Press, 1988), 126ff.

2. Joachim Jeremias, *The Parables of Jesus*, 2nd rev. ed. (New York: Charles Scribner's Sons, 1972), 198ff.

3. Donahue, *The Gospel in Parable*, 12–13.

4. Jeremias, *The Parables of Jesus*, 204.

5. Donahue, *The Gospel in Parable*, 130–31, supplies a short history of the relations between Jews and Samaritans to show why they were such enemies.

6. Jeremias, *The Parables of Jesus*, 202.

7. Donahue, *The Gospel in Parable*, tells us that the Samaritan's extra help at the inn is more than just a sign of the supererogatory: "As a paradigm for compassionate entry into the world of an injured brother or sister, this final action is indispensable. According to the law at the time, a person with an unpaid debt could be enslaved until the debt was paid (see Matt. 18:23-35). Since the injured man was robbed and stripped—deprived of all resources—he could have been at the mercy of the innkeeper, a profession that had a bad reputation for dishonesty and violence. The parable assures the injured man's freedom and independence" (133).

8. Actually, Niebuhr said it more abstractly than that: "An immediately felt obligation towards obvious need may be prompted by the emotion of pity. But a continued sense of obligation rests upon and expresses itself in rational calculations of the needs of others as compared with our own interests. A relation between the self and one other may be partly ecstatic; and in any case the calculation of relative interests may be reduced to a minimum. But as soon as a third person is introduced into the relation even the most perfect love requires a rational estimate of conflicting needs and interests" (*The Nature and Destiny of Man: A Christian Interpretation*, vol. 2, *Human Destiny* [New York: Charles Scribner's Sons, 1943], 248.

9. Following the rules of common courtesy can fulfill more than a small part of interpersonal justice on a day to day level. It is amazing how much of the advice that Miss Manners gives in her syndicated newspaper column can be seen as the application of interpersonal justice. She shows an acute sense for the intersection of morality and manners. Though insofar as her rulings on courtesy precipitate a widespread pattern of behavior in society, she is creating a social structure, that is, she is doing the work of social justice.

10. Another retelling of the Good Samaritan story, which makes much the same move to social justice as I make here, is that of Stephen C. Mott in *Biblical Ethics and Social Change* (New York: Oxford University Press, 1982), 58–59. I am not indebted to Mott's retelling, but the parallel is striking. For the Mott reference, I am indebted to Garth L. Hallet, *Christian Neighbor Love: An Assessment of Six Rival Positions* (Washington, D.C.: Georgetown University Press, 1989), 118.

11. On institutionalization, see Peter L. Berger and Thomas Luckmann, *The Social Construction of Reality: A Treatise on the Sociology of Knowledge* (New York: Doubleday Anchor Books, 1967), 54–61.

12. A volunteer patrol is a good example of what Catholic social teaching calls a "mediating structure" or an "intermediate structure." Such structures carry out the "principle of subsidiarity," which could be summed up this way: before creating larger, governmental structures, first create smaller, local, nongovernmental structures. See Fred Kammer, *Doing Faithjustice: An Introduction to Catholic Social Thought* (New York: Paulist Press, 1991), 184.

13. Here we have an example of the twin function of government. On the one hand, it has the more positive function of extending medical help to all who need it. On the other hand, it has the more negative function of countering violence with violence, of enforcing order against the forces of anarchy and destruction. There are two traditions in Western political theory that tend to focus on one function at the expense of the other. Martin Luther (and, before him, Augustine, after him, Hobbes) tends to reduce government to the "negative" function, that is, "to bear the secular sword and punish the wicked" (see "Secular Authority: To What Extent Should It Be Obeyed" [first published in 1523], in John Dillenberger, ed., *Martin Luther: Selections from His Writings* [New York: Doubleday Anchor Books, 1961] 363–402, here, 374). Government indeed is willed by God, according to Luther, but by God's "left hand." Its work is God's work, yet an "alien work" (377). If there had been no sin, there would be no government. The scriptural source for this tradition can be found in Rom. 13:4 and 1 Pet. 1:13. Another tradition, going back to Plato and Aristotle, stresses that government is a good and is natural to human life. Christian socialists and welfare state liberals add to this the agapic motivation and welcome government structures in their "positive" function of meeting a broad range of human needs. Reinhold Niebuhr keeps these two traditions in good balance: "All structures of justice do indeed presuppose the sinfulness of man, and are all partly systems of restraint which prevent the conflict of wills and interests from resulting in a consistent anarchy. But they are also all mechanisms by which men fulfill their obligations to their fellow men, beyond the possibilities offered in direct and personal relationships. The Kingdom of God and the demands of perfect love are therefore relevant to every political system and impinge upon every social situation in which the self seeks to come to terms with the claims of other life." See *The Nature and Destiny of Man* 2.192.

14. One of the effects of the widespread indebtedness among the peasants in Palestine was virtual slavery for those who could not pay their debts. Many took to banditry. See Richard A. Horsley, *Sociology and the Jesus Movement* (New York: Crossroad, 1989), 88–90.

15. I am not saying that people in Jesus' time lacked a political vision in the broad sense: they dreamed of a new world where life would be radically different. Jesus had that vision, as did many other millenarian prophets of his time. What I do not see is the combination of political vision and social analysis, which I think is a modern phenomenon.

16. In the words of Fred Kammer: "Instead of a tension between love and justice, love as the soul of justice gives the Christian passion for building a more just order" (*Doing Faithjustice*, 181).

17. An extraordinary example of agapic love practiced spontaneously more because of communal ethos than individual heroic virtue is the story of the French mountain village of Le Chambon, whose five thousand inhabitants sheltered five thousand Jews during World War II. The documentary *Weapons of the Spirit* (1990), produced by Pierre Sauvage, contains many interviews with individuals who participated in this good work. What is remarkable is how self-effacing they are. Indeed, they are baffled by the attention. What emerges out of the interviews is

that these people performed individual acts of love because that is what one does if one is a member of that community. There appears to have been very little agonizing over the risks. It was the triumph of an ethos and thus was the work of social justice. See also Philip P. Hallie, *Lest Innocent Blood Be Shed: The Story of the Village of Le Chambon and How Goodness Happened There* (New York: Harper and Row, 1979). And yet reading Hallie's book reveals how mysteriously complex all this is. For the ethos of Le Chambon would not have attained its spontaneous strength without the inspired work of two individuals, the pastor and his wife, André and Magda Trocmé. For a very interesting philosophical examination of both the village ethos and the moral achievement of the Trocmés, see Lawrence A. Blum, *Moral Perception and Particularity* (New York: Cambridge University Press, 1994), 73–74, 85–89, 91–92, 151–52, 175–80.

18. Within the public sphere of social justice, there are several subspheres that correspond to different kinds of social justice: (1) basic human rights and freedoms, such as freedom of speech, of worship, of movement, and so on; (2) economic justice, the duty of society to ensure that goods and services are fairly and equally distributed and the duty of individuals to contribute to the production of goods and services; (3) political justice, the duty of society to ensure that political power is fairly and equally distributed and the duty of individuals to contribute to political decision making; (4) criminal justice, the duty of the society to fairly and equally enforce the law and the duty of individuals to obey the law; (5) environmental justice, the duty to protect the inorganic and organic world so that all being will flourish, not just human being; (6) intergenerational justice, the duty of the present generation to pass on just social structures to the next generation and not overburden the next generation with debt and environmental degradation; and (7) international justice, the duty of nations to live in comity with other nations and to create international social structures to solve social problems that are global in their effects. To all these duties are corresponding rights; indeed, one of the tasks of social justice is to find the proper balance of duties (responsibilities) and rights (entitlements), or, to put it another way, to find the proper mix of what the larger society should distribute to subsocieties and individuals, and what individuals and subsocieties should contribute to the larger society.

19. The works of two contemporary theorists of agapic love show these two tendencies. Gene Outka, in his *Agape: An Ethical Analysis* (New Haven, Conn.: Yale University Press, 1972), defines agapic love as "universal equal regard." Although he does accept mutuality as a proper fulfillment of agape, his understanding of agape leads his analysis more naturally toward justice. Stephen Post, in his *A Theory of Agape: On the Meaning of Christian Love* (Lewisburg, Pa.: Bucknell University Press, 1990), shows agapic love as seeking out mutual response in "special relations." My own view is that both tendencies must be kept together in dialectical unity. I like the words of Gilbert Meilander: "We ought not give up the desire for mutual love and try to be stoics. Neither ought we permit our love to be limited to the small circle of those who return it" (*Friendship: A Study in Theological Ethics* [Notre Dame, Ind.: University of Notre Dame Press, 1981], 50).

10. The Human Response of Hope

1. So strong is the element of self-commitment on the part of the person
promising that John Searle refers to the promissory function as the "commissive"
function (*Expression and Meaning: Studies in the Theory of Speech Acts* [Cam-
bridge: Cambridge University Press, 1979], 1–29, especially 22–23.

2. See Margaret A. Farley, *Personal Commitments: Beginning, Keeping, Changing* (San Francisco: Harper & Row, 1986), 34. Her book is a beautiful reflection on
the promissory function.

3. The word *confident* is important here, for hope can vary from the very shaky
("I hope, for once, he arrives on time") to the very confident ("I have every hope
that he will come on time"). But within a developing love relationship, the lover
aims to arouse a *confident* hope. In the words of Thomas Aquinas: "Hope is excited
by a good which can be secured—indeed hope wears an air of confidence" (*Theological Texts*, selected and trans. Thomas Gilby [Durham, N.C.: Labyrinth Press,
1982], 203).

4. The German philosopher Ernst Bloch built a whole ontology on the hope
for a reality that is "not-yet." See especially his *Tübinger Einleitung in die Philosophie* (Frankfurt: Suhrkamp Verlag, 1970). For an analysis, see Thomas H. West, *Ultimate Hope without God: The Atheistic Eschatology of Ernst Bloch* (New York: Peter
Lang Publishing, Inc., 1991), 269–328.

5. There are many New Testament passages that anchor hope in Jesus' resurrection: "If Christ has not been raised, your faith is futile and you are still in your
sins. Then those also who have died in Christ have perished. If for this life only
we have hoped in Christ, we are of all people most to be pitied. But in fact Christ
has been raised from the dead, the first fruits of those who have died. For since
death came through a human being, the resurrection of the dead has also come
through a human being; for as all die in Adam, so all will be made alive in Christ"
(1 Cor. 15:17-22). "By [God's] great mercy he has given us a new birth into a living
hope through the resurrection of Jesus Christ from the dead" (1 Pet. 1:3). "We
have this hope, a sure and steadfast anchor of the soul, a hope that enters the
inner shrine behind the curtain, where Jesus, a forerunner on our behalf, has
entered, having become a high priest forever according to the order of
Melchizedek" (Heb. 6:19-20).

6. According to William Lynch: "Hope comes close to being the very heart and
center of a human being" (*Images of Hope: Imagination as the Healer of the Hopeless* [Notre Dame, Ind.: University of Notre Dame Press, 1965], 31). But neither
Lynch nor I wish to say that hope is the core of the human being, because the tendency to meaning *does* seek fulfillment and rest and, indeed, finds it ultimately in
a relationship of mutuality with God, cosmos, and others: "The final object of our
hopes is love" (171). And it is the clear implication of Paul's teaching on hope that
hope comes to its rest in love. For this reason, among faith, love, and hope, the
"greatest is love" (1 Cor. 13:13).

7. Love can still be unconditional, that is, offered even if the receiver does not accept it. This does not mean, however, that the one offering love cannot or should not feel a lively desire and hope that her love be accepted and returned. In this sense, unconditional love is not "disinterested." Stephen Post says it well: "The ideal of disinterested love makes folly of the theological virtue of hope" (*A Theory of Agape: On the Meaning of Christian Love* [Lewisburg, Pa.: Bucknell University Press, 1990], 22).

8. With respect to the relation between *agape* and friendship love (*philia*), Gene Outka has these insightful words: "Unqualified regard [*agape* in Outka's terminology] promotes *philia*, however, by liberating us, for example, from certain anxieties that tend to block full reciprocity. As a consequence of such anxieties, our concern for others is held hostage to our concern that others confirm us. We care *about* them but not in the first instance *for* them. We start by caring about the effect their approvals and disapprovals have on our own self-esteem, not by revering their lives in their otherness. Two elements coexist in these anxieties. Others matter too little: their approval of us proves to be a condition for whether we care or continue to care about them at all. Others matter too much: in seeking to secure their approval, we are problematically liable to do their bidding, to be controlled by their appraisals of us. Agape gives us independence from these anxieties: from not caring unless they care and from caring unduly what others think of us and thus allowing them to set the terms for the confirmation of ourselves we want, above all, to obtain. I suspect that in the deepest friendships *both* parties always display an ingredient of unqualified regard" ("Theocentric Agape and the Self: An Asymmetrical Affirmation in Response to Colin Grant's Either/Or," *Journal of Religious Ethics* 24 [1996]: 35–42, here, 38).

9. In the words of Sebastian Moore: "Desire is love trying to happen" (*Jesus the Liberator of Desire* [New York: Crossroad, 1989], 93).

10. William Lynch says: "We can love others only if we put the absolute in the right place. We must keep the absolute out of things, rather like good, homely atheists. This comes close to the religious teaching that we cannot love anything unless we love God first. In this light, religion is the reverse of an inhibiting reality. Rather, it makes clear thinking and clear, accurate wishing possible" (*Images of Hope*, 139–40).

11. I think it is important to counter the accusation leveled by process theists such as Charles Hartshorne that individual ultimate hope is selfish. We should be concerned, he says, only with contributing to God's joy and glory; all hope on our part for sharing God's joy and glory as individuals in the next life is self-centered and irreligious. The language of Eugene Fontinell's critique of Hartshorne's views is too harsh, but I agree with his basic point: "In spite of Hartshorne's prodigious intellectual powers, I find it difficult to avoid a response characterized by both repugnance and frivolity. He softens the picture somewhat by maintaining that we 'will serve God, not as puppets in His hands, but as, in humble measure, co-creators with Him.' The bottom line, however, is still that we are to act in such a way as to make life interesting and enjoyable for the divine spectator-participant" (*Self, God, and Immortality: A Jamesian Investigation* [Philadelphia: Temple

University Press, 1986], 186. For Hartshorne's views, see his *Omnipotence and Other Theological Mistakes* (Albany, N.Y.: SUNY Press, 1984), 34–35, 97–98, 121–22. In Hartshorne's defense, his opposition to the individual afterlife is motivated in part by the crude and not infrequent Christian practice of motivating people to do good by dangling before them the rewards of heaven and punishments of hell.

12. Against those who reject Christian hope for the next life because the object of such a hope is merely invented to compensate for a miserable life here below, Fontinell rightly stresses the positive desire to continue living a life of meaning: "It is not because life is so bad that we must seek meaning for it in another life. It is because life is so good that we desire to extend, deepen, and enrich it without limit" (*Self, God, and Immortality,* 230). In an article comparing the views of Hartshorne and Rahner, Norman J. King and Barry L. Whitney sum up the key difference: "For Rahner, the longing for personal fulfillment beyond the confines of this life, the longing in effect for oneness with Mystery, is not egotistical but inevitable, insofar as it is built into the very structure of the human being. In his view, this thirst for enduring meaning contains a hope for conscious personal immortality" ("Rahner and Hartshorne on Death and Eternal Life," *Horizons* 15 [fall 1988]: 239–61, here, 259).

13. *Eschatology* is that area of theology that studies what comes after the end (the Greek word for *end* is *eschaton*) of penultimate life. An *eschatological symbol* is an image or metaphor or analogical concept referring to next life. Symbols point to a reality without fully capturing it. All theological language is symbolic, but eschatological language is especially so. In the famous dictum of Reinhold Niebuhr, the eschatological symbols must be taken "seriously" but never "literally" (*The Nature and Destiny of Man: A Christian Interpretation,* vol. 2, *Human Destiny* [New York: Charles Scribner's Sons, 1943], 289). And thus the theologian uses these symbols with great modesty and trepidation. John Shea says it well: "All linguistic efforts to elaborate Christian hope are betrayals. They are not the deliberate betrayals of malice but the inevitable betrayals of the poet. The hope for a future life, precisely because it is the resonance of God's prodigal love, is too great for the human heart. Every symbol this hope gives birth to is to a degree adequate and to a larger degree inadequate" (*What a Modern Catholic Believes about Heaven and Hell* [Chicago: Thomas More Press, 1972], 52).

14. Jewish eschatology of the individual afterlife develops after 300 B.C.E. Some strains were influenced by Greek eschatology, to the point that talk of a soul separated from the body at death could be found in some Jewish writings. See for example the Wisdom of Solomon 2:23-34 and the Testament of Abraham 12–13. When Luke in 23:43 has Jesus on the cross say to the crucified bandit next to him, "Truly I tell you, today you will be with me in Paradise," it would be compatible with the eschatology of some Jews to imagine that the bandit's soul, not his body, would be going to paradise immediately at death and to reside there in the interim state until the end of time when his soul would be reunited with his body at the universal resurrection of the dead. When, therefore, contemporary theologians urge a return to the holism of Jewish thought, they really mean going back to that strain of Jewish thought that preserved the traditional holism of Jewish thought

before 300 B.C.E. For a brilliant historical survey of early Jewish views of the after-life, see Alan F. Segal, "Life after Death: The Social Sources," *The Resurrection: An Interdisciplinary Symposium on the Resurrection of Jesus*, ed. Stephen T. Davis, Daniel Kendall, S.J., and Gerald O'Collins, S.J. (Oxford: Oxford University Press, 1997), 90–125. For a clear presentation of the recent theological tendency to see the individual's resurrection as occurring immediately at death, see Dermot Lane, *Keeping Hope Alive: Stirrings in Christian Theology* (Mahwah, N.J.: Paulist Press, 1996), 151–62. Lane follows Karl Rahner in claiming that the teaching about the intermediate state should be open for reformulation. Lane finds strong hints in certain Pauline passages (Rom. 6:3-4; 2 Cor. 5:1-4; Phil. 3:2-12) that at death the physical body is immediately transformed into a "spiritual body" (1 Cor. 15:44).

15. Cremation was forbidden by the Catholic Church until 1963. See Peter C. Phan, *Responses to 101 Questions on Death and Eternal Life* (Mahwah, N.J.: Paulist Press, 1997), 58–59.

16. Thomas Nagel has written a book completely given over to the theme of the human being as situated both immanent in, and transcendent to, the world, *The View from Nowhere* (New York: Oxford University Press, 1986). Unfortunately, Nagel, like virtually all U.S. philosophers, is totally ignorant of the work of theologians, who have often written on this theme with great depth and insight. See, for example, Reinhold Niebuhr, *The Nature and Destiny of Man: A Christian Interpretation*, vol. 1, *Human Nature* (New York: Charles Scribner's Sons, 1941).

17. See Karl Rahner, *On the Theology of Death* (New York: Herder and Herder, 1961), 16–26. See also Ladislaus Boros, *The Moment of Truth: Mysterium Mortis* (London: Burns and Oates, 1962), 77–79.

18. If our bodies are the principle of self-communication, it would seem that they also are the principle of individual identity. This at least is the view of Louis Dupre who in his *Transcendent Selfhood: The Rediscovery of the Inner Life* (New York: Crossroad, 1976) writes: "Bodiliness of some sort, then, appears to be an essential condition for preserving individuality after death" (91). It is difficult, however, to see how individuality based on bodiliness could be preserved in the risen life if the body is the whole material cosmos. Thomas Aquinas, like his men-tor Aristotle, believed that matter was the principle of individuation. But he also believed with the church that in the intermediate state the soul was separated from the body. Aquinas drew the stark conclusion: "A human soul naturally desires his own salvation; but the soul, since it is part of the body of a human being, is not the whole human being, and my soul is not I; so even if a soul gains salvation in another life, that is not I or any other human being" (*Super Priman epistolam ad Corinthios c. 15*, Cai edition, 924). For this astonishing quotation, I am indebted to Lane, *Keeping Hope Alive*, 40.

19. For a fascinating history of the ways Christians have pictured heaven, see Colleen McDannell and Bernhard Lang, *Heaven: A History* (New Haven, Conn.: Yale University Press, 1988).

20. Jesus clearly preaches a doctrine of hell. See the parable of the sheep and goats (Matt. 25:31-45) and the verse in Mark 3:29 about the unforgivable sin

against the Holy Spirit. Also Mark 9:43-47; Matt. 10:29; 23:33. Before 300 B.C.E., the Jews did not have a fully developed eschatology for the individual. Those who died went to Sheol (Greek, *hades*), a kind of twilight zone where they existed as shades of their former selves. It was not a place of punishment, nor was it a desirable place. By the time of Jesus, Sheol had ceased to be regarded by many Jews as a neutral place, having been divided into Gehenna (see 1 Enoch 22:1-14), the hell of the damned, and paradise, the abode of the righteous (or "Abraham's Bosom"—see Luke 16:23). Jesus appears to have had this view of Gehenna as divided. Yet the view of Sheol as a neutral place where the dead went to await the resurrection persisted through the New Testament period (see Matt. 16:18; Acts 2:27; 2:31; Rev. 1:18; 6:8; 20:13; 20:14). I should warn the reader: New Testament eschatology is a thicket. All the New Testament writers share the belief in Jesus' bodily resurrection, and all await the collective resurrection of the dead, but apart from that, there is great diversity of views, especially about the interim state. For the information on Sheol, I am in part indebted to Bo Recke, "Sheol," on the CD-rom Mac Complex Version 2.1.1 of *The Oxford Companion to the Bible* (1995).

21. John R. Sachs refers to the continuing presence of "God's inviting, forgiving love" to the person in hell. See "Current Eschatology: Universal Salvation and the Problem of Hell," *Theological Studies* 52 (1991), 227–54, here, 248. As loved by God, the person in hell continues to have the supernatural existential, that is, the profound orientation to God. In the words of Karl Rahner: "[The human person] must have it [the supernatural existential, the *potentia obedientialis*] *always*; for even one of the damned, who has turned away from this Love and made himself incapable of receiving this Love (which being scorned now burns like fire) as that to which he is ordained in the ground of his concrete being: he must consequently always remain what he was created as: the burning longing for God in the immediacy of his [God's] own threefold life." ("Concerning the Relationship between Nature and Grace," *Theological Investigations*, vol. 1, trans. Cornelius Ernst [Baltimore: Helicon Press, 1961], 297–317, here 311–12). It goes without saying that neither Sachs nor Rahner regards as certain the presence of any one individual in hell. Both, indeed, hold out the hope for universal salvation.

22. For a brilliant analysis of the way we human beings crucify our best self and then out of guilt "crucify" Jesus as the realized ideal of our best self, see Sebastian Moore, *The Crucified Jesus Is No Stranger* (New York: Seabury Press, 1977).

23. My use of the masculine and feminine pronouns is deliberate here. It is an allusion to the discussion among feminist theologians (male and female) of whether the masculine and feminine experiences of sin have different modalities. For centuries, sin at its root has been defined as pride, as the radical assertion of the self against and over others. But is not this view a reflection of the way men have sinned because they have had all the power? Is not sin also the ceding of power to another, the allowing of the other to take over and run one's life, the evading of one's freedom and responsibility to forge a self of one's own? In the words of the Catholic feminist Elizabeth Johnson: "Analysis of women's experi-

ence is replete with the realization that within patriarchal systems women's primordial temptation is not to pride and self-assertion but rather to a lack of it, to diffuseness of personal center, overdependence on others for self-identity, drifting, and fear of recognizing one's own competence" (*She Who Is: The Mystery of God in Feminist Theological Discourse* [New York: Crossroad, 1992], 64). Women have been deprived of power and thus are more tempted to find a self in those who have power. This analysis does not say that a person of one gender cannot commit the sin of the other gender, nor does it say that women are therefore anywhere nearly as responsible for their oppression as men are for oppressing them. It says rather that feminine experience can lead to a deeper appreciation of sin as both domineering self-assertion and abject self-relinquishment and help convince men and women that there are spiritually mature ways of both self-assertion and self-relinquishment. The book that spurred much of this discussion is that by Judith Plaskow, *Sex, Sin, and Grace: Women's Experience and the Theologies of Reinhold Niebuhr and Paul Tillich* (Washington, D.C.: University Press of America, 1980). As the liberation of women moves ahead and women come into their fair share of social power, I should think that opportunities for both modalities of sin will become more equal.

24. Thus the choice of evil, says Jeffrey L. Walls, is not wholly unintelligible. He quotes Satan's words in Milton's *Paradise Lost* (I, 263): "Better to reign in Hell, than to serve in Heaven." Hell, then, is *psychologically* possible. "Those in hell may be almost happy, and this may explain why they insist on staying there. They do not, of course, experience even a shred of genuine happiness. But perhaps they experience a certain perverse sense of satisfaction, a distorted sort of pleasure" (*Hell: The Logic of Damnation* [Notre Dame, Ind.: University of Notre Dame Press, 1992], 126). See also the riveting book by Jack Katz, *Seductions of Crime: Moral and Sensual Attractions in Doing Evil* (New York: Basic Books, 1988). The attractions of sin then easily combine with our capacity to rationalize, to pretend that what we are really doing is good, not evil. Thomas Aquinas says that "evil as such cannot be desired" (*Theological Texts*, selected and trans. Thomas Gilby [Durham, N.C.: Labyrinth Press, 1982], 87) and therefore, we give a "positive tone" (127) to what attracts us and yet what in fact is evil.

25. For my way of framing these questions, I am indebted to Sachs, "Current Eschatology."

26. This definition of evil receives classical expression in the writings of Augustine (354–430 C.E.). He writes: "Vice and death do no damage to anything except by depriving it of soundness, and vice would not be vice if it did no damage. All things are good which have vice opposed to them, and vice vitiates them. Things which are vitiated are therefore good, but are vitiated because they are not supremely good." There is therefore no "substantial evil" (as taught by the Manicheans); evil is not something in itself but simply the lack of something that ought to be there. See "Of True Religion," *Augustine: Earlier Writings*, ed. J. H. S. Burleigh (Philadelphia: Westminster Press, 1953), 225–83, here, 242. The essay was originally published in Latin in 390.

27. Sachs, "Current Eschatology," 248: "One could imagine that freedom could persist in such a decision *indefinitely* without for that reason attributing eternal definiteness to it; it would persist, quite literally, *nondefinitely*. In this sense one could say that the human person can 'decide against God forever,' but that would be something like a state of lasting indefiniteness and nondefiniteness, not an eternally fixed negative. Moreover, its persistence in a stance of rejection would have to be something which at every moment was an active 'effort' against the power of God's inviting, forgiving love, something quite different from the final 'rest' of human freedom which freely and finally surrenders to the power of that love."

28. Keith Ward believes that God loves us so much that God suffers when we sin. He argues, therefore, against the eternity of hell in this way: "Even if one holds that souls have put themselves beyond the possibility of repentance, the existence of unending frustration and agony would seem to entail a permanent diminution of the bliss of God. Can one really accept that God and the saints will be happy to see the justice of God done, in the punishment of sinners, when this entails the existence of unending pain?" Though he leaves open the possibility that some persons could persist in their no, he suggests that because this no is against the fullness of being, it is finally an embrace of nonbeing, and that if it persists, the naysayers may "fall into a progressive disintegration, until they cease to exist as personalities" (*Religion and Human Nature* [Oxford: Clarendon Press, 1998], 252–53).

29. The doctrine of purgatory first found official dogmatic expression in the thirteenth century, but the belief in some kind of purification after death had been part of Christian piety since about 200 C.E. and was defended by reference to 2 Macc. 12:42-45 and 1 Cor. 3:12-15 (though Catholic theologians today agree that these texts do not prove the existence of purgatory). The belief emerged out of the practices of praying for the dead and of doing penance for sin. Penance was done because it was felt that forgiveness of sin should be followed by further purification and satisfaction, and if this purification is left incomplete in this life, it must be completed in the next life, in purgatory (the noun *purgatory* did not come into use until the twelfth century), which at first was not thought to be a place but rather a condition. Purgatory was imagined as a cleansing fire, and it was painful, though this pain was commingled with the joy that one's salvation and heavenly destiny were assured. Meanwhile, Christians had long been offering prayers for the dead, and purgatory became a theological explanation for these prayers: in some way, these prayers must help the departed souls who are undergoing purification. The departed would not need prayers if they were in heaven or hell; they must be in a third condition or place.

Penances in the early church were so severe and lengthy (thus the term *temporal punishment*) that many adults delayed baptism until late in life, and over time the church instituted a more lenient system that indulged penitents by allowing them to perform their penance through designated pious actions (prayers, worship, charitable works, pilgrimages, financial donations, and so on) and have these credited against their temporal punishment. If not enough of these penances were performed in this life, the penitent had to undergo purgation in the next life. Thus it happened that these less severe penitential actions, eventually called indulgences, became a large part of medieval piety. Attached to each indulgence was a time period that represented the amount of penitential or purgatorial time remitted. For example, one might make a financial contribution to the church and receive an indulgence of five years. All this was very convenient for bishops and popes who needed to raise money for their enormous projects (for example, building St. Peter's Church in Rome). In this way, indulgences came to be sold, as in the case of the Dominican priest Johann Tetzel, who came to Luther's town on one of his sales trips. The whole business so scandalized Luther that he initiated a public protest (that is, the famous Ninety-five Theses in 1517) that eventually resulted in the Reformation. On the history of the doctrine of purgatory, see Jacques Le Goff, *The Birth of Purgatory* (Chicago: University of Chicago Press, 1984).

30. According to Ladislaus Boros, at death we encounter "a love so devouring that it causes acute suffering to the unpurified man" (*The Moment of Truth*, 141).

31. This is the so-called rapture, from the Latin word *rapere*, which means to seize, to catch up.

32. However, some forms of apocalypticism (based on a literal reading of Rev. 20:1-15) envision two comings of Christ, one bringing an end to history as we know it but issuing in the millennium, a thousand-year reign of the saints on earth. At the end of the millennium, evil will be unleashed again, and Jesus will fight the final battle. Those who do not lose faith during this final battle will be brought by Christ into an ultimate fulfillment that exceeds the limits of the earth as we know it. It should be said here in fairness that apocalyptic views of the eschaton have strengths that should be preserved. One strength is that such views insist on a cosmic dimension to salvation, and another is their insistence on preserving the tension between this age and the next, preventing the illusion that the world, as it is, is just fine. Finally, they focus on God's work, not ours, and protect us from the Promethean pride that we human beings by ourselves can create the fulfilled world to come.

33. Agapic love comes to be understood primarily as "missionary love," that is, love that is practiced only as a means to converting people, which historically is the work of missionaries. See Post, *A Theory of Agape*, 69.

34. One of the ironies of Western intellectual history is that millennialism, once the sole possession of apocalyptic pessimists, underwent in the minds of other more optimistic Christians a series of fascinating transpositions, and became the foundation for a much more optimistic view of penultimate history. These Christian optimists dropped the first abrupt premillennial coming of Christ, making the transition to the millennium much smoother and more gradual. And then they made the transition from the millennium to the ultimate fulfillment smoother and more gradual. Apocalyptic millennialism became in their hands a progressivist view of history. With some, it led to a totally secularized progressivism. This riveting story is brilliantly told by Ernest Lee Tuveson in the books *Millennium and Utopia: A Study in the Background of the Idea of Progress* (New York: Harper and Row, 1964) and *Redeemer Nation: The Idea of America's Millennial Role* (Chicago: University of Chicago Press, 1968).

35. See W. Warren Wagar, *Good Tidings: The Belief in Progress from Darwin to Marcuse* (Bloomington: Indiana University Press, 1972).

36. Liberation theologians have often been accused of blurring the distinction between penultimate history and ultimate fulfillment and thereby falling into a naive and even dangerous religious utopianism. This accusation is not without merit, but the best of them can defend themselves against it. For example, Gustavo Gutierrez says in his most famous work: "Christian hope opens us, in an attitude of spiritual childhood, to the gift of the future promised by God. It keeps us from any confusion of the Kingdom with any one historical stage, from any idolatry toward unavoidably ambiguous human achievement, from any absolutizing of revolution" (*A Theology of Liberation: History, Politics and Salvation* [Maryknoll, N.Y.: Orbis Books, 1973], 238).

37. "The Kingdom of God . . . lies beyond history. But the Kingdom of God is not some realm of eternity that negates time. It is a realm of eternity that fulfills time" (Reinhold Niebuhr, *Beyond Tragedy: Essays on the Christian Interpretation of History* [New York: Charles Scribner's Sons, 1937], 192). One of the great themes of the Vatican II document *Gaudium et Spes* is that the growth of Christ's kingdom or reign in the penultimate is in continuity with the ultimate reign to come. Thus "on this earth that kingdom is already mysteriously present and when the Lord returns it will enter into full flower" (Art. 39 of *The Church Today*, in Walter M. Abbott, ed., *Documents of Vatican II* [New York: America Press, 1966], 237–38).

38. In a nifty maneuver, women theologians have exploited patriarchy's consignment of them to the bodily, the natural, and the earthly, and have become the most persuasive builders of theologies sensitive to the natural environment. Among the best of them is Rosemary Radford Ruether. See *Gaia & God: An Ecofeminist Theology of Earth Healing* (San Francisco: HarperSanFrancisco, 1992).

Selected Bibliography

[Author's note: I list here only the references that I have cited in the end-notes. The bibliography is not a complete record of all the works and sources I have consulted. A more complete bibliography is available for download at www.fortresspress.com (search for *Jesus and the Quest for Meaning*) or can be procured directly from me via e-mail at THWest@stkate. edu.]

Abbott, Walter M. *Documents of Vatican II.* New York: America Press, 1966.

Adler, Mortimer. *Some Questions about Language.* La Salle, Ill.: Open Court, 1976.

Ahlstrom, Sydney E. *A Religious History of the American People.* New Haven, Conn.: Yale Univ. Press, 1972.

Allan, Keith. *Linguistic Meaning.* 2 vols. New York: Routledge and Kegan Paul, 1986.

Allison, Dale. *Jesus of Nazareth: Millenarian Prophet.* Minneapolis: Fortress Press, 1998.

Anderson, George H., T. Austin Murphy, and Joseph A. Burgess. *Justification by Faith: Lutherans and Catholics in Dialogue, VII.* Minneapolis: Augsburg, 1985.

Aquinas, Thomas. *Theological Texts.* Trans. T. Gilby. Durham, N.C.: Labyrinth, 1982.

Aranguren, J. L. *Human Communication.* Trans. F. Partridge. New York: McGraw-Hill, 1967.

Arndt, William F. and F. Wilbur Gingrich. *A Greek-English Lexicon of the New Testament and Other Early Christian Literature.* Rev. and ed. Frederick W. Donker. Chicago: Univ. of Chicago Press, 2000.

Augustine. "Of True Religion." In *Augustine: Earlier Writings.* Ed. J. H. S. Burleigh, 225–83. Philadelphia: Westminster, 1953.

———. *The Trinity.* Trans. E. Hill, O.P. Brooklyn: New City, 1990.

Aulén, Gustav. *Christus Victor: An Historical Study of the Three Main Types of the Ideas of the Atonement.* Trans. A. G. Herbert. New York: MacMillan, 1969.

Austin, J. L. *How to Do Things with Words.* 2nd ed. Cambridge: Harvard Univ. Press, 1975.

Barad, Judith. "Aquinas on the Role of Emotion in Moral Judgment and Activity." *Thomist* 55 (1991): 397–413.

Barbour, Ian G. *Religion in an Age of Science: The Gifford Lectures.* Vol. 1. San Francisco: Harper and Row, 1990.

273

Barr, James. "Words for Love in Biblical Greek." In *The Glory of Christ in the New Testament*. Ed. L. D. Hurt and N. T. Wright, 3–18. New York: Clarendon, 1987.

Bausch, William J. *A New Look at Sacraments*. Rev. ed. Mystic, Conn.: Twenty-Third, 1983.

Beeck, Frans Jozef van. *Christ Proclaimed: Christology as Rhetoric*. New York: Paulist, 1978.

———. *God Encountered: A Contemporary Catholic Systematic Theology*. Vol. 2, pt. 1 of *The Revelation and the Glory*. Collegeville, Minn.: Liturgical, 1993.

Beggiani, Seely. "A Case for Logocentric Theology." *Theological Studies* 32 (1971): 371–406.

Benveniste, Emile. *Problems in General Linguistics*. Coral Gables, Fl.: Univ. of Miami Press, 1971.

Berger, Peter L. *A Rumor of Angels: Modern Society and the Rediscovery of the Supernatural*. 2nd ed. New York: Doubleday, 1990.

———. *The Sacred Canopy: Elements of a Sociological Theory of Religion*. Garden City, N.Y.: Doubleday, 1969.

Berger, Peter L., and Thomas Luckmann. *The Social Construction of the Reality: A Treatise on the Sociology of Knowledge*. New York: Doubleday, 1967.

Bershady, Harold J., ed. *Max Scheler: On Feeling, Knowing, and Valuing: Selected Writings*. Chicago: Univ. of Chicago Press, 1992.

Bloch, Ernst. *The Principle of Hope*. Trans. N. Plaice and P. Knight. Cambridge, Mass.: MIT Press, 1986.

———. *Tübinger Einleitung in die Philosophie*. Frankfurt am Main: Suhrkamp, 1970.

Blum, Lawrence A. *Moral Perception and Particularity*. New York: Cambridge Univ. Press, 1994.

Boff, Leonardo. *Trinity and Society*. Trans. P. Burns. Maryknoll, N.Y.: Orbis, 1993.

Bokenkotter, Thomas. *A Concise History of the Catholic Church*. Rev. ed. New York: Doubleday, 1990.

Borg, Marcus J. *Jesus: A New Vision*. San Francisco: Harper and Row, 1988.

Borg, Marcus J., and N. T. Wright. *The Meaning of Jesus: Two Visions*. San Francisco: HarperSanFrancisco, 1998.

Boros, Ladislaus. *The Moment of Truth: Mysterium Mortis*. London: Burns and Oates, 1962.

Brandon, S. G. F. *Jesus and the Zealots: A Study of the Political Factor in Primitive Christianity*. Manchester, England: Manchester Univ. Press, 1967.

Brown, Raymond E. *The Birth of the Messiah: A Commentary on the Infancy Narratives in Matthew and Luke*. Rev. ed. New York: Doubleday, 1993.

———. *The Community of the Beloved Disciple*. New York: Paulist, 1979.

———. *The Death of the Messiah: From Gethsemane to the Grave, a Commentary on the Passion Narratives in the Four Gospels*. 2 vols. New York: Doubleday, 1994.

Brown, Raymond E., and Raymond F. Collins. "Canonicity." In *The New Jerome Biblical Commentary*. Ed. Brown et al., 1034–54. Englewood Cliffs, N.J.: Prentice Hall, 1990.

Brown, Raymond E., John R. Donahue, Daniel Senior, and Adela Yarbro Collins. "The Resurrection of Jesus." In *The New Jerome Biblical Commentary*. Ed. Brown et al., 1373–77. Englewood Cliffs, N.J.: Prentice Hall, 1990.

Brown, Raymond E., Joseph A. Fitzmyer, and Roland E. Murphy, eds. *The New Jerome Biblical Commentary*. Englewood Cliffs, N.J.: Prentice Hall, 1990.

Brown, Robert McAfee. *Elie Wiesel: Messenger to All Humanity.* Notre Dame, Ind.: Univ. of Notre Dame Press, 1983.

Buber, Martin. *I and Thou.* Trans. W. Kaufmann. New York: Scribner's, 1970.

Bultmann, Rudolf. *Jesus and the Word.* Trans. L. P. Smith and E. H. Lantero. New York: Charles Scribner's Sons, 1958. [First German ed. 1926.]

———. "New Testament and Mythology." In *Kerygma and Myth: Rudolf Bultmann and Five Critics.* Ed. Hans Werner Bartsch, 1-44. New York: Harper, 1961.

Burkitt, Ian. *Social Selves: Theories of the Social Formation of Personality.* London: Sage, 1991.

Bushnell, Horace. *On Christian Nurture.* Grand Rapids, Mich.: Baker, 1971. Rpt. of the 1861 ed.

Buss, Arnold H., and Robert Plomin. *Temperament: Early Developing Personality Traits.* Hillsdale, N.J.: Lawrence Erlbaum, 1984.

———. *A Temperament Theory of Personality Development.* Wiley Series in Behavior. New York: John Wiley and Sons, 1975.

Cahill, Lisa Sowle. *Sex, Gender, and Christian Ethics.* New York: Cambridge Univ. Press, 1996.

Camus, Albert. *The Myth of Sisyphus and Other Essays.* Trans. J. O'Brien. New York: Random House, 1955.

Carnley, Peter F. "Response to Gerald O'Collins." In *The Resurrection: An Interdisciplinary Symposium on the Resurrection of Jesus.* Ed. Stephen T. Davis, Daniel Kendall, S. J., and Gerald O'Collins, S. J., 29–40. New York: Oxford, 1997.

———. *The Structure of Resurrection Belief.* Oxford: Oxford Univ. Press, 1987.

Carr, Anne E. *Transforming Grace: Christian Tradition and Women's Experience.* San Francisco: Harper and Row, 1988.

Charlesworth, James H. *Jesus Within Judaism: New Light from Exciting Archeological Discoveries.* New York: Doubleday, 1988.

———. "The Righteous Teacher and the Historical Jesus." In *Earthing Christologies: From Jesus' Parables to Jesus the Parable.* Ed. James H. Charlesworth and Walter P. Weaver, 46–61. Valley Forge, Pa.: Trinity Press International, 1995.

Cobb, John B., Jr. "Toward a Christocentric Catholic Theology." In *Toward a Universal Theology of Religion.* Ed. Leonard Swidler, 86–101. Maryknoll, N.Y.: Orbis, 1988.

Cobb, John B. Jr., and David Griffin. *Process Theology: An Introductory Exposition.* Philadelphia: Westminster, 1976.

Comstock, Gary L. "Two Types of Narrative Theology." *Journal of the American Academy of Religion* 55 (1987): 687–717.

Congar, Yves. *The Word and the Spirit.* Trans. D. Smith. San Francisco: Harper and Row, 1984.

Connerton, Paul. *How Societies Remember.* Cambridge: Cambridge Univ. Press, 1989.

Cook, Michael L. *Responses to 101 Questions about Jesus.* New York: Paulist, 1993.

Cooke, Bernard. *Christian Sacraments and Christian Personality.* New York: Holt, Rinehart, and Winston, 1965.

———. "The Experiential 'Word of God'." In *Consensus in Theology? A Dialogue with Hans Küng and Edward Schillebeeckx.* Ed. Leonard Swidler, 69–74. Philadelphia: Westminster, 1980.

———. *God's Beloved: Jesus' Experience of the Transcendent.* Philadelphia: Trinity Press International, 1992.

————. *Ministry to Word and Sacraments: History and Theology.* Philadelphia: Fortress Press, 1976.

————. *Sacraments and Sacramentality.* 2nd ed. Mystic, Conn.: Twenty-Third, 1994.

————. "Synoptic Presentation of the Eucharist as Covenant Sacrifice." *Theological Studies* 21 (1960): 1–44.

Crossan, John Dominic. *The Historical Jesus: The Life of a Mediterranean Jewish Peasant.* San Francisco: HarperSanFrancisco, 1991.

Dahl, Nils Alstrup. *Jesus the Christ: The Historical Origins of Christological Doctrine.* Minneapolis: Fortress Press, 1991.

Davies, Horton. *Bread of Life and Cup of Joy: Newer Ecumenical Perspectives on the Eucharist.* Grand Rapids, Mich.: Eerdmans, 1993.

Davis, Leo Donald. *The First Seven Ecumenical Councils (325–787): Their History and Theology.* Wilmington, Del.: Michael Glazier, 1987.

Davis, Stephen T. "'Seeing' the Risen Jesus." In *The Resurrection: An Interdisciplinary Symposium on the Resurrection of Jesus.* Ed. Stephen T. Davis, Daniel Kendall S. J., and Gerald O'Collins S. J., 126–47. New York: Oxford Univ. Press, 1997.

Detmer, David. *Freedom as Value: A Critique of the Ethical Theory of Jean-Paul Sartre.* La Salle, Ill.: Open Court, 1986.

Donahue, John. *The Gospel in Parable: Metaphor, Narrative, and Theology in the Synoptic Gospels.* Philadelphia: Fortress Press, 1988.

Dorner, Isaak. "The Dogmatic Concept of the Immutability of God." In *God and Incarnation in Mid-Nineteenth-Century German Theology.* Trans. and ed. C. Welch, 115–79. New York: Oxford Univ. Press, 1965.

————. "System of Christian Doctrine. Part II. Special Doctrines: The Doctrine of Christ." In *God and Incarnation in Mid-Nineteenth-Century German Theology.* Trans. and ed. C. Welch, 180–284. New York: Oxford Univ. Press, 1965.

Dostoyevsky, Fyodor. *Crime and Punishment.* Trans. C. Garnett. New York: Modern Library, 1950.

————. *The Brothers Karamazov.* Trans. C. Garnett. New York: Modern Library, 1950.

Duffy, Stephen. "Our Hearts of Darkness: Original Sin Revisited." *Theological Studies* 49 (1988): 597–622.

Dufrenne, Mikel. *Language and Philosophy.* Bloomington: Indiana Univ. Press, 1963.

Dulles, Avery. *Apologetics and the Biblical Christ.* Baltimore: Newman, 1966.

————. *Models of the Church.* New York: Doubleday, 1978.

Dunn, James D. G. *New Testament Theology in Dialogue: Christology and Ministry.* Philadelphia: Westminster, 1987.

Dupre, Louis. *Transcendent Selfhood: The Rediscovery of the Inner Life.* New York: Crossroad, 1976.

Edwards, Jonathan. *Religious Affections: The Works of Jonathan Edwards.* Vol. 2. Ed. John E. Smith. New Haven: Yale Univ. Press, 1959.

Erikson, Erik H. *Young Man Luther: A Study in Psychoanalysis and History.* New York: Norton, 1962.

Evangelical Lutheran Church of America. *The Joint Declaration on the Doctrine of Justification* (1999). Internet: http://www.elca.org/ea/ecumenical/romancatholic/jddj/index.html

Evans, Donald. *Faith, Authenticity, and Morality.* Toronto: Univ. of Toronto Press, 1980.

————. *Struggle and Fulfillment: The Inner Dynamics of Religion and Morality.* Philadelphia: Fortress Press, 1979.

Fabry, Joseph B. *The Pursuit of Meaning: Viktor Frankl, Logotherapy, and Life*. 2nd rev. ed. New York: Harper and Row, 1980.

Farley, Margaret A. *Personal Commitments: Beginning, Keeping, Changing*. San Francisco: Harper and Row, 1986.

Feeley-Harnik, Gillian. *The Lord's Table: Eucharist and Passover in Early Christianity*. Philadelphia: Univ. of Pennsylvania Press, 1981.

Ferrara, Dennis Michael. "Representation or Self-Effacement: The Axiom *in Persona Christi* in St. Thomas and the Magisterium." *Theological Studies* 55 (1994): 195–224.

Ferré, Nels F. S. *Christ and the Christian*. New York: Harper, 1958.

Fiddes, Paul S. *The Creative Suffering of God*. Oxford: Oxford Univ. Press, 1988.

———. *Past Event and Present Salvation: The Christian Idea of the Atonement*. Louisville: Westminster John Knox, 1989.

Fingarette, Herbert. *The Self in Transformation: Psychoanalysis, Philosophy and the Life of the Spirit*. New York: Harper, 1965.

Fish, Stanley. *Doing What Comes Naturally: Change, Rhetoric, and the Practice of Theory in Literary and Legal Studies*. Oxford: Clarendon, 1989.

Flusser, David. *Jesus*. 2nd ed. Jerusalem: Magnes, 1998.

Fontinell, Eugene. *Self, God, and Immortality: A Jamesian Investigation*. Philadelphia: Temple Univ. Press, 1986.

Fowler, Roger. *Understanding Language*. London: Routledge and Kegan Paul, 1974.

Frankenberry, Nancy K. *Religion and Radical Empiricism*. Albany: SUNY Press, 1987.

Frankl, Viktor E. *The Doctor and the Soul: From Psychotherapy to Logotherapy*. New York: Random House, 1973.

———. *Man's Search for Meaning*. 3rd ed. New York: Pocket, 1984.

———. *Recollections: An Autobiography*. New York: Plenum, 1997.

———. *The Unconscious God: Psychotherapy and Theology*. New York: Simon and Schuster, 1975.

———. *The Unheard Cry for Meaning: Psychotherapy and Humanism*. New York: Simon and Schuster, 1978.

———. *The Will to Meaning: Foundations and Applications of Logotherapy*. New York: New American Library, 1969.

Frings, Manfred S. *Max Scheler: A Concise Introduction into the World of a Great Thinker*. Pittsburgh: Duquesne Univ. Press, 1965.

Galvin, John P. "The Death of Jesus in Contemporary Theology: Systematic Perspectives and Historical Issues." *Horizons* 13 (1986): 239–52.

———. "From the Humanity of Christ to the Jesus of History: A Paradigm Shift in Catholic Christology." *Theological Studies* 55 (1994): 252–73.

Ganoczy, Alexandre. *An Introduction to Catholic Sacramental Theology*. New York: Paulist, 1984.

Gide, André. *The Vatican Swindle*. Trans. D. Bussy. New York: Knopf, 1925.

Griffin, David Ray. *Evil Revisited: Responses and Reconsiderations*. Albany: SUNY Press, 1991.

———. *God, Power, and Evil: A Process Theodicy*. Lanham, Md.: Univ. Press of America, 1976.

Grimes, Ronald L. "Defining Nascent Ritual." *The Journal of the American Academy of Religion* 50 (1982): 539–55.

Gutierrez, Gustavo. *A Theology of Liberation: History, Politics and Salvation*. Maryknoll, N.Y.: Orbis, 1973.

Habermas, Jürgen. "What Is Universal Pragmatics," 1-68. In *Communication and the Evolution of Society.* Boston: Beacon, 1979.

Haight, Roger. *Jesus, Symbol of God.* Maryknoll, N.Y.: Orbis, 1999.

Hallet, Garth L. *Christian Neighbor Love: An Assessment of Six Rival Positions.* Washington, D.C.: Georgetown Univ. Press, 1989.

Hallie, Philip P. *Lest Innocent Blood Be Shed: The Story of the Village of Le Chambon, and How Goodness Happened There.* New York: Harper and Row, 1979.

Harrington, Daniel J. "The Jewishness of Jesus: Facing Some Problems." In *Jesus' Jewishness: Exploring the Place of Jesus within Early Judaism.* Ed. James H. Charlesworth, 123–52. New York: Crossroad, 1991.

Harris, Errol E. *Cosmos and Anthropos: A Philosophical Interpretation of the Anthropic Cosmological Principle.* Atlantic Highlands, N.J.: Humanities, 1966.

Hartshorne, Charles. *The Divine Relativity: The Social Conception of God.* New Haven, Conn.: Yale Univ. Press, 1948.

———. *Omnipotence and Other Theological Mistakes.* Albany, N.Y.: SUNY Press, 1984.

Haught, John F. *What Is God?: How to Think about the Divine.* New York: Paulist, 1986.

Havel, Václav. *Letters to Olga: July 1979–September 1982.* Trans. P. Wilson. New York: Henry Holt, 1989.

Hebblethwaite, Brian. *The Incarnation: Collected Essays in Christology.* Cambridge: Cambridge Univ. Press, 1987.

Hegel, G. W. F. *Lectures on the Philosophy of World History: Introduction.* Trans. H. B. Nisbet. Cambridge: Cambridge Univ. Press, 1975.

Heidegger, Martin. *Being and Time.* Trans. J. MacQuarrie and E. Robinson. London: SCM, 1962.

Hick, John. *A Christian Theology of World Religions: The Rainbow of Faiths.* Louisville: Westminster John Knox, 1995.

———. *God Has Many Names.* Philadelphia: Westminster Press, 1982.

———. *An Interpretation of Religion: Human Responses to the Transcendent.* New Haven, Conn.: Yale Univ. Press, 1989.

Hildebrand, Dietrich von. *Christian Ethics.* New York: David McKay, 1953.

Hodgson, Peter. *Jesus—Word and Presence: An Essay in Christology.* Philadelphia: Fortress Press, 1971.

Hopkins, Julie M. *Towards a Feminist Christology: Jesus of Nazareth, European Women, and the Christological Crisis.* Grand Rapids, Mich.: Eerdmans, 1994.

Horsley, Richard A. *Sociology and the Jesus Movement.* New York: Crossroad, 1989.

Irwin, Alexander C. *Eros Toward the World: Paul Tillich's Theology of the Erotic.* Minneapolis: Fortress Press, 1991.

Jenson, Robert W. *Visible Words: The Interpretation and Practice of Christian Sacraments.* Philadelphia: Fortress Press, 1978.

Jeremias, Joachim. *The Parables of Jesus.* 2nd rev. ed. Trans. S. H. Hooke. New York: Charles Scribner's Sons, 1972.

Johnson, Elizabeth A. *Consider Jesus: Waves of Renewal in Christology.* New York: Crossroad, 1990.

———. "Jesus, Wisdom of God: A Biblical Basis for Non-Androcentric Christology." *Emphemerides Theologicae Lovanienses* 61 (1985): 261–94.

———. *She Who Is: The Mystery of God in Feminist Theological Discourse.* New York: Crossroad, 1992.

Jung, C. G. *Psychological Types.* Rev. by F. C. Hull. Princeton: Princeton Univ. Press, 1971.

Kammer, Fred. *Doing Faithjustice: An Introduction to Catholic Social Thought.* New York: Paulist, 1991.

Karris, Robert A. "The Gospel according to Luke." In *The New Jerome Biblical Commentary.* Ed. Brown et al., 675–721. Englewood Cliffs, N.J.: Prentice Hall, 1990.

Käsemann, Ernst. *Essays on New Testament Themes.* Trans. W. J. Montague. Studies in Biblical Theology 1/41. London: SCM, 1964.

Katz, Jack. *Seductions of Crime: Moral and Sensual Attractions in Doing Evil.* New York: Basic, 1988.

Kilmartin, Edward. "Sacraments as Liturgy of the Church." *Theological Studies* 50 (1989): 527–47.

Konner, Melvin. "Darwin's Truth, Jefferson's Vision: Sociobiology and the Politics of Human Nature." *The American Prospect* July–August (1999): 30–38.

Kroeger, Otto, and Janet M. Thuesen. *Type Talk: The 16 Personality Types That Determine How We Live, Love, and Work.* New York: Delta, 1988.

Küng, Hans. *Does God Exist? An Answer for Today.* Trans. E. Quinn. Garden City, N.Y.: Doubleday, 1980.

Kushner, Harold. *When Bad Things Happen to Good People.* New York: Avon, 1981.

LaCugna, Catherine Mowry. *God for Us: The Trinity and Christian Life.* San Francisco: HarperSan Francisco, 1993.

Lakeland, Paul. *Postmodernity: Christian Identity in a Fragmented Age.* Minneapolis: Fortress Press, 1997.

Lakoff, George, and Mark Turner. *More Than Cool Reason: A Field Guide to Poetic Metaphor.* Chicago: Univ. of Chicago Press, 1989.

Lane, Dermot A. *Keeping Hope Alive: Stirrings in Christian Theology.* Mahwah, N.J.: Paulist, 1996.

Lawler, Michael G. *Symbol and Sacrament: A Contemporary Sacramental Theology.* New York: Paulist, 1987.

Lee, Bernard J. *Jesus and the Metaphors of God: The Christs of the New Testament.* New York: Paulist, 1993.

Le Goff, Jacques. *The Birth of Purgatory.* Trans. A. Goldhammer. Chicago: Univ. of Chicago Press, 1984.

Le Senne, René. *Obstacle and Value.* Trans. B. Dauenhauer. Evanston, Ill.: Northwestern Univ. Press, 1972.

Levinson, Stephen C. *Pragmatics.* Cambridge Textbooks in Linguistics. Cambridge: Cambridge Univ. Press, 1983.

Lifton, Robert Jay. *The Protean Self: Human Resilience in an Age of Fragmentation.* New York: Basic, 1993.

Livingston, James. *The Enlightenment and the Nineteenth Century.* Vol. 1 of *Modern Christian Thought.* 2nd ed. Upper Saddle River, N.J.: Prentice Hall, 1997.

Lonergan, Bernard J. F. *Method in Theology.* 2nd ed. New York: Herder and Herder, 1972.
———. *Verbum: Word and Idea in Aquinas.* Ed. D. B. Burrell. Notre Dame, Ind.: Univ. of Notre Dame Press, 1967.

Lüdemann, Gerd. *What Really Happened to Jesus: A Historical Approach to the Resurrection.* Trans. J. Bowden. Louisville: Westminster John Knox, 1995.

Luther, Martin. *The Bondage of the Will.* Trans. of the Latin ed. (1525) by J. I. Packer and A. R. Johnson. London: James Clarke, 1957.
———. "Secular Authority: To What Extent Should It Be Obeyed." In *Martin Luther: Selections from His Writings.* Ed. John Dillenberger, 363–402. New York: Doubleday, 1961.

Lynch, William. *Images of Hope: Imagination as the Healer of the Hopeless.* Notre Dame, Ind.: Univ. of Notre Dame Press, 1965.

Lyons, John. *Semantics.* 2 vols. Cambridge: Cambridge Univ. Press, 1977.

Mackey, James P. "Christian Faith and Critical History." In *Critical History and Biblical Faith: New Testament Perspectives.* Ed. Thomas J. Ryan, 59–90. Villanova, Pa.: College Theology Society, 1979.

———. *Jesus, the Man and the Myth.* New York: Paulist, 1979.

Macquarrie, John. *Thinking about God.* New York: Harper and Row, 1975.

Martos, Joseph. *Doors to the Sacred: A Historical Introduction to Sacraments in the Catholic Church.* Tarrytown, N.Y.: Triumph, 1991.

Marxsen, Willi. *The Resurrection of Jesus of Nazareth.* Trans. M. Kohl. Philadelphia: Fortress Press, 1970.

Maslow, Abraham H. *Toward a Psychology of Being.* Princeton: Van Nostrand, 1962.

May, Rollo. *Freedom and Destiny.* New York: Norton, 1981.

McDannell, Colleen, and Bernhard Lang. *Heaven: A History.* New Haven, Conn.: Yale Univ. Press, 1988.

McDermott, Brian O. "The Theology of Original Sin: Recent Developments." *Theological Studies* 38 (1977): 478–512.

McFague, Sallie. *Metaphorical Theology: Models of God in Religious Language.* Philadelphia: Fortress Press, 1982.

McGrayen, Sharon Bertsch. *Nobel Prize Women in Science.* 2nd ed. Secaucus, N.J.: Carol, 1998.

Meier, John P. *The Roots of the Problem and the Person.* Vol. 1 of *A Marginal Jew: Rethinking the Historical Jesus.* New York: Doubleday, 1991.

———. *Mentor, Message, and Miracles.* Vol. 2 of *A Marginal Jew: Rethinking the Historical Jesus.* New York: Doubleday, 1994.

Meilander, Gilbert. *Friendship: A Study in Theological Ethics.* Notre Dame, Ind.: Univ. of Notre Dame Press, 1981.

Meyer, Ben F. *The Aims of Jesus.* London: SCM, 1979.

Moltmann, Jürgen. *Theology of Hope: On the Ground and the Implications of a Christian Eschatology.* Trans. J. W. Leitch. New York: Harper and Row, 1967.

Moore, Sebastian. *The Crucified Jesus Is No Stranger.* New York: Seabury, 1977.

———. *Jesus the Liberator of Desire.* New York: Crossroad, 1989.

Mott, Stephen C. *Biblical Ethics and Social Change.* New York: Oxford Univ. Press, 1982.

———. "The Use of the New Testament for Social Ethics." *The Journal of Religious Ethics,* 15 (1987): 225–59.

Murdoch, Iris. *The Sovereignty of the Good.* New York: Schocken, 1971.

Nagel, Thomas. *The View from Nowhere.* New York: Oxford Univ. Press, 1986.

Niebuhr, H. Richard. "Value-Theory and Theology: The Nature of Religious Experience." In *Essays in Honor of Douglas Clyde Macintosh,* 93–116. New York: Harper and Brothers, 1937.

Niebuhr, Reinhold. *Beyond Tragedy: Essays on the Christian Interpretation of History.* New York: Charles Scribner's Sons, 1937.

———. *The Children of Light and the Children of Darkness: A Vindication of Democracy and a Critique of Its Traditional Defense.* New York: Charles Scribner's Sons, 1944.

———. *An Interpretation of Christian Ethics.* New York: Crossroad, 1979. Orig. ed., 1935.

————. *Human Destiny.* Vol. 2 of *The Nature and Destiny of Man: A Christian Inter-pretation.* New York: Charles Scribner's Sons, 1943.

Norris, Christopher. *What's Wrong with Postmodernism: Critical Theory and the Ends of Philosophy.* Parallax. Baltimore: Johns Hopkins Univ. Press, 1990.

Nussbaum, Martha. *Sex and Social Justice.* New York: Oxford Univ. Press, 1999.

Ogden, Schubert M. *Doing Theology Today.* Valley Forge, Pa.: Trinity Press Interna-tional, 1996.

————. *The Point of Christology.* San Francisco: Harper and Row, 1982.

————. *The Reality of God and Other Essays.* New York: Harper and Row, 1966.

O'Grady, John F. *Models of Jesus Revisited.* 2nd rev. ed. New York: Paulist, 1993.

O'Neill, Tip, with Gary Hymel. *All Politics Is Local, and Other Rules of the Game.* New York: Times Books, 1994.

Osborne, Kenan B. *The Christian Sacraments of Initiation: Baptism, Confirmation, Eucharist.* New York: Paulist, 1987.

————. *The Resurrection of Jesus: New Considerations for Its Theological Interpreta-tion.* Mahwah, N.J.: Paulist, 1997.

Otto, Rudolf. *The Idea of the Holy.* Trans. J. W. Harvey. 2nd ed. Oxford: Oxford Univ. Press, 1950.

Outka, Gene. *Agape: An Ethical Analysis.* New Haven, Conn.: Yale Univ. Press, 1972.

————. "Theocentric Agape and the Self: An Asymmetrical Affirmation in Response to Colin Grant's *Either/Or." Journal of Religious Ethics* 24 (1996): 35–42.

Pelikan, Jaroslav. *The Emergence of the Catholic Tradition (100–600).* Vol. 1 of *The Christian Tradition: A History of the Development of Doctrine.* Chicago: Univ. of Chicago Press, 1971.

Percy, Walker. *The Message in the Bottle: How Queer Man Is, How Queer Language Is, and What One Has to Do with the Other.* New York: Farrar, Straus, and Giroux, 1975.

Perkins, Pheme. *Love Commandments in the New Testament.* New York: Paulist, 1982.

————. *Resurrection: New Testament Witness and Contemporary Reflection.* Garden City, N.Y.: Doubleday, 1984.

Phan, Peter C. *Responses to 101 Questions on Death and Eternal Life.* Mahwah, N.J.: Paulist, 1997.

Plaskow, Judith. *Sex, Sin, and Grace: Women's Experience and the Theologies of Rein-hold Niebuhr and Paul Tillich.* Washington, D.C.: Univ. Press of America, 1980.

Polkinghorne, John. *Quarks, Chaos, and Christianity: Questions to Science and Religion.* New York: Crossroad, 1997.

Pope, Stephen J. *The Evolution of Altruism and the Ordering of Love.* Washington, D. C.: Georgetown Univ. Press, 1994.

Post, Stephen. *A Theory of Agape: On the Meaning of Christian Love.* Lewisburg, Pa.: Bucknell Univ. Press, 1990.

Power, David N. *Sacrament: The Language of God's Giving.* New York: Crossroad, 1999.

Powers, Joseph. *Eucharistic Theology.* New York: Herder and Herder, 1967.

Rahner, Karl. "Anonymous Christians." In *Theological Investigations.* Vol. 6. Trans. K. H. and B. Kruger, 390–98. New York: Seabury, 1969.

————. "Concerning the Relationship between Nature and Grace," 297–317. In *Theological Investigations.* Vol. 1. Trans. C. Ernst. Baltimore: Helicon, 1961.

————. "The Dignity and Freedom of Man." In *Theological Investigations.* Vol. 1. Trans. C. Ernst, 235–63. Baltimore: Helicon, 1963.

———. "Following the Crucified." In *Theological Investigations.* Vol. 18. Trans. E. Quinn, 157–70. New York: Crossroad, 1983.

———. *Foundations of Christian Faith: An Introduction to the Idea of Christianity.* Trans. W. V. Dych. New York: Seabury, 1978.

———. "Observations on the Problem of the 'Anonymous Christian'." In *Theological Investigations.* Vol. 14. Trans. D. Bourke, 280–94. New York: Crossroad, 1976.

———. *On the Theology of Death.* New York: Herder and Herder, 1961.

———. "The One Christ and the Universality of Salvation." In *Theological Investigations.* Vol. 16. Trans. D. Morland, 199–224. New York: Seabury, 1979.

———. "Reflections on the Unity of Love of Neighbor and Love of God." In *Theological Investigations.* Vol. 6. Trans. K. H. and B. Kruger, 231–49. New York: Crossroad, 1974.

———. *The Trinity.* Trans. J. Donceel. New York: Herder and Herder, 1970.

———. "Virginitas in Partu." In *Theological Investigations.* Vol. 4. Trans. K. Smyth, 134–62. Baltimore: Helicon, 1966.

Reck, Andrew J. *The New American Philosophers: An Exploration of Thought since World War II.* New York: Delta, 1970.

Recke, Bo. *The Oxford Companion to the Bible.* Mac Complex CD-ROM, version 2.1.1m, 1995.

Reimarus, Herman S. *Fragments.* Trans. R. Fraser. Ed. Charles H. Talbert. Lives of Jesus Series. Philadelphia: Fortress Press, 1970.

Reiser, Marius. *Jesus and Judgment: The Eschatological Proclamation in Its Jewish Context.* Trans. L. M. Maloney. Minneapolis: Fortress Press, 1997.

Rist, John M. *Human Value: A Study in Ancient Philosophical Ethics.* Leiden: E. J. Brill, 1982.

Rivkin, Ellis. *A Hidden Revolution: The Pharisees' Search for the Kingdom Within.* Nashville: Abingdon, 1978.

———. *What Crucified Jesus?* Nashville: Abingdon, 1984.

Rock, Paul. *The Making of Symbolic Interactionism.* Totowa, N.J.: Rowman and Littlefield, 1979.

Rolf, Eckhard. "On the Concept of Action in Illocutionary Logic." In *Speech Acts, Meanings and Intentions.* Ed. Armin Burkhardt, 147–65. Berlin: de Gruyter, 1990.

Rorty, Amélie, and David Wong. "Aspects of Identity and Agency." In *Identity, Character, and Morality: Essays in Moral Psychology.* Ed. Amélie Rorty and Owen Flanagan, 19–36. Cambridge: MIT Press, 1990.

Rorty, Richard. *Consequences of Pragmatism: Essays, 1972–1980.* Minneapolis: Univ. of Minnesota Press, 1982.

———. *Contingency, Irony, and Solidarity.* Cambridge: Cambridge Univ. Press, 1989.

———. *Objectivity, Relativism, and Truth. Philosophical Papers.* Vol. 1. Cambridge: Cambridge Univ. Press, 1991.

———. *Philosophy and the Mirror of Nature.* Princeton: Princeton Univ. Press, 1979.

———. "Postmodernist Bourgeois Liberalism." In *Objectivity, Relativism, and Truth. Philosophical Papers.* Vol. 1, 197–202. Cambridge: Cambridge Univ. Press, 1991.

Ross, Susan. *Extravagant Affections: A Feminist Sacramental Theology.* New York: Continuum, 1998.

———. "Feminist Theology: A Review of the Literature." *Theological Studies* 56 (1995): 327–41.

Rubin, Lillian B. *The Transcendent Child: Tales of Triumph over the Past*. New York: HarperCollins, 1997.

Ruether, Rosemary Radford. *Gaia & God: An Ecofeminist Theology of Earth Healing*. San Francisco: HarperSanFrancisco, 1992.

———. *Sexism and God-Talk: Toward a Feminist Theology*. Boston: Beacon, 1983.

———. *To Change the World: Christology and Cultural Criticism*. New York: Crossroad, 1983.

———. *Women and Redemption: A Theological History*. Minneapolis: Fortress Press, 1998.

Sachs, John R. "Current Eschatology: Universal Salvation and the Problem of Hell." *Theological Studies* 52 (1991): 227–54.

Sanders, E. P. *The Historical Figure of Jesus*. London: Penguin, 1993.

———. *Jesus and Judaism*. Philadelphia: Fortress Press, 1985.

Sartre, Jean-Paul. *Being and Nothingness: An Essay on Phenomenological Ontology*. Trans. H. E. Barnes. New York: Washington Square, 1966.

———. *Existentialism and Human Emotions*. Trans. B. Frechtman and H. E. Barnes. New York: Philosophical Library, 1957.

Schaberg, Jane. *The Illegitimacy of Jesus: A Feminist Theological Interpretation of the Infancy Narratives*. New York: Harper and Row, 1987.

Scheler, Max. *Man's Place in Nature*. Trans. H. Meyerhoff. New York: Noonday, 1961.

Schillebeeckx, Edward. *Jesus: An Experiment in Christology*. Trans. H. Hoskins. New York: Crossroad, 1979.

Schleiermacher, Friedrich. *The Christian Faith*. Edinburgh: T. & T. Clark, 1928.

———. *On Religion: Addresses in Response to Its Cultured Critics*. Trans. and ed. Terrence M. Tice. Richmond, Va.: John Knox, 1969.

Schneiders, Sandra M. *Women and the Word: The Gender of God in the New Testament and the Spirituality of Women*. New York: Paulist, 1986.

Schoonenberg, Piet. *Der Geist, Das Wort und Der Sohn: Eine Geist-Christologie*. Trans. from Dutch by W. Immler. Regensburg: Friedrich Pustet, 1991.

———. "Spirit Christology and Logos Christology." *Bijdragen* 38 (1977): 350–75.

———. "Trinity—The Consummated Covenant: Theses on the Doctrine of the Trinitarian God." *Studies in Religion* 5 (1975-76): 111–16.

Schottroff, Luise, Silvia Schoer, and Marie-Theres Wacker. *Feminist Interpretation: The Bible in Women's Perspective*. Trans. M. and B. Rumscheidt. Minneapolis: Fortress Press, 1998.

Schrein, Shannon. *Quilting and Braiding: The Feminist Christologies of Sallie McFague and Elizabeth A. Johnson in Conversation*. Collegeville, Minn.: Liturgical Press, 1998.

Schüssler Fiorenza, Elizabeth. *In Memory of Her: A Feminist Theological Reconstruction of Christian Origins*. New York: Crossroad, 1983.

———. "Wisdom Mythology and the Christological Hymns of the New Testament." In *Aspects of Wisdom in Judaism and Early Christianity*. Ed. Robert L. Wilken. Notre Dame, Ind.: Univ. of Notre Dame Press, 1975.

Schutz, Alfred. "Max Scheler's Philosophy." In *Collected Papers*. Vol. 3, 133–44. The Hague: Martinus Nijhoff, 1966.

Schwager, Raymund. *Jesus of Nazareth: How He Understood His Life*. New York: Crossroad, 1998.

Schwarz, Hans. *Christology*. Grand Rapids, Mich.: Eerdmans, 1998.

Schweitzer, Albert. *The Quest of the Historical Jesus: A Critical Telling of Its Progress from Reimarus to Wrede*. New ed. Baltimore: Johns Hopkins, 1906, 1998.

Searle, John. *Expression and Meaning: Studies in the Theory of Speech Acts*. Cambridge: Cambridge Univ. Press, 1979.

———. *Speech Acts: An Essay in the Philosophy of Language*. Cambridge: Cambridge Univ. Press, 1969.

Segal, Alan F. "Life after Death: The Social Sources." In *The Resurrection: An Interdisciplinary Symposium on the Resurrection of Jesus*. Ed. Stephen T. Davis, Daniel Kendall, S. J., and Gerald O'Collins, S. J., 90–125. Oxford: Oxford Univ. Press, 1997.

Shaw, Marvin C. *The Paradox of Intention: Reaching the Goal by Giving Up the Attempt to Reach It*. Atlanta: Scholars, 1988.

Shea, John. *What a Modern Catholic Believes about Heaven and Hell*. Chicago: Thomas More, 1972.

Sherry, Patrick. *Spirit and Beauty: An Introduction to Theological Aesthetics*. Oxford: Clarendon, 1992.

Sigal, Phillip. *The Halakhah of Jesus of Nazareth according to the Gospel of Matthew*. Lanham, Md.: Univ. Press of America, 1987.

Sills, Chip, and George H. Jensen, eds. *The Philosophy of Discourse: The Rhetorical Turn in Twentieth-Century Thought*. 2 vols. Portsmouth, N.H.: Boyton/Cook, 1992.

Skinner, B. F. *Beyond Freedom and Dignity*. New York: Knopf, 1971.

Smith, Barry. "Towards a History of Speech Act Theory." In *Speech Acts, Meaning and Intentions*. Ed. Armin Burkhardt, 29–61. Berlin: Walter de Gruyter, 1990.

Smith, John E. *The Analogy of Experience: An Approach to Understanding Religious Truth*. New York: Harper and Row, 1973.

Sobrino, Jon. *Christology at the Crossroads*. Trans. J. Drury. Maryknoll, N.Y.: Orbis, 1978.

———. *Jesus the Liberator: A Historical-Theological Reading of Jesus of Nazareth*. Trans. P. Burns and F. McDonagh. Maryknoll, N.Y.: Orbis, 1993.

Sölle, Dorothee. *Christ the Representative: An Essay in Theology after Auschwitz*. London: SCM, 1967.

Solomon, Maynard. *Beethoven*. 2nd rev. ed. New York: Schirmer, 1999.

Sperber, Dan. *Rethinking Symbolism*. Trans. A. L. Morton. Cambridge: Cambridge Univ. Press, 1975.

Spiegelberg, Herbert. *Phenomenology in Psychology and Psychiatry: A Historical Introduction*. Evanston, Ill.: Northwestern Univ. Press, 1972.

Staal, Frits. "The Meaninglessness of Ritual." *Numen* 26 (1979): 2–22.

Stoffer, Dale R. *The Lord's Supper: Believers Church Perspective*. Scottdale, Pa.: Herald, 1997.

Swidler, Leonard. *After the Absolute: The Dialogical Future of Religious Reflection*. Minneapolis: Fortress Press, 1990.

———. *Yeshua: A Model for Moderns*. Kansas City, Mo.: Sheed and Ward, 1988.

Swidler, Leonard, and Paul Mojzes, eds. *The Uniqueness of Jesus: A Dialogue with Paul F. Knitter*. Maryknoll, N.Y.: Orbis, 1997.

Tallon, Andrew. *Head and Heart: Affection, Cognition, Volition as Triune Consciousness*. New York: Fordham Univ. Press, 1997.

———. "The Heart in Rahner's Philosophy of Mysticism." *Theological Studies* 53 (1992): 700–728.

Taylor, Charles. "The Nature and Scope of Distributive Justice." In *Justice and Equality Here and Now*. Ed. Frank S. Lucash, 34–67. Ithaca, N.Y.: Cornell Univ. Press, 1986.

———. "Rorty in the Epistemological Tradition." In *Reading Rorty: Critical Responses to "Philosophy and the Mirror of Nature" (and Beyond)*. Ed. Alan R. Malachowski, 257–75. Oxford: Blackwell, 1990.

TeSelle, Eugene. *Christ in Context: Divine Purpose and Human Possibility.* Philadelphia: Fortress Press, 1975.

Theissen, Gerd, and Annette Merz. *The Historical Jesus: A Comprehensive Guide.* Trans. J. Bowden. Minneapolis: Fortress Press, 1998.

Thiel, John E. *Nonfoundationalism*. Guides to Theological Inquiry. Minneapolis: Fortress Press, 1994.

Tillich, Paul. *The Shaking of the Foundations*. New York: Charles Scribner's Sons, 1948.

———. *Systematic Theology*. 3 vols. in 1. New York: Harper and Row, Univ. of Chicago Press, 1967.

Tindall, Matthew. "Christianity as Old as Creation." In *Deism and Natural Religion: A Source Book*. Ed. E. Graham Waring, 107–70. 1st ed. 1730. New York: Ungar, 1967.

Todorow, Tzvetan. *Facing the Extreme: Moral Life in the Concentration Camps.* New York: Henry Holt, 1996.

Torrance, T. F. "The Relevance of the Doctrine of the Spirit for Ecumenical Theology." In *Theology in Reconstruction*. Grand Rapids, Mich.: Eerdmans, 1965.

Tracy, David. *Blessed Rage for Order: The New Pluralism in Theology.* New York: Crossroad, 1975.

———. "The Hidden God: The Divine Other of Liberation." *CrossCurrents* 46 (1996): 5–16.

Trager, G. L. "Paralanguage: A First Approximation." *Studies in Linguistics* 13 (1958): 1–12.

Tuveson, Ernest Lee. *Millennium and Utopia: A Study in the Background of the Idea of Progress.* New York: Harper and Row, 1964.

———. *Redeemer Nation: The Idea of America's Millennial Role.* Chicago: Univ. of Chicago Press, 1968.

Vawter, Bruce. "Introduction to Prophetic Literature." In *The New Jerome Biblical Commentary*. Ed. Brown et al., 186–200. Englewood Cliffs, N.J.: Prentice Hall, 1990.

Vermes, Geza. *Jesus and the World of Judaism*. Philadelphia: Fortress Press, 1984.

———. *The Religion of Jesus the Jew*. Minneapolis: Fortress Press, 1993.

Via, Dan O. Jr. *The Parables: Their Literary and Existential Dimension*. Philadelphia: Fortress Press, 1979.

Viviano, Benedict T. "The Gospel according to Matthew." In *The New Jerome Biblical Commentary*. Ed. Brown et al., 630–74. Englewood Cliffs, N.J.: Prentice Hall, 1990.

Vorgrimler, Herbert. *Commentary on the Documents of Vatican II*. Vol. 2. New York: Herder and Herder, 1968.

Wagar, W. Warren. *Good Tidings: The Belief in Progress from Darwin to Marcuse.* Bloomington: Indiana Univ. Press, 1972.

Wahlberg, Rachel. *Jesus according to a Woman*. 2nd rev. ed. New York: Paulist, 1986.

Walls, Jerry L. *Hell: The Logic of Damnation*. Notre Dame, Ind.: Univ. of Notre Dame Press, 1992.

Ward, Keith. *The Concept of God.* New York: St. Martin's, 1974.

———. *Rational Theology and the Creativity of God.* New York: Pilgrim, 1982.

———. *Religion and Human Nature.* Oxford: Clarendon, 1998.

———. *Religion and Revelation: A Theology of Revelation in the World's Religions.* Oxford: Clarendon, 1994.

———. *A Vision to Pursue: Beyond the Crisis in Christianity.* London: SCM, 1991.

Weingart, Richard E. *The Logic of Divine Love: A Critical Analysis of the Soteriology of Peter Abelard.* Oxford: Oxford Univ. Press, 1970.

West, Thomas H. *Ultimate Hope without God: The Atheistic Eschatology of Ernst Bloch.* New York: Peter Lang, 1991.

Whitehead, Alfred North. *Process and Reality: An Essay in Cosmology.* Corrected and ed. David Ray Griffin and Donald W. Sherburne. New York: Free Press, 1967.

Whitney, Barry L., and Norman J. King. "Rahner and Hartshorne on Death and Eternal Life." *Horizons* 15 (1988): 239–61.

Wiesel, Elie. *All Rivers Run to the Sea: Memoirs.* New York: Schocken, 1995.

Wieseltier, Leon. "Washington Diarist." *New Republic* (January 24, 1994), 42.

Wildman, Wesley J. *Fidelity and Plausibility: Modest Christologies in the Twentieth Century.* Albany, N.Y.: SUNY Press, 1998.

Williams, Daniel Day. *The Spirit and the Forms of Love.* New York: Harper and Row, 1968.

Williams, H. A. *True Resurrection.* Springfield, Ill.: Templegate, 1972.

Wilson, Edward O. *Sociobiology: The New Synthesis.* Cambridge, Mass.: Harvard Univ. Press, 1975.

Wink, Walter. *Engaging the Powers: Discernment and Resistance in a World of Domination.* Minneapolis: Fortress Press, 1992.

———. *Naming the Powers: The Language of Power in the New Testament.* Philadelphia: Fortress Press, 1984.

———. *The Powers That Be: Theology for a New Millennium.* New York: Doubleday, 1998.

———. *Unmasking the Powers: The Invisible Forces That Determine Human Existence.* Philadelphia: Fortress Press, 1986.

Witherington, Ben, III. *The Christology of Jesus.* Minneapolis: Fortress Press, 1990.

Wood, W. Jay. *Epistemology: Becoming Intellectually Virtuous.* Downers Grove, Ill.: InterVarsity, 1998.

Wrede, William. *The Messianic Secret.* Trans. J. C. G. Greig. Greenwood, S.C.: Attic, 1971. [Orig. German ed., 1901.]

Wright, John H. *A Theology of Christian Prayer.* New York: Pueblo, 1987.

Wright, N. T. "Christian Origins and the Resurrection of Jesus as a Historical Problem." *Sewanee Theological Review* 41 (1988): 107–23.

———. "Early Tradition and the Origins of Christianity." *Sewanee Theological Review* 41 (1988): 125–40.

———. *Jesus and the Victory of God.* Minneapolis: Fortress Press, 1996.

———. *The New Testament and People of God.* Minneapolis: Fortress Press, 1992.

Wright, Robert. *Moral Animal: Evolutionary Psychology and Everyday Life.* New York: Vintage, 1995.

Index

Abelard, atonement theory of, 235n32
adoptionism, 56
Adler, Mortimer, 199n1
agapē, agapic love. *See* love
Ahlstrom, Sidney E., 248n24
Allan, Keith, 200n6, 201n9
Allison, Dale, 209n13, 226n31
Anabaptist, 251–252n34
Anderson, George H., 256n20
Anselm of Canterbury, 234n28
anti-foundationalism, 15–20
apocalyptic, 67, 209n13, 219n49; and mil-
    lennialism, 270n32n34
apocalyptic pessimism: and Billy Graham,
    185; as a view of penultimate history,
    184–88; and social justice, 185–86
Aquinas, Thomas. *See* Thomas Aquinas
Aranguren, J. L., 201n10
argument from design, 142–43
Aristotle, 262n13
Arius, 66
Arndt, William E., 221n6, 234n28
atonement theory, subjective and
    objective, 235n32
Augustine, 204n21, 254n7, 262n13; on
    evil as the privation of being, 269n26;
    on sacrament, 246–247n18
Aulén, Gustav, 236n35
Austin, J. L., 200n5n7

baptism, sacrament of, 127–29,
    247–248nn19–24; and original sin,
    129, 248n24. *See also* ritual;
    sacrament
Barad, Judith, 257n24
Barbour, Ian G., 210–211n18
Barr, James, 257n27
Barth, Karl, 213n30
Bausch, William J., 247n20
Beeck, Frans Jozef van, 218n46,
    254–255n13
Beethoven, Ludwig van, 12
Beggiani, Seely, 204–205n21, 215n34
Benveniste, Emile, 199n1
bereavement theory, and resurrection,
    111; 239n10
Berger, Peter, 144, 194n45, 203n20,
    261n11; and the anthropological
    approach to God's existence,
    254n7; on methodological
    atheism, 208n7
Bershady, Harold J., 198n66
Bloch, Ernst: and the melancholy of
    fulfillment, 19, 194n47, 264n4
Blum, Lawrence A., 262–263n17
body: the functions of, and resurrection,
    176–77
Boff, Leonardo, 213–214n30
Bokenkotter, Thomas, 212n23

287